Moving to Office 365

Planning and Migration Guide

Matt Katzer

Apress®

Moving to Office 365: Planning and Migration Guide

ISBN-13 (pbk): 978-1-4842-1198-4

ISBN-13 (electronic): 978-1-4842-1197-7

Managing Director: Welmoed Spahr
Lead Editor: Gwenan Spearing
Development Editor: Douglas Pundick
Editorial Board: Steve Anglin, Louise Corrigan, Jim DeWolf, Jonathan Gennick, Robert Hutchinson, Michelle Lowman, James Markham, Susan McDermott, Matthew Moodie, Jeff Olson, Jeffrey Pepper, Douglas Pundick, Ben Renow-Clarke, Gwenan Spearing, Steve Weiss
Coordinating Editor: Melissa Maldonado
Copy Editor: Kimberly Burton
Compositor: SPi Global
Indexer: SPi Global
Artist: SPi Global

Distributed to the book trade worldwide by Springer Science+Business Media New York, 233 Spring Street, 6th Floor, New York, NY 10013. Phone 1-800-SPRINGER, fax (201) 348-4505, e-mail orders-ny@springer-sbm.com, or visit www.springer.com. Apress Media, LLC is a California LLC and the sole member (owner) is Springer Science + Business Media Finance Inc (SSBM Finance Inc). SSBM Finance Inc is a Delaware corporation.

For information on translations, please e-mail rights@apress.com, or visit www.apress.com.

Apress and friends of ED books may be purchased in bulk for academic, corporate, or promotional use. eBook versions and licenses are also available for most titles. For more information, reference our Special Bulk Sales–eBook Licensing web page at www.apress.com/bulk-sales.

Any source code or other supplementary material referenced by the author in this text is available to readers at www.apress.com. For detailed information about how to locate your book's source code, go to www.apress.com/source-code/.

Contents at a Glance

Contents

About the Author

Matt Katzer is the president of KAMIND IT, a Microsoft Gold Partner, and author of the best-selling cloud book *Office 365: Managing and Migrating Your Business in the Cloud* (Apress, 2013). He is currently the president of the local chapter of IAMCP (International Association of Microsoft Channel Partners) and active in local business communities.

Matt's focus with cloud solutions started in 2008, as he was looking at ways that businesses could grow quickly and with reduced operating costs. Matt holds a BSEE from the University of Michigan and an Executive MBA from the University of Oregon.

Matt's greatest satisfaction comes from helping his customers become competitive in an increasingly technology-driven world.

About the Technical Reviewers

We at KAMIND IT have taken a different approach to the technical review of this book. This book is a collection of "notes from the field"—documents that we have generated to help us educate our customers as we partner with them to move to Microsoft Office 365, a cloud service that simply works. These chapters are a collection of the experiences of more than 8,200 users as they migrated to Office 365. Their tireless feedback and the questions from our customers have helped us hone this book to be a practical reference document, not only for moving to Office 365, but also as a tool to manage businesses on Office 365.

Acknowledgments

I want to thank all of my customers; my editor, Gwenan Spearing; Robyn Schutz, our Microsoft Business Development Manager; Eugene Chi, General Manager SMB West Region and the countless support staff at Microsoft; my team at KAMIND IT who allowed me the time to write this book, especially Hakim Spears and David Tollefsen for their reviews of the chapters, helping to improve the final product; Brian Geraths, photographer extraordinaire; and last but by no means least, my wife, Barbara, for her encouragement and support. Without the assistance of all these individuals and companies, this book would never have been written.

Each of the chapters includes additional information culled from various blogs and Internet postings, to assist readers in searching out information on Office 365 and Microsoft's other cloud services.

Introduction

Why Office 365 and why this book? The answer is simple: for me it has always been about giving back to the community. Office 365 users are a community. It is important for those who are passionate about Office 365 to help the community grow. This Office 365 book is a combination of my experiences and questions that I am constantly being asked about moving customers to Office 365. Customers who move to Office 365 improve their productivity and reduce operation costs. Why use Office 365? It just makes business sense. It is about what people want to do, and how they work.

Office 365 is a cloud-based service; using it is what you know—the Microsoft Office suite. It simply works, plus you do not have to give up your intellectual property to use the service. This is important. Not all cloud solutions are this forthright. Our customers who use Office 365 have significantly reduced their IT services costs and their concerns in the areas of data security, compliance, and discovery.

This is a living book. We approached Apress, our publisher, with the idea that this book should morph over time. We suggested that a living book could be created about Microsoft cloud services, based on our experience both now and in the future. Apress agreed.

KAMIND IT, a Microsoft Cloud Solution Provider and Cloud Champion and a multiyear Microsoft Partner award winner, presents a unique value proposition for our Office 365 customers. Our approach has been to partner with our clients to journey to the cloud together. That experience is reflected in this book and will continue to be.

Join us in this journey to the cloud with Office 365.

Chapter 1: What Is Office 365?

This chapter focuses on why you should move your organization to Office 365. The decision to move to Office 365 is a business, rather than a technical, decision. Like any business change, the objective is to reduce your operational costs and to improve your organization's productivity to gain a competitive advantage. The chapter ends with a hypothetical customer making the business trade-offs toward moving to the cloud.

Chapter 2: Understanding the End User Experience

The best way to understand Office 365 is to experience it. You explore Office 365 capabilities in the Contoso demonstration site, with a focus on how this helps your business productivity. A day in the life of a user demonstrates the capabilities of Office 365.

Chapter 3: The Apps

Office 365 is owned by the business, and the data is only available to the business for business use. Office 365 takes advantage of social enterprise through the different data mining capabilities that are present in services like Gmail, Dropbox, Facebook, LinkedIn, and other social media sites. These capabilities are applied to your Office 365 site to improve your business productivity. This chapter describes Office 365 apps and discusses how you use them in your business to improve communications and productivity.

Chapter 4: Cloud Security Best Practices

One of the issues that all managers are faced with is the management of data and security and learning best practices. In this chapter, you explore the different capabilities of Office 365 and the monitoring that is in place to manage your Office 365 company to ensure that your data remains private. This chapter covers the most common approaches to Office 365 migration.

Chapter 5: Office 365 Deployment Step by Step

The secret to a successful deployment to Office 365 is picking the correct plan that supports your business. The key to a successful migration to Office 365 is the planning and purchase process. Once you select a plan, your primary consideration must be to ensure that the migration process is seamless for your organization. This chapter describes the basic purchase information and it details the choices. It concludes with information about pre-deployment, deployment, and post-deployment.

Chapter 6: Workstation Setup and Configuration

Office 365 supports many different systems and capabilities, depending on your business needs. The issue that IT managers constantly face is how to set up and manage the client environment. This chapter is focused on the configuration of an Office 365 desktop environment. This is the go-to reference chapter on the configuration of your desktop and mobile phones.

Chapter 7: Managing Office 365

This chapter describes the different administration centers in Office 365 and the most common tools that you use to administer Office 365. Depending on your Office 365 plan, there are five possible administration tools. This chapter focuses on the Office 365, Exchange, and Skype for Business administration centers. The chapter closes with using PowerShell to manage your Office 365 environment.

CHAPTER 1

■ ■ ■

Why Office 365

We plan and design for change. After it happens, we plan for the next change. What drives change? With information technology, there are many factors—lower cost of equipment, better computing power, greater bandwidth, new software, and so on.

Office 365 is a cloud solution that is having a significant impact on information technology and its role in business. Office 365 represents change—change from the way we used to work to a new way of working. Its proven benefits include lowering the cost of IT services and enabling higher user productivity.

The profit factor is a universal driving force for business. Profit generation also drives the information technology function to become more efficient. When times are good, organizations have more resources and there is less pressure on the IT function to become more efficient. However, when a downturn in business happens, IT is frequently the first to suffer budgets cut. The only option is to become more efficient in the use of resources. IT people, whether staff or contractors, are often viewed as "the first to be cut, and the last ones around to turn off the lights."

Small businesses are particularly sensitive to change. Most do not have the capital to handle long downturns, and many look at IT as an "optional" expense. To combat this perception, many IT partner programs (like the Microsoft Partner Network, which is made up of hundreds of independent IT service providers) encourage their partners to become trusted business advisors as well as IT experts. The clear objective is to change the business owner's view of IT from an optional expenditure to an essential investment.

The challenge for IT professionals, whether they are staff or contractors, is to evaluate the business processes and technologies available and apply those that improve business efficiency. Cloud computing is one technology that can make a big difference quickly. Why Office 365? There are three reasons why Office 365 is the choice for businesses.

- You do not assign your intellectual property rights to a third party to use its cloud service. You own the data in Office 365, and when you leave the Microsoft service, the data is destroyed after 90 days.

- It is what you know—Microsoft Office.

- Microsoft cloud services reduce operating costs and increase worker productivity.

This book addresses these issues. It also outlines a host of business efficiency opportunities that are to be realized with cloud computing and demonstrates how to make this happen. This book is a collection of our Best Known Methods (BKM) and processes. We want to provide you with the knowledge and tools necessary so you can move your business to the cloud using Microsoft Office 365.

Office 365: The New Cloud Challenge

When commercial cloud services were introduced more than 10 years ago, initial prices were high. Products were, admittedly, not mature and robust. This is the case with most innovations. Customer feedback was mixed and there were issues with how services were delivered and what customers really needed or wanted. In the early days of cloud services, Internet connections were slow (~56Kbits to 1.2Mbits); today, Internet connections are extremely fast (1000Mbits), which leads to a better user experience. Looking at today's environment, there is a lot of opportunity to fine-tune product services to meet the needs of small businesses in particular. The opportunities for small businesses include the ability to improve worker productivity and reduce (and control) IT operations costs. With this in mind, this book will use examples of integrated cloud migration solutions that we at KAMIND (IT cloud advisors and provider of services for Office 365) have engaged for this tier of user.

Like other companies, over the years, Microsoft has developed an increasingly more complete set of services for businesses—from small (less than 250) to large enterprises with a scalable solution offering. The current Microsoft cloud solutions have evolved from the Microsoft on-premises offerings for the 2007–2016 class of server and application products and Hotmail cloud services offering. Microsoft's first commercial service was Microsoft's Online Services (2007–2010), known as the Business Productivity Online Standard Suite (BPOS), which included Exchange, SharePoint, Office Communicator, and Live Meeting.

In February 2013, Microsoft deployed Office 365 Wave 15, the third generation of online services. This generation of Office 365 supports client desktop software for PC (Office Professional Plus) and Macs (Mac Office 2011). The service also allows installation of desktop software on five desktop and five mobile devices per user. This is the new Office 365 (see Figure 1-1).

Full plan lineup

		Business			Enterprise		
		Business	Business Essentials	Business Premium	ProPlus	E1	E3
Customer	Price	$8.25	$5	$12.5	$12	$8	$20
	Seat Cap	300 (for each plan)			Unlimited		
	24/7 phone support from Microsoft	Critical issues			All issues		
Office	Word, PowerPoint, Excel, Outlook, OneNote, Publisher	•		•	•²		•²
	iPad, Windows RT & smartphone apps	•		•	•		•
	Office Online	•	•	•	•	•	•
	Access				•		•
Standard services	1TB cloud storage (OneDrive for Business)	•	•	•	•	•	•
	Email, calendar (Exchange)		•	•		•	•
	Online meetings, IM (Lync)		•	•		•	•
	Team sites, internal portals (SharePoint)		•	•		•	•
	Enterprise social (Yammer)		•	•		•	•
Advanced services	Active Directory integration	•	•	•	•	•	•
	Supports hybrid deployment				•	•	•
	Office shared computer activation support (RDS)				•		•
	Upcoming services – Video content management					•	•
	Compliance – Archiving, eDiscovery, mailbox hold						•
	Information protection – message encryption, RMS, DLP						•

Figure 1-1. *Office 365 feature set (courtesy of Microsoft)*

Office 365 continues to be enhanced with new productivity features. In July 2015, Microsoft introduced a new voice communication product, which integrates Skype consumer and Lync/Office communicator. The new product offerings—Skype for Business services—are integrated into the Office 2016 August 2015 release (supporting Mac and PC). The Office 2016 Skype for Business component allows Office 365 users to integrate new voice services with Skype meeting Broadcast (up to 10,000 attendees), PSTN Conferencing, and Cloud PBX. Microsoft's new business phone service integrates both domestic and international callers under the Cloud PBX option. Microsoft Cloud PBX can be added to any Enterprise plan or purchased via a bundled E5 suite. This new product offering is being rolled out in late 2015.

Customer Segments

When KAMIND IT migrates customers with fewer than 250 users, our approach differs based on workforce size. We have developed distinct service packages for businesses smaller than 25 end users (be they employees, contractors, or others in the network), 26–75 end users, and 75–250 end users. This helps maintain focus on one of the main deciding factors for small business—cost. It also accommodates growth trajectory, allowing small companies to start small and invest more in cloud IT services only when the return on investment (ROI) justifies it. These are considerations that KAMIND IT customers say are key to their decision making. Enterprise customers, those with more than 250 users, have different requirements than the smaller clusters, but the needs are very much the same—to reduce ongoing operation costs.

Developing affordable, flexible, and powerful cloud solutions has involved a number of interim approaches. Knowing the evolution of today's IT landscape provides some insight into the current tools available from the major suppliers. For example, prior to 2013, Microsoft served the less-than-75-end-users market with Microsoft Small Business server. Enterprises with more than 75 end users tended to use Microsoft traditional server products, such as Windows Server 2012R2 and 2016. For a short period between 2008 and 2010, Microsoft offered the Essential Business Server (EBS) product family, which was not a good fit for the 75–350 end-users market. EBS was designed to provide a graceful path between Small Business Servers (SBS) and traditional Microsoft server products. An EBS version 2 was under development until it was canceled on March 4, 2010.

The EBS server product offering was one of the first solutions that addressed both on-premises and cloud integration of cloud computing. Its cancelation was a precursor to a change introduced by Office 365. The EBS solution was a three-server solution. It was designed for virtualization and integration of all SBS product features, with remote access and the management tools of System Center essentials. When EBS was aborted, Microsoft lost its leading integrated solution for the 75-plus end-user market. This left the traditional Microsoft server products and the Microsoft Online Services to do the job.

The less-than-75 user market has a large set of solutions, including Microsoft Home Server, Foundation Server, Windows Server, and Small Business Server. In July 2009, KAMIND IT made a comparison of SBS, EBS, and Microsoft Online Services to determine the return on investment. The crossover point was identified at about 15 users. In other words, with fewer than 15 users, it appeared to be less expensive to deploy Microsoft Online Services than it was to use on-premises services.

As we moved into 2010 and incorporated the March 2010 pricing of $10 per user for Microsoft Online Services, the crossover point shifted to between 100 and 150 users. Microsoft Online Services' price was at $22.50 per user at this time. The corresponding Office 365 subscription E1 is $8 per user today, demonstrating a 65 percent cost reduction.

There have been a number of changes since 2010. Microsoft has introduced at least four significant version changes in Office 365. Office 365 is simpler to operate and the return on investment is significantly better than it was in 2010. Microsoft changed the yearly Office 365 new-feature release into an agile development, releasing new features every 90 days to all Office 365 users. In October 2014, a Microsoft/Forester[1]

---

[1]Microsoft Forester Research study published in October 2014. See http://www.whymicrosoft.com/see-why/office-365-tei-study-forrester/

total-cost-of-ownership study was released. This study looked at the migration and support costs of companies moving to Office 365. The Microsoft/Forester study showed that there is a seven-month payback on the migration to Office 365 from an on-premises solution.

The Forester/Microsoft study is interesting. Forester collected information on a number of companies, then compared the information and built a couple of different scenarios. In one case, a fictitious 150-person company moved from an on-premises Exchange Server solution to Office 365. The interesting conclusion was the calculated payback after migration to Office 365. This is in line with the migration results for customers moved to Office 365. Small clients (for example, a 15-person company) in a managed services program see monthly IT support costs reduced by ~$1,000 a month. Larger companies, (like a 500-seat migration recently completed) see a very significant return. It is not uncommon to have a 50% reduction in IT costs, and receive a two-to-six month ROI payback on the investment in Office 365. It doesn't matter how you slice it, Office 365 saves you money and provides end users a higher level of service.

If you look at the pricing and features of Office 365 today (see Figure 1-2), there is no longer a business case to stay on-premises. The cloud-based Office 365 solution is currently the most cost-effective direction for any size business. Office 365 adapts to small one-site enterprises, as well as global operations, and it is growing every day. As of late 2013, a reported 69 percent of companies with 20 or fewer employees were using some type of cloud-based IT solution. At the upper end, costs for an enterprise with an on-premises server supporting 2,500 users are reduced by 52 percent with the deployment of an Enterprise E3 license ($20 per user per month), with a seven-month payback.

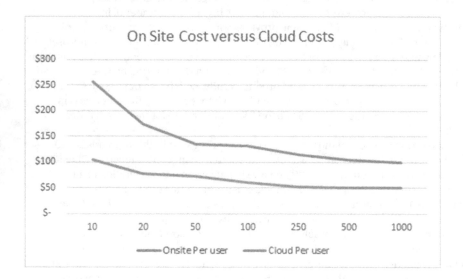

Figure 1-2. *2015 cost comparison of on-site vs. the cloud (no cloud deployment costs included)*

Unless there is a compelling reason to use an on-premises solution, it is more cost-effective to use a cloud service. There are advantages and disadvantages to whichever solution you use, and you need to understand your business requirements and how well a particular IT approach integrates with your business strategy.

Microsoft defines small business as an enterprise with fewer than 250 end users. A few other definitions will be useful at this point. The following terms aid in further understanding cloud migration and how it applies to business:

- *On-premises*: Software and hardware devices located at a user's physical location; for example, an on-premises Exchange Server handling mail services.

- *Off-premises*: Often used as a synonym for the cloud, this actually denotes software and hardware devices that are located off-site. Users of cloud services have outsourced physical hardware and software maintenance. For example, with Microsoft Online Services, the user owns and is responsible for the data, but not the software or the physical server. Microsoft is responsible for backups and server maintenance.

- *Cloud*: Any cloud service that is maintained by a third party. Examples are Hotmail, Gmail, and Microsoft Online Services (called Office 365).

- *Office 365*: The Microsoft cloud services suite solution supports collaboration sites, dynamic document synchronization, enterprise voice, compliance, and Office software subscriptions (Word, Excel, PowerPoint, etc.) for the PC and the Mac, as well as Office productivity subscriptions for Project and Visio.

- *Cloud PBX*: Skype for Business with local and international dialing is part of the Microsoft E5 subscription; it provides a full cloud-based PBX for inbound and outbound call handling.

- *Intel server*: The next-generation high-density compute server that supports an integrated SAN and switch control modules. These servers handle virtualization of line-of-business applications. These servers may be the on-premises or off-premises physical hardware.

- *Hosted*: Any cloud service owned by the user but maintained by a third party; for example, the user may host web servers on either third-party equipment or customer-owned equipment.

- *Virtualization*: A server or desktop operating system running on a virtual host. The server or desktop operating systems are run in a hardware-agnostic mode, since the hardware services are supplied by the virtual host.

- *Virtual host*: The hosted operating environment that allows virtualization of the operating systems. Microsoft Azure is an example of a cloud-based virtual host.

Those of us who own or run a business would like to increase efficiency and reduce operational costs. It does not matter the business size. What matters is what customers want. Most customers want the businesses they use for services to be competitive in terms of services and price. In order to be competitive, owners want capability at the lowest possible price. As business owners, we make investments and want our businesses to scale, so we can grow the business and generate resources for expansion.

Table 1-1 details an example of the on-premises cost of a business that has 50–250 users. It includes a set of core functions that all businesses have: mail, document storage, web conferencing, and line of business (LOB) applications (such as a payroll application or accounting packages). In this example, the IT costs for a small business with 50 end users are about $269 per user per month. The IT cost for a business with 250 end users is about $67 per user per month. The infrastructure required to support the business is roughly the same. Cloud migration clearly enables IT infrastructure cost reduction. Table 1-2 shows the expected costs for a 50-user company, comparing on-premises and cloud services.

Table 1-1. *On-Premises Infrastructure Costs for 50 and 250 Users (Courtesy of Microsoft)*

	50 Users Cost (USD)	250 Users Cost (USD)
Hardware and Maintenance	70,413	73,123
Software	107,738	128,078
Operations	207,297	298,827
Deployment	98,951	101,802
	$484,399	$601,830
Cost per user	$269	$67

■ **Note** Core services costs are provided by Microsoft Online Services.

Table 1-2. *On-Premises vs. Cloud Comparison for a 50-User Company*

	On-Premises 50 Users Cost (USD)	Cloud 50 Users Cost (USD)
Hardware and Maintenance	$70,413	$0
Software	107,738	36,270
Operations	207,297	100,456
Deployment	98,951	28,886
	$484,399	$165,612
Cost per user	$269	$92

■ **Note** The 250-user company on-premises cost is $67 per user and the cost for the cloud is $30 per user.

When a business moves to Office 365, there are three driving factors.

- The business retains ownership of its intellectual property.
- It is what they know (Microsoft Office).
- Business productivity increases and operating costs decrease.

In Table 1-2, note that the cost for a 50-user company drops from $269 per user per month to $92 per user per month when you move to Office 365. Expand this to a 250-user company, and the cost per user per month drops from $67 per user per month to $30 per user per month for an Office 365 user. This is a cost savings of more than 50 percent. The following are the reasons for this:

- Elimination of in-house maintenance and upgrades to new server software.
- Shortening the time and expense for rollouts of new features.
- Gaining the efficiency of IT services and software features that are usable anywhere.
- Reduction in IT operation costs for energy consumption and hardware updates.
- Moving voice communications to Skype for Business (Cloud PBX).

Once Microsoft reduced the entry prices for online services to as low as $2 per user/month, it became more expensive to deploy on-premises equipment in virtually every enterprise. The challenge for the IT professional is how to help businesses adapt to change while balancing on-premises and cloud requirements. Our approach with all businesses is to examine the business processes of the company to understand the balance. Once the business processes are known, we examine the steps required to deploy a cloud solution to meet the business needs. This is why the approach to the cloud as a solution is so different from a traditional IT solution. The cloud solution for a business is a business process change that reduces the operating costs of the business and improves productivity.

To assist in your understanding, we have created a small company called Ready Design Custom Cupcakes (RDCC). You will look at how RDCC's business requirements compare against on-premises and cloud services.

RDCC's IT Requirements

RDCC has a unique business model compared to other cupcake bakers. Years ago, RDCC discovered that it could simulate the cupcake design and place the simulated cupcakes of various designs into a virtual environment to gauge consumer reactions. The company discovered that cupcakes that were simulated and later baked enjoyed four times the sales of "regular" cupcakes.

RDCC corporate headquarters supports 20 retail cupcake outlets. The IT organization has deployed Microsoft Exchange Server 2010 and a WebEx video conferencing solution. The remote locations use Microsoft Outlook web access, and documents are e-mailed to all franchise owners. To meet the demands of the cupcake design team, the IT organization deploys LOB applications with a clustered SQL Server 2008R2 to support the cupcake simulation. The RDCC IT infrastructure consists of seven servers: three support the LOB simulation application and four support core operations. The current IT department has deployed the following solutions:

- One server for the LOB with an Access simulation database

- One server for Microsoft Exchange Server 2010 with 18 local users and 150 remote web mail accounts

- One server for Microsoft Systems Management Server for application deployment and management

- One Microsoft SharePoint 2007 server

- Support of 150 remote mail users with iPhone and Windows 10 Mobile

- 30 WebEx accounts and 25 GoToMeeting accounts

- Traditional phone systems with a 10-year-old PBX

Strategic Overview

RDCC management wants an IT system focused on supporting the LOB applications rather than supporting commodity software. The IT staff at RDCC has submitted a capital expenditure (CAPEX) spending request to upgrade the aging RDCC servers. RDCC management is seeking alternatives to reduce both CAPEX and operational expenses (OPEX).

RDCC's corporate objective is to make the organization more agile and increase productivity. Management evaluated one of the online alternatives, Microsoft Office 365, to host its core software. RDCC management summarizes its priorities as follows:

- 100% ownership of the company's intellectual property (IP); no IP rights assignments to use third-party services.

- Reduce capital equipment expenditures.

- Reduce operational expenditures with predictable IT costs.

- Work on the business with a focus on market differentiation.

- Reduce energy consumption; become more energy-efficient.

- Access latest software versions with no server upgrade.

- Achieve the ability to share cupcake recipes with the franchises from the internal document storage site.

- Replace the PBX with a cloud-based phone system.

The following is a summary of RDCC's IT management requirements with a focus on determining potential commodity products, plus a comparison of them with the various business needs to design a solution addressing both on-premises and cloud needs.

On-Premises and Cloud Resource Requirements

Many different arguments are made to justify keeping servers on-premises vs. moving them into the cloud. They range from control over the data (intellectual property rights) to reducing costs. The secret is to look at the problem from a service level, to differentiate services that provide a competitive advantage from those that are a commodity. In other words, identify the business processes and look at those processes from an IT services point of view that promotes business growth. Differentiate those capabilities from those that are core to the business, but have no strategic value. Commodity services (those that are not core to the business) move to the cloud.

If a cloud migration is approached correctly, you can achieve both objectives—promoting business and reducing cost for core commodity services. This seems like a simple problem, but it is actually very complex. To help address this, we look at the business from a capability point of view, and we will use that point of view to help us in our decision process.

The following core IT considerations are common to all businesses when viewed from the perspective of an IT solution. When looking at cloud solutions, it helps to look at each distinctive business unit and business processes before deciding what is best for the whole enterprise.

- Core business software

- LOB solutions

- Requirements for on-premises and cloud data

- E-mail utilization and retention

- Network infrastructure

- Desktop support and upgrade

- Information security

- Monitoring

- Budget: CAPEX vs. OPEX

- Hosted web site

Which IT elements will help sustain a competitive advantage? That is the overriding question in each of these categories. Each business is different, depending on its needs. An obvious example is the e-mail capabilities for business. A few years ago, a business needed to place on-site servers to have ownership and control of their e-mail (intellectual property). This need drove the Microsoft Small Business Server market. Today, e-mail is a commodity, so unless there is a different business need for an on-site mail server, it no longer makes business sense (see Figure 1-3) to manage.

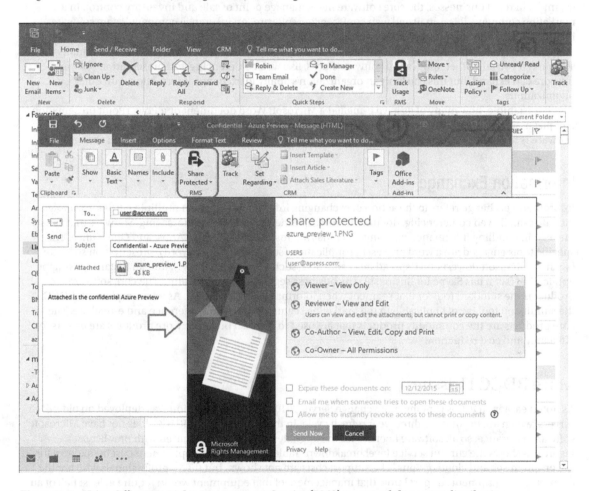

Figure 1-3. Using Office 365 Rights Management Service (RMS) to control document distribution

In all cases, it is wise to seriously look at the cloud and the impact on the business. At KAMIND IT, we looked at our customers, from the small five-person law firm to the larger 2,000-employee business. We looked at the impact from a commodity services perspective, and in all cases, we found that the cloud cost at least 50 percent less than on-premises equipment. The only caveat was bandwidth (the ability to transfer large amounts of data at fast speeds to cloud services). If the bandwidth was not available, then it did not make sense to migrate to the cloud.

Core Business Software

What is core software? Core software has many different meanings, depending on the business. As an example, in retail businesses, the core software helps manage point of sale and inventory control. In a marketing company, it is e-mail and web conferencing software. An insurance company's core software includes e-mail and an application for managing the insurance offerings.

Core software products are usually word processing, spreadsheet, phone integration, and e-mail software. If you add other application software stacks, like web conferencing and presentation software, the core can expand, but this can limit an organization's ability to exchange information with other organizations.

For example, how many of us have e-mailed a Microsoft Word document or a PowerPoint presentation and just assumed that the other party could read the file? The simplest definition you can use for core software is to define it as "those software programs and services that facilitate information exchange."

Information Exchange

Information exchange refers to the action of exchanging information between multiple parties. Examples include e-mail, web conferencing, document storage/retrieval, and instant messaging. Software that assists the user in handling information exchange includes Microsoft Office, Google Apps, and OpenOffice. The specific tools engaged are a word processing application (such as Microsoft Word), presentation software (such as Microsoft PowerPoint), spreadsheet software (such as Microsoft Excel), and an instant-messaging application (such has Skype for Business). The business segment does not matter. The core software product is the standard tool for that segment when information is exchanged. As an example, with RDCC, the simulation tool is not applicable to the marketing segments, but web conference and e-mail are. The core products are the commodity products that are used to conduct business. Core products are drivers for efficiency and cost reduction.

More RDCC IT Issues

As noted earlier, RDCC is running on Exchange Server 2010. The RDCC solution was deployed on older Dell servers, which are beyond the three-year refresh cycle. In this configuration, RDCC does not have Microsoft software assurance, so all software licenses for the upgrades need to be purchased with new licenses. Figure 1-3 shows the current service level breakdown. Table 1-3 shows the deployment cost breakdown for the on-premises and cloud options. The support costs are not shown, but the IT professionals who handle on-premises equipment support know that management of that equipment would require at least half of an IT professional's time. Both options are listed in Table 1-3.

Table 1-3. *RDCC Deployment Comparison*

Microsoft Online Services: Office 365						
Description	Users	Service	Cost per User (USD)	Deployment Costs (USD)	One-Time Cost (USD)	Monthly Cost(USD)
Franchise owner	100	E2	16	10 per user	1,000	1,600
Users	50	E3	24	100 per user	5,000	1,200
					$6,000	$2,800

Onsite Server					
Description	Users		Deployment Costs (USD)	One-Time Cost (USD)	Monthly Cost (USD)
Users	150		200 per user	30,000	2,500
Server installation				15,000	1,250
Server hardware (Intel-based Dell PowerEdge Server)				29,392	2,449
Microsoft software (Exchange + Enterprise + Client Access Licenses – CAL)				49,309	4,109
				$123,701	$10,308

The RDCC IT manager reviewed the support requested and proposed a budget of $123,000, or approximately $10,000 per month. The IT manager expects this will consume half of the on-staff IT professional time at a cost of about $70,000. RDCC management looked at the cost and requested the IT manager do a comparison against the monthly costs using a subscription (cloud) model.

The IT manager reviewed the information and was shocked to see that the on-premises solution costs $7,000 per month more than the Microsoft Office 365 solution. He also became aware that he could free up half of his time by not having to manage an on-premises server. RDCC's management reviewed the financials and chose the Microsoft Office 365 solution, saving $150,000 in a one-year period. RDCC management also committed to having all of its franchise users use Microsoft Office applications as the office standard. Management also decided to deploy two distinct offerings for franchises. At the franchise level, they specified the E1 service with Office web applications. This allows the franchise owner either to use the web applications or to purchase the retail version of the Office software. RDCC corporate offices can either use the Office subscription service (E3) or deploy the Office 2013 software through a volume license.

The IT manager looked at the different programs to purchase Office 365. Office 365 subscriptions can be purchased directly from Microsoft, through a local Microsoft Partner, or through a cloud solution provider, (such as Dell). The Office 365 purchase process depends more on the support model and who owns the billing relationship with RDCC. If RDCC purchases the software through the Cloud Solution Provider (CSP) program, the first line of support will be the CSP (in this example, Dell) and the invoices for the Office 365 services will come directly through Dell. If RDCC purchases the Office 365 software (from the Microsoft web site and assigns a partner), the first level of support is with Microsoft (and/or the Microsoft partner).

The IT manager presented an overview of the different purchasing processes to the CFO, who remarked that he should look into the CSP program in greater detail. The CFO was thinking about the payment that the franchise owners make to RDCC, as well as the demands for IT services. The CSP program may be used to allow the CSP to directly bill the franchise owners for the Office 365 subscriptions. This would allow the franchise owners to scale their IT services to meet local business needs, without draining RDCC's resources. RDCC would own the base Office 365 subscriptions and control the base level of services. The CFO and the IT manager agreed to further investigate this option.

RDCC's decision to use Microsoft Online Services reduced the CAPEX and OPEX for the fiscal year. RDCC IT staff estimated that the deployment costs were between $50 and $100 per person in one-time fees, for a total of $6,000. The $6,000 migration cost for the RDCC deployment was one-fifth the estimated cost of the Exchange 2010 deployment. RDCC management realized that the selection of online services significantly reduced the cash outlay for the organization.

Line-of-Business Applications

LOB applications are unique to a business or a business segment. A good example of an LOB application is an insurance documentation archive system designed to handle insurance agency data. This LOB application is not relevant to, for example, a retail segment that does not handle insurance agency documents. Likewise, an LOB application of a point-of-sale (POS) system would not be a relevant application for an RDCC cupcake simulation.

RDCC's LOB application consists of the simulation application and the Microsoft Access database used in the simulation. The Access database is known to consume network bandwidth. However, with Office 365, the Access database can be shared from the cloud SharePoint service, so the database that is used locally is cached, and changes are replicated to the cloud. The Access database can also be linked to Microsoft Azure (an extension of Office 365 cloud services) and integrated with Office 365. Thus, the user accesses the database locally, and transaction change records are replicated to the cloud. This allows multiple users to have access to the information in real time without over-using available bandwidth. This is possible because updates are driven to client desktops only as they are "cached."

RDCC IT staff concluded that the LOB application no longer needed a server to support the application. The IT manager reviewed SharePoint online services and decided that this software only needed minor customization to make it useful. This decision allows the IT management to reduce the server "farm" by one more server, at a savings of about $20,000 on top of the budget savings of $90,000—all made possible by cloud services and not deploying on-premises equipment.

Requirements for On-Premises and Cloud Data

The final concern for RDCC was how to address backup data issues. RDCC has a business requirement under Sarbanes-Oxley (SOX) that all financial data needs to be recoverable. RDCC has also been involved in litigation, so they are well aware of the e-discovery impact to the business. In recent litigation, RDCC was required to process all the e-mails on its Exchange Server and turn over the e-mail data as part of the litigation. Because RDCC did not have an archive retention policy, it received a notice of document retention prior to a stipulated court order that mandated a freeze in the deletion of all RDCC electronic and physical documents. The IT staff had to recall all laptops from the field and copy the users' personal archives to the server so the data could be processed for electronic discovery. This was extremely expensive.

E-mail Utilization and Retention

RDCC management sought to avoid this type of expense in the future and to make any discovery process more automated and less labor intensive. RDCC's policy is to have a ten-year compliance archive segmented into different groups: the factory workers' archive is one year, the middle managers' archive is two years, and sales' and managements' archives are ten years.

■ **Note**   Microsoft views an archive as a duplicate mailbox where data is copied from the primary mailbox. In the E1/E2 versions of Office 365, the archive is 50GB; in versions E3/E5, it is unlimited in size.

There are three types of archives in Office 365: personal archives (local PST and cloud). Personal archives (local or PST) are files in which the content is controlled by the user. A compliance archive must have data immutability; the user cannot change the data. The Office 365 (versions E1 and E2) personal archives are limited to 50GB. Office 365 archives in E3 and E4 are unlimited in size and can be made immutable (for compliance requirements). The compliance archive is controlled by business policies governed by the organization business processes and federal regulation. Office 365 makes it easy to control and track documents using Azure Rights Management (see Figure 1-3). Documents can be blocked from distribution by setting the document template. This allows documents to be restricted from distribution and sets a document expiration date. The Microsoft Azure Rights Management plug-in for Outlook 2016 can be downloaded at https://portal.aadrm.com.

Network Infrastructure

RDCC has a large, robust network infrastructure to support the user requirements of 200-plus employees and franchise owners. The franchise owners' businesses run seven days a week, from 5 a.m. to 10 p.m. (Pacific Standard Time).

To keep the network capability as it is, RDCC IT staff was faced with upgrading an aging on-premises data center with the latest Intel processor-based servers from Intel, Dell, or IBM. The IT design staff proposed replacing the data center shown in Figure 1-4 with an Intel server. The RDCC IT staff felt that this approach would provide the most comprehensive set of features for the cupcake virtualization and it would accommodate growth. The unresolved issue was how much to deploy on an Intel server vs. the cloud.

Figure 1-4. RDCC private data center

The Intel server is 6U in size and allows up to 14 high-speed SAS drives to be arranged in a data storage pool. RDCC IT staff is planning to use the 1TB SAS drives, which allows a storage pool size of 14,366GB, with an online hot spare. As far as RDCC IT staff is concerned, this allows them to reduce the size of the data center (see Figure 1-4) to a single 82-inch rack. RDCC IT staff selects the Intel server over other vendors' products based on the following considerations:

- Lower power consumption

- More flexibility in adding computing capacity

- Intel Xeon 6-core processors enable support for 12–24 virtual machines with a combined memory size of over 256GB

- Fault-tolerant compute module support with autofailover

- Fault-tolerant storage module with external SAN support

To help them in their decision process, RDCC IT staff modeled storage pool consumption on the Intel server test-drive site. This site allows them to try different configurations and out-of-band management systems to develop the best solution. Figure 1-5 shows a storage pool view of the Intel server with a RAID 1 and a RAID 5 subsystem.

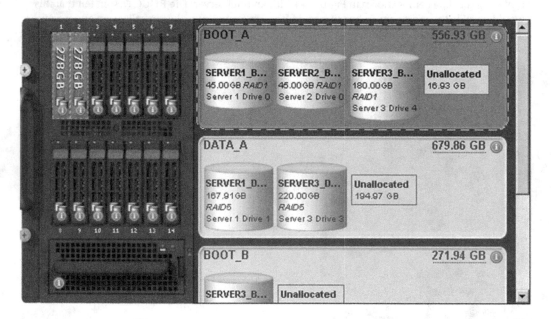

Figure 1-5. *Storage pool organization and allocation*

The Intel server allows for organizing the Storage Access Network (SAN) or the attached SAN into a set of storage pools. The storage pools are then allocated to the individual *compute module*. In Figure 1-5, two SAS drives were added to the storage pool. However, when building their virtual drives, the IT staff decided to organize the data in a RAID 1 configuration. KAMIND recommends that the RDCC IT staff deploy the Intel server storage with a global hot spare.

Desktop Support and Upgrade

The RDCC IT staff needs to complete not only a data center upgrade, but also a software upgrade. In the past, they purchased a Microsoft Open License that did not include software assurance, so they had a group of deployed desktops using Office 2003 software under Windows XP. Some of the newer software uses Windows 8, so RDCC is faced with replacing all XP systems before the end of support from Microsoft, which is less than a year away.

RDCC IT examined the different pricing options for the new software. The software deployment cost is the same in all cases except for the retail product. The retail product requires that the IT staff physically enter a different serial number for each version of Office 365 software installed.

Office 2013/2016 prices range from $144 to $957 (see Table 1-4) for Office 2013 software. The breakeven between the retail software ($399) and the subscription is 2.7 years. The software that costs the most is the retail version. The cost will be higher since it requires an IT professional to install the software on every desktop and deploy a unique serial number key; RDCC IT staff cannot do an automated "push" install for mass deployment of the software and upgrades with the retail ($399) version.

Table 1-4. *Office 2016 Professional Plus License Prices (as of Publication Date, Prices Subject to Change)*

Office 2016 Professional Plus			
Option	3-Yr Cost (USD)	Yearly Costs (USD)	Notes
Full retail product	$399	$399	No upgrade, limited installs
Volume license (L/SA)	$975	$325	Three-year agreement, with upgrade rights
Volume license (SA)	$444	$148	Agreement exists for license portion
Volume license subscription	$432	$144	Three-year subscription, upgrades included
Office 365 subscription	$12 per user/month	$144	One-year Microsoft online agreement

Information Security

RDCC's information security requirements are similar to those of most companies. RDCC wants to make sure its data is kept private. The company wants to control access to its data and the computing resources. These are its business needs. It doesn't want to use any cloud service that requires an intellectual property transfer. Some cloud services companies use IP rights assignment as a way to sell additional products and services to the companies' employees.

All of us have heard reports of credit card numbers being stolen from retail store point-of-sale computers. What about the government employee losing a laptop that contained thousands of Social Security numbers? There are countless stories of identity theft. The stories all come down to this: How safe is your data? The safety of your data is what information security is all about, and the crux of the problem is data access and control.

Realistically, it does not matter where your data is located. It can be safe anywhere—with the right precautions. The processes and security around your data and the way that it is controlled is what matters. As an example, does the network administrator have access to your e-mail? What password policies are in place to ensure that your data is under control? What is the physical security like? Who picks up the trash in the evening at your data center? Who has after-hours access to the information? All that matters is how data is managed. Data loss prevention is critical to RDCC's business. RDCC wants to ensure that confidential information stays inside the company and that there is no intellectual property rights assignment to use the Office 365 cloud service.

There are many aspects of physical data security. All server access should be controlled and limited to a few select individuals. Microsoft also has controls on who accesses data, which is a critical aspect of data security that is often overlooked. Microsoft manages access for more than 1 billion users (see Figure 1-6).

Azure global datacenters

Global datacenters ○
Global support ●
Local account teams 👤
Local currencies ⑨

24 x 7 x 365 support Over 1 billion customers, 20 million businesses 90 markets worldwide

Figure 1-6. Microsoft modern data center locations (courtesy of Microsoft)

■ **Note**   Microsoft's policy is that the customer owns the data, not Microsoft. Microsoft is planning to provide data-at-rest encryption keys to its customers as part of a security upgrade to Office 365.

Microsoft believes that the data is owned by the customer, and the customer has 100 percent control over the data. To put this in perspective, the customer must grant Microsoft permission to access the data. This philosophy limits data access and establishes the controls necessary for data security.

The next part of data security is built around the standards necessary for access and control. The Microsoft software design philosophy is developed from an idea of secure code design. Secure code design means that the software is designed by using best practices from the ground up. To put this in perspective, the code in the data centers is formed from a best-practice software design known as *code secure*. Michael Howard and David LeBlanc wrote *Writing Secure Code* (Microsoft Press, 2002). This is a must-read book if you are doing any software development.

Writing Secure Code walks through the process of software development and describes how to prevent attacks on software. This book provides examples of how software developers must padlock their code to prevent unknown attacks. The philosophy of Microsoft security begins at the core of the product design life cycle—the developer. If you do not put the correct processes in place, then the products built on top of those products will not be secure. This philosophy of security permeates modern Microsoft products, as well as the data center.

■ **Note**　Employ a risk-based, multidimensional approach to safeguarding services and data. All products must go through the secure development cycle to release code publicly. The secure development life cycle ensures threat development management.

Microsoft supplies a multitenant architecture based on Active Directory and built from secure code design. Microsoft has scaled the data security problem and discovered the weaknesses of various security products. Microsoft discovered that when a deployment is scaled beyond certain practical limits, security issues that no one else has thought of emerge. Microsoft deployment of the Exchange data infrastructure goes beyond the limits of whatever has been tested before. Microsoft has more than 40 million mailboxes that use Windows Azure Active Directory security. Microsoft augments the design with data access policies that prohibit the unauthorized access of data. To ensure compliance, these policies are automatically monitored within Microsoft Office 365 software, a feature that meets RDCC design goals.

With its security requirements met, RDCC is ready to use the Microsoft Azure Active Directory services (see Figure 1-7) to manage the entire business and ultimately move all on-site servers to the cloud and Office 365.

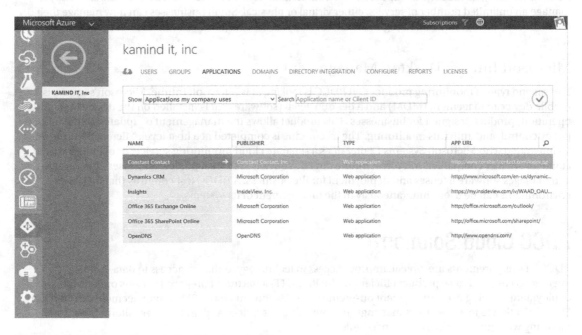

Figure 1-7. *Windows Azure Active Directory Services*

The following sections cover the approaches to achieving this phased "migration." RDCC's long-term plan is to move the database to a hosted service in Azure and add a WordPress site that is integrated to the Office 365 environment. RDCC believes that Azure allows the company to expand to the cloud for all commuting services in a secured manner.

Monitoring

There are two different monitoring approaches used to manage the on-site equipment and off-site equipment. These involve Microsoft Systems Center and Microsoft Intune. Each has different capabilities and features that depend on the needs of the client and the type of existing on-premises equipment.

Microsoft Systems Center

There are several services available for systems monitoring. There are those available from managed service providers like Level Platforms or ConnectWise and on-premises monitoring using Microsoft Systems Center (SCC). The objective of both is the proactive monitoring of servers and clients. Why proactive monitoring? The simplest explanation is productivity. As users become more dependent on computers for daily activity, there is an expectation that it "just works."

SCC is a software management tool that runs on-premises equipment and provides complete monitoring and updates management. This software is typically used in environments with 150–500 client PCs. SCC's goal is to unify the organization under one management console and thus reduce IT costs. From an IT perspective, SCC provides a proactive view of the on-premises network and has the capabilities to distribute patches (temporary fixes), install software updates, and troubleshoot network issues. SCC also has the capability to manage an unlimited number of servers, either virtual or physical. Small businesses can now manage their on-premises desktops and remaining servers at a fraction of the cost per user available to larger enterprises.

Microsoft Intune: Desktop Management

The second type of monitoring product that RDCC is looking at is Microsoft Intune. Microsoft's Intune is a mobile device management (MDM) and a desktop agent (software that is installed on the device to monitor operation) product designed for businesses. This product allows the management of updates, limited group policy control, and antivirus monitoring. The monitoring is completed at a host level. Microsoft Intune may be integrated with Microsoft Systems Center or as a separate cloud monitoring service, or operated via the cloud for smaller companies. Microsoft Intune directly controls systems updates, addresses virus issues, and manages software licenses and deployment for the business. A RDCC test confirms that these two environments can be used simultaneously in the management of its systems.

RDCC Cloud Solution

RDCC's IT requirements are typical: improve access to technology, enhance access to data, lower operations cost, and raise product efficiency. The RDCC IT department prepared various options for deployment, ranging from 100 percent on-premises to 100 percent cloud. RDCC management directed the IT organization to focus on areas that engage commodity IT services and find the best alternatives. The following was agreed upon as a balanced solution:

- Migrate all e-mail users to Microsoft Office 365–hosted Exchange mail services. There are 18 local users and 150 remote mail users.

- Move the SharePoint services to SharePoint online as part of the Exchange Mail migration.

- Move the 55 web conferencing accounts (WebEx or GoToMeeting) to Microsoft Skype for Business as part of the migration. Skype for Business will handle upward of web conferences for 10,000 users.

- Change the current phone supplier to Skype for Business – Cloud PBX (E5 subscription).

- Eliminate the need for a software security server and replace this with local firewalls (Fortinet or SonicWALL) since remote users will use the cloud and use Microsoft Enterprise Mobility Management for cloud security.

Cloud Requirements

The commodity products that are readily available externally include Microsoft Exchange, SharePoint, web conferencing, virus management, and spam/virus filters. RDCC IT estimates that it could immediately save 35 percent in IT resources by moving to the cloud.

Office 365 Business Savings for RDCC

The principal savings come from reducing the number of servers from twelve to three. This would also eliminate some corresponding upgrades of Windows 2012, Exchange 2013, SharePoint Services, Exchange CALs, and SharePoint CALs. Other "hidden" costs eliminated included the expense for backup software from the Exchange and SharePoint servers and the off-site disaster recovery backup. RDCC IT management realizes that they are allocating three-quarters of the time of a full-time IT employee to managing these environments, and skipping the expenses on server refresh.

Summary of RDCC On-Premises Requirements

Moving RDCC's core IT services to the cloud frees up budget for additional development. RDCC IT wants to migrate the cupcake simulation tool from an Access database to SQL Server, and implement some other management and consolidation projects. The following summarizes RDCC's IT needs for on-premises services:

- Use Active Directory (password synchronization) for on-site security integration to Microsoft Online Services (they only have to manage 19 users; the 150 users are franchise owners).

- Use Microsoft Intune for antivirus and update management.

- Deploy the Microsoft Enterprise Mobility Suite (EMS) for mobile device management.

- Deploy a blade server with two virtual machines to support the LOB application.

- Contract with a third-party managed service provider to provide a monitoring solution and hosted backup.

With the savings realized by the proposed cloud solution, RDCC is able to significantly restructure its business process and focus the organization on business productivity gains. The company will be able to realize two big priorities: upgrading its servers to the new Intel server and cleaning up its data center. RDCC will also be able to dispose of two of its three computer racks and reduce all servers to one 6U unit with an integrated SAN.

RDCC IT presents the comprehensive plan to management, which is thrilled with the direction to reallocating IT resources to improve the cupcake design simulation by moving it from Access/SQL Server Express to SQL Azure and Microsoft Azure.

Migration Cost and Approaches

Granted, Table 1-4 makes many assumptions about hardware and software costs and support. However, it provides a good illustration that the total cost of ownership is quite different if the costs of server upgrades and software upgrades are considered. That is, when one compares apples with apples.

If it takes at least three years to receive a payoff from an on-premises solution, it is worthwhile to look at the cost trade-offs and other business and technical assumptions. As an example, Table 1-2 illustrates cloud deployment costs to be less than 30 percent of the deployment costs for an equivalent on-premises solution for 50 people.

It is possible to overlook the deployment costs associated with hardware, software, infrastructure, and security required for a server-based solution. The other factor for migration to the cloud depends on employees. Small business migration can be greatly aided by IT skillsets among employees—and on whether they have accepted the migration as a positive thing. It is good practice to involve end users in the planning and transition, and to thoroughly communicate its benefits at key points in the process.

The cloud migration cost for small organizations varies depending upon the organization's skills. Office 365 migrations are about business process changes. In organizations that tend to have well-known business process, migration is quick. Organizations that change the business process experience longer cloud migration.

The business process change for a 20-user business may involve creating a program to train administrative assistants in handling the day-to-day issues like password changes, spam issues, and Outlook configurations. In the RDCC case, there was an initial cost in setting up the training, but rapidly dropped as soon as trained administrators took over.

Contrast this migration with an international organization that is more end-user literate with computers and technology; it was a 35-person company that migrated to online services across four different countries within three days. The users were migrated from an on-premises solution to Microsoft Online Services.

Larger companies are business process driven. As an example, the migration of a 400-person public library in Denver, Colorado, had two business goals: to reduce operation costs and to retrain IT staff on new technologies. The technical migration was simple: move mail from server X to the cloud. However, the business process change was complex. In this case, a program was designed to grow grassroots support in the company and build a peer-user support network. The migration, which was originally forecasted for four months, reduced the schedule by one month. Office 365 is about business process changes and empowering organizations to embrace the change.

These are just some examples. There are different costs associated with all migration. You need to look at the business processes of the organization. This book is designed to address components in each of these costs areas. Looking at migrations, they fall into three categories: low, medium, and high. The migration costs are directly related to the organization's skills.

- *Low.* This is a do-it-yourself (DIY) migration. The IT professional (or business owner) provides the basic configuration and setup, and acts as backup support if needed. Usually, mail is uploaded using PST (since the source environment is usually POP mail).

- *Medium.* The IT professionals partner with customers for the migration, direct customer resources remotely to complete the migration, and train the local IT staff. The organization may need password synchronization and has a local LOB server resource.

- *High.* The IT professionals handle the migration from start to finish. The cost depends on the security requirements and the configuration of the on-site mail server and SharePoint usage. For, there may be a need for tightly integrated security; in the RDCC case, an Enterprise Mobility Suite (EMS) was installed.

The migration environment differs by business. Some businesses run under the Microsoft Active Domain architecture. In cases where there is a non-Microsoft OS, the mail migration costs depend on where the mail and documents reside. There are other factors in the migration costs, and the solution comes down to the business processes.

Remote Monitoring with Microsoft Intune and Systems Center

Remote monitoring and management allows a group of computers to be managed and controlled from a central location. The rationale for remote management and monitoring is to contain operation costs. As organizations' computing infrastructure becomes more complex, we are looking for ways to reduce the complexity of the environment. There are many different sets of remote management and monitoring tools. Typically, remote monitoring looks for a way to aggregate data to allow a proactive analysis of the work environment. Figure 1-8 replicates the Microsoft Intune Monitoring dashboard of a typical small business.

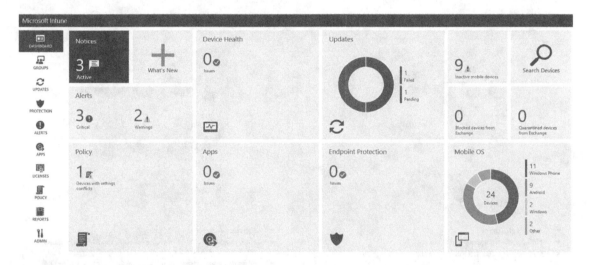

Figure 1-8. *Microsoft Intune monitoring dashboard*

Microsoft recently introduced Microsoft Intune, a desktop management tool for inventory, updates, and security policies, which can be purchased by end users through Microsoft Online Services. The Office 365 user accounts are linked into Microsoft Intune, providing better desktop management. It is highly recommended to deploy some type of tool to determine the system's health. Office 365 requires that desktop user systems be up-to-date and patched with the latest security patches. These desktop management tools are used to identify problems so that proactive action may be taken to resolve issues before they become serious problems and affect business continuity.

The Big Decision: On-Premises or Cloud Solutions?

The line in the sand for IT change is whether to keep data on-site or off-site. The most frequent motivator for data migration to the cloud is cost. Whether it is savings realized through reduced labor, more efficient equipment, or general "operations" expenses, cost is king. Still, the best solution sometimes straddles the line, because there can be a case for equipment and services that are both on-premises and hosted by the cloud. The decision process is known as *resource optimization*, which consists of the following:

- *Server consolidation:* Reducing the number of servers to improve overall operations costs (see Figure 1-10).

- *Hardware consolidation:* Optimizing the server hardware to reduce overall systems cost.

- *Core services consolidation:* Removing core services that can be purchased in the cloud at a lower rate than keeping those services on-premises.

As part of this process (illustrated in Figure 1-9), the server was optimized, enabling it to handle a more integrated workload. In this case, the server is a high-density blade server, such as the Intel server platform. Many different types of servers can be used for hardware consolidation. Dell, HP, and Lenovo offer other choices. The driving factor in the optimization decision should be the integration cost.

Before:

After:

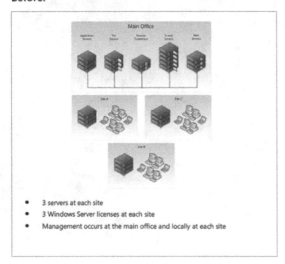 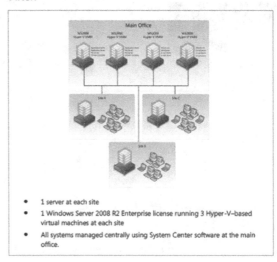

Figure 1-9. *Virtualization and branch office design (courtesy of Microsoft)*

The branch office design (see Figure 1-9) demonstrates a reduction of the on-premises servers from three to one Intel server, with six compute modules hosting the virtual machines. The Intel server (see Figure 1-10) allows the addition of an integrated SAN with 14 SAS (1TB) drives in a RAID 10 configuration (providing a raw space of 14TB). A second integrated networked switch is also added.

Figure 1-10. *High-density server (courtesy of Intel)*

The server also supports six compute modules with 32GB to 512GB memory and dual Intel Xeon E5-2600 v3 processors. Each compute module host OS is either Windows 2012R2 Enterprise or Microsoft Windows Server 2012R2. The Microsoft Hyper-V software can support up to 15 additional virtual machines, with the appropriate licenses, or three additional licensed Windows Enterprise VMs. The redesign reduces the number of servers to one device and adds capabilities to support disaster recovery and business continuity.

Optimizing Core Services with the Cloud

Core services are those basic services that all businesses require, including e-mail, file and print services, and document storage/management. Internal web sites, web/video conferencing, and instant messages are core cloud services that are also used in day-to-day business. All other services used to conduct business can be best described as LOB applications or on-premises services. When we look at the core services, we are looking for ways to optimize the business's productivity and operating efficiency.

Business Efficiency

Optimizing business efficiency involves looking at the core services that make businesses work and making them work as well as possible (see Figure 1-11). Supporting core IT services on-premises involves hiring information technology workers, ordering new server software, and planning the migration of users on workstation software to support the new software releases. This is an ongoing struggle in all businesses, and it costs resources to perform it adequately.

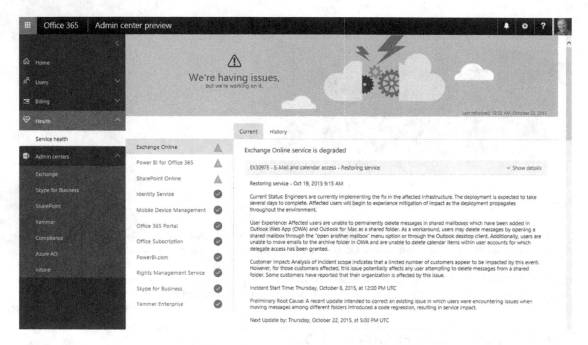

Figure 1-11. Service dashboard—Office 365 services

A complete cloud services migration involves moving the on-premises infrastructure to the cloud. As noted earlier, moving to the cloud can allow businesses to either reduce the IT support staff necessary to maintain the on-premises solution or to reallocate the resources for different IT projects. Operational costs can be reduced for additional services, such as business continuity and disaster recovery. These services are standard with all cloud services partners. Microsoft Online Services offers 30-day mailbox content and SharePoint recoverability, and 14-day recoverability on a mailbox deletion. Additional Microsoft Online Services include e-mail point-to-point encryption and immutable compliance archive (such as Litigation Hold and the FINRA–the Financial Industry Regulatory Authority (www.finra.org)).

Typical migrations involve removing on-premises e-mail (the internal SharePoint web site) to Microsoft Online Services and centralizing conferencing from a third-party supplier to Microsoft Live Meeting. There are sometimes differences in the user interface, but the Microsoft Online Services Business Productivity Online Standard Suite helps resolve them. Services that are left on-site are designed around existing LOB applications using CRM systems and SQL LOB applications, as well as the traditional file/print services.

Next Steps for RDCC

Before RDCC migrates their business to the cloud and Office 365, there is planning to be done. To help plan for the migration, the management team attended a demonstration event as participants in the Microsoft Experience Center (MEC). The MEC demo walks the user through the experience using different persona to fully understand the capabilities of Office 365. This is a key step in the planning cycle for Office 365 migration. As RDCC looks at their business in detail, they will go through a typical planning and evaluation process. Office 365 migration is smooth, but it is essential to plan and test. The next few chapters will detail RDCC's experience.

Summary

This chapter focused on why businesses move to Office 365. It included a review of the business reasons and provided a cost comparison of different approaches. Like any business change, the objective is to reduce operating costs and improve productivity to build a competitive advantage. The conclusion is that Office 365 solutions can provide that competitive advantage.

Next Steps

Your Office 365 systems have been set up and configured. At this point, you understand the features of Office 365 and you are ready to move forward. However, your work is not yet complete. There is more to do, depending on your Office 365 configuration. It is recommended that you review Chapters 2, 5, and 6 in preparation for deployment.

Chapter 2: Understanding the End User Experience. The best way to understand Office 365 is to experience it. You explore the Office 365 capabilities in the Contoso demonstration site, with a focus on how this helps your business productivity. A day in the life of a user demonstrates the capabilities of Office 365.

Chapter 3: The Apps. Office 365 is owned by the business, and the data is only available to the business for business use. Office 365 takes advantage of social enterprise through the different data mining capabilities that are present in services like Gmail, Dropbox, Facebook, LinkedIn, and other social media sites. Those capabilities are applied to your Office 365 site to improve your business productivity. This chapter describes Office 365 apps and discusses how you use them in your business to improve communications and productivity.

Chapter 4: Cloud Security Best Practices. One of the issues that all managers are faced with is the management of data and security and learning best practices. In this chapter, you explore the different capabilities of Office 365 and the monitoring that is in place to manage your Office 365 company to ensure that your data remains private. This chapter covers the most common approaches to Office 365 migration.

Chapter 5: Office 365 Deployment Step by Step. The secret to a successful deployment to Office 365 is picking the correct plan that supports your business. The key to a successful migration to Office 365 is the planning and purchase process. Once you select a plan, your primary consideration must be to ensure that the migration process is seamless for your organization. This chapter describes the basic purchase information and it details the choices. It concludes with information about pre-deployment, deployment, and post-deployment.

Chapter 6: Workstation Setup and Configuration. Office 365 supports many different systems and capabilities, depending on your business needs. The issue that IT managers constantly face is how to setup and manage the client environment. This chapter is focused on the configuration of an Office 365 desktop environment. This is the go-to reference chapter on the configuration of your desktop and mobile phones.

Chapter 7: Managing Office 365. This chapter describes the different administration centers in Office 365 and the most common tools that you use to administer Office 365. Depending on your Office 365 plan, there are five possible administration tools. This chapter focuses on the Office 365, Exchange, and Skype for Business administration centers. The chapter closes with using PowerShell to manage your Office 365 environment.

CHAPTER 2

■ ■ ■

Understanding the End User Experience Using Office 365

Office 365 is scalable for all businesses. An Office 365 subscription can be created for 1 user or 100,000 users. Office 365 is the only service that allows any business to have the same capabilities as a Fortune 100 company, at a low monthly subscription. As a business owner, you are no longer restricted from using tools that were only available to large corporations—you have the same capabilities.

After the user logs in to the Office 365 service (see Figure 2-1), Office 365 displays the features available to the user (based on the plan that the administrator has assigned). Each plan is designed with features to best meet the needs of businesses based upon business size or other factors. All business and users are different. Office 365 allows the administrator to mix and match different plans to meet the individual user needs in the organization. The popular plans are Business Essential, Business Premium, and E3. There is no longer a requirement to have everyone on the same plan; you can mix all types of plans in your Office 365 subscription.

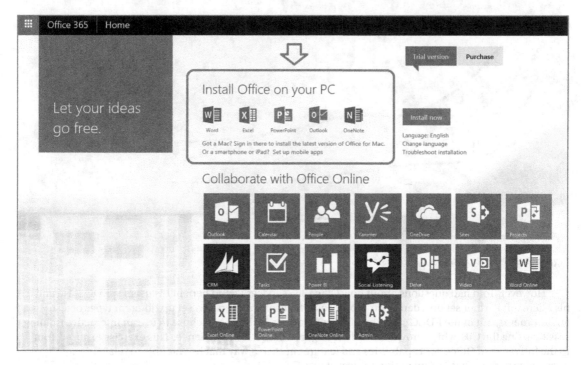

Figure 2-1. *Office 365 login page*

The administrator can select the plan mix that makes business sense for the users in the company. Office 365 supports Macs, PCs, iPads/tablets, and mobile devices. All the user needs to do is log in using the Company Credentials at http://office.microsoft.com (or http://portal.microsoftonline.com). Our approach to an Office 365 configuration is to select the subscription that best matches the roles of the employees and the needs of the organization.

This chapter details a day in the life of an Office 365 user and the materials needed for setting up one computer to use Office 365. This approach enables most end users to start an Office 365 trial subscription and successfully configure the service. We have placed additional information about the Microsoft Customer Immersion Experience (CIE) center and the Microsoft FastTrack service in the reference section of the chapter.

The "A Day in the Life of an Office 365 User" section explores Office 365 capabilities in the Microsoft demonstration site and details the features of Office 365. Taking the time to test service offerings in this way tends to result in the most successful migrations. With a basic understanding of the service offerings, identifying the ones that match your business needs becomes simple.

A Day in the Life of an Office 365 User

In the previous chapter, the Ready Design Custom Cupcakes (RDCC) company completed a business analysis of Office 365 cloud services and was ready to move to Office 365. The IT manager (let's call him Tom) looked at his total company spending, and with the help of his Microsoft Partner, determined that his on-site cost was about $115 per user, per month; and the Office 365 cost was approximately $53 per user, per month (see Figure 2-2). These costs included ongoing support.

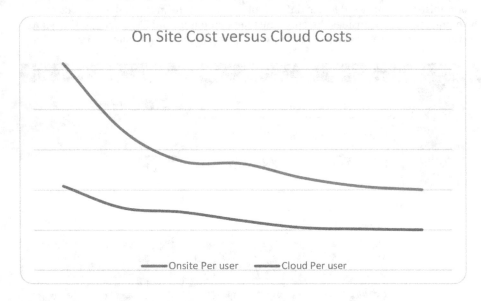

Figure 2-2. On-site costs vs. cloud costs

However, Tom had questions about how Office 365 services would benefit his users at RDCC. He and his Microsoft Partner set up a demonstration. Most Microsoft Partners can set up different types of test environments, but in the RDCC case, the Microsoft Partner, KAMIND IT, chose to use an interactive training session using the CIE, which provides a fully configured Office 365 experience. This exercise exposed Tom to the full range of Office 365 capabilities and features in such a way that he was able to relate his new knowledge to the Office 365 migration project at RDCC.

The CIE is a preconfigured Office 365 organization that supports all of the Office 365 services, including Yammer, Project, Exchange, Skype for Business, SharePoint, OneDrive for Business, Delve, Video, CRM, Enterprise Mobility Suite, and Microsoft Intune.

Now Tom is looking for ways to reduce the costs of managing the Office 365 user's devices with a cloud solution so that RDCC does not need to manage an on-premises solution using Microsoft System Center. KAMIND IT suggests that Tom play the role of an end user in the Microsoft demonstration company, Contoso, Inc. Tom is assigned an Office 365 user account, and he assumes the hypothetical identity of a Contoso sales associate, Karen Berg.

■ **Note** The "Where to start with Office 365" section is a *hands-on tutorial*, not a *configuration guide*. We have dedicated a specific chapter and all of the necessary configuration information to set up your desktop. The tutorial serves only to show the features of Office 365; the ones that you really need can be selected and applied to your specific work environment.

Where to Start with Office 365? A Hands-on Tutorial

Start by opening up a web browser and logging in to the Office 365 site at **http://portal.office.com** *or* **http://portal.microsoftonline.com** (see Figure 2-3).

Figure 2-3. *Log in to Office 365: login screen*

Once you have entered your e-mail address, Microsoft Online Services determines if there are multiple accounts for different Microsoft services under your e-mail address. Microsoft offers two different services for users: consumer services and company or business services. These services are represented as a Microsoft account and a Work (or Organization) account. The Microsoft account is for Microsoft services that require a unique ID, such as your e-mail address. Examples of these accounts are Hotmail, Microsoft Outlook.com, Xbox Live, Windows Phone 8.1, and volume license services (to name a few; there are other consumer services). A Microsoft account can be any e-mail address (for example, you can have a Gmail account as a Microsoft account) and is used to provide secure access to Microsoft services.

The Work account is your Office 365 company business service account. The services of these two accounts are different and isolated from each other on different servers in one or more Microsoft datacenters. It is very common that a user will have both a Work account and a Microsoft account. When you access Office 365 services, you always use the Work account.

■ **Note**   You do not need to have a Microsoft account to use Office 365, only a Work account.

Logging in to Office 365

After you have opened a browser to either office.microsoft.com or login.microsoft.com, select the sign-in and enter your Office 365 work e-mail address. If you have added consumer capabilities to your e-mail address (found at account.live.com), then you are presented with two choices (see Figure 2-4). If you are going to access Office 365, then select the **Work account**.

Figure 2-4. *Access Office 365 using a Work account*

Once you have entered your password, you log in to Office 365 services. The next step is to explore the interface of Office 365.

RDCC's IT manger, Tom, chooses to use the hypothetical persona of Karen Berg, a sales associate in the Contoso Company. Tom wants to experience the operation of Office 365 from a productivity point of view as a user. When you log in to Office 365 for the first time, a normal Office 365 user (like Karen Berg) sees an initial configuration screen that introduces Office 365 services to the user in the self-service portal (see Figure 2-5). Tom likes this approach because the self-service portal reduces the calls to his help desk and improves his users' satisfaction.

Figure 2-5. *Office 365 first-time login*

Tom, acting as Karen Berg, sees that he can continue to install the Office 365 software for his PC/Mac, phone, and tablet without any help desk support. He sees the Install Now button and realizes that he can install Office ProPlus for his PC. Tom is interested in Mac support as well, so he logs in from his Mac and selects installs it too. The correct Office 2016 for Mac software is supplied as part of the download. Tom realizes that this self-service feature will help him deploy Office ProPlus and Office for the Mac to his clients.

Tom's Office 365 partner, KAMIND IT (partner ID 4471503), recommends that Tom start with Outlook. KAMIND IT configured the demonstration center and his subscription with Microsoft FastTrack SharePoint site for RDCC. FastTrack is a site that includes training material, support video, and deployment plans for moving your business to Office 365. KAMIND IT's business practice is to deploy all customers with the Microsoft FastTrack site to help empower users with migrating to and using Office 365.

■ **Note**   KAMIND IT uses a 93-point checklist for Office 365 deployments. KAMIND IT believes that all users need to understand the capabilities of Office 365. It deploys FastTrack SharePoint sites to speed the deployment and to provide training resources to IT managers to reduce the cost of support with using Office 365. KAMIND IT has deployed more than 300 Office 365 and Microsoft Intune customers.

Tom selects the Outlook icon (see Figure 2-6) to begin to exploring the online services. Tom notices the nine-block grid in the upper-left corner (with the description "Looking for your apps") of the browser and discovers that he can navigate to the various Office 365 web applications. Tom's goal is to launch Outlook. He notices that if the web applications are missing, he can select the nine-block grid to return to the application choice. Tom explores the different services, such as Web Outlook and his personal cloud document storage, OneDrive for Business. Tom selects the Outlook tab (see Figure 2-6) to see Karen's e-mail.

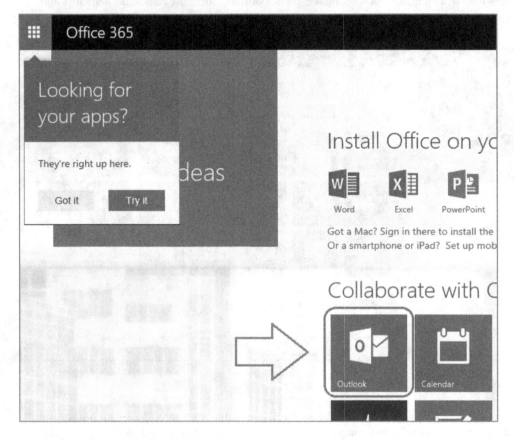

Figure 2-6. *Accessing Outlook: Office 365*

Office 365 Outlook mail services are designed to provide data synchronization between all devices that are using Office 365. The simplest way to look at this is that all information is synchronized, so in using e-mail on his smartphone, web browser, or local Outlook, Tom only needs to "read once" and/or "delete once" and all devices connected to Office 365 e-mail services will sync his actions. The e-mail that Tom sees on his tablet is the same on his smartphone and in the cloud (see Figure 2-7). The information is updated and in sync with the data sources, line-of-business applications, and user devices (smartphones, tablets, laptops, or desktop systems).

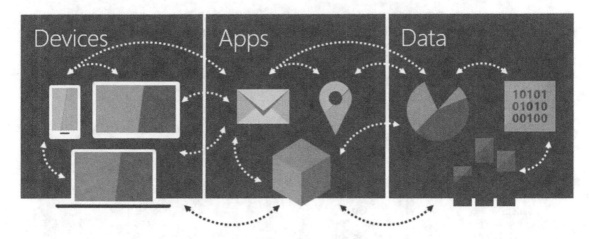

Figure 2-7. *Accessing Outlook from a tablet (courtesy of Microsoft)*

Accessing Outlook Web Application (OWA)

Tom begins to explore the Office 365 web site. The Microsoft Partner, KAMIND IT, informs him that after the initial login, all future logins to Office 365 replace the user start page to either use Outlook or the Team Site, depending on the license that is assigned to the user. As an example, if the user only has a SharePoint license, she will land on the Sites page. If the user has an e-mail license, then he will land on the Outlook page (see Figure 2-8). Karen's license is a full Office 365 subscription that includes access to SharePoint and Office 2016, so her default page is the Outlook Web Application, or OWA.

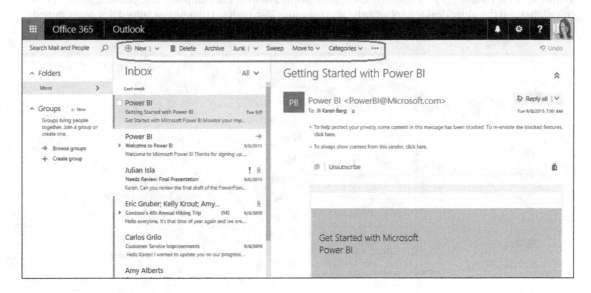

Figure 2-8. *Office 365 landing page for user with an e-mail account*

Tom notices that the Office 365 OWA looks very similar to the Outlook desktop client. The interface is crisp and simple to understand. When you select an e-mail, you can easily move the e-mail to different folders or set into color-coded categories. The Outlook e-mail, calendar, and People (contacts) are easily navigated. Tom notices that the OWA supports right-click actions on the interface (see Figure 2-9). This is important to Tom so that the sales staff can color-code their customer e-mail into different categories.

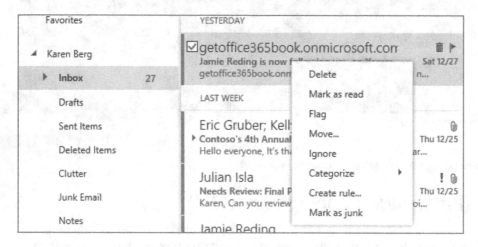

Figure 2-9. *OWA with right-click support*

Tom also notices that he can assign individual categories to e-mail, and that these categories are updated on both OWA and the desktop Outlook (see Figure 2-10). He quickly realizes that this is a big benefit to his users. He constantly gets midnight calls from the president of the company, complaining about the color tabs with the older desktop software he was running. Tom realizes that he has solved this one problem through migration and provides full compatibility moving forward.

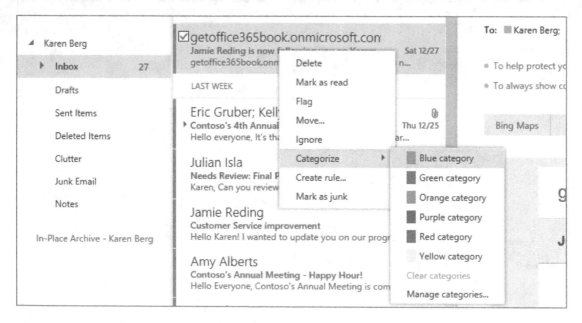

Figure 2-10. *Outlook Web Application (OWA) with e-mail category tabs*

■ **Note**   IT polices can override individual polices on e-mail retention. The default is to allow the user to determine the best way to save e-mail. We have seen corporate e-mail retention polices provide as little as 90 days' history. Many of us expect to retain years of old e-mails.

Setting Outlook Options

One of the capabilities that Tom is looking for is the ability for his users to make the necessary configuration changes, such as adding a signature, and setting the e-mail retention policy and out-of-office messages. Tom speaks to his Microsoft Partner, who explains that Office 365 OWA has configuration settings. To access these settings, the partner instructs Tom to select the gear icon next to the user picture in the browser (see Figure 2-11) and then select the Options. For example, the e-mail options include automatic processing, account configuration, customization of the e-mail template, checking on delivery reports, and managing personal encryption.

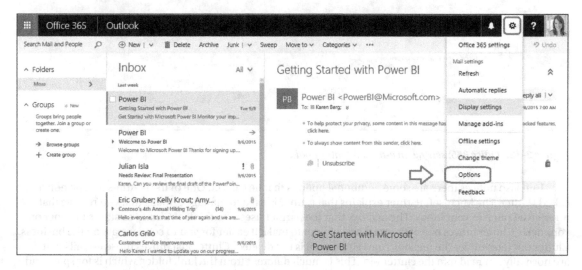

Figure 2-11. *Office 365: Selecting the e-mail options settings*

One of the problems that Tom is dealing with is the personal e-mail retention policy. Tom has set the corporate e-mail retention policy and compliance requirements, but allow the users to have some granular control. As an example, the corporate e-mail policy is set to move e-mail from the main mailbox into the archive folders after two years. Tom has individual users that want to move their e-mail into an archive folder after 90 days.

Tom quickly sees that he can provide individual users more freedom to manage their own inbox and to add their own individual retention policy. He selects the Options, and then selects Retention Policies (see Figure 2-12) for e-mail retention. In this case, he sees that "never delete" is enforced on the mailbox. The Microsoft Partner informs Tom the e-mail size is 50 GB per user, and the per-user archive is unlimited. Tom quickly realizes that this is a big benefit to his users. He also often gets midnight calls from the president of the company, complaining about the limited size of user mailboxes. At some point, most of us have suffered the frustration of an over-full mailbox, either as a sender or as a receiver. Office 365 removes this frustration.

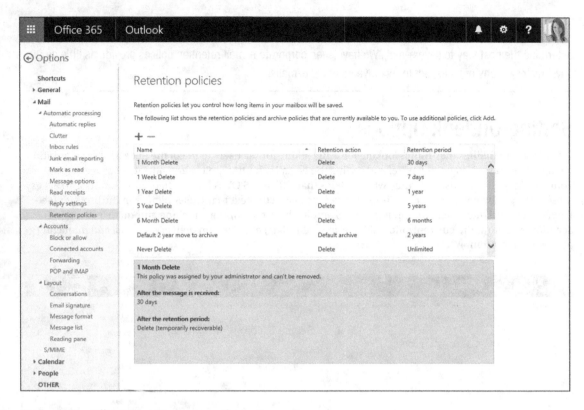

Figure 2-12. Office 365: setting an e-mail retention policy

Tom also notices there are some additional options that he can set. One of the features that he notices is called Clutter. The Microsoft Partner explains that Clutter is used to manage e-mails that you receive that are not viewed often in your inbox. The analogy that the partner uses is to think of Clutter as stacks of paper on your desk. Clutter moves one of the stacks to a folder to make it easier for you to concentrate on the business. Clutter operates under the mailbox rules and e-mail is not deleted. Clutter just moves those e-mails that are normally not read into the clutter bin. This is much different from the Junk folder, which is for spam and where e-mail is deleted after 30 days (assuming you have the default retention policies in place).

There are additional features that Tom sees that are very valuable for his users. Distribution groups for instance. The users can create their own distribution groups for various team meetings. He also notices that the user can adjust the viewing panes and customize the panes for the device that they are using. Tom thinks about how he likes to read e-mail on his iPad. He can now set the view pane to reflect his device style (see Figure 2-13).

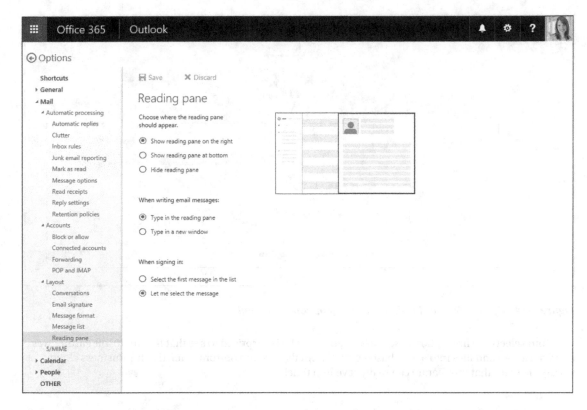

Figure 2-13. *Office 365: Setting the OWA viewing pane under options*

Tom is also interested in the way e-mail attachments are handled in the OWA. The current web mail tool that he is using makes it almost impossible to send e-mail attachments to other users. When Tom is using his iPad, he just gives up and pulls out his laptop, which is simpler than using the iPad. Tom would like to use a web browser and just attach a document in a new e-mail, rather than forwarding an e-mail that has the attachment but the e-mail content is a different subject. Currently, he does not have an option to do this and he was looking to solve this problem. Tom speaks to the Microsoft Partner, who informs him that he can attach documents from OneDrive or from his desktop.

Tom decides to test this capability, so he creates a new e-mail and selects the "insert file" icon. He discovers that he can send a document from the OneDrive for Business cloud storage. He creates an e-mail and selects the Attach icon (see Figure 2-14). He sees that he can add pictures inline and insert files from OneDrive, his local desktop, and group mailboxes.

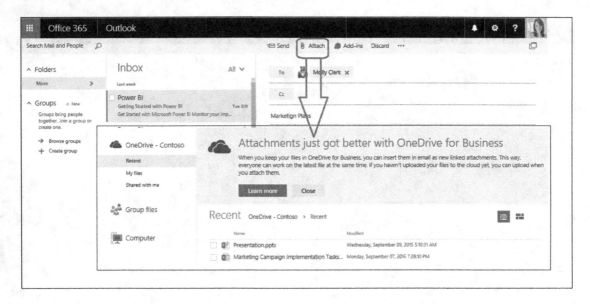

Figure 2-14. *Office 365: Selecting the attachment options for e-mail*

Tom selects the first option to see how to add files; he is surprised to see that the Microsoft Partner was correct. He can add files into a web-based e-mail from the desktop or from OneDrive for Business cloud storage. He sees that this feature can really save him time!

OneDrive for Business: Overview

Tom reviews the Office 365 features and notices that there is support for OneDrive, Sites, and Yammer. The Microsoft Partner explains that Office 365 document synchronization is part of OneDrive. OneDrive is a Microsoft tool that synchronizes documents with Office 365 and all of the user's desktop or mobile devices. This allows the user Karen to access work documents on her phone, laptop, or desktop computer. The Microsoft Partner instructs Tom to access OneDrive from the App menu (the nine-block grid in left-hand corner) and select the OneDrive menu item (see Figure 2-15) to edit documents in the Office 365 cloud.

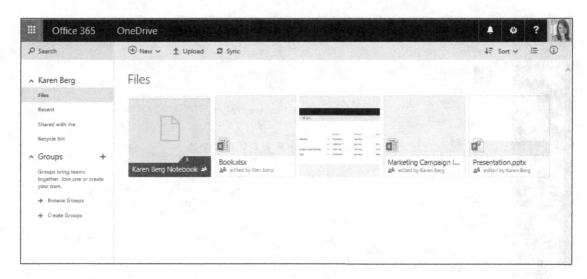

Figure 2-15. *Karen's personal document storage in OneDrive (tablet view)*

■ **Note** If this is the first time you are accessing OneDrive, setting up can take a few minutes.

Once the setup is completed, Karen's private OneDrive for Business cloud storage is built. Karen's initial OneDrive for Business storage capacity is set at 1 TB (1,000 GB). Tom thinks of RDCC sales associates who have a mobile laptop, iPad, and smartphone, and considers that they are located in several different parts of the world. He realizes that OneDrive for Business storage solves a problem for RDCC by easily maintaining control of company documents in centralized team storage, without the associated overhead costs. Tom starts Word 2016 and looks at the account settings (located under File menu) to see the different services that he can use (see Figure 2-16).

Figure 2-16. *Using Word 2013, selecting files from OneDrive, OneDrive for Business, or Office 365 SharePoint*

Tom's Microsoft Partner informs him that OneDrive for Business is included in the subscription he plans to use for RDCC, at no additional cost. He realizes that OneDrive for Business combined with web-based Outlook (OWA) solves a lot of problems for his users.

Tom explores other aspects of using documents in the cloud and discovers that any document that is uploaded to the cloud can be used in any collaboration. Office 365 has two document storage areas. One is the personal OneDrive site and the other is the company's Team Site. The difference between the two is that the personal OneDrive site is managed by the user (Karen) and the Team Site is managed by the IT department.

Document Collaboration

The Office 365 OneDrive and Team Site allow Tom to create documents specifically for collaboration. He can just select the **New** dropdown menu shown in Figure 2-17, then select the type of document he needs.

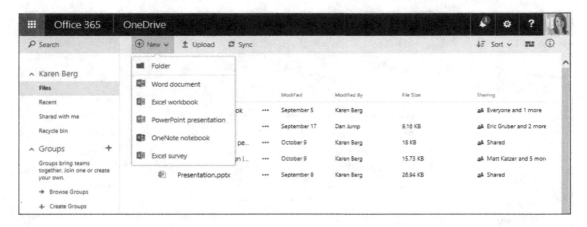

Figure 2-17. *Office 365 document creation*

Tom can also upload documents from other systems to Office 365 using a drag-and-drop interface. He discovers that when he uses Windows 8.1 and Windows 10, he can easily drag documents (see Figure 2-18) to the OneDrive for Business site in the web browser and place those documents in his personal area on Office 365. Tom also experiments with the Team Site and discovers that he has the same capability there.

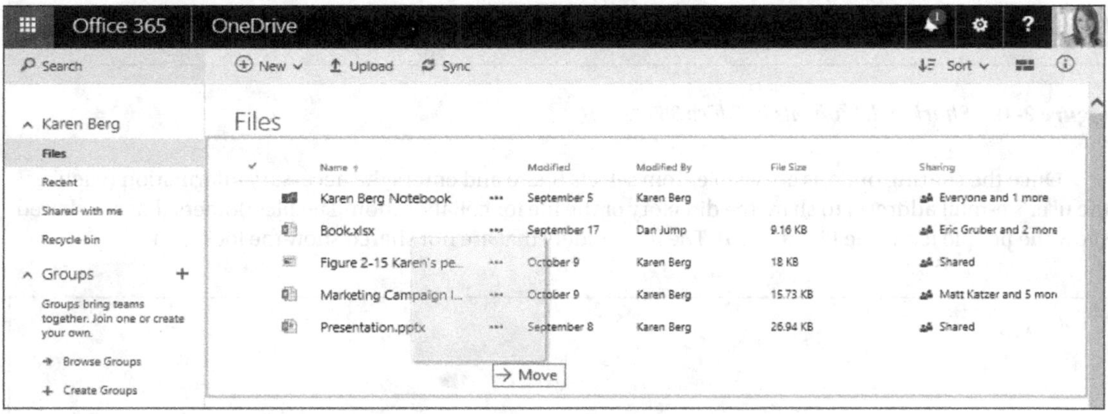

Figure 2-18. *Uploading documents to Office 365*

Once a document is saved in Tom's personal area of Office 365, it could be shared with other members of the team as needed. Once documents are uploaded, they also can be edited with Office 365 web applications (Word, Excel, OneNote, PowerPoint) or with the desktop (or mobile) Office Professional Plus software, which supports PC, Mac, and Android devices).

Tom discovers that Office 365 documents can be shared between designated team members using the personal shared folder, or externally to users outside the company. Tom experiments with sharing documents by selecting the ellipses (…) for additional options, and later the Share option in the menu bar. Tom is surprised to see a preview of the file with an option to allow him to explicitly share the document (see Figure 2-19).

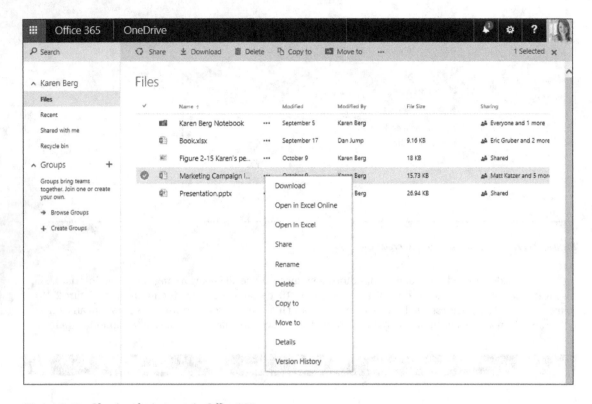

Figure 2-19. *Sharing documents in Office 365*

Once the sharing options are visible, Tom selects Share and enters the necessary information (such as the user's e-mail address) to share the directory or the file for collaboration. The files/folders that are shared show the people icon (see Figure 2-20). The files/folders that are not shared show the lock icon.

	Name ↑		Modified	Modified By	File Size	Sharing
✓						
	Karen Berg Notebook	•••	September 5	Karen Berg		👥 Everyone and 1 more
	Book.xlsx	•••	September 17	Dan Jump	9.16 KB	👥 Eric Gruber and 2 more
	Figure 2-15 Karen's pe...	•••	October 9	Karen Berg	18 KB	👥 Shared
✓	Marketing Campaign I...	•••	October 9	Karen Berg	15.73 KB	👥 Matt Katzer and 5 more
	Presentation.pptx	•••	September 8	Karen Berg	26.94 KB	👥 Shared

Figure 2-20. *Office 365 sharing icons*

Office 365 Delve Configuration

Tom looks at the Office 365 applications that are available (on the nine-block grid), and comes across two new collaboration applications: Delve and Video. He has been looking into these collaboration applications. He comes across information from Microsoft (see Figure 2-21) that describes Delve as a visual tool that links content based on relevancy. Tom has always been fascinated by Facebook and LinkedIn, and the way that these tools display information to the user based on relevancy. The CIO of RDCC has asked Tom if it made sense to create a private Facebook site for the RDCC organization, rather than trying to build something from scratch that would relate information.

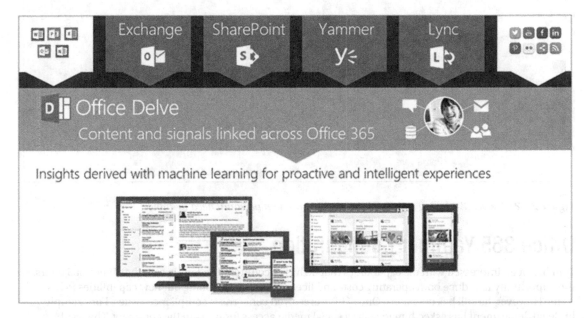

Figure 2-21. *Delve: linking Office 365 content from multiple sources in one spot (courtesy of Microsoft)*

Tom further explores Delve and Yammer and discovers that the Office documents are linked by relevancy and user permissions. In other words, Office 365 users start searching for documents in SharePoint, Yammer, or e-mail, and Delve finds the documents that the user is searching. Delve links data that is linked (Office documents). E-mail, Yammer, and SharePoint can easily be related to the user.

Tom looks at different users in the test account and notices that the data is different in Delve, when using "Karen B" account login, than when using the "Molly C" account login in the test account (see Figure 2-22). Delve is about user trending of what is relevant to that user based on the e-mail, OneDrive for Business, Yammer, and the SharePoint site. Tom thinks about the conversation that he had with his CIO, who was concerned that a user's individual data would be made generally available. Tom is pleased to find that data is isolated and only shown if other users have permissions to see it. Delve could help him deploy the Office 365 OneDrive for Business.

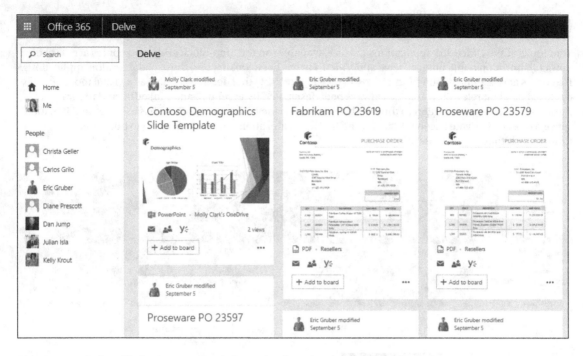

Figure 2-22. Delve: displaying trending information based on personal need to know

Office 365 Yammer Configuration

Tom has been impressed with the capabilities that he has encountered so far. He sees that Office 365 offers the opportunity to reduce both operating costs and license costs while rolling out new capabilities to his users. However, he still has questions. One of his unresolved concerns is compliance issues. For example, his legal department has asked him to restrict social media access for users in the company. The legal department feels that too much proprietary information (company confidential information) is being discussed on external social media sites such as Facebook and Google Plus.

The legal department advises that loss of company information could hurt business growth and give RDCC competitors advance information on the direction of RDCC products. The Microsoft Partner suggested that Tom consider the Yammer social media service, which is part of Office 365, as a solution. Yammer is a service similar to Facebook that is used to handle group interactions in a free-form manner. It is explained that company information exchanged on Yammer is owned by the company and not licensed to a third party. Usually, a free service has intellectual property rights assignment that overrides the confidentiality of the company information.

Tom selects the Yammer login on the Office 365 page (see Figure 2-23) and logs in to it using Karen Berg's Office 365 account. The first thing that he notices (see Figure 2-24) is the interaction of the different teams and the discussion groups. There were discussion groups for events, HR, and using Yammer itself. Tom could see that Yammer addresses one of RDCC business objectives: to make the company more integrated in their internal communications to improve productivity. The productivity gain addressed this directive and Yammer received full endorsement by the legal department.

Figure 2-23. *Yammer access: Office 365 menu option*

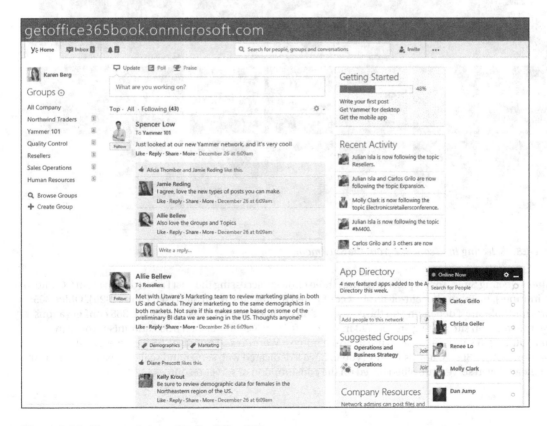

Figure 2-24. *Yammer integration for Office 365*

Tom quickly realizes that one of the benefits of Yammer is that the service provides a tool for the group's communications that can be kept internal to the company. The problem with traditional social media solutions is that RDCC's proprietary information can be accidentally leaked to the public. Legal informed Tom that last year, some employees used free social media sites to share information about a project. The legal department discovered the project discussed in the trade press. Tom was informed about the data leak of company information at a company senior management meeting. He feels that Yammer will allow RDCC to control potential data leaks.

Accessing the SharePoint Team Site

The final service that Tom reviews is the Team Site. Tom has a business requirement to create a new company intranet and to help the company reduce its carbon footprint. He has a secondary objective to reduce the use of other file-sharing services, enabling the exchange of information with external parties. To access the Team Site, Tom returns to the main Office 365 page and selects Sites (see Figure 2-25).

Figure 2-25. *Selecting the Team Site from the Sites menu*

After selecting Sites, Tom is presented with three choices: accessing the FastTrack (deployment), Contoso (demo intranet), or Team Site (out-of-the-box configured SharePoint Team Site) (see Figure 2-26). Office 365 supports multiple sites, depending on the configuration of Office 365 services. The Office 365 configurations that use the free web site hosting are located in Microsoft Azure Cloud. All Office 365 administrators can link their Office 365 subscription to Azure to host a no-cost WordPress, Drupal, or IIS web site in a shared environment. Office 365/Azure also allows you to have a dedicated web server and scale the web server to any size. Dedicated web servers are billed based on the consumption of server resources.

Figure 2-26. Sites that are promoted for users

■ **Note**   FastTrack is optional and it is not configured into all Office 365 accounts. To add FastTrack, you need to use an E3 or E5 trial, go to deploy.office.com, and select the "Getting started with FastTrack" option.

Office 365 Team Site: "FastTrack"

Tom selects the FastTrack site icon to see the capabilities of the FastTrack site. His FastTrack SharePoint site has information on how to manage the migration to Office 365. The Microsoft Partner helping Tom manage Office 365 arranges for Microsoft to deploy the FastTrack content so that Tom can understand the Office 365 migration process and provide the necessary educational material to his end users to speed the transition to Office 365.

Tom discovers that Office 365 SharePoint sites are easy to use and share. He explores FastTrack and selects the Video Learning section. The Video Learning section has additional material on the how to use various features of Office 365. As an example, his users are looking at ways to use SharePoint and OneDrive for Business and learn how to use these Office 365 services (see Figure 2-28). Tom wants to make the site available to all users and finds that the best way to do this is to share the site (see Figure 2-29).

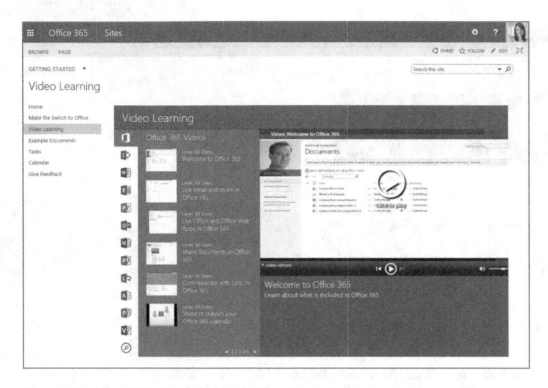

Figure 2-27. *Office 365 FastTrack deployment SharePoint video learning site*

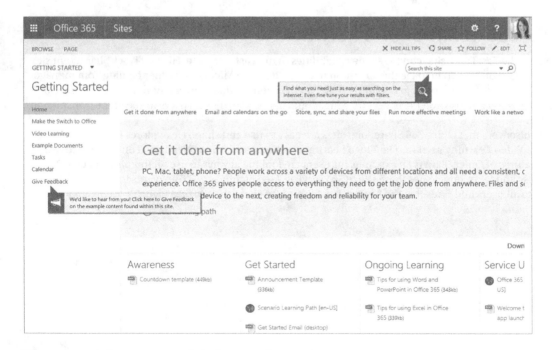

Figure 2-28. *Office 365 FastTrack deployment SharePoint site*

Figure 2-29. *Inviting other users to a SharePoint Team site by sharing the site*

The Microsoft Partner explains to Tom that the Office 365 account he is using is the Microsoft Immersion Experience Center (MEC) demo Contoso site, a fully functional SharePoint site complete with document retention polices, workflows, and other productivity features. The Partner also explains that these capabilities can be used to improve the operation of RDCC business. Tom selects the Team Site icon and launches the intranet site (see Figure 2-30).

■ **Note**   Office 365 default configurations do not include the Contoso demonstration site or the FastTrack site. KAMIND IT deploys the FastTrack site to all the Office 365 subscriptions that they manage. Please contact your Microsoft Partner or KAMIND IT if you would like to access this preconfigured demonstration site.

Office 365 Team Site: "Contoso"

The Microsoft Partner explains to Tom that the MEC demo Contoso site is a fully functional SharePoint site complete with document retention polices, work flows, and other productivity features. The Partner also explains that these capabilities can be used to improve the operation of RDCC business. Tom selects the Team Site icon and launches the intranet site.

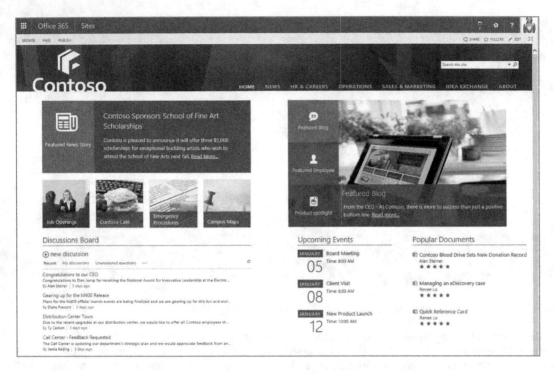

Figure 2-30. *Office 365 Team Site*

Tom looks at the team site and the capabilities that Office 365 has, and then compares this to the amount of servers they use in RDCC to achieve the same capabilities. He realizes that he can add the functionality to his Office 365 SharePoint Team Site and reduce his capital and operating costs at RDCC. In addition to reducing costs (by removing server hardware), Tom realizes that he can assign user permissions, so that individuals can have access to the different business areas. For example, Karen can access the sales resources but can have access to HR, IT, operations, and the account team only as each relates to her business role.

Office 365 Desktop Tools

The only issue that Tom has not reviewed is desktop tools for Office 365. He returns to the Office 365 portal and installs the client software. He was under the misconception that Office 365 tools only run in the cloud and that there is no desktop software. He learns that Office 365 is a suite of products—namely, desktop and cloud services—that are integrated to work together. Tom looks at editing an Excel spreadsheet in the cloud and discovers that he had the option to edit it in the cloud or on the desktop (see Figure 2-31).

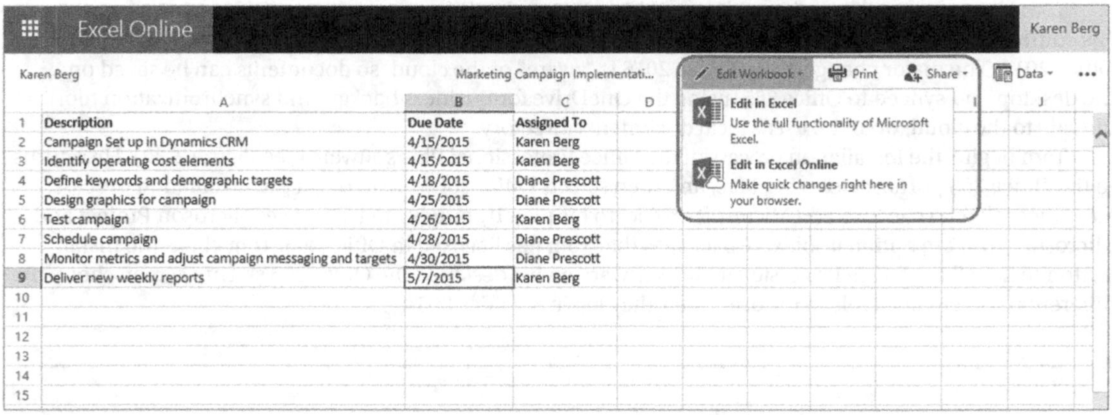

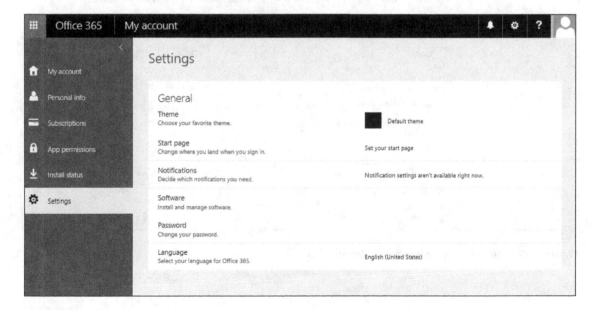

Figure 2-31. *Editing documents with Desktop Office 2016 Professional Plus*

While using the "Karen Berg" login account, Tom is able to use the cloud tools on Office 365 and the desktop office software without being hooked to the Internet. He can work offline on his PC or on his home Mac (see Figure 2-32). The Microsoft Partner explains that Office 365 allows each user to have up to five copies of Office desktop software installed under the subscription. Tom thinks about the cost savings from using subscription services to manage his software assets. He realizes that he would no longer need to manage serial numbers or manage employees installing software on their own computers. Office 365 allows Tom to remove the user software subscription when an employee leaves the company and no longer has any responsibility to remove the software. This is a business liability and huge labor effort that Tom realizes he no longer needs to manage. Office 365 will significantly reduce his operating costs.

Figure 2-32. *Selecting Office 365 Settings to install Office Professional Plus desktop software*

Tom remembers a discussion with one of his users on the differences between Office 2007 and 2010. His comment was that Office is Office; only the menus are different. The 2016 Office 365 is very similar to Office 2010. The major change is that Office 2016 is "aware" of the cloud, so documents can be saved on the desktop and synced to Office 365 (using the OneDrive for Business background synchronization tool), directly to the cloud, or in the user's local documents directory.

Tom begins the installation process of the Office Professional Plus software (see Figure 2-33). He returns to the Office 365 portal, selects PC/Mac, and then selects Office software to begin the installation process. He notices that he can also add Microsoft Project to his plan by purchasing a license. Microsoft Project and Microsoft CRM are optional software packages that Tom has licensed in Office 365. Tom clicks the Install button to install the Office Professional Plus software on his desktop. The Office 365 startup screen shows the different packages available to the users after they log in to Office 365.

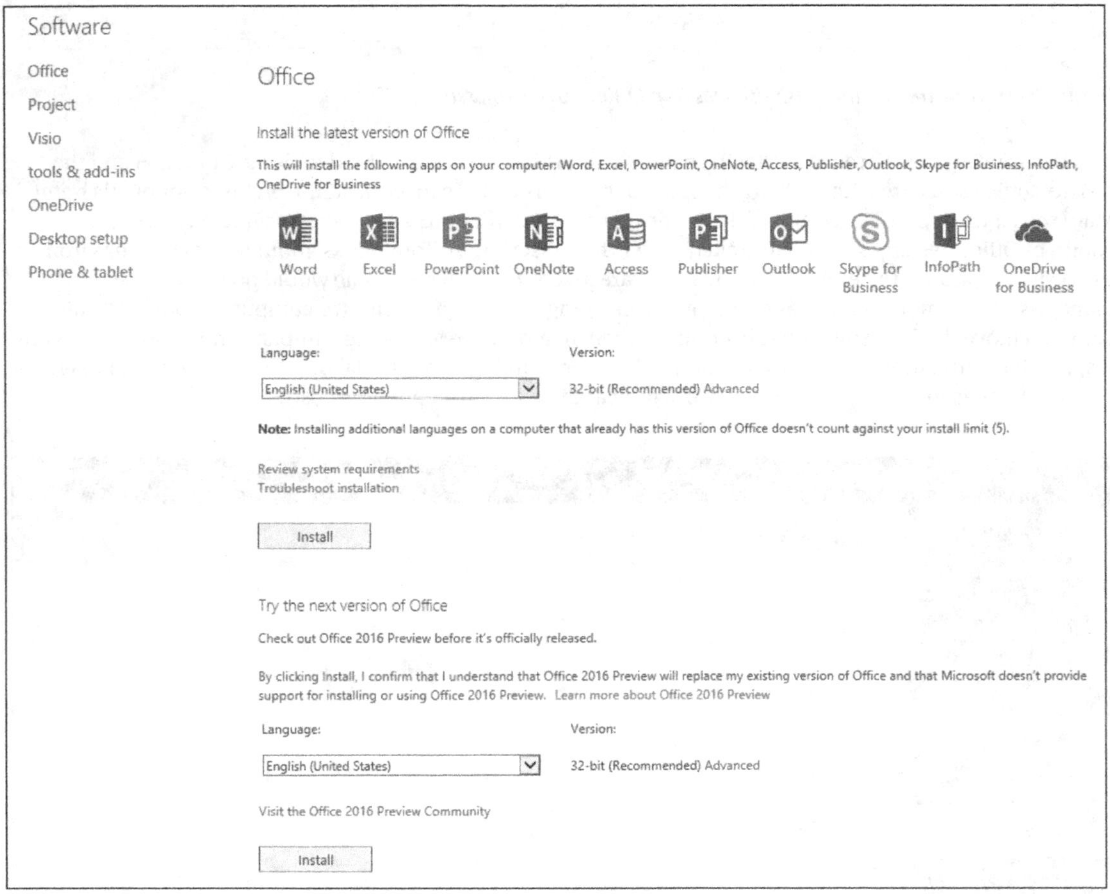

Figure 2-33. *Office desktop software installation*

The Office installation software is streamed (see Figure 2-34). Streaming means that the user can continue to work while the new software is being delivered from the Microsoft Office servers.

Figure 2-34. Streaming Office 365

After the Office Professional Plus installation completed, Tom starts Outlook using Karen Berg's e-mail address for the demonstration account. He selects a New Profile. The installation process requires Tom to enter Karen's e-mail address, name, and password (see Figure 2-35). Outlook discovers the cloud service and downloads Karen's e-mail.

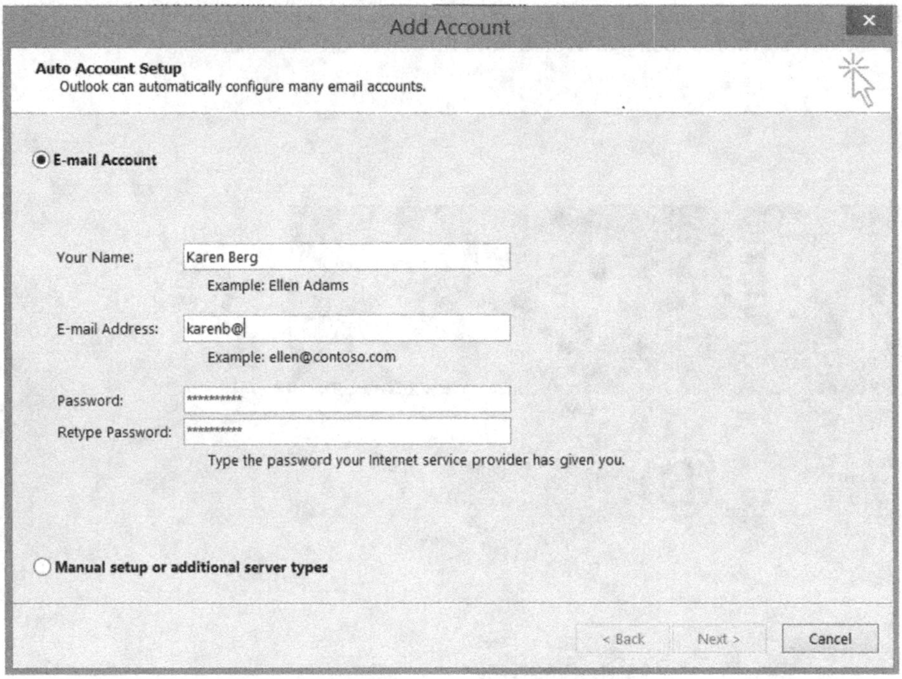

Figure 2-35. *Outlook startup screen: creating new profile*

Tom is off and running with Outlook. He selects Finish (when prompted) and starts Outlook. Karen's e-mail downloads to Tom's client. In desktop Outlook (see Figure 2-36), Tom notices that when he reads an e-mail, the Office 365 Outlook Web App had the same changes. Then, Tom notices that his actions to e-mail (read, delete, move) were synced to the cloud. His users have always complained that smartphones do not update the e-mail status after a message was read or deleted. Tom no longer has to worry about this issue; all e-mail is synced to the latest activity. He wants to try one other test, so he disconnects his network connection, creates a new e-mail in Outlook, and sends it. Tom then connects his laptop back into the network and discovers that the offline e-mail sent to Outlook was updated in the cloud.

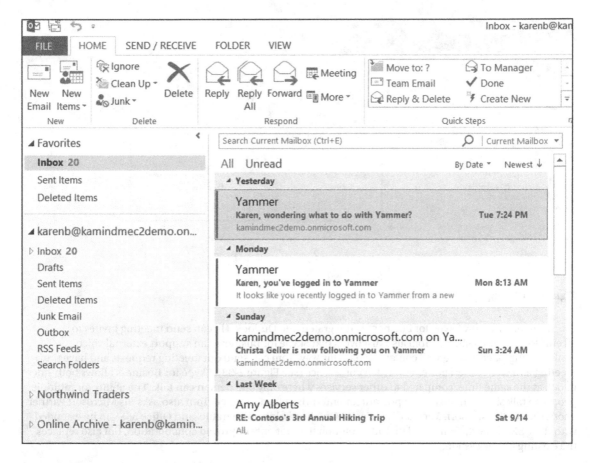

Figure 2-36. *Karen's desktop Outlook*

This solved a big problem for his users. Tom now had full business e-mail, calendar, and contacts synchronization, not only to his desktop version of Outlook, but also to his smartphone and iPad. He realizes that the variety of third-party programs that his users are using to synchronize their contacts and calendars are no longer needed.

Using Skype for Business

Tom also has a problem with web conferencing. When he installed Office on the desktop, Skype for Business, the web video conferencing tool, was installed. His users currently use Skype over the public network to discuss business needs and issues. As Tom explores Skype of Business, he realizes that he can now use it to talk to external Lync/Skype for Business users, Skype users outside of the company, as well as internal RDCC employees. Using Skype, conversations (and text in instant messaging windows) can be recorded (see Figure 2-37). Tom also notices that Skype for Business is an Enterprise voice solution, where both users can speak at the same time. Skype for Business can also replace a desktop phone and it can be placed on a user's mobile devices (laptop, iPad, and smartphone). Tom is pleased to see this, since many new federal regulations require conversation recording to meet compliance rules.

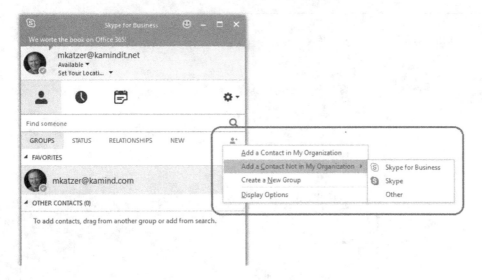

Figure 2-37. *Skype for Business linking Skype users*

Tom looks at how Skype for Business is integrated into Outlook. He can send meeting invites to all employees from Outlook. Tom also discovers that Skype for Business can support external voice conferencing, such as InterCall conferencing. This way, Tom can send out meeting requests and have the meeting as a web conference or as a video conference (see Figure 2-38). Skype for Business allows both sides to talk at the same time, compared to other services where only one person can talk. The ability for multiple people to talk simultaneously is important for enterprise business voice. Tom also asks his Microsoft Partner about Cloud PBX support. Microsoft carries 40% of the world's voice traffic, and Office 365 can be extended with the PBX support. Tom is told to find a solution that not only improved collaboration, but also replaces the existing phone system.

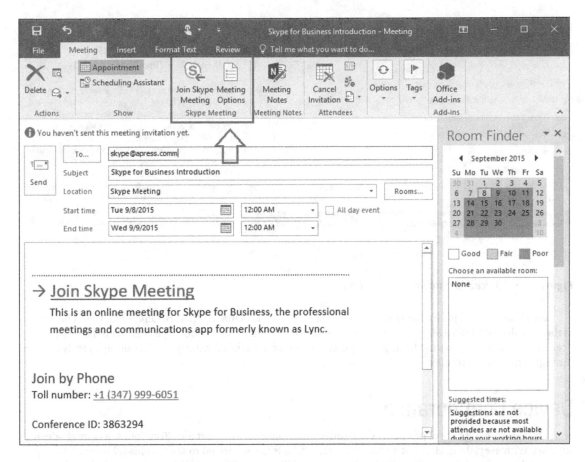

Figure 2-38. Outlook scheduling a video conference call using Skype for Business

Data Loss Prevention

Tom explores additional features in Office 365. One item he wants to verify is what happens if credit card information (embedded in e-mails or documents) is e-mailed externally from RDCC. So he e-mails a test message to an external user, and the e-mail is rejected (not delivered to the external user).

The Microsoft Partner explains that data loss prevention (DLP) is a configured service that is part of Office 365. This service processes an e-mail message's content against various rules. One of the rules that e-mails can be processed against is a personally identifiable information (PII) rule that detects credit card numbers in e-mail and documents. Microsoft supplies a standard set of DLP template rules, but you can also have custom DLP templates built. As an example, if RDCC has internal proprietary information, you can construct a Word template for those documents, as well as an appropriate DLP rule that manages the information so that it is not e-mailed externally. This way, RDCC has maximum control (as much as possible) over its external communications to ensure that only appropriate information is delivered. The Partner shows Tom the available DLP rules (see Figure 2-39), which can be easily added to Office 365.

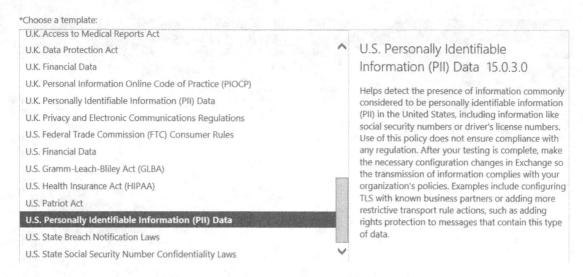

*Choose a template:

U.K. Access to Medical Reports Act	**U.S. Personally Identifiable Information (PII) Data** 15.0.3.0
U.K. Data Protection Act	
U.K. Financial Data	Helps detect the presence of information commonly considered to be personally identifiable information (PII) in the United States, including information like social security numbers or driver's license numbers. Use of this policy does not ensure compliance with any regulation. After your testing is complete, make the necessary configuration changes in Exchange so the transmission of information complies with your organization's policies. Examples include configuring TLS with known business partners or adding more restrictive transport rule actions, such as adding rights protection to messages that contain this type of data.
U.K. Personal Information Online Code of Practice (PIOCP)	
U.K. Personally Identifiable Information (PII) Data	
U.K. Privacy and Electronic Communications Regulations	
U.S. Federal Trade Commission (FTC) Consumer Rules	
U.S. Financial Data	
U.S. Gramm-Leach-Bliley Act (GLBA)	
U.S. Health Insurance Act (HIPAA)	
U.S. Patriot Act	
U.S. Personally Identifiable Information (PII) Data	
U.S. State Breach Notification Laws	
U.S. State Social Security Number Confidentiality Laws	

Figure 2-39. *Office 365 data loss standard rules*

Tom thinks about his business requirements and the services that are part of Office 365. When he looks at the overall costs, Office 365 makes business sense and it reduces his overall expenses. With the different licensing models, Tom has the flexibility to purchase the services on a monthly invoice, or on a yearly invoice through a traditional reseller.

Device Configuration

Tom has been having a lot of problems configuring smartphones. The next area Tom looks at is smart-device support. With everything else that he has experienced, he is not surprised to see that his iPhone is fully supported by Office 365, as well as Android devices and iPads (see Figure 2-40). Tom accesses the IPhone software by selecting the gear icon (next to the picture of Karen in the right-hand corner), and then the Office 365 Settings and the software he wants to download. Office 365 supports the major smartphones. This resolves one of the other issues that Tom was facing. The VP of sales is an avid iPhone and Mac user. Tom is relieved that Office 365 supports iPhone, iPad, and the Mac as part of the standard offering.

Figure 2-40. *Selecting the iPhone software to install form Office365*

As Tom looks over Office 365, he becomes aware of its different configurations. Office 365 is a cloud-based service that does discriminate the manufacturer of the user's device. Tom's users have iPhones, Macs, PCs, laptops, and Chrome notebooks. He sees that Office 365 supports all of these devices.

Office 365 and Enterprise Mobility Suite

Tom looks into the security in more detail and realizes that he can use either his on-premises servers' Active Directory to manage security, or the Office 365 security groups to grant permissions. As an IT manager, Tom must have maximum flexibility to restrict information as appropriate for individuals' roles. The Microsoft Partner suggests that Tom review Microsoft's Azure Active Directory integration (see Figure 2-41). Through the web site at `https://myapps.microsoft.com`, Tom uses his Office 365 test account to access the portal. Once logged in, he notices that there are four tabs and a set of applications that correspond to the business applications in Office 365.

Figure 2-41. *Microsoft application portal (myapps.microsoft.com)*

The Microsoft Partner explains that once you enable the Azure Active Directory interface and deploy the Microsoft Enterprise Mobility Suite, there are additional security features available to the user. For example (see Figure 2-42), Tom uses LogMeIn Rescue for desktop management. The Partner explains that he can link third-party cloud accounts and give permission to the user to access the account, without giving the password to individual users. Once Tom configures the password, all he needs to do is grant user access to the third-party cloud services app.

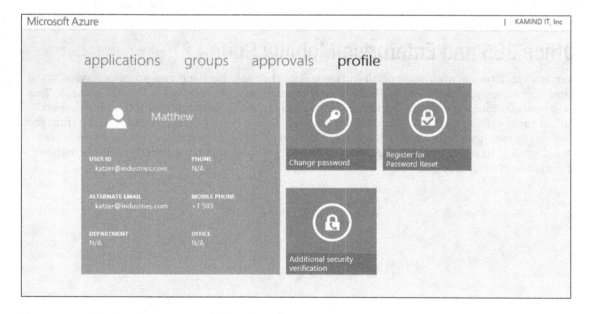

Figure 2-42. *Windows Enterprise Mobility Suite self-service portal*

The Enterprise Mobility Suite also provides additional security analytics that can be used to log information about an account. In Figure 2-43, Enterprise Mobility Suite (EMS) has been enabled to provide a monitoring function on access to the Office 365 tenant. In this example, Azure audits login to the cloud from different geographies. This way, Tom can monitor an account that has been breached.

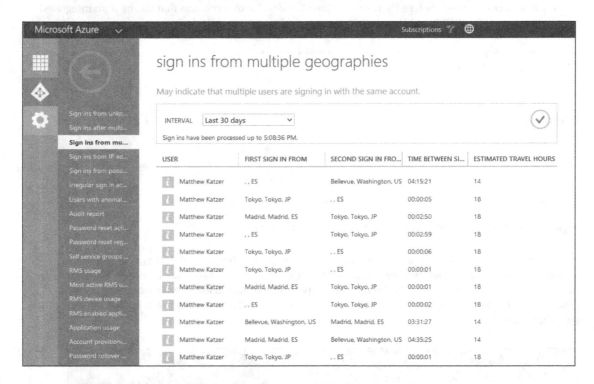

Figure 2-43. *Azure account management portal*

Azure Active Directory is integrated into Office 365. This makes it simpler to have a single sign-on for RDCC users. When an on-premises server is integrated into Office 365 (using any Active Directory integration tools), the security objects are also copied into Azure. Tom feels that with this integration approach, he can manage the user security access using either on-premises services or Office 365. For example, Tom was thinking of placing the accounting line of the business in a Virtual Windows Azure Server and integrating that server into Office 365 Active Directory. Tom accesses the self-service portal by looking at `mypass.microsoft.com` and logging in to Office 365/Azure with his Office 365 account.

RDCC's long-term strategy is to remove all on-premises servers and move them to the cloud. Tom feels there is no longer a business need for an on-premises Active Directory server. After looking at Azure Active Directory integration and virtual server management, Tom recognizes that he may accomplish the server migration to the cloud as part of the RDCC move to Office 365. This will significantly reduce RDCC's operating costs. Tom makes a note of this to discuss with the Microsoft Partner after the migration to Office 365 is completed.

Microsoft Intune

Enterprise Mobility Suite includes both Microsoft Azure Premium and Microsoft Intune. The Microsoft Partner suggests that Tom look at Intune, so Tom enters the URL (`https://account.manage.microsoft.com`) and starts to access the service (see Figure 2-44). The Microsoft Partner remarks that Intune is an integrated service that uses Office 365 Active Directory to manage desktop and mobile devices.

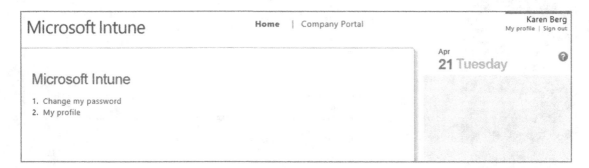

Figure 2-44. *Intune user page at account.manage.microsoft.com*

Intune allows an IT department to fully manage users' mobile devices and desktop devices with antivirus, policy management, updated management, and hardware and software inventory management. Intune monitors end-user devices and sends notifications to the administrator when there are issues associated with the user's system. Tom looks at the Start screen and proceeds to log in to the company portal (see Figure 2-45).

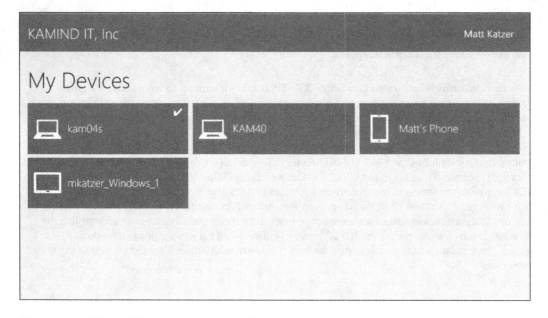

Figure 2-45. *Microsoft Intune company portal*

The Microsoft Partner explains that Intune is designed for the IT staff to reduce the cost of desktop management deployment. Intune has a self-service portal that allows users to register their devices (mobile, laptops, desktop) into the Intune deployment center. This allows IT staff to manage those systems. Intune also supports custom application deployment for mobile devices. Controlling the deployment of custom applications is a key benefit for RDCC, because they no longer need to publish the mobile application to the public cloud.

Tom looks at what Intune can do. He briefly looks at the admin center (see Figure 2-46) to see how the mobile devices are managed. Tom discovers that he has the ability to remotely wipe the portions of an employee's cell phone that contains customers' information, if the employee leaves the organization.

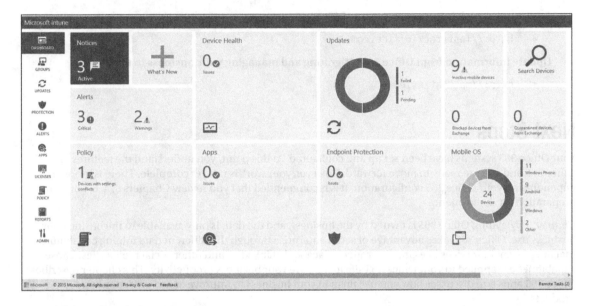

Figure 2-46. *Intune administration console*

Summary

Using a "walk-through" approach has exposed you to the different capabilities of Office 365 from a very practical point of view of how you use the features. There is much more to Office 365 than we discussed, and we will cover that information in subsequent chapters. At this point, if you have a trial subscription, you are ready to try Office 365.

Reference Links

There is a lot of information about Office 365 on the Web, but the issue is finding the right site. The information contained in this chapter is a combination of our experiences in doing deployments and knowledge of support information that has been published by third parties.

Office 365 Learning Center

- http://office.microsoft.com/en-us/office-home-for-office-365-FX102821134.aspx

Office 365 Cloud Solution Provider Information

- http://www.kamind.com/csp

Adding OneDrive for Business for Office 2010 and 2007

- http://www.microsoft.com/en-US/download/details.aspx?id=39050

Adding FastTrack information to your Office 365 Company

- http://fasttrack.office.com

Update information from Office 365: Migrating and managing your business in the cloud

- http://mattkatzer.com

Next Steps

Your Office 365 systems have been set up and configured. At this point, you understand the features of Office 365 and you are ready to move forward. However, your work is not yet complete. There is more to do, depending on your Office 365 configuration. It is recommended that you review Chapters 3, 4, 6, and 7 in preparation for deployment.

Chapter 3: The Apps. Office 365 is owned by the business, and the data is only available to the business for business use. Office 365 takes advantage of social enterprise through the different data mining capabilities that are present in services like Gmail, Dropbox, Facebook, LinkedIn, and other social media sites. Those capabilities are applied to your Office 365 site to improve your business productivity. This chapter describes Office 365 apps and discusses how you use them in your business to improve communications and productivity.

Chapter 4: Cloud Security Best Practices. One of the issues that all managers are faced with is the management of data and security and learning best practices. In this chapter, you explore the different capabilities of Office 365 and the monitoring that is in place to manage your Office 365 company to ensure that your data remains private. This chapter covers the most common approaches to Office 365 migration.

Chapter 6: Workstation Setup and Configuration. Office 365 supports many different systems and capabilities, depending on your business needs. The issue that IT managers constantly face is how to setup and manage the client environment. This chapter is focused on the configuration of an Office 365 desktop environment. This is the go-to reference chapter on the configuration of your desktop and mobile phones.

Chapter 7: Managing Office 365. This chapter describes the different administration centers in Office 365 and the most common tools that you use to administer Office 365. Depending on your Office 365 plan, there are five possible administration tools. This chapter focuses on the Office 365, Exchange, and Skype for Business administration centers. The chapter closes with using PowerShell to manage your Office 365 environment.

CHAPTER 3

■ ■ ■

Office 365: The Apps

The business environment around us has changed. In today's workplace, we see that there are at least four age-based demographics that IT services need to support. These demographics have different needs, different views on business collaboration, and different views on how a business needs to commutate with employees, vendors, and contractors. The common bond among all of these groups is apps. As funny as it sounds, when we look at today's work environment, collaboration, sharing information, and simplification of the job and productivity, it all comes down to apps. The previous chapter offered an overview of a typical workday using the various tools to conduct business. This chapter takes a deeper dive into using the apps, with a focus on collaboration.

It Is All About the Apps!

The apps in Office 365 are designed with collaboration in mind (see Figure 3-1). There are different forms of collaboration and work sharing. Office 365's approach is to enable this with apps. If you have an iPhone or an iPad, you are using apps—so why not in Office 365?

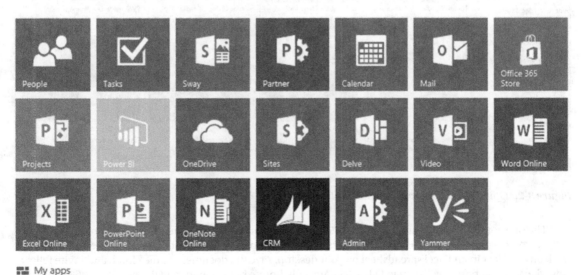

Figure 3-1. *Office 365 collaboration applications*

There are two sets of apps that can be loaded into Office 365: those downloaded from the Office 365 Store and those that your administrator adds. These apps appear on your dashboard or in the **My apps** window. These are the approved apps that your administrator allows you to have based on your business role. In this chapter, the focus is on the Office 365 applications and using them to collaborate.

When you think of apps on Office 365, you must also think of data. In the previous chapter, you walked through a day in the life of an Office 365 user. The user stored documents on Office 365 in OneDrive for Business and on the team site. Both of these cloud storage locations are built on SharePoint. The apps in the Store are used to improve the productivity and manageability of Office 365. There are apps for every aspect of Office 365 (see Figure 3-2).

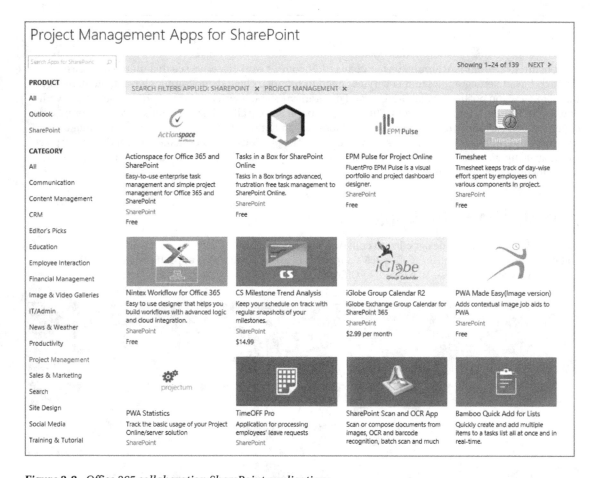

Figure 3-2. *Office 365 collaboration SharePoint applications*

The one common thread around Office 365 is collaboration. Collaboration is the sharing of information with coworkers and external business associates. Office 365 allows you to collaborate everywhere. You can work on a project in an Excel spreadsheet on your desktop, save the document to the cloud, and invite fellow coworkers to collaborate with you in Office 365. You collaborate in the cloud in real time. Office 365 can be set up to notify you when other users have stopped editing the document. All documents in the cloud can be access with your desktop Office 2016 applications.

■ **Note** With Office 365, you are not restricted to only use the cloud for collaboration. You can now run Office 2016 on your desktop and share the Office productivity app with someone who does not have Word installed on her computing (Mac or PC) device. Desktop and cloud editing is on the roadmap.

Where to Start?

You are going to focus on the apps in Office 365. The first step is to log in to Office 365. As an E3 user, you should see the dashboard displayed in Figure 3-3.

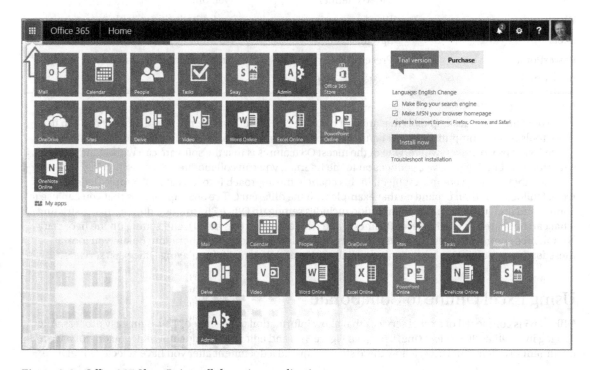

Figure 3-3. Office 365 SharePoint collaboration applications

Office 365 is a collection of apps (described in Table 3-1). In Figure 3-3, the applications that you see are based on an Office 365 E3 subscription and use Microsoft Free Power BI (see https://app.powerbi.com). The Office 365 subscription shown here provides both desktop applications and cloud-based applications. You can install up to five copies of Office desktop software on Apple or Microsoft laptops. You never need to purchase another copy of desktop Office software.

Table 3-1. *Office 365 App Descriptions*

Name	Description	Distribution
Outlook (Caldera, people Task)	E-mail integration tool	No limitations, available everywhere
Sway	PowerPoint replacement	Web only
OneDrive for business	Sync tool to cloud storage	No limitations, available everywhere
Sites	Team site shortcuts	Web only
Delve	Displays most recent access documents	Web only
Video	Video channel	Web only
Word	Word processing	No limitations, available everywhere
Excel	Spreadsheet	No limitations, available everywhere
PowerPoint	Presentation maker	No limitations, available everywhere
Power BI	Decision-making tool	Web only

There are other desktop tools that are part of Office 2016, but these are the primary ones. You can use these tools on any computing device: laptops, Chromebooks, iPhones, smartphones, iPads, and tablets. Office 365 apps work everywhere. One of the nicest OS features is that the software can work stand-alone or with the Web, and if you have a connection to the Internet, you can collaborate.

Collaboration is a complex subject. In this chapter, the approach is to look at an example (let's use Excel Online), and then expand on that example with the different Office 365 capabilities that you can use to control and limit user access. This limitation includes setting up Office 365 to share documents, restricting what can be shared in OneDrive for Business (and where this can be synced), and setting up the necessary compliance controls to keep the version history of the files you use for collaboration. Before you look at these features, you need to look at online collaboration and then review managing Office 365 services.

Using Excel Online to Collaborate

Office 365 is composed of a set of services that allow information to be shared. This is an easy process. After you log in to Office 365, select **OneDrive** (see Figure 3-3) and edit an Excel document. If you do not have a document to edit in OneDrive, follow these steps to upload a document after you have selected OneDrive.

1. In OneDrive, select **Upload** (see Figure 3-4).

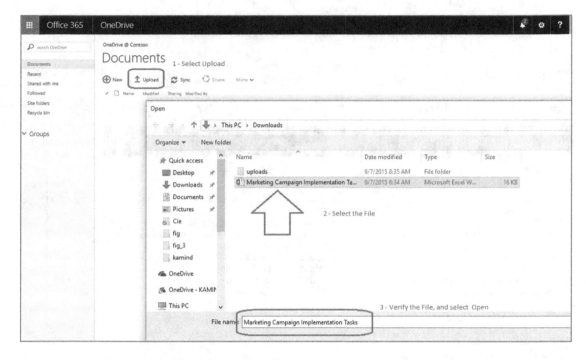

Figure 3-4. *Uploading a file to OneDrive for Business*

2. Browse to the file name to upload.

3. Verify the file name and select **Open**.

4. Once you have uploaded the document (it should look similar to Figure 3-5), select it to launch the Excel Online editor.

Figure 3-5. *Using Excel Online to edit the document*

5. Once you have launched Excel Online, select **Edit Workbook** (see Figure 3-6) to edit the workbook. Then select the **Edit in Excel Online** option.

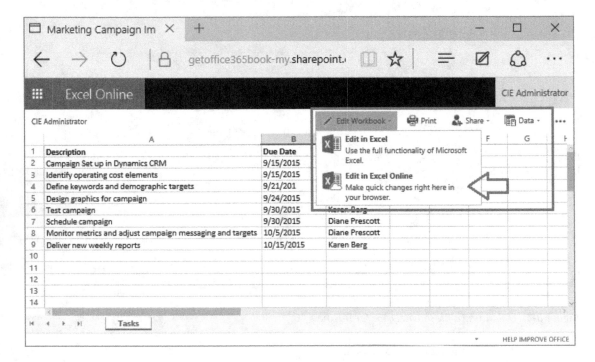

Figure 3-6. *Editing the document*

6. Sharing is a function that works either online or from your desktop version of Excel. To share Excel Online with your coworkers, select **Share** (see Figure 3-7).

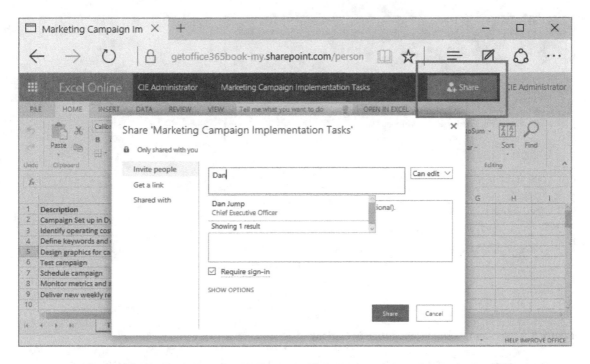

Figure 3-7. *Sharing the document*

Once you select Share, an e-mail is sent to the user whom you choose to share the document with. It will be similar to what's shown in Figure 3-8 and Figure 3-9.

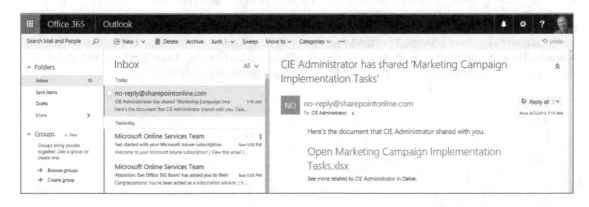

Figure 3-8. *Receiving a shared invitation in Outlook Web Access (OWA)*

Figure 3-9. *Receiving a shared invitation in Outlook*

There are two types of sharing allowed: anonymous and required login. If you are an Office 365 user, then access to a shared invite is straightforward: just click the link and log in with your Office 365 credentials. But what happens if you are external to the Office 365 company? In this case, you need to log in with a Microsoft account, which is no different than using a Gmail account or an Apple.me account to log in to Google Drive or Apple's iCloud storage. It uses a set of security credentials to access the online services. To access the share resource, click the link in the e-mail and enter your login credentials.

What is different is that with a Microsoft account, you no longer need to use a Hotmail account or a live. com e-mail account to access shared resources on Microsoft servers. Microsoft account security credentials can be added to any user account. To extend your work e-mail to have Microsoft security credentials, go to **account.live.com** (additional instructions are discussed later in this chapter). Once you have added the security credentials to your account, pay attention to the login prompts (see Figure 3-10).

Figure 3-10. *Selecting the correct credentials to access Office 365*

■ **Note** Once you have added Microsoft account security to your Office 365 account, you need to correctly respond to the login prompts. (I have run into situations where I thought I was logging into Office 365, but I was logging into a personal OneDrive account.) Keep the passwords different to make life easier later on; otherwise, you may mistakenly use credentials on the wrong account.

As you can see in Figure 3-10, after logging into Office 365, I was prompted about which set of credentials I wanted to use to access Microsoft Services. In this case, my personal e-mail address has both Microsoft account security credentials and Office 365 account security credentials. Which credentials I use depends on the services that I am using. Office 365 is a business service, not a personal service, so I select **Work or school account** (the one with the badge) to access my Office 365 services. Keep in mind that the passwords on a personal account or a work account are not the same. If they are the same, it is because you chose to make them the same. Changing a password on Office 365 does not change the password on a Microsoft account.

As you can see in Figure 3-11, I accepted the invite and logged into the Office 365 service. When you log in to the server to collaborate, you can only use the URL that is sent to you. If you forward the e-mail with the URL to another user, and you give this person your password, the login will fail. Collaboration works only with the intended target. Security is paramount to Office 365, along with digital rights management. Office 365 has the ability to restrict data to internal and external users.

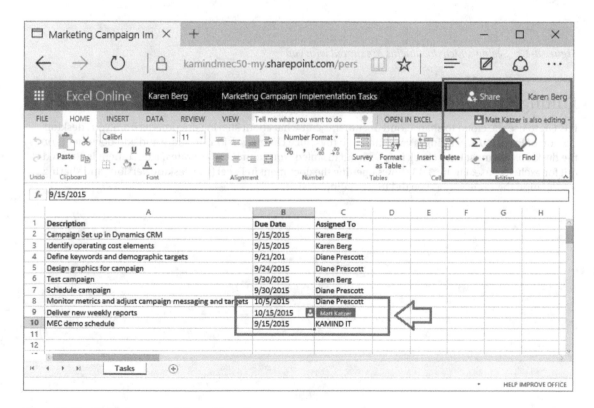

Figure 3-11. Multiple users editing a file online

■ **Note** Once you have accepted the invitation, the document location information is maintained in your OneDrive for Business site—once you use the link and accept the sharing request.

As you can tell, over time, you tend to share a lot of documents and have documents shared with you. To determine which documents are shared, select **OneDrive**, and under Documents (on the left-hand side), select **Shared with me** (see Figure 3-12). These are the valid documents that you have accepted.

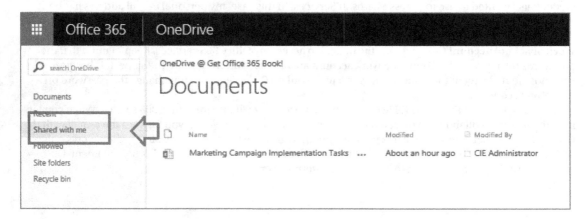

Figure 3-12. Seeing which documents are shared with you

Editing Excel files in Office 365

It is OK to use the cloud to share cloud documents, but what about sharing documents from your desktop version of Excel 2016? Sharing is very similar to the Office Online version. To share and edit documents on the desktop, you must have check in/check out disabled. You cannot collaborate if a document is checked out for exclusive use. Figure 3-13 shows opening the document in Excel (the desktop version) and sharing information the same way as you did in the online version.

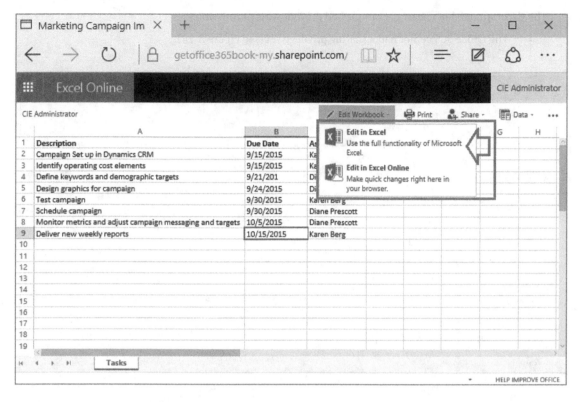

Figure 3-13. *Opening Excel as a local file*

You receive two prompts if this is the first time you have opened Excel locally. The first prompt verifies that you want to open the file (a caution for viruses), and the second prompt is for your Office 365 account. Earlier, we talked about Office 365 accounts and Microsoft accounts. You want to use your Office 365 "work" account to open the file. If you do not have an Office 365 account, and you receive a share invite, you want to use your Microsoft account.

■ **Note**   Sharing files only works with the desktop version if the files are not exclusively checked out.

You can share the desktop Excel file in the same way you shared the online version: just select the **Share** menu option (in the right-hand menu on the Excel desktop; see Figure 3-13. The Excel workspace expands. Enter the user e-mail address and send the invite (very similar to the Excel Online). However, at this release, the desktop version does not support real-time editing.

Verify That Sharing Is Enabled

At this point, you were either successful in sharing documents, or you were unsuccessful and perhaps frustrated that you could not send out an external sharing link. The default configuration for an Office 365 setup is to have sharing disabled. To resolve this, you need to review your company's policies and learn who is responsible for sharing external information. Office 365 is designed to have three levels of sharing: (1) globally across all Office 365 data, (2) across independent sites (team sites and My Drive), and (3) individual files (and directories). Sharing is turned off by default; but even when it is enabled, you must explicitly share links.

75

The Excel spreadsheet sharing example had the following permissions:

- The Office 365 center had a sharing privilege set (see Figure 3-14).

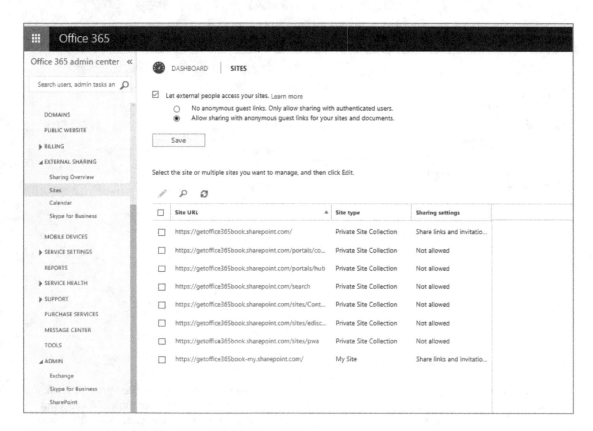

Figure 3-14. *Enabling External Sharing in Office 365*

- The Office 365 SharePoint library (getoffice365book) had sharing enabled.
- An explicit link was sent to an external user to access the Excel spreadsheet.

If you look at Figure 3-14, you can see the sites that are enabled for sharing and the sites that are not enabled for sharing. In this case, My Sites is enabled (the Office 365 OneDrive for Business sites) and the main team site.

■ **Note**   If you receive an error stating that you cannot share information with external users, this is because your sharing permissions have been disabled.

Preventing OneDrive for Business Data from Being Shared

This chapter has spent a lot of time on how to share data. There are also controls to restrict data from being shared, as well as controls to restrict the growth of the OneDrive sites. To control who has data and how data is managed in OneDrive and in the team site requires PowerShell commands. These commands are discussed in Chapter 7. I wanted to mention these commands so that you can make informed decisions on restrictions. The following are some of the PowerShell options for OneDrive.

- Set storage quotas on individual users

- Limit unintentional sharing to Everyone or All users

- Improve auditing of OneDrive access by admins and users

- Restrict OneDrive users to only sync with corporate computers

Protecting Data That Is Shared

You have only looked at one app and seen how the data is shared. But what about protecting the data? Which Office 365 features allow you to protect the data from being destroyed? OneDrive for Business and team site are built on SharePoint, which has a rich feature set of enterprise capabilities that is used to manage information. Figure 3-15 shows the standard version history for OneDrive for Business. These are the file versions from the previous example.

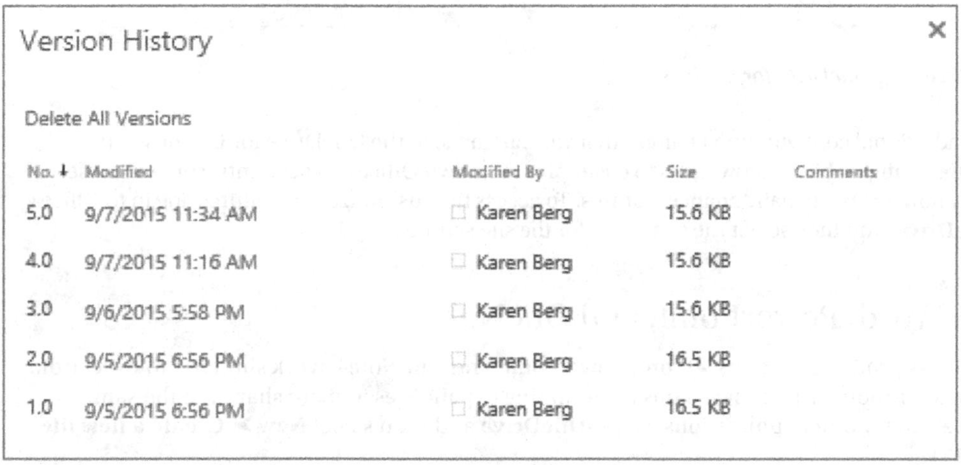

No. ↓	Modified	Modified By	Size	Comments
5.0	9/7/2015 11:34 AM	☐ Karen Berg	15.6 KB	
4.0	9/7/2015 11:16 AM	☐ Karen Berg	15.6 KB	
3.0	9/6/2015 5:58 PM	☐ Karen Berg	15.6 KB	
2.0	9/5/2015 6:56 PM	☐ Karen Berg	16.5 KB	
1.0	9/5/2015 6:56 PM	☐ Karen Berg	16.5 KB	

Version History ✕

Delete All Versions

Figure 3-15. OneDrive for Business versioning

Accessing the version history is simple: all that is needed is to click the **...** (three ellipses) next to the file name and the additional **...** to access the advance configuration features (see Figure 3-16). Editing and saving any version creates another version. The OneDrive version configuration allows up to 500 versions.

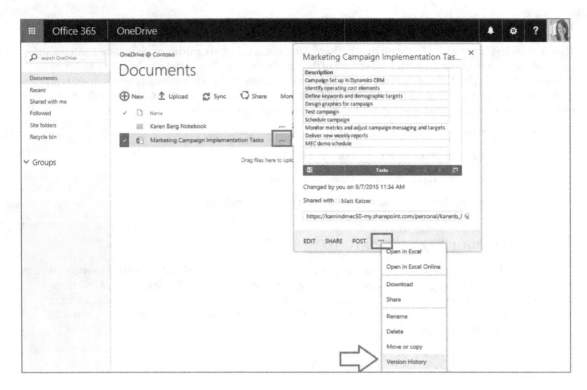

Figure 3-16. *Accessing OneDrive for Business*

There are additional configuration changes that you can make to the OneDrive for Business site. Most of these are configurable to allow users to customize their own Office 365 accounts; some of these configurations allow access to maintenance features. To access the customization features, log in to Office 365, select **OneDrive**, and then select the **gear icon** for the site settings.

Office 365 Word, PowerPoint, and OneNote

The other business productivity apps—Word, PowerPoint, and OneNote—work similarly to Excel from a collaboration standpoint. All of these apps have sharing capabilities and are shared in the same manner as Excel. To try other applications, select **OneDrive** and then select **New ➤ Create a new file** (see Figure 3-17).

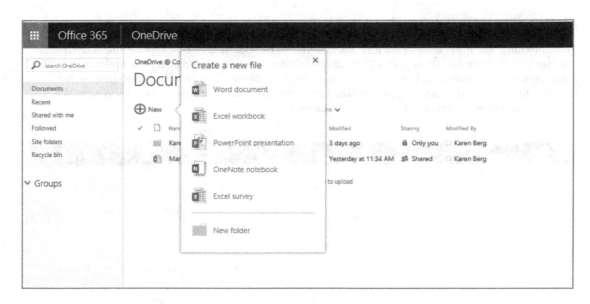

Figure 3-17. *Creating other applications files in OneDrive*

If you create a PowerPoint application, it launches PowerPoint Online, and it is ready to add content or share with other users and associates (see Figure 3-18). All of the other applications work in the same way. Just create the applications and share them with your associates.

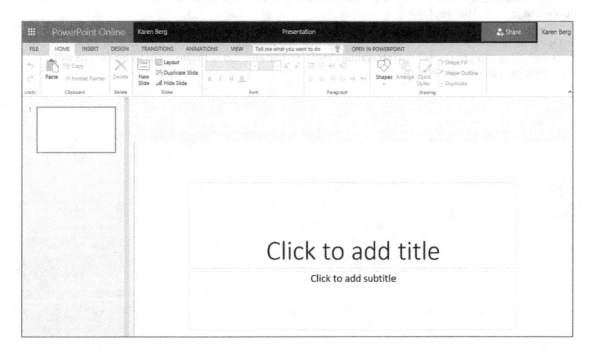

Figure 3-18. *Launching an Office 365 PowerPoint application*

Collaborating with Outlook Web Access

All of the Office 365 apps are designed for collaboration. An Outlook Web Access application, or OWA app, is set up to show team members' status. For example, OWA allows you to send an instant message to other employees in the organization based on their availability (see Figure 3-19). OWA has constantly evolved its capabilities and feature set; for example, when you select an e-mail, you have the ability to move the message to different folders or to tag it with color categories.

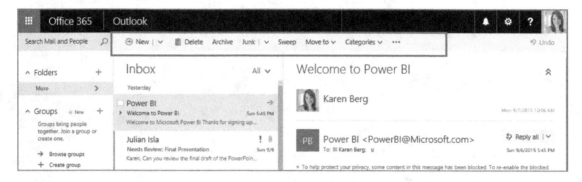

Figure 3-19. *Outlook web app (OWA) message options for e-mail management*

A lot of the features are very similar to desktop Outlook. Looking at the productivity aspect of OWA, the new feature that attracts most users is the instant message (IM) integration and presence. This integration allows instant messages to be sent to all Office 365 users and those users that have a business relationship through Skype with the employee.

Figure 3-20 shows the presence based on the status of the user's calendar. If you receive an e-mail from an Office 365 user who is also a Skype for Business contact, you can respond with an e-mail or an instant message. Office 365 apps are about integrating to remove barriers and to improve communications with team members and business partners.

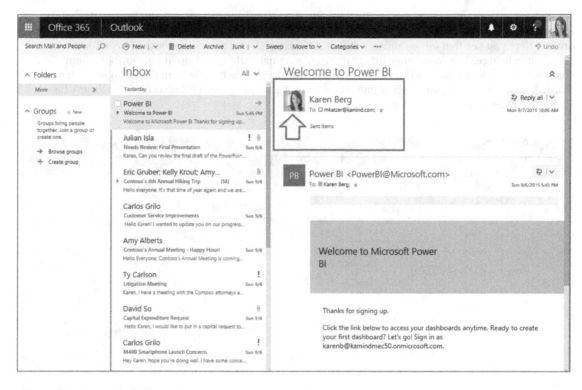

Figure 3-20. *Accessing OneDrive for Business*

Collaborating with Skype for Business

Skype for Business is the next logical extension of collaboration. It raises collaboration to a new level, with integration a part of Office 365. Skype for Business incorporates online meetings, messaging, calls, and video, and integrates into your Office 365 apps. Skype of Business is installed when you install Office 365 E3 subscriptions, or if you have downloaded the client to your desktop from Office 365 (Chapter 6 describes the process of installing Skype for Business). There is very little configuration needed for Skype for Business; as a user, you start the Skype for Business application and enter your password.

■ **Note** Skype for Business external communication settings are set by the Office 365 administrator. Skype for Business described in this section includes the Microsoft conferencing bridge and the Cloud PBX and PSTN calling.

Communications is key in any job; it is important that you have the ability to use your formal tools to communicate to employees in the company (using Skype for Business) and that you can externally communicate and collaborate. This is where Skye for Business helps your personal productivity and collaboration. It is very easy to add external Skype users to Skype for Business (see Figure 3-19). It is as simple as adding a new contact and setting up a meeting (scheduled or ad hoc). Skype for Business is integrated into your Outlook client.

Setting up a meeting in Skype for Business is easy; all you need to do is create an appointment, insert a Skype Meeting notice, and send the notice out to the user. Figure 3-21 shows a **Join by Phone** option; here you see that our company's Office 365 administrator signed up for the Skype for Business conference bridge. The conference bridge number automatically shows up in the Outlook client. The conference bridge is convenient; with it, you have the ability to schedule formal meetings (with a dial-in), have users call your office number (we have the Skype Cloud PBX installed), or simply have a Skype-to-Skype call.

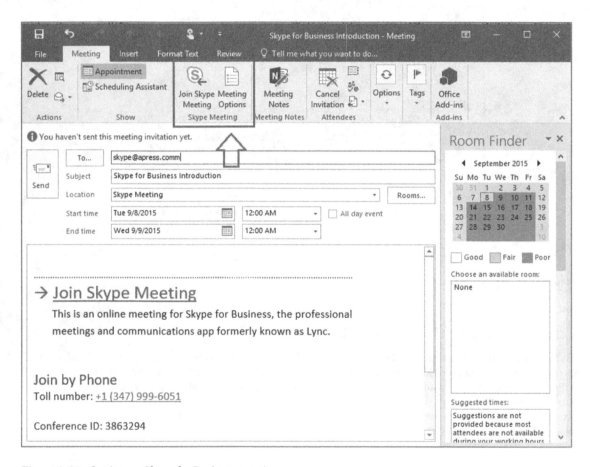

Figure 3-21. *Setting up Skype for Business meetings*

In our company's case of adding Skype users, this was simple: all we did was select the "people" icon (see Figure 3-22), and then we added the appropriate contact (either **Not in My Organization** or as a Skype user). Keep in mind that a Skype contact can only be added if he or she has given you permission. This also applies to Skype for Business contacts being added as Skype users (see Figure 3-23).

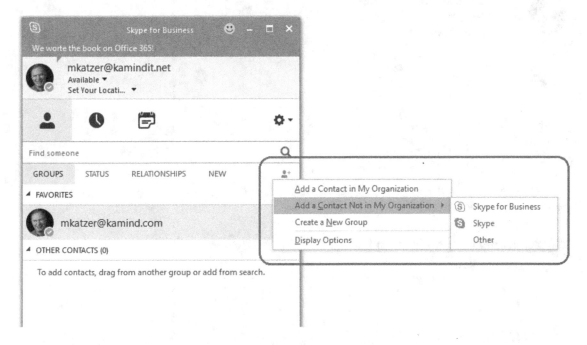

Figure 3-22. *Adding Skype users to Skype for Business client*

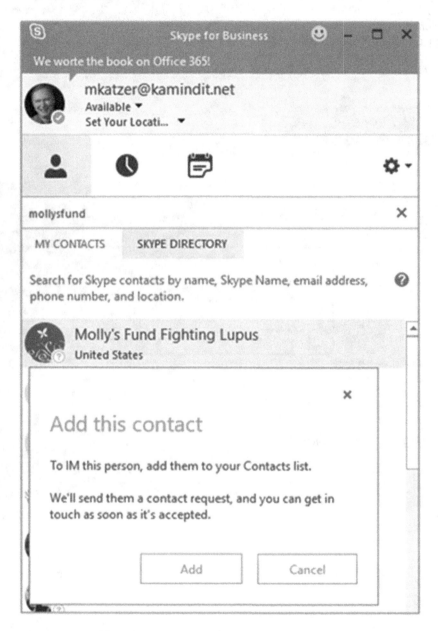

Figure 3-23. *Adding Skype user "Molly's Fund Fighting Lupus" as a Skype user*

Skype for Business with PSTN Calling (Cloud PBX)

In Figure 3-24, notice that there is a dial pad (not shown in Figure 3-23). This dial pad means that the Office 365 administrator added local and international calling to the Skype for Business client. The user does not need to perform any complicated configuration or setup to support Skype for Business local calling. When a user calls into a Skype for Business client (see Figure 3-21), a pop-up icon appears with the user's information, pulled from Outlook contacts. You can select the dial pad to call an external number.

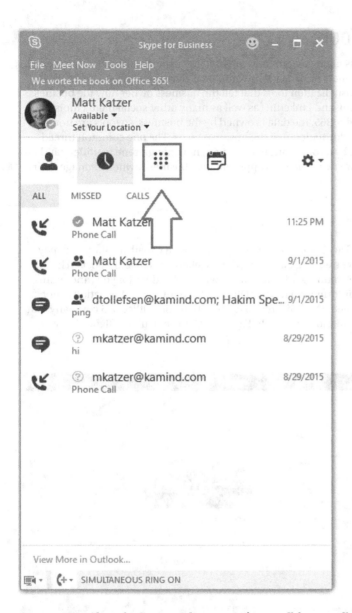

Figure 3-24. Skype for Business client receivi)ng a call from a cell phone

---

■ **Note** External phone numbers in Skype for Business do not change any functionality described in this chapter. Local calling simply allows external customers to use a cell phone or a transitional landline. Granted, it is difficult to have a video conference or share visual material with someone who has called in on the dial-in number.

Business Management Tools

Office 365 has introduced a series of business management tools targeted to business owners to manage Office 365 services. These new management tools provide users a graphical view of the information that is trending in their company, along with data visualization tools that tell the business owner how the business is running. These tools are in used in Facebook and LinkedIn (as well as many other social media tools) to deliver advertising content to the user. In Office 365, the data is owned by the business, so tools are not used to deliver targeted ads, but rather to deliver information that the business owns. The one common thread that you see in all industries is a lack of time. Everyone is super busy, with not enough time to understand the business information presented. There are two Office 365 apps that help business owners manage their business: Delve and Power BI.

Delve

Delve is a data mining tool. If you have used Facebook or LinkedIn, or you have a Gmail account, you may have noticed that the ads presented to you are trending based on your Facebook or LinkedIn posts. The ads reflect the contents of your Gmail. All of this "trending information" is what Delve does for you (and more). The difference is that Delve trends business information in your Office 365 tenant. The information is not resold to third parties. The information is mined and delivered to users within your Office 365 company, but limited to the information that they have permission to view. In Figure 3-25, the default configuration is to present a view of what is trending for the user.

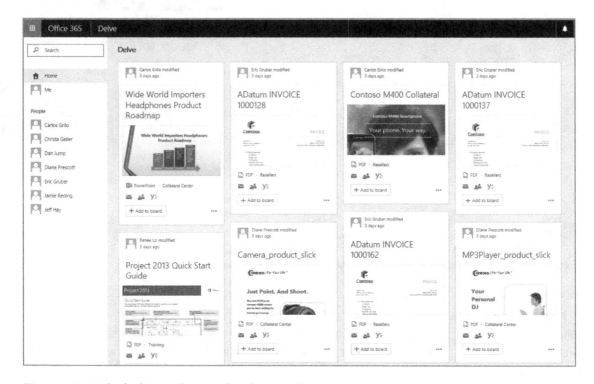

Figure 3-25. *Delve looking at data trending for a specific user*

Delve doesn't only show what is trending, it is also used to find information. Delve is a fully featured search engine designed to look for links between information. For example, in Figure 3-23, if you were looking for a document related to what you recently produced and distributed, you would select **Me**.

In this case, you would see all of those documents. Comparing Figures 3-25 and 3-26, you see the difference. Figure 3-26 shows what is trending in the company, whereas Figure 3-25 shows the documents that you have produced. This is helpful in meetings. You can easily see what is at the top of minds when you go into a meeting. Delve shows trending data, the documents that are being viewed within the company, and the documents that are being distributed in e-mail and on OneDrive for Business.

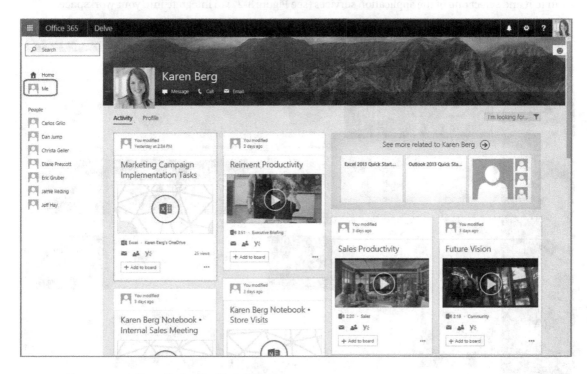

Figure 3-26. *Using Delve to look at published documents*

Delve has additional capabilities. You can search for different documents that are uploaded in Office 365 and those documents that are distributed. Delve provides access to all the information that you have permission to see. The best way to experience Delve is to use it.

■ **Note** Delve only displays the documents and the e-mails that you have permission to see. If you do not have permission to view a document, then it will not show up in your Delve view.

Power BI

Data visualization is the latest trend in helping improve a user's productivity. Data visualization is used to see trends in large data, to see what is current, and to see how you can manage your projects and business differently. Power BI is the Office 365 data visualization application (see `https://app.powerbi.com`). Power BI is an analytical tool that allows you to mine data from multiple sources to speed up the decision-making process. If Power BI is not in your account, go to the Power BI web site and sign up for the free service. Power BI uses your Office 365 organizational account. Once Power BI is enabled in your Office 365 company, just log in to it and select one of the application services (see Figure 3-27) to integrate into your workspace.

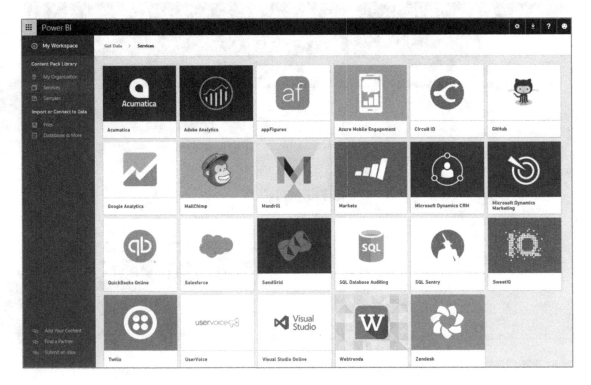

Figure 3-27. *Using Power BI to visualize your data*

Power BI is a management tool that can organize your data so that you can visualize your business. If you are a QuickBooks Online user, start up Power BI and select the QuickBooks Online services. This tool gives you a different perspective of your business; the best way is to compare the raw data to the data processed by Power BI. Figure 3-28 shows the raw data to be processed by Power BI and Figure 3-29 shows the processed data. For a business owner, seeing the data in visual form makes it easier to identify what is affecting the business and determine how to make changes to improve business profits.

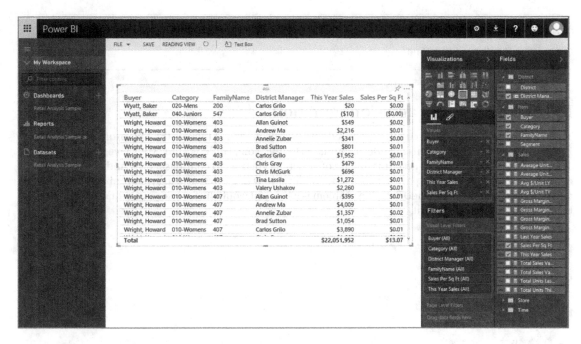

Figure 3-28. *Using Power BI raw data*

Figure 3-29. *Power BI: processed raw data in visualized form*

■ **Note** The preconfigured Power BI service connectors are very useful for giving you a different perspective of how your business is operating.

MS Account: Setup and Configuration

There are two types of login accounts associated with Microsoft; one of these is the Microsoft account (see Figure 3-30). Microsoft accounts include accounts at Hotmail.com, Outlook.com, Xbox Live, and OneDrive. These accounts are consumer accounts. Microsoft accounts are used to control security and access to computing devices. It is this type of account that Windows 10 wants you to use to synchronize your desktop and other features through OneDrive. The problem is when you would like to use your e-mail address as a login to your Microsoft account.

Figure 3-30. *Office 365 prompting a user to choose an account to log in to Microsoft services*

Microsoft, Google, and Apple have unique accounts that are used to map security features with their cloud services. Microsoft accounts are different; you are allowed to add security extensions to your Office 365 account. As an example, I can link two-factor authentication to my Microsoft account and use my business e-mail address. Microsoft account mapping adds Microsoft security credentials to an organization account. Follow these next steps to create a Microsoft account.

1. Go to **http://account.live.com** and select **Don't have a Microsoft Account? Sign up now** (see Figure 3-31).

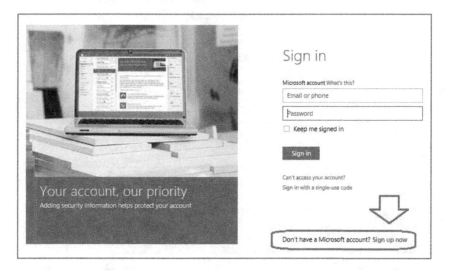

Figure 3-31. *Setting up a Microsoft account*

2. Next, enter your work e-mail address and mobile phone number (see Figure 3-32).

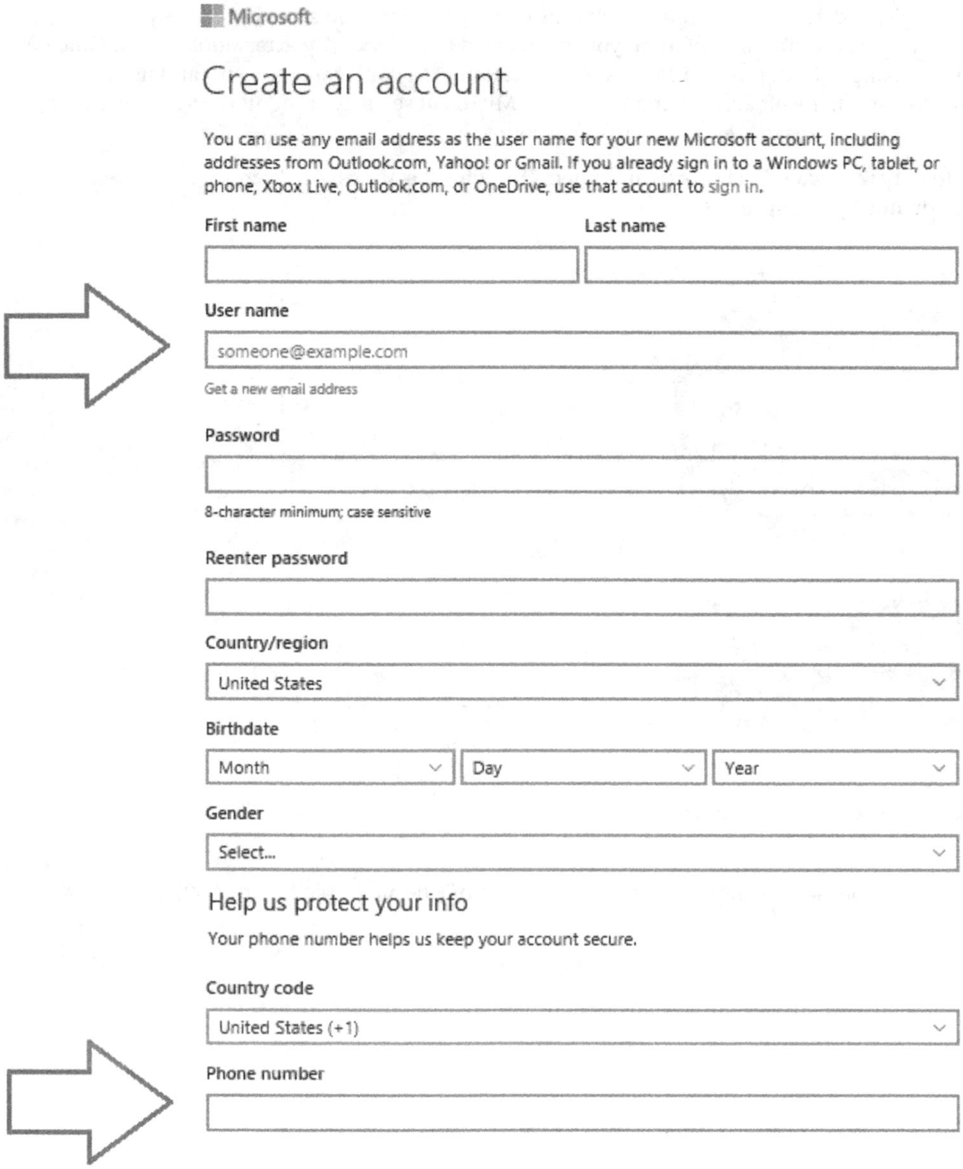

Microsoft

Create an account

You can use any email address as the user name for your new Microsoft account, including addresses from Outlook.com, Yahoo! or Gmail. If you already sign in to a Windows PC, tablet, or phone, Xbox Live, Outlook.com, or OneDrive, use that account to sign in.

First name

Last name

User name

someone@example.com

Get a new email address

Password

8-character minimum; case sensitive

Reenter password

Country/region

United States

Birthdate

Month   Day   Year

Gender

Select...

Help us protect your info

Your phone number helps us keep your account secure.

Country code

United States (+1)

Phone number

Figure 3-32. Entering key data for a Microsoft account

At this point, setup is completed and you have created your Microsoft account. It is important that you correctly enter your mobile phone number; it will be used to reset your password on the Microsoft account. Remember that the passwords are not synchronized with your Office 365 account.

Summary

The information that we cover in subsequent chapters expands on the productive nature of using Office 365. Look at the devices that we use today: our smartphones, tablets, and laptops. We pick the device because it makes our life simpler and our work faster (and easier). As you plan your deployment, be aware of the Office Apps available, and how they will help your users work better and be more productive. As you begin the process of moving to Office 365, remember this chapter, because deployment is all about how your users use the Office 365. It is all about the apps.

Reference Links

There is a lot of information about Office 365 on the Web, but the issue is finding the right site. The information contained in this chapter is a combination of KAMIND IT's deployment experiences and the support information published by other parties.

Office 365 Learning Center

- https://technet.microsoft.com/en-us/library/jj871004.aspx

Office 365 documents and training videos

- http://mattkatzer.com

Using Office 365 OneDrive for Business

- http://www.youtube.com/watch?v=c740qwWR-cs

Office online support configuration

- https://technet.microsoft.com/en-us/library/Excel-online-service-description.aspx

- https://technet.microsoft.com/en-us/library/word-online-service-description.aspx

- https://technet.microsoft.com/en-us/library/powerpoint-online-service-description.aspx

- https://technet.microsoft.com/en-us/library/onenote-online-service-description.aspx

Adding FastTrack information to your Office 365 company

- http://fasttrack.office.com

Adding Skype for Business

- https://products.office.com

Update information from Moving to Office 365

- http://mattkatzer.com

Next Steps

Your Office 365 systems have been set up and configured. At this point, you understand the features of Office 365 and you are ready to move forward. However, your work is not yet complete. There is more to do, depending on your Office 365 configuration. It is recommended that you review Chapters 4, 6, and 7 in preparation for deployment.

Chapter 4: Cloud Security Best Practices. One of the issues that all managers are faced with is the management of data and security and learning best practices. In this chapter, you explore the different capabilities of Office 365 and the monitoring that is in place to manage your Office 365 company to ensure that your data remains private. This chapter covers the most common approaches to Office 365 migration.

Chapter 6: Workstation Setup and Configuration. Office 365 supports many different systems and capabilities, depending on your business needs. The issue that IT managers constantly face is how to setup and manage the client environment. This chapter is focused on the configuration of an Office 365 desktop environment. This is the go-to reference chapter on the configuration of your desktop and mobile phones.

Chapter 7: Managing Office 365. This chapter describes the different administration centers in Office 365 and the most common tools that you use to administer Office 365. Depending on your Office 365 plan, there are five possible administration tools. This chapter focuses on the Office 365, Exchange, and Skype for Business administration centers. The chapter closes with using PowerShell to manage your Office 365 environment.

CHAPTER 4

■ ■ ■

Security Best Practices

The cloud is changing the way our businesses operate. Business owners, employees, and contractors work anywhere in the world, work at any time of the day, and use many types of devices to access business resources. Business owners are always looking for ways to manage those resources. The question is how to manage these resources in our new cloud-based economy. What is the impact if you do not manage your cloud identity? The best way to begin a discussion about security is to take a quick look at the security features that are part of Office 365, and explore a practical example as to why security is important.

Office 365 has extended the capabilities for monitoring different levels of service. As an example, Figure 4-1 shows the additional service monitoring that can be used in Office 365. These services are easy to turn on. At first, they seem only somewhat interesting—just another set of reports. Let's look at one of the reports—**Sign ins from multiple geographies**—to understand why security is important.

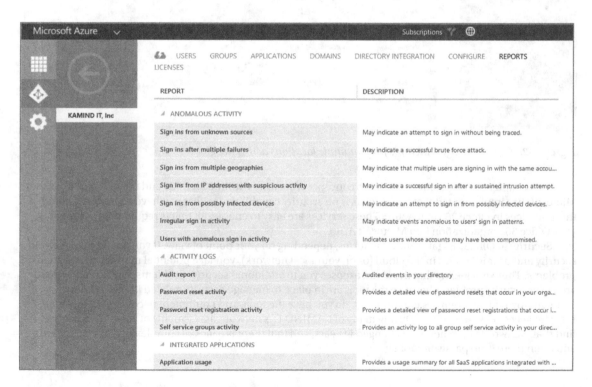

Figure 4-1. *Office 365 security monitoring with Azure Active Directory Premium services*

In Figure 4-2, you see that my personal e-mail account has experienced breach attempts from Estonia, Madrid, Japan, and Bellevue, Washington—all within 5 minutes of each other. The configuration of my company's Office 365 organization includes Azure Premium services. Once these services are enabled, these reports are feasible. In this example, I am ostensibly logging in to the system in multiple places around the world, which would require me to travel 14–18 hours to reach—yet I am logging in to these locations within 5 minutes of each other. This is why cloud security is important and the control of your personal information is critical.

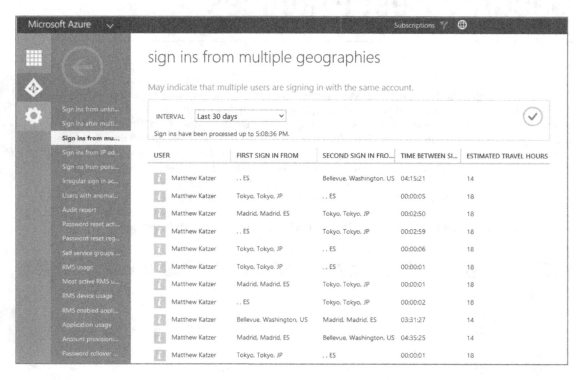

Figure 4-2. *Office 365 login attempts from multiple locations across the globe*

This chapter reviews some of the basic concepts of security within Office 365 and the different ways that Microsoft has implemented them. The focus is on security capabilities so that you have an understanding of these services in Office 365 and Azure. These services are easy to enable; all that is required is that you link your Office 365 organization into Microsoft Azure.

Security in Office 365 takes different forms, depending on your point of view. If you do not manage your security and user identities in the cloud (or on your local network), you face potential network penetration problems. There is a feeling that the cloud exposes you to additional security problems, but in reality, there are fewer security problems because the tools are in place to manage security-related issues. Within a company-owned on-premises environment, do you have the tools and equipment necessary to fully manage Internet access to your servers? During many of KAMIND IT's network assessments of customer sites, we find that passwords have not been changed in years, and that there is a lack of complexity to the passwords and often there is no password policy.

A Step Back in Time

In the pre-cloud days, computer security professionals worried about physical structures and described computer security as a layer of boundaries—known as COMSEC boundaries (communications security boundaries). The US government used this broad definition to establish access classification with levels of security clearance; they used computer security boundaries to control access. For example, a building would be classified as an "A-level building" and you would have a room in the building with a B-level classification. To enter the building, you needed clearance at the A level, and to enter the B-level room, you needed to have a security classification at the B level. In some facilities, there were guards to check and make sure that you were at the correct security level.

As more services moved to the cloud, there was a new problem: the ability to control access to third-party services were limited. Businesses had to control access to their data and grant individuals permission to use the subscription services. No longer was there a guarded building to control access. In the secured building example, what happens if an employee that has access to the B-level room is fired? In a secured building, you can just tell the guards not to let the fired employee into the building; problem solved. In the cloud world, access is controlled with user IDs and passwords. In the fired employee example, you can block the user's access to the business application and data. This works great, but what happens if there are thousands of different applications and multiple users (see Figure 4-3)? What do you do now?

Figure 4-3. *Sample of different cloud identities (courtesy of Microsoft)*

Office 365 is a suite of software products that Microsoft offers as a service subscription. The basis for the service is to reduce the IT costs for business implementation. The major benefit of using Microsoft Office 365 services is that businesses are more focused on building the business than building IT cost centers.

In the past, there were three Office 365 plans: Professional, Midsize Business, and Enterprise. As more customers migrated to the cloud, Microsoft consolidated the plans so that they are all on the Enterprise version of Office 365. Compliance, data loss prevention, encryption, and rights management are available only in Enterprise subscriptions, but they are options in the other subscription mixes (see Figure 4-4). Office 365 offers levels of security. The Enterprise plans are enabled to access some levels of security using the base level of Azure, known as Azure Basic. This service is included in Enterprise E1 and E3/E5 subscriptions. The advanced security features are part of the Azure AD Premium subscription.

Full plan lineup

	Business			Enterprise		
	Business	Business Essentials	Business Premium	ProPlus	E1	E3
Customer Price	$8.25	$5	$12.5	$12	$8	$20
Seat Cap	300 (for each plan)			Unlimited		
24/7 phone support from Microsoft	Critical issues			All issues		
Office Word, PowerPoint, Excel, Outlook, OneNote, Publisher	●		●	●²		●²
iPad, Windows RT & smartphone apps	●		●	●		●
Office Online	●	●	●	●	●	●
Access				●		●
Standard services 1TB cloud storage (OneDrive for Business)	●	●	●	●	●	●
Email, calendar (Exchange)		●	●		●	●
Online meetings, IM (Lync)		●	●		●	●
Team sites, internal portals (SharePoint)		●	●		●	●
Enterprise social (Yammer)		●	●		●	●
Advanced services Active Directory integration	●	●	●	●	●	●
Supports hybrid deployment				●	●	●
Office shared computer activation support (RDS)				●		●
Upcoming services – Video content management					●	●
Compliance – Archiving, eDiscovery, mailbox hold						●
Information protection – message encryption, RMS, DLP						●

Figure 4-4. Office 365 subscription plans (courtesy of Microsoft)

This chapter is a compilation of the best-known methods used to control access to an Office 365 organization. The chapter also reviews some of the other tools integrated into Office 365 and Azure Premium, as well as the Intune Enterprise Mobility Suite. I encourage you to reach out to a Microsoft Tier 1 Champion partner and engage it as a licensed advisor to help with these features in Office 365. This is very important to your business.

What Is Single-User Identity?

Security is a concern. You need to manage user identity in the cloud and in your on-premises environment. This issue has always been one of managing users' passwords and access. From a management perspective, you want to provide flexibility for your employees, and auditable controls for IT management. Employees should only have access to the data that they need to do their job. Single-user identity is a security tool that helps manage users. It is a single-user sign-on that is used to access all cloud services (Microsoft and third parties). It is easy to make security changes for a few people, but extremely complex if you need to make changes for hundreds or even thousands of people. Expand this even further, where each user can access ten different cloud services. This is where single-user identity comes in handy. You configure your cloud services to treat one service as a master. When you change the user password in the master service, all related services' passwords are changed. There are multiple services that all share this capability (such as Ping, Okta, Office 365, and Google Apps). They are similar in that they look at which applications are on your system and which are cloud-based.

Looking at Employees and Their Use of Business Services

If you step back and look at the employees in your business, you can see the changes in the business environment due to the cloud. There is no longer the capability to control the "building" as was done in the early days (in a hypothetically secured building). Rather, today we have employees that bring their own devices to work, run business applications using multiple different cloud services to manage their work (and personal) environment (see Figure 4-5), and work anywhere in the world. IT management has become more complex because employees are now mixing their personal identities and equipment into the business environment.

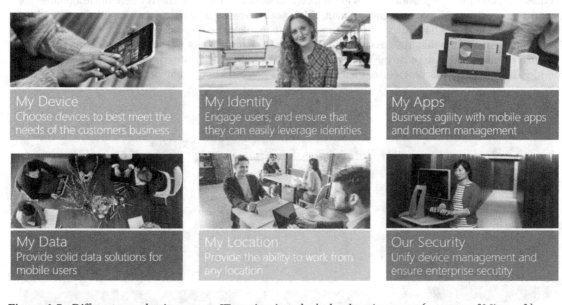

Figure 4-5. *Different ways businesses use IT services in today's cloud environment (courtesy of Microsoft)*

Employers now need to incorporate the necessary controls on employees' personal equipment (and user accounts) to allow employees to perform the required work. One of the issues in today's cloud environment is business intellectual property. How do business owners manage business assets with employees that work from any location and at any time? The common thread in this scenario is the control and the management of employees through a single-user identity. It no longer maters which "identity" you use as the cornerstone (such as a Google Apps ID or a Microsoft Office 365 organization ID).

It is more important that you pick one and use that as the standard in your organization. The organization single-user identity should be derived from your core cloud or on-premises security server. The organization's single-user identity becomes the cornerstone of the business. You are now replacing the building security with a single-user identity that is controlled by the business.

As a business grows and expands its capabilities, those capabilities become more apparent, because a single-user identity can provide a business with control over the following.

- Users can bring any device into the organization

- A user's business identity can be granted to third-party cloud services

- Users can only use approved company applications

- Users can only access company data that has been approved

- Users can access data anywhere approved by the company

- User security and data access is managed by the business through a common identity

As a business expands its operational capabilities, it starts to deliver the control and security of business information at the same level as the old secured building. Single identities allow you to access data and services stored in any cloud solution; it leverages the local security identities (which may be referred to as domain or Active Directory credentials) and works across any device. If you make things easier for your employees (with appropriate security governance issues fully addressed), the employees will perform to their potential and the business will grow.

In Figure 4-6, you see a typical user that has different business needs and requires access to different levels of services. This user must be provided access to the tools necessary to do her job. This is where single identities are used to manage the employee work environment. This is not a new idea; it just hasn't been applied to the public cloud. Large enterprises have always had the capability to manage the resources inside a secured building. What's different today is that businesses (of any size) need to manage these resources for their organization. Business owners need to manage the cloud services for which they have subscriptions and to use single-user identity. The benefit is that single-user identity becomes a powerful management tool for our businesses.

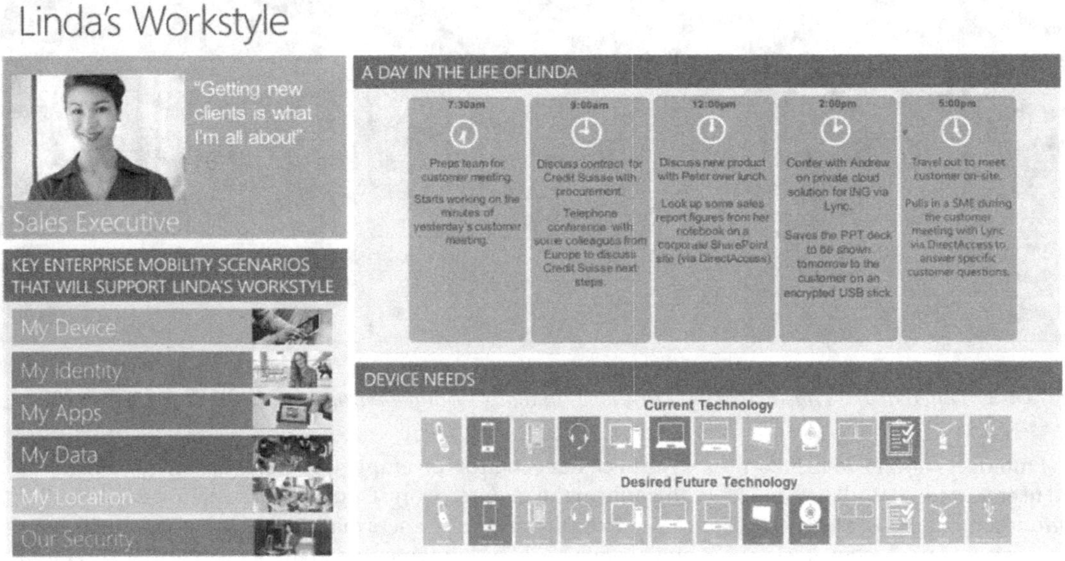

Figure 4-6. *Typical user business life mapped to the single identity (courtesy of Microsoft)*

How Does Single Identity Work?

Single identity is simply the linking of on-site resources to cloud services (such as Microsoft Office 365), and using the cloud services as the information broker to coordinate with other external business services. How businesses accomplish this depends on the business's size. Larger enterprises have the resources to manage these activities from their own data centers. Smaller businesses manage this activity from third-party services such as Microsoft Office 365 and Azure user identity services. As you can see in Figure 4-7, the KAMIND IT team linked our on-site security servicers (known as Active Directory) to Microsoft Azure services to access third-party software applications; when we linked these resources, we enabled a new level of security.

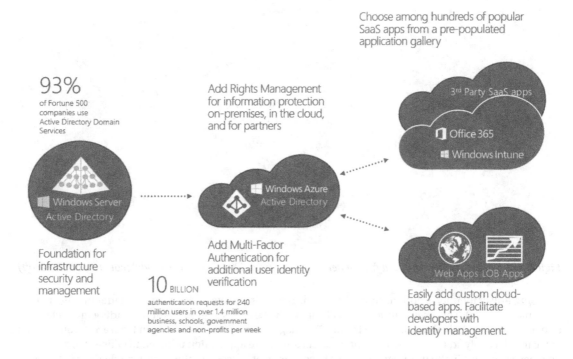

Figure 4-7. Linking onsite and cloud services for single identity access (courtesy of Microsoft)

The first step in the deployment of single-user identity is to look at what you are trying to accomplish. For example, a company might use the following business applications: Dropbox, QuickBooks Online, Twitter, and Pinterest. These services build security for their own use and there is no convenient way to manage these applications. For example, suppose you have developed a social media presence in the market, and a key employee leaves the company. How do you manage the user account of the employee who left? What about his Dropbox account or his Google Drive data? Now expand this across many employees; you can easily see the problem. In most cases, you have a friendly employee who turns over the information to you and you can change the passwords. However, in some cases, you may need to use legal measures to get access to business data, because the ex-employee was using a personal account. This is why single-user identity is so important in today's cloud-based company. A business owner must control the information in the business for it to survive and grow.

Single-User Identity vs. Device Management

When you look at single-user identity, you see the resources used in your communication to external parties and the way that you manage the activities. You have to step back and look at the basic structure that the single identity is built upon. Too many times businesses try to place a security strategy around a device, when the security must be built around the user. This is the fundamental switch that you see in today's business environment (see Figure 4-8)—a switch from a device-centric model to a user-centric model. This is what is meant by single-user identity: the ability to focus on the businesses' most important assets—the business data and the people.

Changing the focus

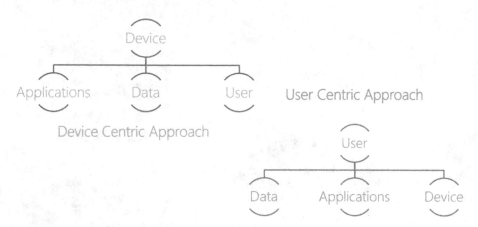

Figure 4-8. *Single identity changed from a device-centric model to user-centric model (courtesy of Microsoft)*

Single-user identity is nothing more than managing those assets under a common identity (usually an e-mail address). This user-centric approach allows the business to grow securely. Adding more cloud applications is easy; they can be added by the IT manager or the business owner. In Figure 4-9, you see that you can selectively add a link to a third-party application. The application is linked to Office 365, and users who have accounts in the third-party services have immediate access. In this case, Google Docs is added and managed by Microsoft Office 365. The implementation in Microsoft Office 365 uses Microsoft Azure services.

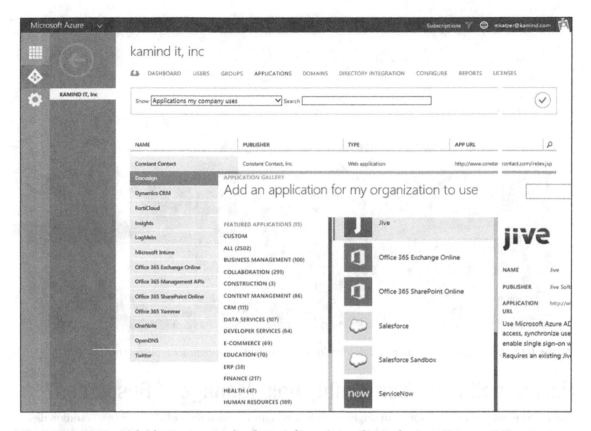

Figure 4-9. *Using single identity to centralized user information under one business ID*

Microsoft Azure provides tools that you can run on user workstations to determine the types and number of business cloud applications (or you can add them directly from your gallery of cloud applications). In this example, we added a DocuSign business account and linked the account to our Office 365 account. The business user (who has subscribed to DocuSign) is automatically linked to the DocuSign services with a single-user account and sign-in. You can add a Google Apps account and link it to Microsoft Office 365. In all of these examples, we are linking business assets to the user to enable the user to complete the job tasks. As a business owner, you can selectively provide your employees access to cloud services based on the business needs (see Figure 4-10).

Accessing Company Information?

- ▶ Classify data according to sensitivity and business impact
- ▶ Differentiate access to data based on identity & role
- ▶ Offer an "Opt-in" model for readying devices to access corporate resources
- ▶ Deploy robust firewall and perimeter protection; maintain an 'assume breach' model

Changing perspective: From device control to data governance

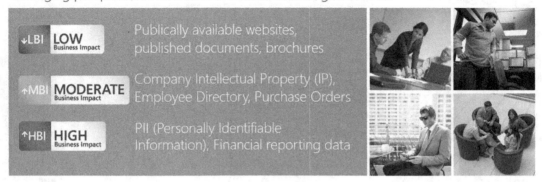

Figure 4-10. *Limiting access in using single identity to manage data governance (courtesy of Microsoft)*

How Can Single-User Identity Help Manage IT Resources?

One of the most overlooked aspects of single-user identity is the consumption of IT resources. Traditionally, single-user identity has not been used because of the amount of overhead associated with using it. Usually, this happens when user passwords are not linked to a cloud service. Cloud services such as Microsoft Azure and Office 365 make this linking easy and transparent to the users.

Figure 4-11 shows that we have linked the common applications to the company's Office 365 cloud account; for example, we are linking the Microsoft Office 365 services to DocuSign. This is the way users can access applications with a common identity. Once you develop a single-user identity (or cloud identity), there are additional services that you can make available to your users. In Figure 4-12, we provided a way that the user can have local control over the password reset and add additional applications to the inventory (subject to the organization's permissions). The user can register to self-manage password reset, and the process requires the user to register their cell phone. Microsoft's self-managed password reset is a two-factor approach. Two-factor password reset is built around something that you have (your cell phone) and something that you know (your e-mail address or phone number). The combination provides a very strong approach to allow the user to self-manage password resets.

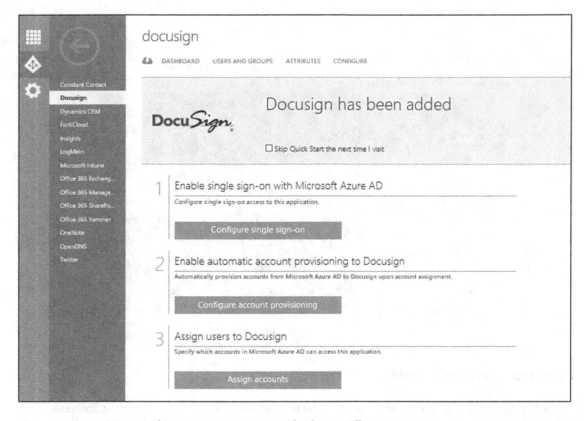

Figure 4-11. *Assignment of DocuSign service to a single identity Office 365 account*

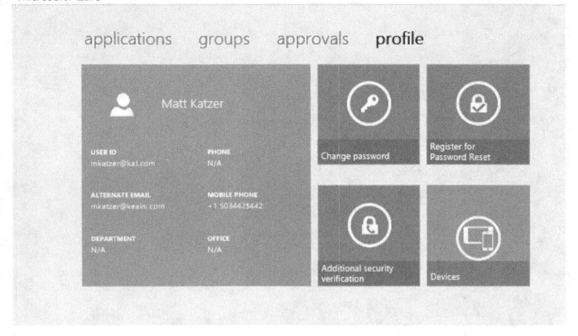

Figure 4-12. *User control over password reset and single identity*

Self-managed cloud identities also allow the user to control access. The user can request access to groups and applications on demand. This allows a seamless management of user permissions and service permissions without the direct knowledge of user accounts. This provides the manager/business owner the ability to control information and access for the employees in the organization.

Cloud Identity and Single-User Identity

You looked at why single-user identity is important and how it leverages the third-party applications that are available to the business. Business owners that use a single-user identity service have the ability to manage all resources that the business uses. The single-user identities can easily be transformed to a cloud identity (which uses the same security structure, but no on-premises resources) to manage thousands of third-party services. In Figure 4-13, a cloud identity is used to control access to documents for those subscriptions that include Azure rights management and Azure Premium services.

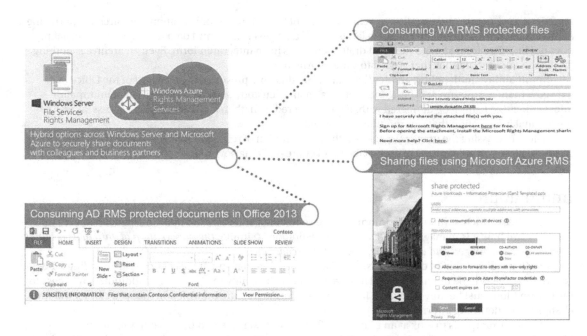

Figure 4-13. *Rights management with a single identity or cloud identity (courtesy of Microsoft)*

The examples here are based on using Microsoft Office 365 and Azure Active Directory management services. There are other services that you can use; however, the Microsoft approach is more seamless for the end user and it has scaled companies ranging from 1 to more than 100,000 employees.

Data Governance Concepts

Earlier, you looked at single-user identities and linked those to the user's Office 365 account. This is important, because single-user identities are based on the Microsoft Office 365 account. Once the user subscription is assigned to a user, Office 365 enables different services. As an example, Microsoft provides the management service on Office 365 that meets or exceeds the required regulatory compliance. The management of the data in Office 365 (and the subscription types) are managed and owned by the individual users. Office 365 business owners need to look at the business and decide what makes business sense based on the needs of the business. To put this in perspective, when an external entity looks at e-mail storage, it is considered modifiable by the user and is noncompliant with certain regulations. A compliant system requires that the mail and document storage systems must be incapable of being modified, or *immutable*. The owner of a mailbox must not be able to go in and delete the information or document. These capabilities are options in the Office 365 Enterprise plan and are included at no charge in some of the subscriptions suites (such as the Enterprise E3 subscription).

You are probably familiar with the various *CSI* television shows. A key message that these shows highlight lies in the evidentiary collection of information, and that there must be a "chain of custody" regarding the information collected. Think of data governance in the same context as you would a crime, with the collection of information for the legal prosecution of the suspect. It is all about chain of custody. Data governance on Office 365 is the same. Access to information that is under discovery or access cannot be tampered with. Further, access is recorded and auditable for all those who access the information. This is the data governance model of Office 365.

Archive and retention policies are implementations of our ability to manage the data to meet our data governance needs. Traditional approaches—such as journaling—record information external to the organization structure and usually just contain copies of the e-mail communication. This archaic journaling approach does not address the changing landscape of data governance and data management. Journaling does not link data from storage sites and draft documents in an integrated form. Even an archive is nothing more than another mailbox that is used to store information.

Immutability, audit policy, archive/retention, and data loss prevention are all part of the Office 365 data governance structure. It is designed around a chain of custody and the preservation of information—information that cannot be tampered with. If it is tampered with, then a full audit trail of access, as well as the original information that was modified, is created.

Before discussing the practical aspects of the configuration of retention policy and eDiscovery, let's frame the discussion with a definition of each of the four key areas of data governance, to put them in perspective.

Immutability

There has been much written about information immutability, and there are many misconceptions as to what it is and how it is managed in Office 365. The definition is simple: *the preservation of data in its original form cannot be changed and is kept in a form that is discoverable.*

Recall the discussion of chain of custody. The information that you are accessing and providing for data governance needs to be unchanged and no one must have the ability to change it. In addition, any access to the information must be fully traceable. If you access information, the information that you extract will not change the underlining information.

The best example is to look at an e-mail that flows in or that is created by a user in the cloud (see Figure 4-14). In this case, information that arrives or is in a user mailbox can be changed and modified by the user. This is the normal process used in writing an e-mail. An e-mail that is immutable, on the other hand, keeps all parts of the message in a form that can be fully discoverable through searches. When an e-mail message is drafted, all changes and drafts are kept and not deleted. Nothing is purged—all information remains intact and is fully discoverable in its original form.

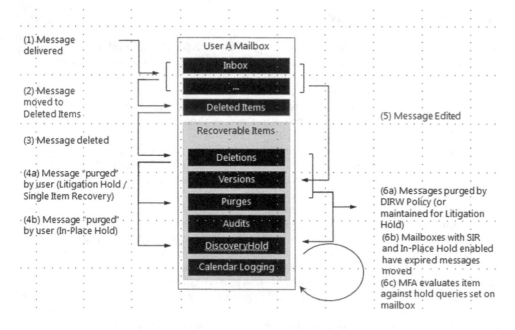

Figure 4-14. Life of an e-mail message (courtesy of Microsoft)

Compliance means the ability to access communications and documents that are immutable. Retention rules are based on business policies in the management of e-mail communications—specifically, which e-mails are visible to the user in the mailbox and what is kept in the archive. For example, you may have a business policy that dictates the movement of e-mail from a user mailbox to an archive if the e-mail is too old, or if the user deletes an e-mail. One company has a retention policy of 90 days; after 90 days, user incoming e-mail is moved into the compliance archive. These retention rules move the mail from the user's mailbox (or delete folder) into the archive. These rules can be systems level (the user has no control), or they can be local level (the user has complete control), or any combination.

Litigation Hold is an action that is placed on a mailbox to meet compliance requirements for future discovery and searching. Litigation Hold ensures that the data in a user's mailbox is immutable. For example, if the user tries to delete an e-mail, it is deleted (or purged) from the user's view, but the Litigation Hold function blocks the e-mail from being deleted in the system and is fully discoverable by the administrator (or a compliance officer).

Referring back to Figure 4-14, you see the life of an e-mail in a user mailbox. In this figure, the user only sees the message in steps 1–3. The compliance officer has access to all transactions in steps 1–6. When a discovery action—a search—is executed, all information is displayed in the search request, including the information in the deleted items, purges, and draft folders.

Audit Policy

Companies in the cloud need to know who has access to their company data. Monitoring and producing related reports are part of the Office 365 audit capability. Companies need to do the following:

- Verify that their mailbox data isn't being accessed by Microsoft or another third party.

- Enforce compliance and privacy regulations and access by non-owners.

- Determine who has access to data at a given time in a specific mailbox.

- Identify unauthorized access to mailbox data by users inside and outside the organization.

The ability to monitor mailbox data is a fundamental part of the Office 365 organization (see Figure 4-15). Once the audit capabilities are enabled, the audit reports can be generated by the administrator or an individual who has been given access permission.

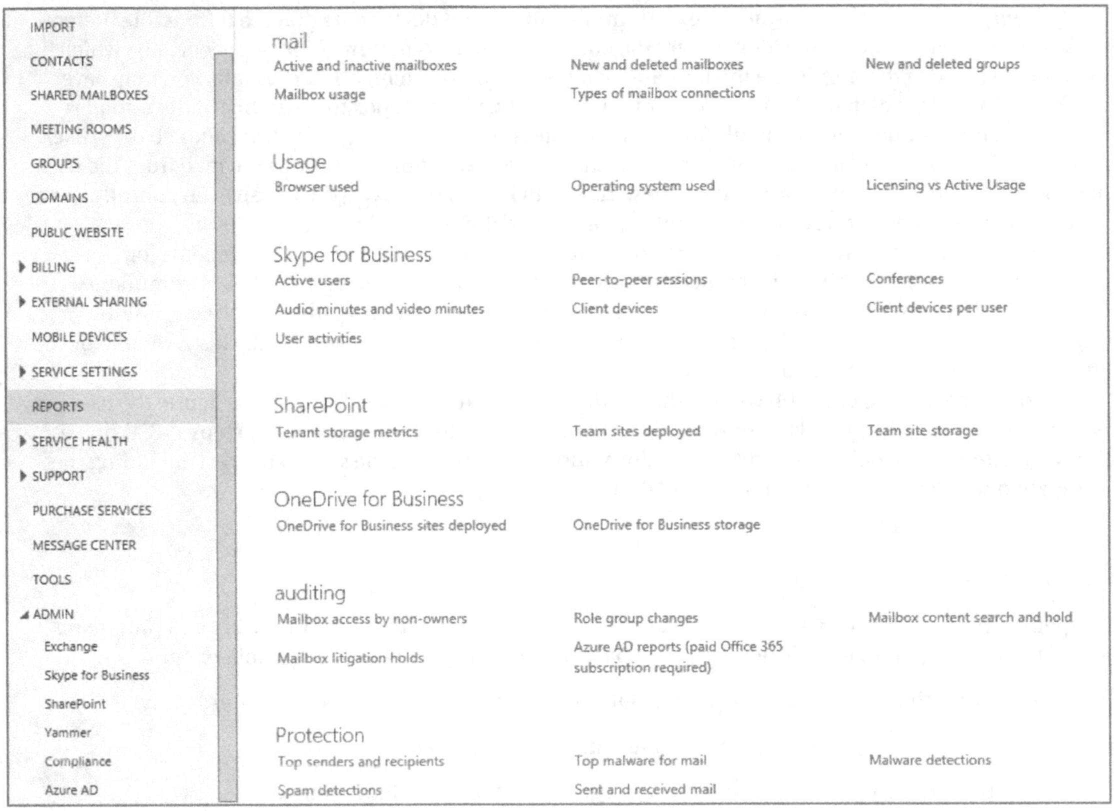

mail

Active and inactive mailboxes	New and deleted mailboxes	New and deleted groups
Mailbox usage	Types of mailbox connections	

Usage

Browser used	Operating system used	Licensing vs Active Usage

Skype for Business

Active users	Peer-to-peer sessions	Conferences
Audio minutes and video minutes	Client devices	Client devices per user
User activities		

SharePoint

Tenant storage metrics	Team sites deployed	Team site storage

OneDrive for Business

OneDrive for Business sites deployed	OneDrive for Business storage

auditing

Mailbox access by non-owners	Role group changes	Mailbox content search and hold
Mailbox litigation holds	Azure AD reports (paid Office 365 subscription required)	

Protection

Top senders and recipients	Top malware for mail	Malware detections
Spam detections	Sent and received mail	

Side navigation menu:
IMPORT
CONTACTS
SHARED MAILBOXES
MEETING ROOMS
GROUPS
DOMAINS
PUBLIC WEBSITE
▶ BILLING
▶ EXTERNAL SHARING
MOBILE DEVICES
▶ SERVICE SETTINGS
REPORTS
▶ SERVICE HEALTH
▶ SUPPORT
PURCHASE SERVICES
MESSAGE CENTER
TOOLS
⊿ ADMIN
  Exchange
  Skype for Business
  SharePoint
  Yammer
  Compliance
  Azure AD

Figure 4-15. *Report capability for Office 365*

■ **Note** audit logs must be turned on via PowerShell. The default audit logs for admin and delegated admin are off. We recommend that audit logs be turned on for 360 days. The audit logs on user mailboxes need to be turned on for each mailbox.

There are additional audit reports available in the Exchange Admin panel (see Figure 4-16). These reports are the standard Exchange 2013/2016 administration audit reports. However, if the audit reports are not enabled, the information is not logged. Each audit report contains the following information:

- Who accessed the mailbox and when
- The actions performed by the non-owner
- The affected message and its folder location
- Whether or not the action was successful

Exchange admin center

dashboard

recipients

permissions

compliance management

organization

protection

mail flow

mobile

public folders

unified messaging

in-place eDiscovery & hold   **auditing**   data loss prevention   retention policies   retention tags   journal rules

Use these reports and audit logs to view information about mailboxes accessed by someone other than the owner and changes made by administrators to your Exchange organization. You can also export search results to a file that is sent to you or other users. Learn more

○ **Run a non-owner mailbox access report...**
Search mailbox audit logs for mailboxes that have been opened by someone other than the owner. You have to enable mailbox audit logging for each mailbox that you want to run a non-owner mailbox access report for. If mailbox audit logging isn't enabled for a mailbox, you won't get any results for it when you run this report. Learn more

○ **Run an administrator role group report...**
Search the admin audit log for changes made to role groups, which are used to assign administrative permissions to users. Learn more

○ **Run an In-Place eDiscovery & Hold report...**
Search the admin audit log for changes made to In-Place eDiscovery searches and In-Place Holds. Learn more

○ **Run a per-mailbox Litigation Hold report...**
Search the admin audit log to determine if a Litigation Hold was enabled or disabled for a user's mailbox. Learn more

○ **Export mailbox audit logs...**
Export entries from mailbox audit logs about non-owner access to user mailboxes. Audit log entries are saved to an XML file that is attached to a message and sent to the specified recipients within 24 hours. Learn more

○ **Run the admin audit log report...**
View entries from the admin audit log about configuration changes made by administrators in your organization. Learn more

○ **Export the admin audit log...**
Export entries from the admin audit log for any configuration change made to your organization. Audit log entries are saved to an XML file that is attached to a message and sent to the specified recipients within 24 hours. Learn more

○ **Run the external admin audit log report...**
View entries from the admin audit log about configuration changes made to your Exchange Online services by Microsoft or by a delegated admin. Learn more

Figure 4-16. Audit reports available on Exchange Server admin panel for Office 365

■ **Note**   Microsoft is deploying a new audit feature on Office 365 recently call the "Office 365 lock box". The Office 365 lock box is used to grant Microsoft access to the customer's data. The customer can either grant Microsoft permission or deny access.

The first step in setting up a compliant organization is enabling the audit capabilities to ensure that you have a complete record of all accesses to user mailbox data by non-owner users. This information is used to supplement future reports. Figure 4-17 provides a descriptive explanation of the terms in the audit reports.

The audit reports that are generated contain detailed information about who has accessed the information and how they have changed it. As you can see in Figure 4-17, users have different levels of access, and that access can be tracked in audit logs. If a Litigation Hold was placed on the user mailbox, then a search of the user mailbox will show the history of any non-mailbox-owner access. The areas marked **Yes** are those that can be tracked in the audit logs. This is different than tracking information in the discovery center. The discovery center can track all information that is placed on Litigation Hold. The audit logs track the non–mailbox owners who access information.

Action	Description	Administrators	Delegated Users
Update	A message was changed.	Yes	Yes
Copy	A message was copied to another folder.	No	No
Soft-delete	A message was deleted from the Deleted Items folder.	Yes	Yes
Hard-delete	A message is purged from the Recoverable Items folder. For more information, see Recover Deleted Items.	Yes	Yes
FolderBind	A mailbox folder was accessed.	Yes	No
Send as	A message was sent using SendAs permission. This means another user sent the message as though it came from the mailbox owner.	Yes	Yes
Send on behalf of	A message is sent using SendOnBehalf permission. This means another user sent the message on behalf of the mailbox owner. The message will indicate to the recipient who the message was sent on behalf of and who actually sent the message.	Yes	No
MessageBind	A message is viewed in the preview pane or opened.	No	No

Figure 4-17. Office 365 audit information (courtesy of Microsoft)

Information Immutability

Information immutability takes this one step further and integrates Skype for Business communications, and SharePoint documents (as well as OneDrive for Business document synchronization), into the equation. The Office 365 approach is designed to reduce the amount of information by removing duplicate information. This reduces the complexity of the searches and allows the compliance officer to clearly see the thread of the information and the root cause (if any) of the discovery request. The searched data can be exported in the industry Electronic Discover Reference Model (EDRM) standard in an XML format to provide content to a third party. The Office 365 approach is designed to remove duplicate data from searches and does not remove any data from the user SharePoint or e-mail mailbox. The data stays where it is and is immutable.

In Office 365, data governance and compliance is simplified. The scope of the discovery is reduced to the specific set of keywords and can be easily restricted to a few users in question. It is not uncommon that an eDiscovery request on Office 365 would cost 90 percent less than an eDiscovery request using an older journaling system for e-mail communications management.

The discussion on archive and retention polices are built around data immutability to manage an organization's compliance needs. In Office 365, this is referred to as *compliance management*. Administrators are able to set up controls based on the business polices of the organization.

Office 365 Archiving and Retention

The term *archive* is overused. It often implies more than what it really is. An archive is nothing more than a second mailbox designed for long-term storage. The relevancy of an archive is based on the business process rules that are used to manage it. This is where immutability and retention policies come into play. Immutability refers to how information is retained (in a form that can't be changed) in the mailbox and the archive. Retention polices (see Figure 4-18) describe the length of time you need to keep the data that is not subject to any legal action (a legal hold to guarantee immutability).

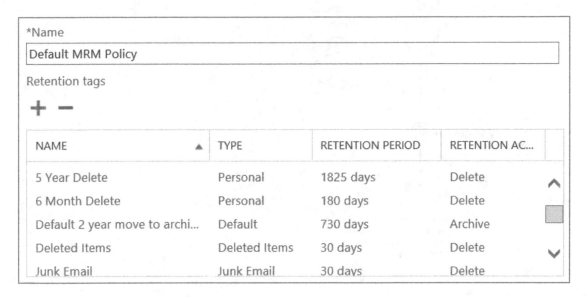

Figure 4-18. Sample retention policies

There are two types of archives in Office 365: personal archives and server archives (see Table 4-1). Server archives can be immutable (meaning they can be configured to ignore any change using Litigation Hold or In-Place Hold). Personal archives are stored locally on the user's desktop and are not immutable (users can change the contents). The retention policies only refer to the moving of data from the user mailbox to the archive.

Table 4-1. Archive Size

Archive Type	Size	Immutable	Retention Policies
Personal	User dependent	No	Personal rules
Server-based	50 GB (E1)or unlimited (E3)	E3 or Exchange Plan 2	Server retention rules

Retention Policy

Retention policy is nothing more than the business processes that define the movement of data. Retention polices are a set of rules that are executed concerning a message (see Figure 4-19). Retention policy is a combination of different *retention tags*, which are actions placed on a message. You can have only one retention policy applied to a mailbox. In an organization where you have compliance requirements, retention tags are used to manage the user mailbox information and to control mailbox sizes.

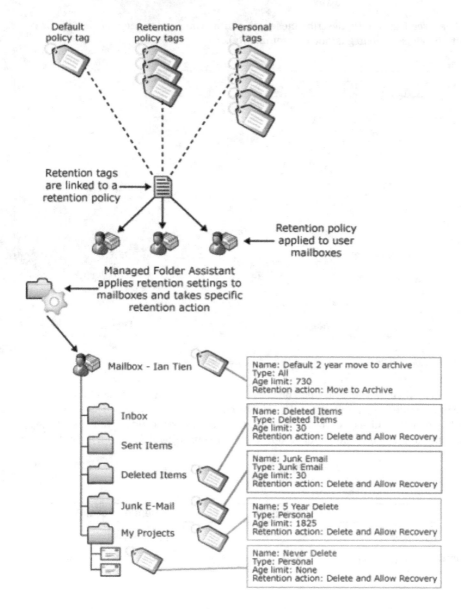

Figure 4-19. *Office 365 retention tags (courtesy of Microsoft)*

Retention tags define and apply the retention settings to messages and folders in the user mailbox. These tags specify how long a message is kept and what action is taken when a message reaches the retention age. Retention tags are used to control the amount of information that is on the user's desktop. Typically, this means that the message is moved to the archive folder or it is deleted. Looking at Figure 4-19, you can see three types of retention tags: default retention tags, policy retention tags, and personal retention tags (described in Table 4-2).

Table 4-2. *Retention Tag Policy*

Type	Description
Default	The default policy applies to all items in a mailbox that do not have a retention tag applied.
Policy	Policy tags are applied to folders (inbox, deleted items, and so on) and override the default policy tags. The only retention action for policy is to delete items.
Personal	Personal tags are only used for Outlook clients to move data to customer folders in the user's mailbox.

The best way to understand retention policy is to look at the default policy and remote retention tags. Keep in mind that the implementation of a retention policy is this execution of individual retention tags. Retention tags are used to reduce the amount of information kept in a user's mailbox. Retention tags (which make up the retention policy) are just another tool used for information management. Depending on your business needs, you may have different retention polices to manage the information of different groups in your organization. In one organization that KAMIND IT managed, the data retention policy was 90 days, unless the mailbox was placed on in-place hold for litigation or discovery.

Compliance archives may or may not have a retention policy applied to them, but they will have the mailbox placed under Litigation Hold; the data retention policy of the SharePoint site will also be placed under Litigation Hold. User mailboxes that are placed under Litigation Hold with the external audit enabled meet all compliance requirements, because the data is immutable.

Data Loss Prevention

Data loss prevention (DLP) operates with either a template rule (see Figure 4-20), or with a trigger from the rights management service based on business policy. The purpose of DLP is to execute an action based on rules. DLP does not prevent an individual from doing something bad. DLP simply limits the information flow in case someone sends electronic communications to a third party that violates business policy.

*Choose a template:

U.K. Access to Medical Reports Act	**U.S. Federal Trade**
U.K. Data Protection Act	**Commission (FTC)**
U.K. Financial Data	**Consumer Rules 15.0.3.0**
U.K. Personal Information Online Code of Practice (PIOCP)	
U.K. Personally Identifiable Information (PII) Data	Helps detect the presence of information subject to U.S. Federal
U.K. Privacy and Electronic Communications Regulations	Trade Commission (FTC) Consumer
U.S. Federal Trade Commission (FTC) Consumer Rules	Rules, including data like credit card numbers. Use of this policy does not
U.S. Financial Data	ensure compliance with any regulation.
U.S. Gramm-Leach-Bliley Act (GLBA)	After your testing is complete, make the necessary configuration changes in
U.S. Health Insurance Act (HIPAA)	Exchange so the transmission of
U.S. Patriot Act	information complies with your organization's policies. Examples
U.S. Personally Identifiable Information (PII) Data	include configuring TLS with known
U.S. State Breach Notification Laws	business partners or adding more
U.S. State Social Security Number Confidentiality Laws	restrictive transport rule actions, such as adding rights protection to

Figure 4-20. *Data Loss Prevention (DLP) templates*

DLP minimizes th)e mistakes that individuals make in sending information to individuals that do not have a business need to know the information. Add auditing and discovery to this capability, and you are able to determine which individual had last access to the information.

There are many rules that you can select to implement in addition to the rights management rules on Office 365. Figure 4-20 shows the different templates that can be managed in your organization to control information to meet federal and state regulations. Rights management is the extension of DLP to manage internal documents and information using Active Directory. DLP functions are managed using both the Office 365 interface and PowerShell commands (see Figure 4-21).

If you need to...	...use the following cmdlets
Connect to or disconnect from the Rights Management service for your organization.	**Connect-AadrmService** **Disconnect-AadrmService** For more information, see Connecting to the rights management service and Disconnecting from the rights management service
Disable (or re-enable after disabling) the Rights Management service for your organization.	**Enable-Aadrm** **Disable-Aadrm** For more information, see Enabling the rights management service and Disabling the rights management service
Manage the super user feature within the Rights Management for your organization.	**Enable–AadrmSuperUserFeature** **Disable–AadrmSuperUserFeature** **Add–AadrmSuperUser** **Get–AadrmSuperUser** **Remove–AadrmSuperUser** For more information, see Manage super users for rights managed content
Manage users and groups who are authorized to administer the Rights Management service for your organization.	**Add–AadrmRoleBasedAdministrator** **Get–AadrmRoleBasedAdministrator** **Remove–AadrmRoleBasedAdministrator** For more information, see Add, list or remove role-based administrators for rights management
Get a log of administrative tasks that have been performed against the Rights Management service for your organization.	**Get-AadrmAdminLog** For more information, see Download audit logs for Windows Azure AD Rights Management
Migrate your organization to an on-premises AD RMS deployment from the Rights Management service.	**Set-AadrmMigrationUrl** **Get-AadrmMigrationUrl** For more information, see List or set the URL for use in migrating rights managed content to AD RMS
Displays the current Rights Management service configuration for your organization.	**Get-AadrmConfiguration** For more information, see Display the current rights management configuration

Figure 4-21. Rights management capabilities (courtesy of Microsoft)

Overview of Office 365 Compliance and Discovery

Office 365 is built on the principle that the information contained in the cloud service is owned by the business. The data your company places in Office 365 is your data. Microsoft has as strict policy to not "data mine" or process your data for any business purpose. If you choose to leave Office 365 for some other service, the data you leave behind will be destroyed within 90–120 days of your subscription termination. When you think of security, you need to think of how data is organized in Office 365 and who has access to the information.

There are two parts to compliance: Microsoft's management of the Office 365 service and your business processes in the management of your Office 365 data. Microsoft's management of the Office 365 service and their service standards are published on the Microsoft "trust" web site (see Figure 4-22 and https://products.office.com/en-us/business/office-365-trust-center-cloud-computing-security). If you want a HIPAA (Health Insurance Portability and Accountability Act of 1996) Business Associate Agreement certification or a copy of the service audit logs, you can request those directly from Microsoft. Microsoft is transparent in its process on Office 365 and built the service around the protection of your company information. This is in contrast to other cloud services that require an intellectual property rights assignment, which allows them to use your information to sell advertising, among other things.

Figure 4-22. Office 365 Trust Center (https://products.office.com/en-us/business/office-365-trust-center-cloud-computing-security)

Compliance Settings

Office 365 compliance means the capabilities of Office 365 data governance to preserve and manage information. Compliance and regulatory settings are the services you enable on the Office 365 site and that meet your business needs or regulatory requirements. As an example, you can group information into three different categories: compliance, information review, or business data retention.

- Compliance (HIPAA, for example)
    - Rights management and the protection of personal information
    - Encryption of personal information external to your organization
- Information review (regulatory like FINRA (Financial Industry Regulatory Authority) or judicial order)
    - Litigation Hold and eDiscovery
    - E-mail review to meet FINRA requirements
- Business data retention
    - Business processes on the age of data
    - Data management: how to archive/how to delete

All information that you keep falls into these categories. For example, HIPAA requires you to manage certain types of data in a way to protect information. To meet HIPAA requirements, you must protect personal information by encrypting the information before it is sent externally to the organization. One of the HIPAA requirements is that the service you are using provides a Business Associates Agreement (BAA) for their services.

Information review typically means that the information is subject to an audit and is immutable—meaning it cannot be changed or deleted by the users or the organization—prior to review. Any type of regulator review requires that the data is immutable. The most common is litigation. When an organization enters into litigation, all information is frozen at that period in time. This is referred to as a *Litigation Hold*. Regulator reviews such as FINRA are nothing more than an extension of a Litigation Hold.

Business data retention is nothing more than the business processes used to maintain information, subject to the regulatory requirements. As an example, if the business policy (or user policy) deletes information subject to the retention policy, the information is deleted from the user perspective, but may be kept for a very long time subject to the compliance needs of the organization. The user may delete information, but the compliance setting keeps the information in an area where it is immutable and fully searchable and hidden from the user.

The Office 365 administrator has complete control over the configuration of the compliance and retention polices. The administrator can enable these settings and all actions are auditable. The settings can be changed by using the Exchange Admin Center or using PowerShell commands. As Microsoft enhances the Office 365 service, these settings are simplified in an easy-to-use graphical interface.

■ **Note**   If you find that you need to perform discovery or mailbox searches, all users subject to search must be on the Enterprise subscription Exchange Plan 2. There also needs to be at least one E3 or E5 subscription to use the Electronic Discovery Center.

Summary

Security is about protecting company information. In this chapter, we wanted to expose you to the different tools you can use to protect your cloud data. Office 365 takes security seriously. We briefly covered the different ways you can use single user login, two factor authentication and how to protect your company data using the data loss prevention tools. As you look to deploy Office 365, you need to consider all aspect of the cloud and how you want to manage information. The next chapter uses these concepts to help you make an informed decision on how you want to use Office 365 in your company.

Reference Links

There is a lot of information about Office 365 on the Web—the issue is finding the right site. The information contained in this chapter is a combination of experience in deployments and support information that published by third parties.

Microsoft Office 365 Blog: Latest News about Office 365

- http://blogs.office.com/b/microsoft_office_365_blog/

Searching Mailboxes on Legal Hold

- https://technet.microsoft.com/en-us/library/ff637980(v=exchg.150).aspx

Understanding Legal Hold in Office 365

- http://www.networkworld.com/community/blog/doing-e-discovery-message-retention-legal-rec

Understanding Retention Policy PowerShell Commands

- http://help.outlook.com/en-us/beta/gg271153.aspx

Understanding Permissions on Discovery Mailboxes

- https://technet.microsoft.com/en-us/library/dn790281.aspx

Search for Deleted Messages

- https://support.office.com/en-us/article/Recover-deleted-items-or-email-in-Outlook-Web-App-C3D8FC15-EEEF-4F1C-81DF-E27964B7EDD4

Update to Moving your business to Office 365

- http://www.mattkatzer.com

AQS Query Syntax : Discovery

- http://blogs.technet.com/b/exchangesearch/archive/2012/03/10/how-to-use-aqs-to-construct-complex-discovery-queries.aspx

How to use Office 365 Compliance Hold

- http://www.kamind.com/clio

Next Steps

Your basic Office 365 system has been set up and configured. At this point, you are 100-percent functional and ready to move to the next steps. However, your work is not complete at this time; there is much more to do, depending on your Office 365 configuration. You need to review Chapters 5, 6, and 7 before for your Office 365 deployment.

Chapter 5: Office 365 Deployment Step by Step. The secret to a successful deployment to Office 365 is picking the correct plan that supports your business. The key to a successful migration to Office 365 is the planning and purchase process. Once you select a plan, your primary consideration must be to ensure that the migration process is seamless for your organization. This chapter describes the basic purchase information and it details the choices. It concludes with information about pre-deployment, deployment, and post-deployment.

Chapter 6: Workstation Setup and Configuration. Office 365 supports many different systems and capabilities, depending on your business needs. The issue that IT managers constantly face is how to setup and manage the client environment. This chapter is focused on the configuration of an Office 365 desktop environment. This is the go-to reference chapter on the configuration of your desktop and mobile phones.

Chapter 7: Managing Office 365. This chapter describes the different administration centers in Office 365 and the most common tools that you use to administer Office 365. Depending on your Office 365 plan, there are five possible administration tools. This chapter focuses on the Office 365, Exchange, and Skype for Business administration centers. The chapter closes with using PowerShell to manage your Office 365 environment.

CHAPTER 5

■ ■ ■

Deployment Step by Step

In the previous chapters, we walked through the Office 365 features, most importantly, Office 365 security. At this point, the question that we all ask is: How do I get started with Office 365? There are a variety of different ways to get started with Office 365. The key is to remember that Office 365 is like the soup aisle in the grocery store. You need to make sure that you are purchasing the correct subscription, and not a retail version from your local Office supply store. Office 365 is a subscription business service and it must be purchased from Microsoft or an authorized Cloud Solution Provider (CSP). The focus of this chapter is to leverage the information discussed in the previous chapters so that you can completely configure your Office 365 environment. At the end of this chapter, you will have a fully functional Office 365 solution.

Purchasing Office 365

Office 365 plans are designed for different target markets and are organized in suites. Microsoft has set up suites for different styles of companies, based on business needs. In the early days, theses suites were fixed in the configuration and were very difficult to change. This has changed considerably. You can now mix different suites and Office 365 plans to reflect your business needs. As an example, if you want to purchase a direct-dial number for Skype for Business, you add the Cloud PBX (E5) option to your subscription (or upgrade to a different suite that has a domestic calling option). Subscription upgrades and downgrades are common. It is recommended that you work with a Cloud Solution Partner (CSP) to handle these requests. Most cloud partners make the change for you as a courtesy, if the cloud partner is added as a subscription advisor (or partner of record) on the account. When you decide to move your IT services—mail, phone, or local file storage—from your current supplier to Office 365, this is referred to as *migration* or *onboarding*.

There are two methods used to move to Office 365: cutover migration and hybrid migration. Each of these approaches has their pros and cons. In cutover migrations, the end user can typically lose the Outlook cache e-mail addresses (users call these *contacts*) and local task/categories. Cutover migrations create a new Outlook profile and the local address cache is not migrated. Hybrid migrations maintain the same user profile, but the mailbox move requires an Exchange mailbox move (called a *federated move*). The method you use depends on your business requirements and how fast you want to move to Office 365. Cutover migration is fast: you "cut over" your mail services to Office 365 from the old service. Federation is a stage, or a slower non-intrusive migration. Table 5-1 shows the different migration types and gives you an idea of which type you can use.

Table 5-1. *Office 365 Migration Table*

Source Mail	Migration Option	Notes
POP/IMAP Mail	Cutover	IMAP or a local archive (.pst file)
Google Mail	Cutover	IMAP or a local archive (.pst file)
Hosted Exchange	Cutover	Process Exchange mailbox in server
O365 CSP	Cutover	Process Exchange mailbox in server
Exchange 2003	Cutover	Hybrid not supported
Exchange 2007+	Hybrid/Cutover	Use Exchange Federation 2013 to migrate mail

Once you have made your selection to either hybrid or cutover, the next decision is how to integrate the user accounts into Office 365. If you have chosen a hybrid approach, you need to use Azure Active Directory Connect to link your on-site Windows Active Directory to Office 365. If you do not have an Active Directory, then you manually input the user accounts in Office 365 or use a third-party migration tool. There are multiple different tools in the market for migration. The common two tools are BitTitan's MigrationWiz (www.bittitan.com) and the Skykick migration tool (www.Skykick.com). Each tool has different capabilities and features, so it is best that you look at the tools and decide which one makes sense for your migration. The focus of this chapter is to provide a "how to" approach in moving your business to the cloud, using our 13-step migration process.

■ **Note**   There is an impact to users depending on the migration. Hybrid will move the users' auto complete files; cutover will not move them. The migration process for the autocomplete is a manual process. Most organization do not migrate autocomplete.

There are two versions of Office 365: Home or Business. An earlier chapter discussed the differences between the Microsoft Consumer/Small Business version of Office 365 and the Business version. If you want to use Office 365 in the cloud, always select the Business version. The Office 365 Business version uses your own e-mail domain, not a Microsoft account. (We may sometimes refer to the Enterprise version as a complete Office 365 cloud implementation.) This chapter only addresses the Business version of Office 365. The Office 365 Business version allows you to mix and match the subscription based on the roles in the organization. It also allows the business to reduce deployment costs and support costs.

The Office 365 Business versions (also known as the Enterprise plans) support Macs and PCs, and provide both cloud and desktop productivity software. These productivity tools are needed for businesses of all sizes to control operating costs and to improve productivity. One of the great features of the Business version of Office 365 is the access to all the software components for Microsoft Office desktop client suites. An Office 365 user can install up to ten copies of software. As you can see in Figure 5-1, we have three copies of software installed, and seven more to use.

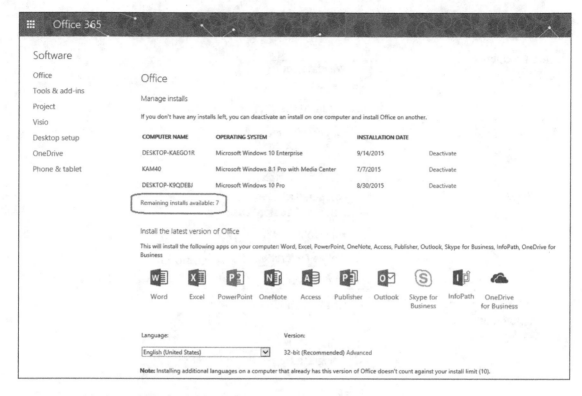

Figure 5-1. *Office 365 Service Administration software download*

All IT changes—no matter how big or small—require planning. Figure 5-2 shows the planning and deployment steps for moving to Office 365. There are various paths to move your users to Office 365, manually or by using Active Directory. If you are using Active Directory, you can use Azure Active Directory Connect to synchronize (copy) your user accounts (e-mail addresses) to Office 365. This is useful, because the other approach requires you to manually enter user e-mail addresses into Office 365 (which is tedious and time-consuming). Once your accounts are in Office 365, you can move your e-mail services to Office 365 and start using the services. Our planning process walks you through the configuration steps to successfully move to Office 365.

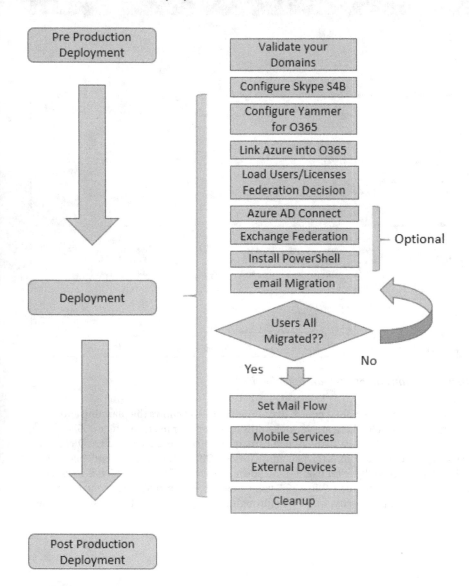

Figure 5-2. *Deployment process overview*

■ **Note** You must have control over your DNS. If you do not have control over your DNS, you cannot move to the cloud or the process will be very time-consuming.

Office 365 is composed of different tools to assist you in running your business better. Once you have moved to Office 365, you can extend your capabilities by using Microsoft Enterprise Mobility Suite (EMS) with Microsoft Intune and Skype for Business Cloud PBX. The combination of these services allows you to manage your desktop and mobile devices with a set of cost-effective and powerful tools designed to improve productivity. Office 365 includes many different services (see Figure 5-3) that can be customized for your business and are configurable, including the following:

- Exchange
- Skype for Business and Cloud PBX
- SharePoint (Team Site)
- OneDrive for Business
- Compliance
- Azure AD
- Bing Places for Business

Figure 5-3. *User portal to Office 365*

There are also numerous option services that you can add to your subscription based on your needs. Typically, these include Project, Business Intelligence (Power BI), and CRM.

Configuring Office 365

Office 365 is simple to configure, as long as you have a plan in place that answers two questions:

- How do you plan to deploy the clients?
- How do you plan to move historical e-mail to Microsoft Online services?

The simplest migration is a cutover migration. The most complex is hybrid coexistence. Our migration approach uses a 13-step plan that you can complete in an evening or over a number of days. If your migration requires Active Directory synchronization (DirSync) or Exchange Federation, see the sections on configuration at the end of this chapter. There are different ways to complete the data migration (third-party tools, an Exchange mailbox move, or shipping the data files to Microsoft for import to Office 365). The direction to take is up to you. The approach that we have taken is to highlight where these migration options are used in the 13-step process outlined next. The areas where you have choices are emphasized.

1. Purchase your Office 365 services.

2. Validate your domain(s) to Microsoft and add DNS records.

3. Configure Skype for Business.

4. Configure Yammer for Office 365.

5. Link Office 365 to Azure Active Directory.

6. Load users and assign licenses or use Federation/Azure AD Connect.

7. Install Azure Active Directory Connect(optional).

8. Install PowerShell (optional).

9. Migrate e-mail (using external tools or with Exchange mailbox move).

10. Set mail flow.

11. Configure mobile services (using Intune)

12. Configure automated devices (copiers, scanners, fax servers).

13. Clean up.

■ **Note**　Are you using single sign-on? If you are planning to implement single sign-on with Active Directory Federation Services (ADFS), this implementation is beyond the scope of this Chapter.

Step 1: Purchase Your Office 365 Services

There are different ways to purchase your subscription, either from the Web (see Figure 5-4) or through a URL supplied to you from your Microsoft Partners. In Figure 5-4, go to **http://www.kamind.com** and select the Office 365 floating web page. Once the web page loads, select **Try Office 365** to launch the 25-user trial subscription (see Figure 5-5).

Figure 5-4. Purchasing Office 365 Business

Once you have launched the trial subscription, you need to enter your company information. After you have done this, enter an administrator name and domain (see Figure 5-5).

Figure 5-5. *Creating the subscription*

Once you have selected **Text me** or **Call me**, enter the verification code and create your account (see Figure 5-6). When your account is created, the screen should look similar to what's shown in Figure 5-7.

Figure 5-6. *Validating the subscription*

Figure 5-7. *Enterprise E3 trial account created*

Step 2: Validate Your Domain(s) to Microsoft and Add DNS Records

After you have created the subscription, the next step is to validate the domain. Validation of the domain proves to Microsoft that you own the domain in Office 365. Sign in at `http://portal.microsoftonline.com` using the account that you created in Step 1. Select the **Admin** icon (or select the nine-block grid in upper-left hand corner to select Admin). You are at the Office 365 dashboard. On the left-hand side (see Figure 5-8), select **DOMAINS**, and then select **Add domain** to start the process of adding your domain to the Microsoft Online environment.

Figure 5-8. *Add a domain in Office 365*

Office 365 requires you to prove that you own the domain you are using. Figure 5-9 explains DNS and outlines the process of Office 365 configuration. Click **Next**.

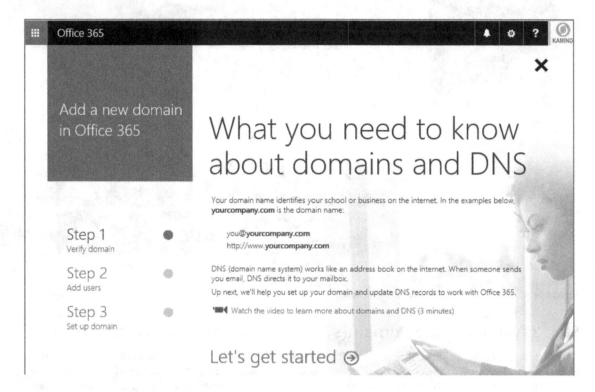

Figure 5-9. *Starting the DNS configuration for Office 365*

Enter the domain you want to use (GetOffice365security in this example) and click **Next** (see Figure 5-10). If you do not have a domain, you can buy one from a 3rd party reseller. Office 365 examines your domain and provides you an automated way to set up your domain. If Office 365 detects that the domain that you want to verify is on GoDaddy, it prompts you to use an automatic configuration of the domain and DNS records.

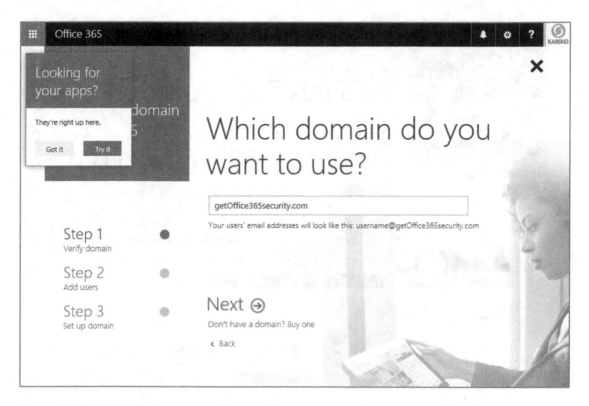

Figure 5-10. *Enter the domain name*

The Office 365 Domain Wizard prompts you to select the service for verification. If you are going to cut over to Office 365 (move all mail services immediately to Office 365), then use the wizard. If you are not planning to use Office 365 this instant, then select **Step-by-step instructions** and manually configure your DNS service (see Figure 5-11), and then select **Okay I've added the record**.

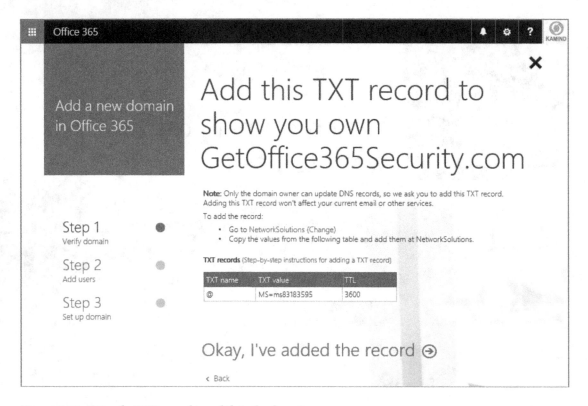

Figure 5-11. *Enter the TXT record to validate the domain name*

Office 365 looks up your DNS information and recommends a record to enter for domain validation. In some cases, you may be prompted to enter a wizard. We recommend that you *do not use the wizard*, unless you are setting up a brand-new Office 365 and have no plans to migrate any e-mail into the Office 365 service.

■ **Note** Only use the wizards if you plan to immediately use Office 365. The wizards configure your domain and move/point your mail records to Office 365. If your mail records are changed to Office 365, your existing mail on the third-party hosting service may be deleted. We only use the wizards if this is a new e-mail domain.

To manually add the domain verification record, follow the directions on the screen. Sign in to your domain registrar and add the TXT record as specified on this screen. Figure 5-12 shows a GoDaddy TXT record and Figure 5-13 shows a TXT record at Network Solutions for the domain getwindowsintunenow.biz. The process is the same for all domain verification.

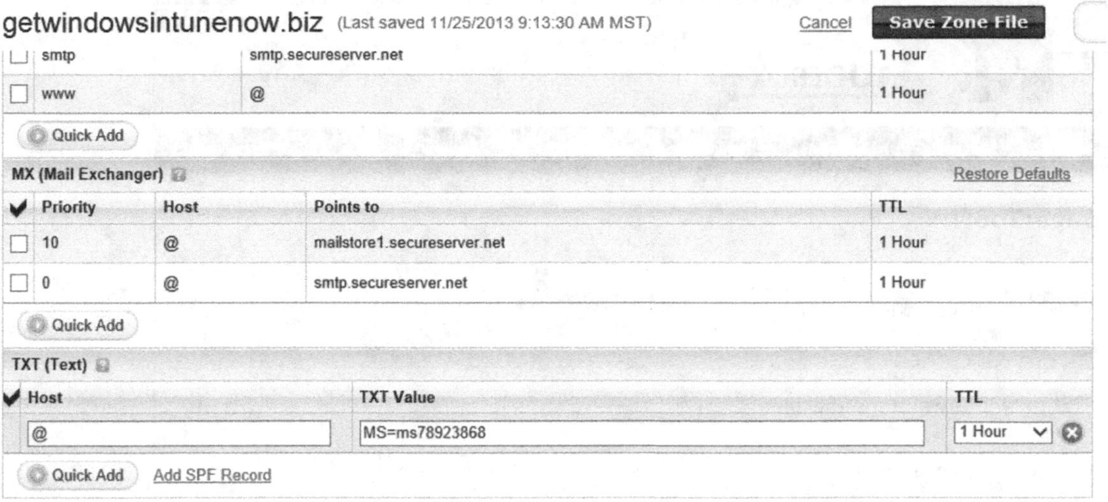

getwindowsintunenow.biz (Last saved 11/25/2013 9:13:30 AM MST)   Cancel   **Save Zone File**

☐ smtp	smtp.secureserver.net		1 Hour
☐ www	@		1 Hour

⊙ Quick Add

MX (Mail Exchanger) 🔲   Restore Defaults

✔ Priority	Host	Points to	TTL
☐ 10	@	mailstore1.secureserver.net	1 Hour
☐ 0	@	smtp.secureserver.net	1 Hour

⊙ Quick Add

TXT (Text) 🔲

✔ Host	TXT Value	TTL
@	MS=ms78923868	1 Hour ∨ ⊗

⊙ Quick Add   Add SPF Record

Figure 5-12. *GoDaddy TXT record configuration*

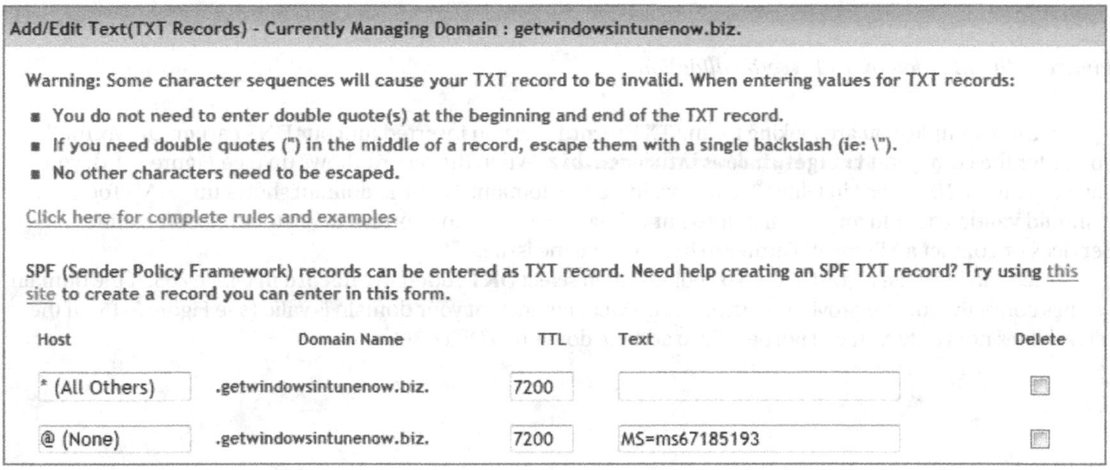

Add/Edit Text(TXT Records) - Currently Managing Domain : getwindowsintunenow.biz.

Warning: Some character sequences will cause your TXT record to be invalid. When entering values for TXT records:

■ You do not need to enter double quote(s) at the beginning and end of the TXT record.

■ If you need double quotes (") in the middle of a record, escape them with a single backslash (ie: \").

■ No other characters need to be escaped.

Click here for complete rules and examples

SPF (Sender Policy Framework) records can be entered as TXT record. Need help creating an SPF TXT record? Try using this site to create a record you can enter in this form.

Host	Domain Name	TTL	Text	Delete
* (All Others)	.getwindowsintunenow.biz.	7200		☐
@ (None)	.getwindowsintunenow.biz.	7200	MS=ms67185193	☐

Figure 5-13. *Network Solutions TXT record domain verification*

Each domain supplier has different tools and processes to add a domain record. You can only add domain records if the domain is managed by the domain supplier. In the GoDaddy case, the name servers are at GoDaddy, so we are adding records in the GoDaddy servers. This is also the case for Network Solutions.

After you have configured the domain for validation, if the domain does not verify, use MxToolbox (www.mxtoolbox.com) to verify that the TXT records have propagated. Once the TXT records show up in MxToolbox, you can validate the domain in Office 365. In Figure 5-14, we verified the record on MxToolbox. The purpose was to check if the changed record in the DNS had replicated to the other World Wide Web DNS servers. These records also replicate to Office 365.

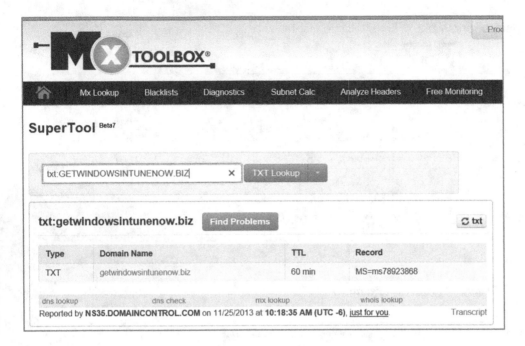

Figure 5-14. *MxToolbox TXT record validation*

In this example, you are looking for the TXT record that you inserted into our DNS earlier. On MxToolbox, you enter the command **txt:getwindowsintunenow.biz**. When the record shows up (see Figure 5-14), you can verify the DNS record in Office 365 and validate the domain. After the domain shows up on MxToolbox, it should validate within an hour. If it does not validate, you need to submit a ticket to Microsoft Online Services or contact a Microsoft Partner to help resolve the issue.

Once you have the record in the MxToolbox, then select **OK I added the Record** in Office 365. If the domain verifies correctly, you are provided with an acknowledgement that your domain is valid (see Figure 5-15). If the record does not verify, you will not be able to add the domain to Office 365.

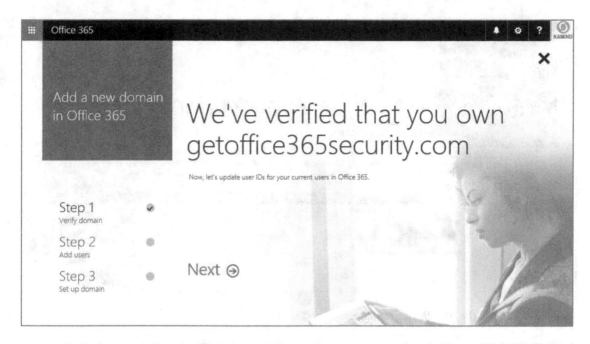

Figure 5-15. *Domain validated, proof of ownership*

The next step is to add users and assign licenses. We have found that it is better to complete the domain configuration (with the exception of changing the MX records) and add users after you have validated the domain. After you click **Next** (as seen in Figure 5-15), then select **skip this step** (as seen in Figure 5-16).

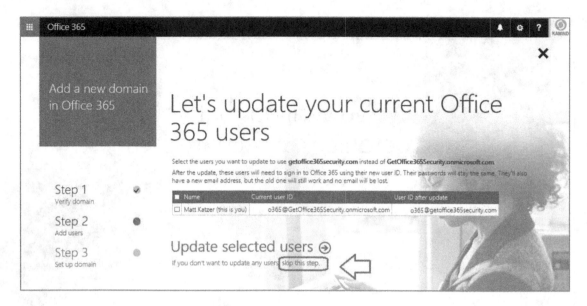

Figure 5-16. *Select the "skip this step" and assign users later*

■ **Note** Unless you are setting up a brand-new Office 365 account, it is best to set up users after you complete the configuration. If you choose to add users, follow the bulk user instructions. The wizard is designed for new users to 365, not for migration of existing accounts.

The first account (shown in Figure 5-16) should be not converted to a user account. This account should be left as a global admin account. If you lose your password to Office 365, having a second account that is linked to your cell phone and e-mail address is very handy.

After you select **skip this step**, you are promoted for similar add-user options. Select **skip this step** to set the domain intent until you see **get ready to update DNS records to work….** Next, you set up the DNS records for Office 365. Keep in mind the following.

- Unless you are cutting over e-mail (at this instant), do not change your MX, SPF, or Autodiscover DNS records. These records are changed when you are ready to receive e-mail services on Office 365.

- Configure all other DNS records, such as Skype for Business and other CNAME records, if these records are not being used in your current environment.

Specifying the domain services is an important step (see Figure 5-17). You are letting Office 365 know how you are planning to use the domain that you just validated. There have been a number of changes in the DNS configuration over the past few years. After you select **Next** (see Figure 5-17), you are asked two questions about your DNS. The purpose of these questions is to determine if you would like to have the DNS transferred to Microsoft name servers. Always select **No** and do not transfer your domain to Microsoft (see Figure 5-18).

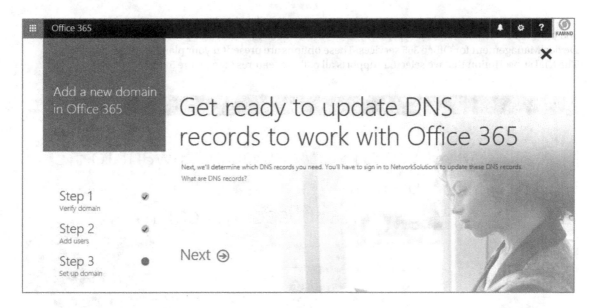

Figure 5-17. *Getting the DNS records ready for Office 365*

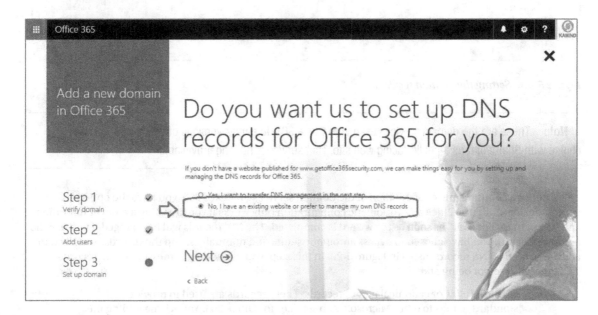

Figure 5-18. *Selecting if you want Microsoft to manage your DNS records; we recommend "no"*

■ **Note** You never want to transfer your DNS to a third party for hosting services. Always maintain the ownership separate from the hosting service. In this case, our domain "DNS" is at the network solutions registrar. We have not transferred the DNS to Microsoft. Instead, we have made changes to the DNS records that point to the Microsoft services.

Once you have selected where the DNS master records will reside, you need to select the services that you plan to use with Office 365. Typically, you choose Outlook for Email, Skype for Business, and Mobile Device Management for Office 365 services. These options are present if your plan has the capabilities. The trial subscription that we selected supports all of these features (see Figure 5-19).

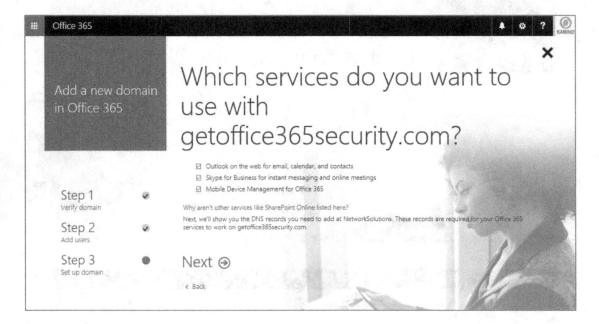

Figure 5-19. *Setting the domain services*

■ **Note** These are the domain services used with Office 365. In earlier versions of Office 365, you had a choice with SharePoint as a public-facing web site. That service is no longer available.

After you complete the configuration of the domain services on Office 365, you have the option to automatically configure Office 365. Automatic configuration only works if you are using a cutover migration and you plan to "cut over" as soon as the wizard is completed. The MX records will be changed if you use the automatic setup. You have chosen to bypass automatic setup, and manually set up the records. You need to add some of the DNS records listed in Figure 5-20. In this step, you are adding some of the DNS records (mail records are not being added).

- CNAME (alias or canonical name) records. These records are used to provide standard names to other Microsoft web services for Office 365. You will be adding the following:

  - lyncdiscover

  - sip

  - msoid

- enterpriseregistration

- enterpriseenrollment

- SRV (service record) records. These records specify information about available services. SRV records are used by Microsoft Lync Online to coordinate the flow of information between Office 365 services.

After the records are added, you verify the records. If the records are entered correctly, they validate with a green check mark. If the records are incorrect, there is a red X. The mail records show up with a red X. In Figure 5-20, we highlighted the Skype for Business and some CNAMES DNS records that you should change for any migration. Leave the mail records alone until you are ready to cut over to Office 365.

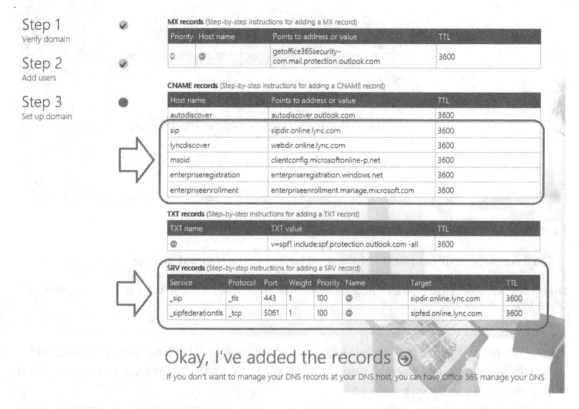

Figure 5-20. DNS records that need to be changed

After you have made the changes in the DNS (only change the records that were highlighted), then click **Okay, I've added the records** and complete the wizard. The wizard indicates errors in the records that you have not changed (see Figure 5-21).

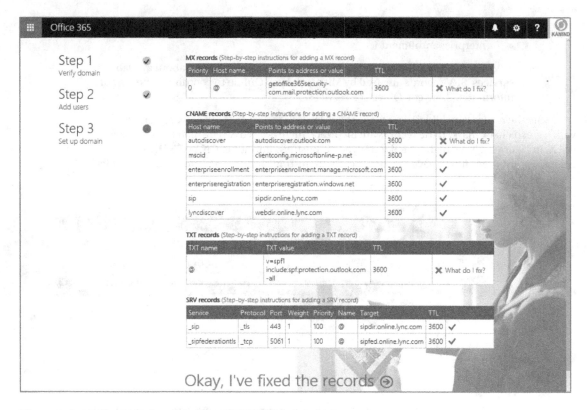

Figure 5-21. *Office 365 wizard showing DNS records that are in correct*

At this point, you are completed with the setup as far as you can proceed. To return to the Office 365 admin center, select the nine-square grid (in the upper left-hand corner next to the Office 365 logo). The other DNS records that have an X next to them will be entered when you start the cutover migration for Office 365.

■ **Note** Do **not** change your DNS MX, Autodiscover, or SPF-TXT records at this time. When you change your MX records, you stop the mail flow to your existing e-mail server. If you change Autodiscover, the Outlook clients cease to work with your current e-mail server.

At any time, you can add additional DNS records. If Office 365 finds a mismatch of the DNS records (with the records that it expects), Office 365 will display the **Complete setup** message (see Figure 5-22). Select **Complete setup** to fix the DNS issues. Office 365 will display the records that need to be added. If Office 365 determines that some of your DNS entries are valid, these valid entries will have green check marks. If there are errors, there are red Xs. Fix the errors until you have green check marks. You may run into a situation where the DNS cannot be fixed because your provider will not support the advance DNS records. You will need to move your DNS to a different provider. Once the records have been validated, you can change the primary domain to the user account domain and add the necessary users to the account.

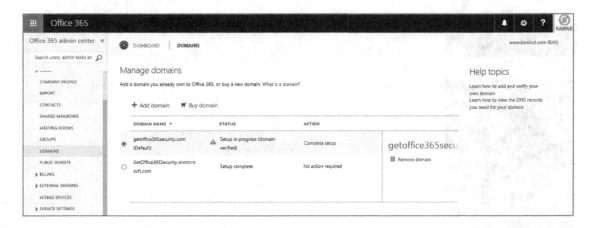

Figure 5-22. *Troubleshooting domain; select domain, then "Complete Setup"*

You should only have three red Xs on the MX, Autodiscover, and SPF-TXT records. All other records should have green check marks. If you have red Xs on records other than the three described, then correct those problems.

■ **Note** The Office 365 automatic DNS wizard configures the DNS and assumes that you are completing a cutover migration, and you have loaded the user accounts into Office 365. If you are not planning to move to Office 365 at this instant, do not use the automatic configuration tool. Once you move the mail records to Office 365, mail will be received on Office 365, not your existing mail server.

Step 3: Configure Skype for Business (S4B)

When your Office 365 site is created, Skype for Business is ready to operate within your intranet. As an administrator, you need to decide if you want to open Skype for Business communications to external users and allow instant messaging. Microsoft calls this "federate the domain." To enable these services, log in to the Office 365 admin center and select **Skype for Business** below the Admin menu (see Figure 5-23). If you have purchased or enabled the trial for Skype for Business calling, there are additional licenses that are assigned to your subscription. Configuration of the phone service is completed after you have migrated your users to Office 365.

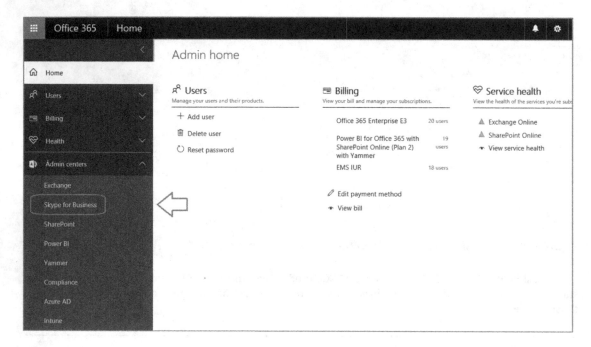

Figure 5-23. *Accessing the new Admin center for Skype for Business*

The Skype for Business "domain federation" allows your intranet to interact with other Office 365 customers and non-Office 365 e-mail addresses that support Microsoft Federation services. For example, domain federation allows your users to see the presence of external vendors (see Figure 5-24). At this point, we are not going to configure Skype voice or dial-in conferencing. These services require that the user accounts be loaded into Office 365.

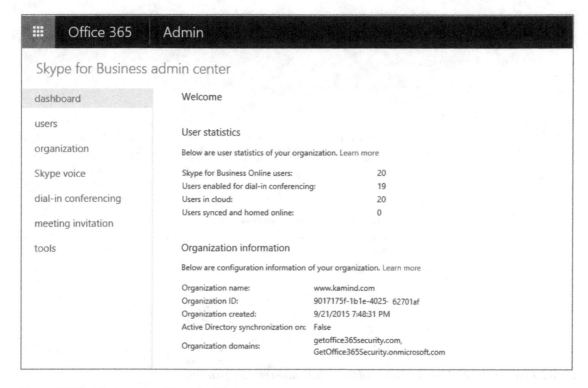

Figure 5-24. Admin screen: Skype for Business setup

The public instant messaging interface allows you to communicate within your intranet with other Office 365 organizations that have federated with Office 365 and Live Messenger. Public IM connectivity is supported with Skype.

In the Skype control panel (see Figure 5-25), select **organization** and then **external communications**. Enable **public IM connectivity**, and set **on except for blocked domains**. This action enables these services. **Enabled** is the recommended setting for both services. The default is off (disabled). After you have made the two selections, click **save**.

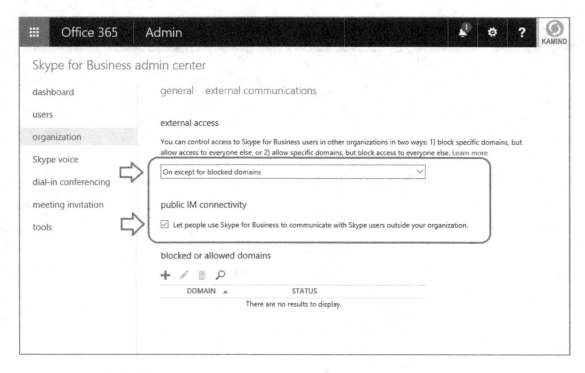

Figure 5-25. *Enabling Skype for Business domain federation and Skype access*

■ **Note** Office 365 users can talk to Skype user via the Skype handle (or Microsoft Live ID). To communicate with Skype users, Skype for Business must add Skype users as a "contact" in their Skype for Business client. If the Skype user is not listed as a contact, you cannot connect with them.

Step 4: Configure Yammer Enterprise for Office 365

After the Office 365 domain is verified, the next step is to configure Yammer so that all users have access to the Yammer network. To configure Yammer, log in to the Office 365 (see Figure 5-26), and select the **Included services**. The next step is to enable the verified domain as your Yammer domain.

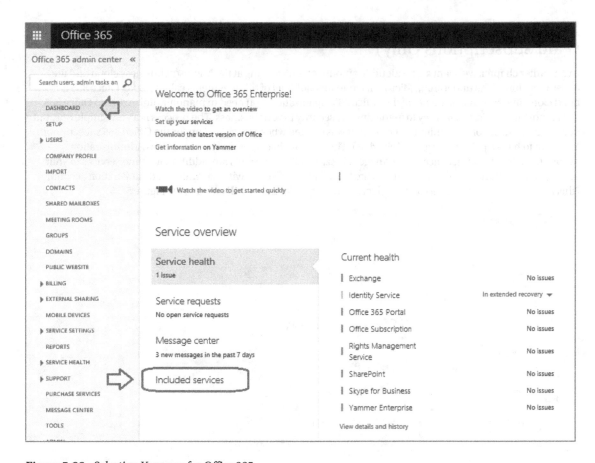

Figure 5-26. *Selecting Yammer for Office 365*

Once you have selected **Included services**, Yammer prompts you for your domain for integration to Office 365. Select the verified domain that you entered earlier, and then activate. In Figure 5-27, we use the verified domain `kamindit.net`.

Figure 5-27. *Enabling Yammer for verified domain*

Step 5: Linking Office 365 into Azure Active Directory and Intune (Paid Subscriptions Only)

In an earlier chapter, we spent a considerable amount of time looking at the Microsoft business cloud and the consumer cloud. The underlining Microsoft cloud that holds all of this together is called Azure. Office 365 is a child cloud in Azure. As the owner of the Office 365 organization, you need to manually link Azure to Office 365. This is not automatic, but it is key to managing the security in your business. The process is a very simple one, but you need to use the original admin account that was created when you signed up for the Office 365 subscription. You have to have a paid subscription (no trials). This account becomes the Azure Services Administration account. The Azure Services account manages all Azure billing and adds any additional online services to your account. To get started, make sure that you are logged in to Office 365 with the original administration account (this is referred to as the *root account*). Select **Azure AD** under the ADMIN menu (see Figure 5-28).

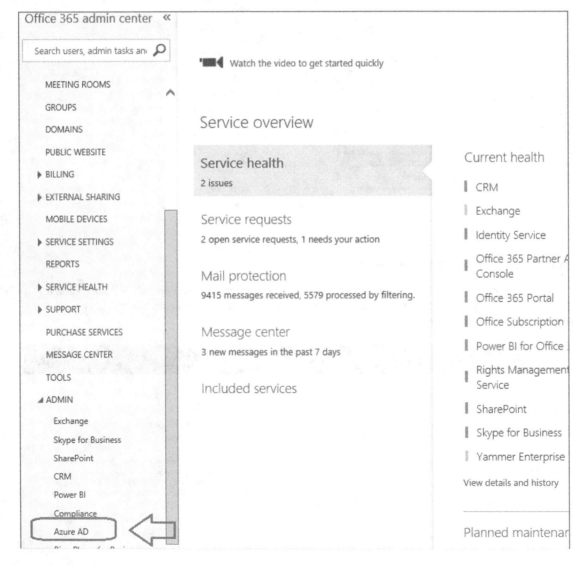

Figure 5-28. *Linking Azure Active Directory to Office 365*

■ **Note** It is best to close all browsers and use Firefox at this step. Internet Explorer (and Chrome) has a "feature" that prohibits the integration of Azure to Office 365. If you try this step and the browser stops working, then switch to Firefox and start over again.

Azure AD and Intune services require that you have a paid Enterprise subscription. If you are using the trial subscription, you need to skip this step or purchase an E3 license.

Azure AD services (basic level) is included as part of your Office 365 subscription. After you have enabled Azure AD, enable the Windows Intune Enterprise Mobility Suite. Azure AD must be activated prior to the activation of any Intune (or EMS) subscription. To begin the process, select the **Azure AD** option and fill in the account information (see Figure 5-29). It is recommended that you use Firefox browser to complete this step.

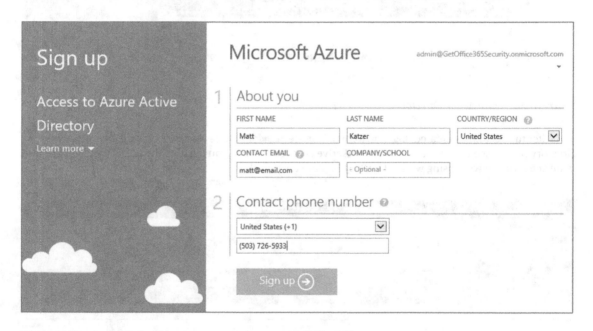

Figure 5-29. Azure Active Directory account setup with Office 365

Fill in the information requested and select **Sign up**. This starts the setup of your Azure account. If the account creation fails using your current browser, try to use Firefox and repeat the process. The account creation may take 4–5 minutes (see Figure 5-30).

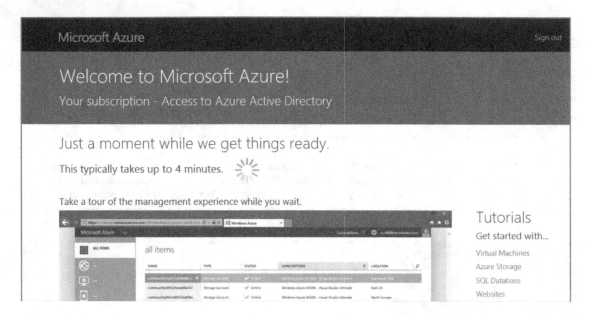

Figure 5-30. *Azure Active Directory account creation*

After the account is created, log in to **http://manage.windowsazure.com** to access the Azure Active directory portal (see Figure 5-31) and access **Active Directory**. Once you log in to the portal (you will use the same account you were using with Office 365), explore the portal.

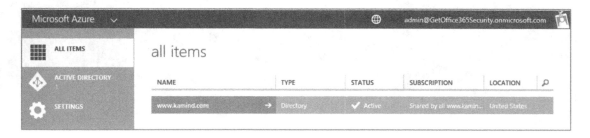

Figure 5-31. *Azure Active Directory portal (via* http://manage.windowsazure.com)

Azure cloud is a parent cloud of the Office 365 account. If you select the Azure account name (in our example, we called our company www.kamind.com), you are able to see the user accounts that were created in Office 365. If you expand the settings, you see this account as the Service Administrator account. You can add additional Azure functionality by purchasing Azure consumption credits for virtual servers. In Step 4, if you are planning to use the Active Directory connector in your Office 365 account, you download the software from Microsoft Azure Active Directory, not through Office 365.

After you have set up the Azure link to Office 365, the next step is to contact a Microsoft Partner and request a trial subscription for Enterprise Mobility suite (see http://www.kamind.com/ems).

> ■ **Note** You need to contact a Microsoft Partner for a 100-user trial subscription to the Enterprise Mobility suite (see Figure 5-32).

KAMIND IT, Inc has configured a custom collection of Microsoft Online Services for you to try.

Review your customized collection here:

https://portal.office.com/partner/partnersignup.aspx?
type=Trial&id=54135447-5c99-4d94-9948-
1c5698eeeb44&msppid=4471503

This trial invitation includes:
- 100 user licenses Enterprise Mobility Suite Direct

Additional partner information:
support@kamind.net
(503) 741-2141
http://www.kamind.com/support-center/

Figure 5-32. EMS trial subscription from a Microsoft Partner

Once you have received the trial subscription for Enterprise Mobility suite, follow these steps to activate the trial subscription.

1. Log in to the Office 365 site that you are setting up.

2. Click the URL and except the trial subscription (see Figure 5-33).

3. Select **Next** and follow the wizard. Assign users to the subscription when you onboard the user accounts.

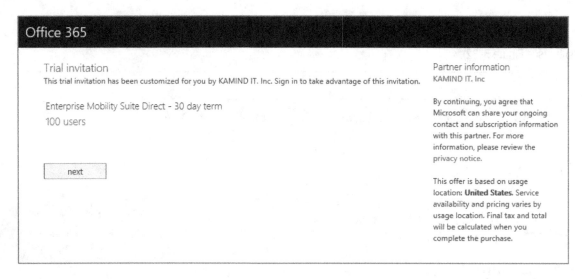

Figure 5-33. Adding a 100-user EMS trial subscription to Office 365

■ **Note**   The Enterprise Mobility Suite (EMS) contains Azure Rights Management Premium, Windows Intune, Azure Rights Management, Azure Active Directory Premium, and Azure Multi-Factor Authentication. You can only purchase EMS through a Microsoft Partner as part of open value enterprise agreement or from a Cloud Solution Partner under the CSP program.

When you add trial EMS licenses to Office 365, there are additional software services that can be used to secure your cloud. These services are managed by Azure security analytics. These services are used to manage and monitor your access to Office 365. Security reporting is discussed in more detail in Chapter 7.

Step 6: Load Users and Assign Licenses or Use Federation/Azure AD Connect

At this point, you are ready to load users, but before you start, you have a decision to make on the migration approach to loading users into Office 365. There are two ways to load users in Office 365. You can use Active Directory (via the Azure AD Connect tool) and Exchange Federation (hybrid) or manually bulk load the user accounts from a spreadsheet. The direction that you choose is based on your business needs. Active Directory sync is required in hybrid, but is optional in cutover. If you choose to use a hybrid migration, your data must be migrated using Exchange Federation or cutover migration, which uses Microsoft migration tools. Third-party tools such as MigrationWiz User Activation or DeploymentPro (see the section on MigrationWiz later in this chapter) are used for cutover migration. Both of these migration options are described next.

■ **Note**   Be careful which migration approach you choose. If there is an Exchange Server on site, and you use Active Directory to load accounts in Office 365, a user mailbox will not be created. This is because the AD sync tool detects that there is an on-site Exchange Server and will not allow you to create two mailboxes.

Hybrid Migration

Hybrid migration is a combination of Active Directory synchronization and Exchange Federation. Hybrid migration does not require Active Directory Federation Services (ADFS). Hybrid is composed of deploying Active Directory synchronization and Exchange Federation (linking the on-site Exchange Server to the cloud). The reason you would use a hybrid migration is to move users to Office 365 to maintain the users Outlook profile, and make the migration 100% transparent to the user. This approach allows you to use a staged migration. The hybrid model leverages the Exchange Server mailbox move function. When an Exchange administrator implements a mailbox move, all the user sees is a message that the user needs to log out and log back in to Outlook when the mailbox move is completed.

If you are looking at hybrid migration, you must visit the Microsoft Exchange Server Deployment Assistant (see Figure 5-34). It is highly recommended that you contact a Microsoft Migration Partner to assist you in this process. Hybrid migration is just a different step in the migration process. Your Exchange Server needs to be up-to-date with all service packs, or the hybrid migration will fail.

Exchange Server Deployment Assistant

The Exchange Server Deployment Assistant is the IT pro's source for Exchange deployment technical guidance. Tell us what kind of deployment you're interested in, answer a few questions about your environment, and then view Exchange deployment instructions created just for you.

Figure 5-34. *Microsoft Exchange Server deployment assistant (courtesy of Microsoft)*

■ **Note** Hybrid is a complex migration. The steps in configuring a hybrid migration are not covered in this chapter. If you choose to use hybrid migration, then follow these additional steps: (1) Review the Exchange Server Deployment Assistant (search for this in the search engine). (2) Complete the step in this chapter on Directory synchronization deployment. (3) Deploy Exchange Server 2013 to move the user mailbox data, and then continue with the remaining steps at the end of this chapter.

Cutover Migration

Cutover migration is named appropriately, because when you deploy a cutover migration, the accounts have already been created on Office 365. The mail records (MX records) are "cut over" from the old mail servers and pointed to the new Office 365 mail servers. The end user loses their profile unless third-party migration tools are used. These third-party tools (such as BitTitan DeploymentPro) mitigate the issues associated with a new Outlook profile. Old e-mail can either be migrated before the cutover event (users in essence have two mailboxes), or can be migrated after the cutover. If you are coming from an older Exchange 2003 server (or any POP/IMAP or other hosted Exchange service), you will use cutover migration.

Cutover or Hybrid: Which One?

At this point, you need to make a decision. If you choose to use cutover as a migration option, and wish to use your Active Directory, there is a process that you need to follow in moving users to Office 365 (described shortly). If you wish to use hybrid migration, you need to deploy Exchange 2013 and use Exchange 2013 servers to move mailboxes to Office 365 (you can use Exchange Server 2010, but there is no need since Microsoft gives you Exchange Server 2013 at no cost for Office 365 migrations).

You want to be careful with using Active Directory synchronization. AD synchronization will disallow the creation of mailboxes in Office 365 if there was an on-site Exchange Server. To get around this, you need to manually load users into Office 365, and then enable Active Directory synchronization. This approach bypasses the AD synchronization checks and forces Active Directory synchronization to process to "soft match" the Office 365 accounts with the on-premises Active Directory. The end result is that you have an Office 365 mailbox ready for migration and password synchronization with the on-site Active Directory—and a destination mailbox created in Office 365. A flow chart summarizing the two migration options is shown in Figure 5-35.

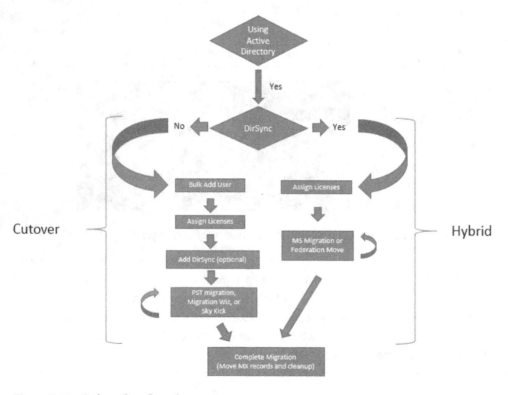

Figure 5-35. *Onboarding flow chart*

Once you have decided on the migration direction (cutover or hybrid), the work follows the process outlined earlier. There are no technical limits on the number of users that you can deploy. If you are using cutover, there is no partial deployment groups (or test groups). If you really want to deploy a test group, see the section on simple coexistence later in this chapter. It can be done, but it is not recommended. If you want a test group, use hybrid.

If you are using hybrid, you can deploy in groups based on departments or other criteria. The deployment group size is a function of the capabilities of the support organization. Technically, you should not have any additional support calls, because you had a good business process for deployment. However, users will call you anyway because they do not like change, so your support team will need to manage the change.

THERE ARE THREE METHODS TO LOAD USERS

1. Add each user (see the "Onboarding Users" section later in this chapter). This method is appropriate for a few users or a test group.

2. Bulk-add users using a specially formatted CSV spreadsheet with the user information. Use the Bulk Import option to load the information into Office 365.

3. Enable Directory Synchronized users for access to Office 365.

Pick your method to load users to Office 365. Once you have selected your method (manual or using Directory synchronization), you are ready to begin moving user data to Office 365. If you choose Directory synchronization, you are restricted to use Microsoft Migration Tools (if you have an Exchange Server in your Active Directory). After you have selected your user-loading approach, then you can begin the mail migration process.

■ **Note** The different user-loading processes are described in the "Onboarding Users" section.

License Assignment

If you selected Active Directory sync (option 3), you do not need to assign licenses until you begin the migration. Directory Synchronized objects from the on-site Active Directory appear as disabled users in Office 365, and no mailbox is created. Once the user object is created in Office 365, you can manually assign licenses or bulk assign them with PowerShell. If you selected the manual loading (option 1 or 2), you need to purchase licenses to create the mailbox for the user. It is not possible to load a disabled user in Office 365.

■ **Note** If you are planning to use third-party tools to migrate users to Office 365, and you have an on-site Exchange Server, you need to load users and assign licenses prior to enabling directory synchronization.

Step 7: Install Directory Synchronization/Azure AD Connect (Optional)

If you have an Active Directory environment (log in to a Windows server) and you are not running a small business server, using Azure AD connect to load users into Office 365 is very simple. It gives you single password log in to Office 365. The caveat on this is the Exchange configuration. If you cannot use Exchange Federation as a method to move mailboxes to Office 365, you need to manually load user accounts into Office 365 before you install the Azure Active Directory Connect tool.

To integrate your local AD and Microsoft cloud, you need to have the following:

- An Office 365 global Admin account (like AdminSyncOnline@domain.onmicrosoft.com)

- A local AD Enterprise Admin account (like AdminSync@domain.com)

- A Windows Server 2008R2 (we recommend you use version 2012R2 or a later server that is domain joined)

Before you begin the configuration of the Active Directory integration, please verify that you have created these user accounts and have a server available to deploy the Active Directory integration tool.

■ **Note** Office 365 Active Directory synchronization tool (DirSync) has been replaced with Azure Active Directory Connect (AD Connect). Microsoft merged the different versions of the Directory synchronization tool into one. The Azure AD Connect tool is downloaded from Azure. If you plan to use Azure Active Directory Connect, you need to complete Step 3 and integrate Office 365 into Azure. This integration requires that you have purchased a license.

Earlier in Step 5, you integrated Office 365 into Azure. At this point, you need to download the Azure Active Directory tool to Office 365. To access the tool, log in to **http://manage.windowsazure.com**, using the service admin account that was used to create the Office 365 tenant. The service admin account is the first account and has the onmicrosoft.com account name. Once you have logged in to manage.windowsazure.com, select **Active Directory** and click the company name. In our example, our company name is www.kamind.com. The name displayed should be the company name that you entered when you created your Office 365 site (see Figure 5-36).

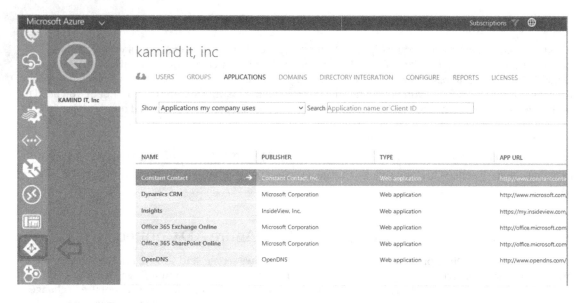

Figure 5-36. *Selecting Azure Active Directory Menu (via http://manage.windowsazure.com)*

CHAPTER 5 ■ DEPLOYMENT STEP BY STEP

After you select the **Azure Active Directory** icon and your company name, you should see a different set of options under the company name. Next select **Directory Integration**, enable Active Directory Integration, and download the Azure Active Directory Connect to your server (see Figure 5-37). The steps to accomplish this are outlined below.

1. Set the UPN to the routable Internet name in the on-premises Active Directory. (In your domain controller, start Active Directory Domains and Trust, select properties, and enter an alternate UPN).

2. Run the IdFix tool to correct any issues with the on-site Active Directory. (Download **IdFix DirSync Error Remediation Tool** from `www.microsoft.com`).

3. Log in to **`http://manage.windowsazure.com`** using the service administrator account used to create the Azure site (see previous Step 5).

4. Select the Azure Active Directory icon.

5. Select the Office 365 company that you will link into Office365/Azure.

6. Select **Directory Integration.**

7. Enable Active Directory Services.

8. Download the Active Directory software to your server (this link moves around so you may need to download AD Connect from `www.microsoft.com`).

9. Install the **Active Directory Connect** tool using the two accounts admin accounts (AdminSync and AdminSyncOnline).

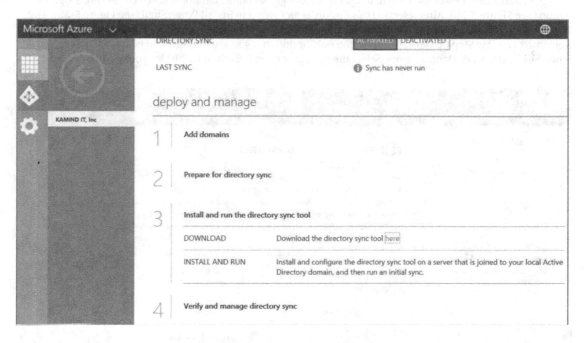

Figure 5-37. *Enabling Azure Active Directory and downloading the Active Directory Connect tool*

Once you have enabled the service and downloaded the Azure Active Directory Connect tool, save the file on your server and follow the installation of Azure Active Directory Connect later in this chapter. After you have completed the installation, return to continue the Office 365 integration. The Azure AD Connect tool installs all necessary software updates and services on your Windows server as part of the installation.

Once you have completed the installation of the Azure AD Connect service, your on-site user accounts will appear in Office 365 (as synced users) and in the Azure Active Directory under the Users tab.

■ **Note** Once you've installed AD Connect, those accounts can be managed from the on-premises Active Directory or Azure Active Directory. Password reset requires the Azure AD Write Back feature. This feature is available if you have deployed either Azure Premium (part of the enterprise suites) or Enterprise Mobility Suite (EMS).

Step 8: Manually Installing PowerShell (Optional)

PowerShell allows you to configure Office 365 features via a command line. This step is an optional step and it depends if you need the capability for your management of Office 365. The simplest way to install the latest version of PowerShell is to select the single sign-on option from the Office 365 admin center. If you already installed Azure Active Directory Connect, your IT administrator sign-in assistant has already been installed. If you have not installed the Azure AD Connect, you will be prompted to install the Microsoft Sign-In Assistant for IT administrators.

To install Azure PowerShell, log in to Office 365 as a global administrator and select the single sign-on option (see Figure 5-38). After selecting this option, select step 3 to install PowerShell (see Figure 5-39). The PowerShell installation verifies the updates required to support the Windows Azure PowerShell. You are welcome to review Steps 1 and 2. However, the only option that you are interested in is the installation of PowerShell on your desktop systems. Select the correct version (32-bit or 64-bit) for your system.

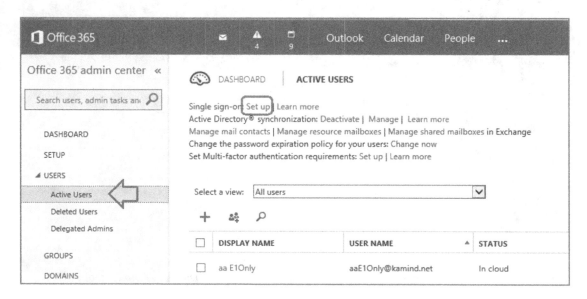

Figure 5-38. *Selecting single sign-on to install PowerShell*

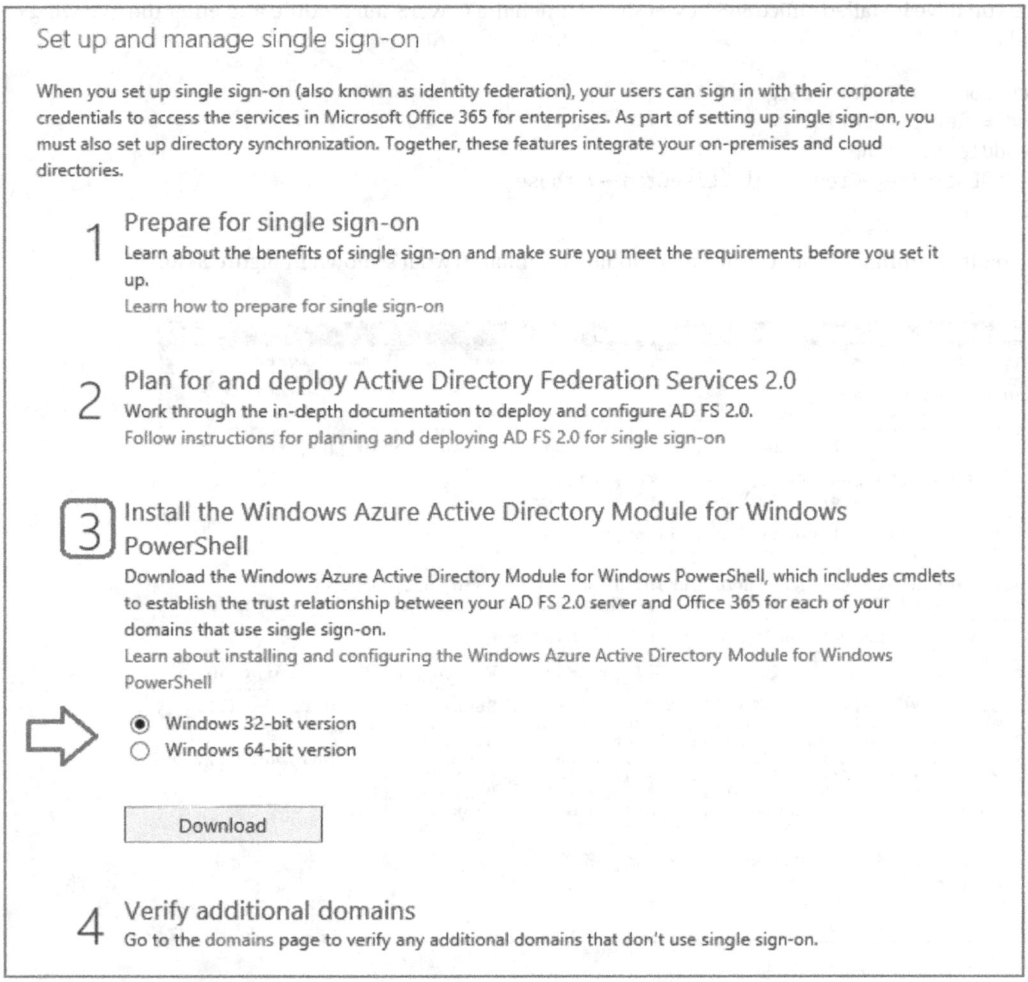

Set up and manage single sign-on

When you set up single sign-on (also known as identity federation), your users can sign in with their corporate credentials to access the services in Microsoft Office 365 for enterprises. As part of setting up single sign-on, you must also set up directory synchronization. Together, these features integrate your on-premises and cloud directories.

1 Prepare for single sign-on
Learn about the benefits of single sign-on and make sure you meet the requirements before you set it up.
Learn how to prepare for single sign-on

2 Plan for and deploy Active Directory Federation Services 2.0
Work through the in-depth documentation to deploy and configure AD FS 2.0.
Follow instructions for planning and deploying AD FS 2.0 for single sign-on

3 Install the Windows Azure Active Directory Module for Windows PowerShell
Download the Windows Azure Active Directory Module for Windows PowerShell, which includes cmdlets to establish the trust relationship between your AD FS 2.0 server and Office 365 for each of your domains that use single sign-on.
Learn about installing and configuring the Windows Azure Active Directory Module for Windows PowerShell

- ⦿ Windows 32-bit version
- ○ Windows 64-bit version

Download

4 Verify additional domains
Go to the domains page to verify any additional domains that don't use single sign-on.

Figure 5-39. Installing Office 365 PowerShell

■ **Note** Before you start, you must install the Microsoft Online Services Sign-In Assistant for IT Professionals BETA. The installation of the Azure PowerShell will fail and give this message: In order to install Windows Azure Active Directory Module for Windows PowerShell, you must have Microsoft Online Services Sign-In Assistant version 7.0 or greater installed on this computer.

Typically, we recommend that if your organization has more than 20 accounts, you may find it more convenient to use PowerShell. This is a command interface in Office 365. In Chapter 7, we offer additional troubleshooting steps and configuration options (such as shared mailboxes) using PowerShell. The account that you will use for PowerShell management is the Global Administrator user account. Users without global administrative privileges will not be able to use this feature.

Once you have installed Office 365 PowerShell, launch the PowerShell module and enter the following commands:

```
Set-ExecutionPolicy RemoteSigned
$LiveCred = Get-Credential
Import-module msonline
Connect-MSOLService -Credential $LiveCred -Verbose
Get-MsolGroup
```

The result of running theses commands should be similar to what's shown in Figure 5-40.

Figure 5-40. *Validating PowerShell commands*

You have completed the base PowerShell setup; now use the preceding command to validate the installation. If the command does not work, you have installed the PowerShell GUI incorrectly, there is a lack of permissions, or you have not installed the desktop connector for Office 365. Using PowerShell requires administrative privileges.

Step 9: Migrate E-mail

We complete a lot of work to lay the groundwork for migrating e-mail to Office 365. At this point, we are using either a cutover migration or a hybrid migration. In Step 6, our method of loading users defines the toolset you should use for copying e-mail to Office 365 (this moving of e-mail is called *migration*). Depending on the method you selected, you can use Microsoft tools or external tools. The key decision factor in the toolset you use is based on Azure Active Directory Connect (AAD Sync Connect) integration. If you use AAD Sync Connect, and there is an on-premises Exchange Server, you are required to use Microsoft migration tools or Exchange Federation. There are cases where you can use AAD Sync Connect (with an on-site Exchange Server) and external tools, but we recommend that you consult a Microsoft Partner if you use this approach.

E-mail Migration

E-mail migration is nothing more than copying the e-mail from the old mail server to the new mail server. The mail is not destroyed in the process. You are just copying the e-mail messages (and other mailbox information) over to Office 365. There are different approaches to moving the e-mail to Office 365 (see Figure 5-41). Depending upon the approach you are using for migration, you may choose to **cut over the mail records before you move e-mail** or move e-mail, and then cut over records. The decision is based more on the source of the mail server and the size of the organization. There is no hard or fast rule on the migration of e-mail, with one exception: if you are running some type of coexistence (such as a stage migration), then place a mail forwarder (to the "long" name) in the older mail system before you start the migration. Once the MX records are moved, there is no need to add a forwarder.

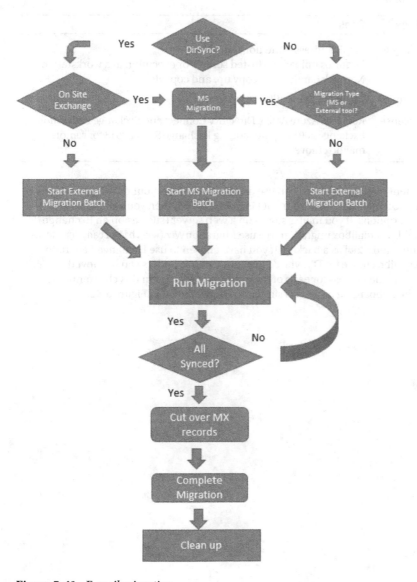

Figure 5-41. *E-mail migration*

■ **Note**   Our policy on e-mail migration is to move at least the first 200 e-mail messages for each user (1 to 2 weeks), along with the contacts, calendars and folder structure into the new mailbox. The older e-mails can come later. We use MigrationWiz to move historical e-mail as our first choice in tools.

There are four tools that you can use for e-mail migration: PST export/import, third-party external tools (such as MigrationWiz), the Microsoft Office 365 migration tool, and moving mailboxes with Exchange Federation. Each tool has its fans and critics (see Table 5-2).

Table 5-2. *Different Migration Methods*

Description	Pros	Cons
PST Migration	Simple	Email addresses are not complete. Requires upload to Hosted service or execution at a workstation. Network bandwidth (copy up, and copy down).
MigrationWiz	Simple	Costs $12 per mailbox to migrate.
Exchange 2007/2010/2013	License	Requires Azure Active Directory Connect and Exchange Federation. Exchange 2007 requires adding Exchange Server 2013 for remote mailbox move.

There are different deployment methods that you can use depending on how your data is kept. As an example, if you have been using POP mail, and all of your data is stored in PST, then you can only use a PST migration. There are no other options. If you mail is stored on a web server (such as on an Exchange Server), you can use the other tools for mailbox migration. We use MigrationWiz (www.bittitan.com) tools and use the Microsoft internal migration tool as a backup. If you have chosen to use Exchange Federation, you can only use the Exchange mailbox move for DirSync'ed accounts. Public folders can be moved with MigrationWiz tools. We discuss the process for each of these approaches later in this chapter in the "Onboarding E-mail" section. The onboarding process is similar to what's shown in Figure 5-42.

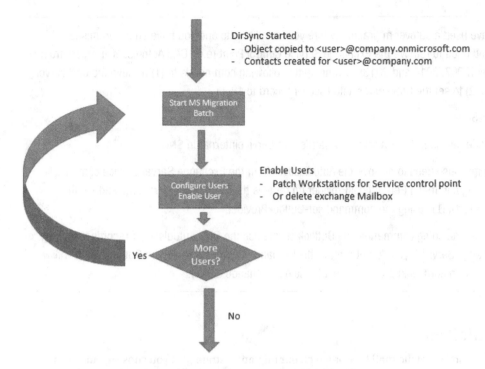

DirSync Started
- Object copied to <user>@company.onmicrosoft.com
- Contacts created for <user>@company.com

Start MS Migration Batch

Enable Users
- Patch Workstations for Service control point
- Or delete exchange Mailbox

Configure Users
Enable User

More Users?

Yes

No

Figure 5-42. *AD Connect synchronization migration approach*

> ■ **Note** If you wish to use MigrationWiz (www.bittitan.com) in your migration, please see the MigrationWiz section later in this chapter. Typically, we use MigrationWiz and DeploymentPro for our cutover migrations.

Exchange Server: Mailbox Changes

When you use the Microsoft migration tools, what the Microsoft tools do at the end of the data sync step is to convert the mailbox from an Exchange mailbox to mail-enabled users. What is really happening is that the Exchange mailbox is converted to a contact and the existing mailbox is placed in a disabled state. When e-mail is received by the on-premises Exchange Server, the server looks up the contact and sends the e-mail to the destination. The contact for the user of the on-site Exchange Server contains the Office 365 long address (*user*@company.onmicrosoft.com).

If you are using a third-party migration tool such as MigrationWiz, you need to manually convert the Exchange mailboxes to mail-enabled users. Microsoft Support has published a set of conversion scripts for Exchange Server 2007 and 2010. These scripts convert a migrated Exchange Server mailbox to mail-enabled users. If you are running SBS server and decide to keep the SBS server around, you will need to add mail forwarder to the Exchange Server.

■ **Note**   If you have used a cutover migration, before you install clients and you have an on-premises Exchange Server, you need to remove the Exchange Service Control Point (e.g., CAS Autodiscover record from the Exchange Server (2007, 2010 and 2013) by running the following commands to (1) retrieve the CAS server identity <name> and (2) to set the CAS server Autodiscover record to $NULL.

(1) Get-ClientAccessServer

(2) Set-ClientAccessServer -Identity "<name>" –AutoDiscoverServiceInternalUri $NULL

In some cases, you may also need to remove the Autodiscover from the Exchange Server service control point. Run the following command Get-OutlookProvider (to retrieve the Autodiscovery records and set the certprincipalName to $null) using the command set-OutlookProvider.

After you have run the preceding commands, the Outlook clients use the DNS Autodiscover records to look up the Office 365 Exchange Server. If you do not remove the Exchange Server CAS role, the Outlook client will bypass the Autodiscover record lookup and connect to the old Exchange Server.

Step 10: Set Mail Flow

At this point, we are ready to set the mail flow based on our migration strategy. If you chose to cut over all users at one time (cutover migration), the Office 365 Global Address List (GAL) contains all the new user accounts. This limited GAL also applies to sharing calendars and free-busy status. If you choose to move users in groups (simple coexistence), the GAL will only contain those users that have been moved.

Earlier, we discussed three possible migration plans:

- *Cutover migration*: All users are loaded, MX and Autodiscover records are changed, and Office 365 receives all e-mail.

- *Test group (non-hybrid)*: Some users are loaded. E-mail is forwarded from on-premises servers to Office 365 (temporary). Not recommended.

- *Hybrid coexistence*: Exchange Server and Office 365 operate in tandem.

The hybrid coexistence migration is a complex migration and is beyond the scope in the chapter. Earlier we directed you to look at the Microsoft Exchange Assistant planning guide. If you have implemented Exchange Federation, the process of moving the MX records is the same for the different migration methods. The other two methods are described next.

Cutover Migration and Hybrid

This is also called a 100% conversion. Cutover means that you have loaded up the users and you point the e-mail records to Office 365 servers. All historical e-mail is brought over in a post-migration process. This is the most common and simplest e-mail migration. If you are at this stage in a hybrid migration, which means that all mail has been moved to Office 365.

■ **Note**   If you have completed loading the users, you can change the DNS records to point to Office 365 services. To determine records that need to change, log in to Office 365 as an administrator, Select the domain, and run the Find and Fix Issues to show the broken DNS records. Make the changes and you are done with your migration.

Coexistence E-mail Flow

When you initially purchase Office 365, one of the items created is the subdomain yourdomain. onmicrosoft.com. This is a valid e-mail domain, and is the "long" e-mail address. You can e-mail to <user>@<yourdomain.onmicrosoft.com> and your e-mail will be delivered into your e-mail box. When you validate a domain and add a user account, the user account is created with two e-mail addresses: <user>@<yourdomain.onmicrosoft.com and <user>@<yourdomain.com.
    Coexistence works as follows:

- E-mail is forwarded from the on-premises domain or other hosted e-mail address to your Office 365 "long" address (i.e. @yourdomain.onmicrosoft.com).

- When e-mail is sent from inside Office 365, it looks to see if the e-mail needs to be delivered to a migrated user (i.e., @yourdomain.com). If not, the e-mail is forwarded to the real e-mail domain (via the DNS MX records).

■ **Note**   After you have moved all users to Office 365 and changed the DNS so the MX records, point to Office 365 and change the domain from Internal Relay to Authoritative (see Figure 5-43). At this point, your e-mail is 100% on Office 365.

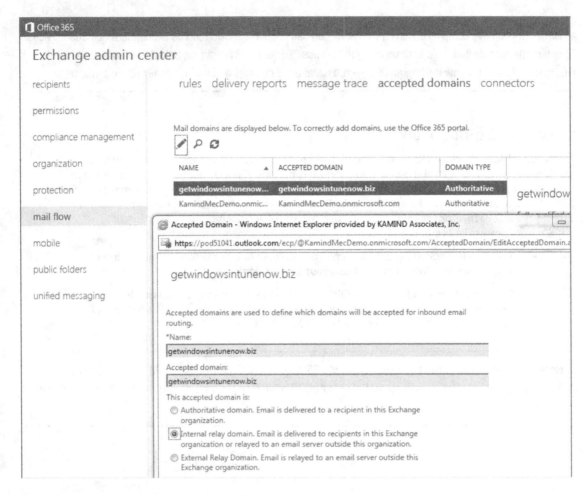

***Figure 5-43.** Setting a domain as a shared domain (some users are on an external server)*

Once you have moved all of the e-mail addresses to Office 365, the MX records are changed to point to Office 365. When the MX records are changed, coexistence mode is completed, and you have implemented your cutover migration or you have completed the hybrid or a cutover migration. That is all that is really needed to move users to Office 365 for mail flow.

■ **Note** Exchange servers may be problematic. You cannot ignore them or turn the power off. At the bare minimum, you will need to add a mail forwarder for each user to send mail to the long address `<user>@<domain>.onmicrosoft.com`. The preferred way is to convert the users to a mail-enabled user, or delete the user mailboxes from the Exchange Server and uninstall the Exchange Server. If you are running SBS, then your only option is a forwarder.

Test Groups (or Simple Coexistence)

This is an iterative coexistence migration. Cutover migration will happen at the point that all users are moved to the cloud. Simple coexistence is used to train IT staff and to build experience using Office 365. In simple coexistence, a "test group" of users are migrated to Office 365, and those users that migrate do not have access to the Global Address list, and shared calendars of the other users who have not migrated. E-mail for converted users is forwarded from the on-premises or hosted e-mail server to their "long" e-mail address (discussed shortly) in the cloud. The iterative approach requires that only a portion of the users are loaded in Step 6, and the Domain Type is set to **Internal Relay**.

■ **Note**   Do not use simple coexistence unless you have no other option. There is no sharing of calendars, contacts, or other information with users that are not on Office 365. The users that are migrated are an island. It is much better to use a cutover migration. Everything just works better.

To set the mail flow, you need to access the Exchange control panel access. To access the Exchange control panel, select the following:

1. Select **Office 365** as an admin.

2. Select **Admin Center**.

3. Select **Exchange**.

4. Select **mail flow**, and then select **accepted domains**. Select the domain and change the record to **Internal relay domain**.

The domain type is set to **Internal relay** until all of the users have been migrated. When the user migration has been completed, the domain is changed to **Hosted** and the MX records are changed to point to Office 365.

■ **Note**   If you have an on-site Exchange Server, and you want to create a Test Group, you will need to manually configure the desktop clients to bypass the on-site Exchange Server. It is not clean, but messy and requires you to edit the registry. These steps are outlined in the Test Group section in this chapter. Test groups will not work in Office 2016.

Step 11: Configure Desktop and Mobile Devices

The desktop configuration for mobile devices and user desktop is in Chapter 6. There are different philosophies on when to configure these services. However, unless you want to manually configure these services, you cannot add them until you have changed the MX and Autodiscover records. Desktop services (Outlook) require the Autodiscover record to be changed. Most mobile devices use the MX record to find the Office 365 mail server.

Configure Desktop Services

Depending upon the subscription (see Figure 5-44), the user will need to log into Office 365 and download the Office Professional Plus software (located under the gear icon and Office 365 settings.)

Figure 5-44. *Office Professional Plus download*

The installation process can be managed by any end user. The workstation setup guide is contained in Chapter 6. We designed Chapter 6 to contain all the Office 365 end-user configuration in one location.

Mobile Device Configuration

The Office 365 supports different mobile devices. The software can be installed at any time and is user driven (see Figure 5-45). To install the Office apps on your smartphone, go to the Office 365 web site, log in, select the **software option** under Office 365 settings), and install. You receive a link in the e-mail on where you can download the information to your smartphone and configure the mobile device.

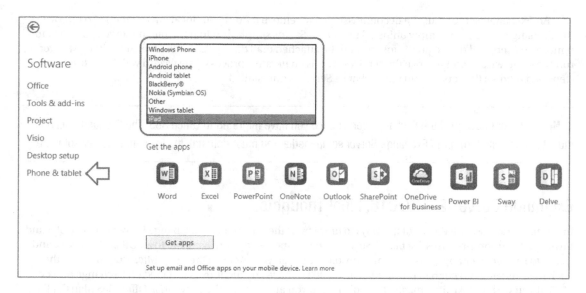

Figure 5-45. *Adding application support for your smartphone*

Complete information on configuring devices for end users is in Chapter 6.

Step 12: Configure External Devices

External devices need to be configured (if there are any devices on your network) to use a different mail server than your Exchange Server. There are different ways that you can configure your devices to send e-mail to Office 365, either directly or through a SMTP server in your network. There are four rules that you need to follow when configuring devices to relay e-mail through Office 365.

- The sending device must have a domain name that is verified in the Office 365 Tenant.

- To send "on behalf" of someone means that you need to create a dedicated "user" in Office 365 and your SMTP relay device will need to login as that user and have permission to send on behalf. You must grant send as to this user to access all internal mailboxes.

- Your static IP address of the on-premises firewall (where the e-mail is being relayed from) must be registered as a connector in Office 365.

- The external IP address that is sending to Office 365 (acting as your relay) must be added as a transport rule with the "bypass" SPAM filter option.

Step 13: Cleanup

The cleanup operation depends on the type of mail system that you have migrated to Office 365. If you are using a hosted e-mail system, or a non-exchange e-mail system, you need to contact the software supplier to determine if there is any special process needed to remove the third-party mail server. Unless the e-mail server is integrated into Microsoft local Active Directory, there is usually no shutdown sequence. The server must be removed from Active Directory.

An Exchange Server must be decommissioned to remove it from your local environment. To remove the Exchange Server, you simply uninstall the server. Seems simple, but to uninstall the server, you need to remove all users and delete public folders and the attached mail database. To remove an Exchange Server, run the setup wizard and remove the services. This is an iterative process. The wizard walks you through the steps and reboots the server until the Exchange Server is uninstalled.

■ **Note**   Do not power off the Exchange server once you have migrated to Office 365. The Exchange Server must be uninstalled from the Exchange Server setup media. You must uninstall the Exchange Server software.

Exchange Server 2013/2016, Final Thoughts

In our migration, we talked about the ways to move from the on-premises Exchange Server to Office 365 and turning off your on-premises Exchange Server. There is another option available to all Office 365 users, and that is to run the Exchange server admin console locally on your Active Directory. Microsoft provides the Exchange Server at no charge, provided that you do not have any mailboxes installed on Exchange Server 2013. If you wish to take advantage of this offer, (and you are running the Enterprise Office 365 plans), all you need to do is log in to https://configure.office.com/Scenario.aspx?sid13 and verify your eligibility (see Figure 5-46).

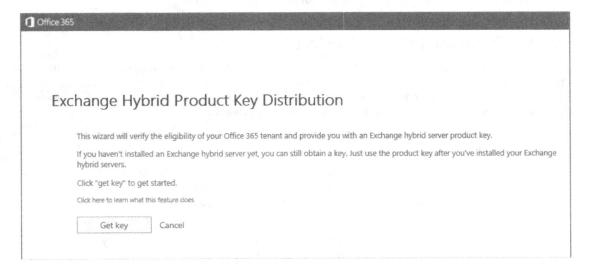

Figure 5-46. Checking the eligibility of Exchange 2013 Enterprise Exchange Management Server

Final Check List

Your Office 365 is ready to be used. At this point, verify the following:

1. If you have a desktop version of Office 2007/2010, and you are using Outlook 2007/2010 (and you are not using Office 2013/2016), run the desktop upgrade for Outlook 2007/2010 from the Office 365 software download. If you do not do this, Outlook 2007/2010 will stop working.

2. Check the domain configuration. If you have any actions to complete, (under the action header) please complete them before you move forward.

3. Verify that your Office 365 domain is set to **Authoritative** and is not shared for e-mail. (This will only be set if you have run a test group).

4. Verify that you have placed a local DNS record in your on-premises DNS server. You will need to add an Autodiscover CNAME to your internal DNS that points to **autodiscover.outlook.com.**

5. If you have an on-premises Exchange Server and you have migrated to Office 365, set the Autodiscover record to **$NULL** with the following command. (Note: once set local clients cannot Autodiscover the local Exchange Server).

    ```
    Set-ClientAccessServer -Identity "<name>" –
    AutoDiscoverServiceInternalUri $NULL
    ```

6. Extend the 14-day delete holding time to a 30-day delete holding time. Run the PowerShell command.

    Extend 30-day delete for a mailbox:

    ```
    Set-mailbox user@contoso.com –retaindeleteditemsfor 30
    ```

    Extend 30-day delete for the organization:

    ```
    Get-mailbox | Set-mailbox –retaindeleteditemsfor 30
    ```

7. Enable the audit logs on all users' mailboxes. The default logs are kept for 30 days and can be extended to multiple years.

    ```
    $UserMailboxes = Get-mailbox -Filter
    {(RecipientTypeDetails -eq 'UserMailbox')}

    $UserMailboxes | ForEach
    {Set-Mailbox $_.Identity -AuditEnabled $true}
    ```

8. The default retention policies *are not enabled* until the archive is enabled. If you **enable the archive** on a user mailbox, the retention polices will begin to execute. As an example, the default retention policy is two years. When the retention policy executes, e-mail will be deleted.

9. Verify the retention tags in the retention policy and remove or create the new policy.

10. Verify that you have enabled Yammer on your subscription. To enable Yammer, select **Dashboard**, followed by included services and select the primary domain for the Yammer Enterprise configuration.

11. Verify that you have transferred all of the distribution groups and contacts over to Office 365.

12. Enable Azure AD and create an Azure account. Different partners provide different capabilities for migration. KAMIND IT enables azure AD and Microsoft Enterprise Mobility Services (EMS) as part of all migrations to Office 365. EMS provides a much higher level of security.

13. (Optional). Create a Global Admin account to be used by the Nuvolex software. Nuvolex is a third-party software package (discussed later in this chapter), that simplifies the administration of Office 365 and Azure.

Test Group or Staged Migration

In the early cloud days, there was a lot of work with test groups to train the IT staff. Now test groups are not really used except in very unique situations. There are two ways to use test groups: hybrid migration or the deployment of a few test mailboxes to test processes, and then discarding the test group when you move to production. Test groups are nothing more than a stage migration. Stage migrations take a lot of work and should only be used for a limited time and for a small number of users. When we discuss test groups, we are using those users to test our deployment processes. A test group is nothing more than placing a group of users on a different mail server that is separate from the existing organization. A test group does not have access to a common calendar or a common address list (unless a hybrid deployment). It is for these reasons that you want to use test groups for a very limited time and with a definite set of objectives. A stage migration is nothing more than a test group.

■ **Note**   If the user accounts are POP or IMAP, stage migration is a viable option because there are no common shared resources (like calendars and address lists).

Client Configuration Changes for Test Group

If you are using a test group with an on-premises Exchange Server (no hybrid, no Exchange Federation), you encounter two problems: Autodiscover (for Outlook client) and the presence of the Exchange Server in the Active Directory. There are only manual workarounds to enable the clients to find the Office 365 mail server. Once you have deployed, you need to remove these "enhancements" to eliminate a future support problem in using Office 365. If you choose to manually configure Outlook, you still need to make these changes, since Outlook will verify the connection via Autodiscover every time it is started.

These are the client steps required to support a test group if there is an on-premises Exchange Server. Also, you cannot use Office 2016 as an Outlook client with a test group. The following are the configuration steps.

1. Add the Autodiscover record in the host file, located at `<drive:>windows/systems32/drivers/etc`.

   a. Ping **autodiscover.outlook.com**.

   b. Add the **Autodiscover** record with the address discovered earlier.

   c. Open a command prompt and enter **ping autodiscover**. This should display the IP address you just entered.

   d. Add the two Autodiscover records: autodiscover and "autodiscover.<yourdomain.com>"

2. Add the registry fixes to ignore the Exchange Server – Service Control Point. The registry entries required to be modified for the clients are listed shortly (see Microsoft KB article – https://support.microsoft.com/en-us/kb/2612922).

   a. Navigate to the following registry key that corresponds to your version of Office (12.0 is Office 2007; 15.0 is Office 2013):

   ```
   HKEY_CURRENT_USER\Software\Microsoft\Office\12.0\Outlook\AutoDiscover
   ```

   b. Set the following values for the Value Names listed:

   ```
   "PreferLocalXML"=dword:1
   "ExcludeHttpRedirect"=dword:0
   "ExcludeHttpsAutodiscoverDomain"=dword:1
   "ExcludeHttpsRootDomain"=dword:1
   "ExcludeScpLookup"=dword:1
   "ExcludeSrvLookup"=dword:1
   "ExcludeSrvRecord"=dword:1
   ```

3. Configure the Outlook profile to prompt for a profile.

4. If there is an existing Exchange Server, you need to manually configure the Outlook client. Outlook clients (MAC & PCs) require an Autodiscover record. Office 2016 cannot be configured. Refer to Chapter 6 for the manual configuration of Office 2007/2010 and Office 2013 clients.

5. Start the Outlook client and create a new profile. In some cases, the client may not start up correctly the first time. Close Outlook and start again.

Test Group Mail Flow

Mail flow in a test group uses a combination of forwarders from the on-site server to Office 365. The on-site server uses onmicrosoft.com as the forwarding address (see Figure 5-47). This approach works, and is useful for testing, but not a recommended practice. Test groups are not integrated into the on-premises Exchange Server.

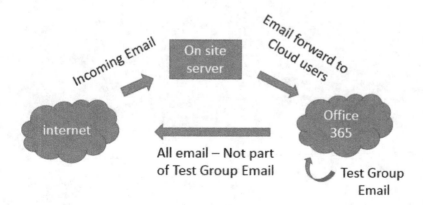

Figure 5-47. *Test group mail flow*

When you add users to Office 365, these users have an active e-mail address. This means the following:

- E-mail that is sent to one of these new Office 365 e-mail accounts from outside Office 365 or from other Office 365 tenants will *not* be received until your MX records are configured and verified by Office 365.

- Any e-mail sent from one of these new accounts will be routed to your other new accounts. (E-mail to outside addresses will route as expected.)

We recommend that you configure mail routing as follows:

- Only load users that are using Office 365 (during test or evaluation).

- If you are using both the Office 365 service and an on-site Exchange Server, you need to set your e-mail Domain Type to **Internal**. You should have e-mail for these Office 365 users forwarded from the on-site Exchange Server to the Office 365 e-mail accounts using the "long" address *user*@<domain>.onmicrosoft.com.

DNS Trouble Shooting

One of the problems associated with the DNS records is who is managing them. In some cases, this may be a web developer who is no longer in business. You may also have it registered with an e-mail address that you no longer use (or can remember). If you cannot access the DNS, how do you find the records?

We use a site at http://who.is. This service gives you a good snapshot of the DNS records for the domain that you are moving (see Figure 5-48). We use this tool in conjunction with mxtoolbox.com. If you do not have access to the actual DNS zone file before you move, you need to use tools like who.is to collect the information before you move the service to a new registrar.

● SOA Record – kamind.net

Name Server	NS97.WORLDNIC.COM
Email	namehost@WORLDNIC.COM
Serial Number	113022613
Refresh	3 hours
Retry	1 hour
Expiry	7 days
Minimum	1 hour

● DNS Records – KAMIND.NET

Record	Type	TTL	Priority	Content
kamind.net	MX	2 hours	0	kamind-net.mail.eo.outlook.com
kamind.net	NS	2 hours		ns97.worldnic.com
kamind.net	NS	2 hours		ns98.worldnic.com
kamind.net	SOA	2 hours		NS97.WORLDNIC.COM. namehost.WORLDNIC.COM. 113022613 10800 3600 604800 3600
kamind.net	TXT	2 hours		v=spf1 include:spf.protection.outlook.com -all

Figure 5-48. DNS records from who.is for kamind.net

■ **Caution**   If you move the DNS from some suppliers, the web site may go offline.

Onboarding Users

There are three ways to load users: (1) Azure Active Directory synchronization, (2) the Office 365 graphical user interface, or (3) using the bulk-load process. The GUI is great for maintenance and small numbers of user accounts (see Figure 5-49), but it is not an effective tool for loading a large number of user accounts. If you chose to use Directory sync and you have an on-premises Exchange Server, you need to use the Office 365 migration tools.

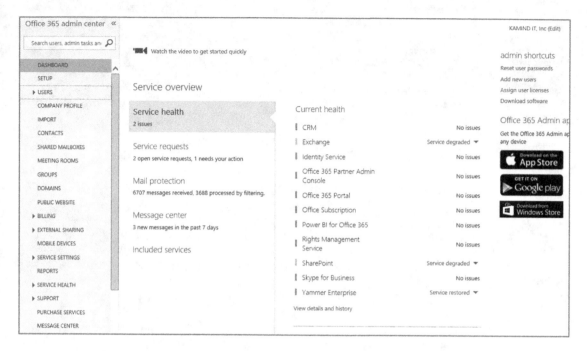

Figure 5-49. *Office 365 administration screen*

Bulk-loading Users Through Azure AD Connect

DirSync links your on-premises Active Directory to Office 365. This allows you to import existing e-mail addresses, contacts, and distribution list into Office 365 through a process called Directory synchronization.

Figure 5-50 shows two types of objects: manually created objects in the cloud and DirSync objects from the on-premises server. There is no loading of users with Directory synchronization.

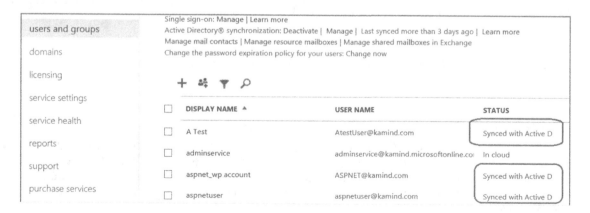

Figure 5-50. *Directory sync objects synced with Active Directory*

Manually Bulk-Loading Users

There are two ways to manually load users: with the Office 365 graphical user interface or using the bulk-load process. The GUI is great for maintenance and a small number of user accounts, but it is not an effective tool for loading a large number of user accounts. The process that we use is the **Bulk add users** process.

Log in as an administrator at http://office.microsoft.com or http://portal.microsoftonline.com, and then select **Users and Groups** (under the dashboard, click the **New** drop-down menu, and select **Bulk add**). The menu has two options: add a single user (use the plus sign), or bulk add users (use the people icon highlighted in Figure 5-51).

Figure 5-51. *Adding users with the bulk add users*

The first step is to build and then select the CSV file with the appropriate users to be added. Download a blank CSV file to get the format. You can open this file in Excel (be sure to save it as a CSV file, without extra lines or columns), or edit it with the text editor.

We recommend that you use the optional fields and enter all the data possible. If you are accurate at this step, it significantly reduces the amount of work necessary to manually fix user profiles.

After you have built the CSV file, select **Browse...** to find it and open it. Click **next** (see Figure 5-52).

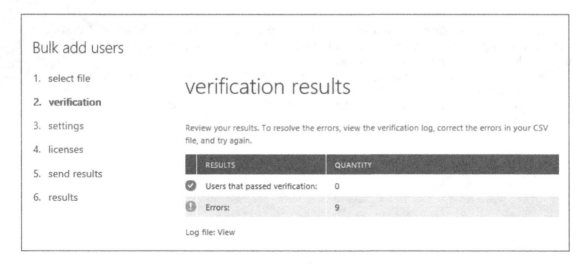

Figure 5-52. *Bulk add users—select CSV file to bulk load*

You should see verification results like what's shown in Figure 5-53.

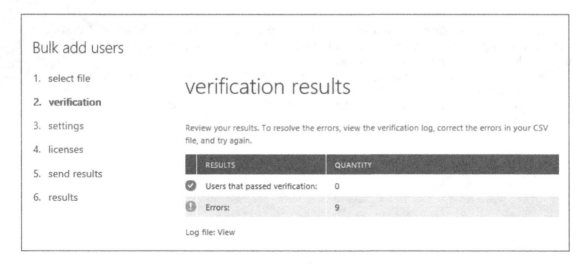

Figure 5-53. *Bulk add users—verification of loaded data*

The users should pass verification. If not, repair the CSV file and try again (see Figure 5-54). Click **next**.

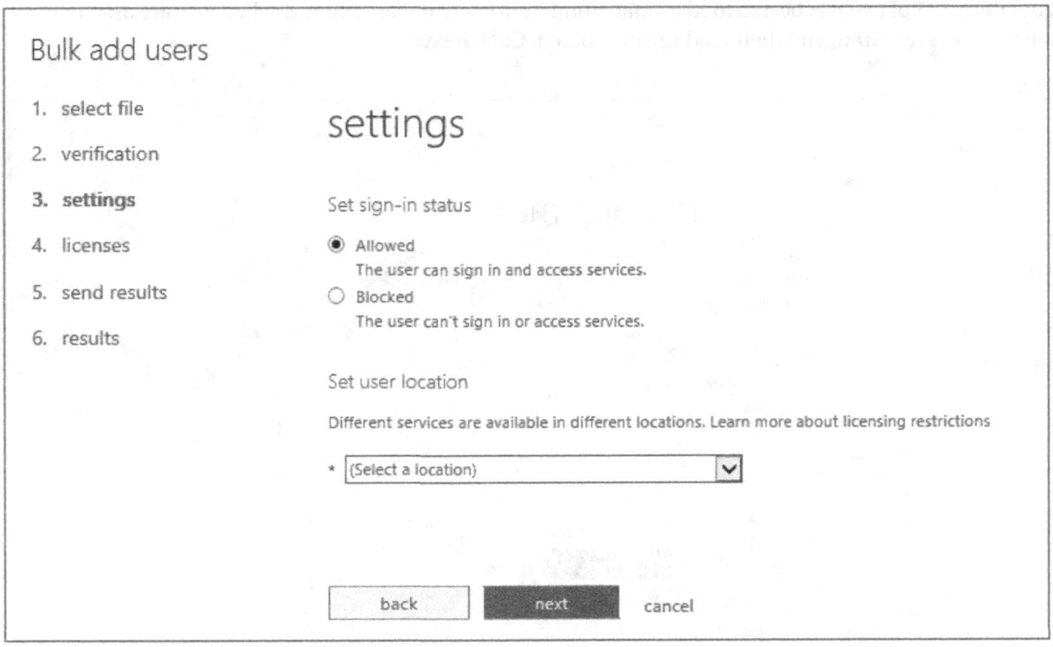

Figure 5-54. *Bulk add users—set locations*

Set the sign-in status and the user location (for all the users being added; see Figure 5-55). Click **next**.

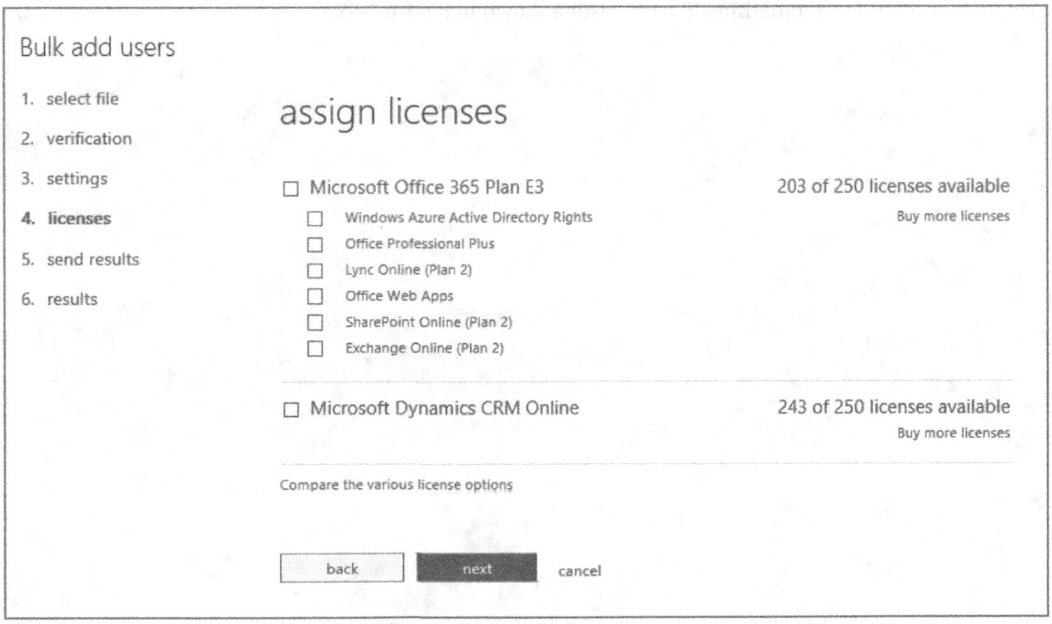

Figure 5-55. *Bulk add users—assign licenses*

Assign licenses (see Figure 5-56). If you do not have enough licenses for the users you are loading, those users will not be loaded and will show up as an error. License assignment can be tricky if you are using different Office 365 plans. It is best to load a small number of users to verify how the licenses are assigned. Assign licenses as required, and then load the next batch. Click **next**.

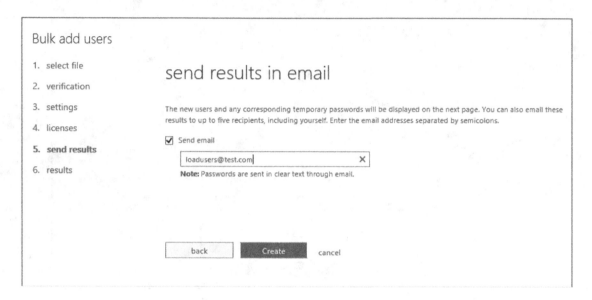

Figure 5-56. *Bulk add users—send e-mail*

Change the send e-mail to whateveryouchoose@yourdomain.com to document the users' creation. This is a complete list and comes in handy if you need to bulk sign on the users and present the passwords. Click **Create**. You should see something like the results shown in Figure 5-57.

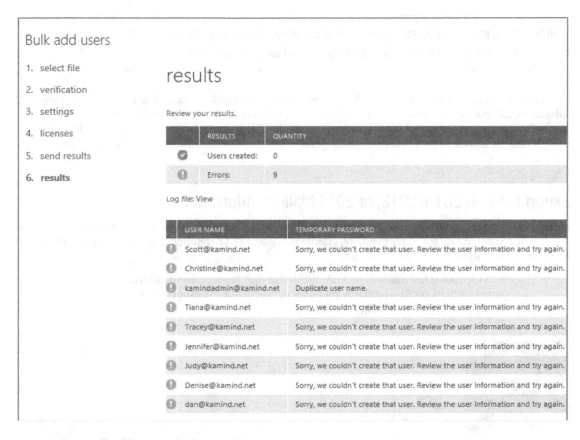

Figure 5-57. Bulk add users—display results

Copy the temporary passwords back into your user's spreadsheet. You will need the passwords to notify your users. Click **close**.

Onboarding E-mail

After you have loaded the user account to Office 365, you need to copy the e-mail from the current mail servers to Office 365. There are different ways to do this, depending on the method you used for loading users. As an example, if you have an on-premises Exchange Server and you enabled DirSync, your only option is to use Microsoft migration tools. If you do not have an existing Exchange Server, you can use different migration tools to move mail to Office 365. The three methods discussed here are (1) PST migration, (2) third-party tool migration, and (3) using Microsoft Office 365 migration tools.

PST Mail Migration to Office 365

PST migration is the importing of the existing PST file into your Office 365 mailbox. A PST export/import is performed at each user's workstation, with data from their Outlook. PST migrations are the simplest, but should be used as a last resort. When you migrate PST data, you need to export the old mailbox at the root, and import the data into Office 365 at the root. If the PST data already exists, then import the data at the level that you wish to see the data in Office 365.

■ **Note**   If you start a PST migration, you need to complete it. There is no real error checking on data imports or duplicates. If you stop and restart a PST migration, you have duplicate data.

Typical user data in a PST contains all the information in the mailbox, including e-mails, folders and subfolders, calendars, and contacts. To install the calendar and contacts into Office 365, you can either manually copy over to Office 365 (drag and drop), or overlay the Office 365 calendar and contact information using an export and an import data command, specifying the root inbox. Next are the two options for this command.

Export Outlook 2010, 2013, or 2016 Mailbox Information

Follow these steps on exporting the PST data into Outlook. If you already have your PST files as an archive, refer to the import. When you export Outlook information into a PST for import into Office 365, you must export the root mailbox.

1. Start Outlook (Outlook 2010 or 2013/2016). Use your on-premises Exchange Server Outlook profile (probably your default profile) for the export of PST mailbox information (see Figure 5-58).

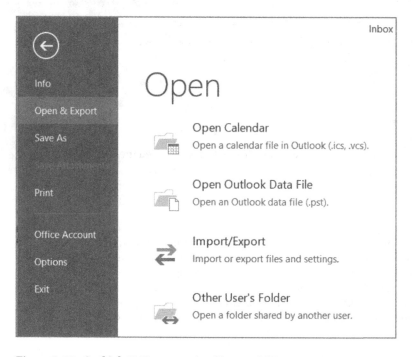

Figure 5-58. *Outlook 2013—exporting files to a PST*

2.   In Outlook 2013/2016, click **File ➤ Open ➤ Import** (this includes file export as well).

3.   Select **Export to a file**, and then **Outlook Data File (.pst)**, as shown in Figure 5-59.

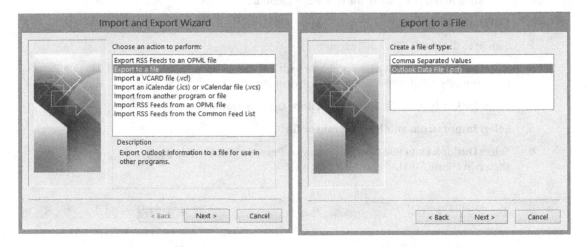

Figure 5-59. *Exporting Outlook files as a PST*

4.   Select the Mail location to export (normally, you want to select the very top item, the mailbox account) and the export options: enter a filename and (normally) select **Replace duplicates with items exported** (see Figure 5-60).

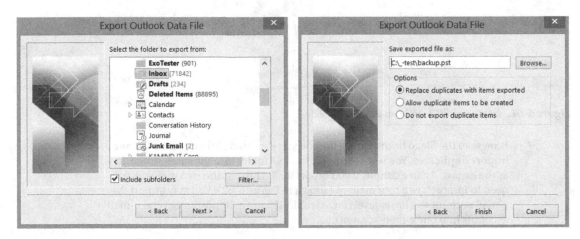

Figure 5-60. *Selecting Outlook mail and file save location*

5.   Once you have exported the documents, write down the location where the PST file is located. The next step is to import the PST file.

Import Outlook 2010, 2013, or 2016 Mailbox Information

Follow these steps to import your exported PST e-mail data into your Office 365 e-mail account. This is done by loading the existing mailbox on top of the Office 365 mailbox.

1. Exit Outlook.

2. Sign in to the user's Office 365 account.

3. Start Outlook either with a new profile or with the user's Office 365 profile. (We normally call the new profile **O365** to distinguish it.)

4. In Outlook 2010 (or 2013/2016), click **File ➤ Open ➤ Import**.

5. Select **Import from another program or file**.

6. Select **Outlook Data File (.pst)** (or it may be **Personal Folder File (.pst)**, as shown in Figure 5-61).

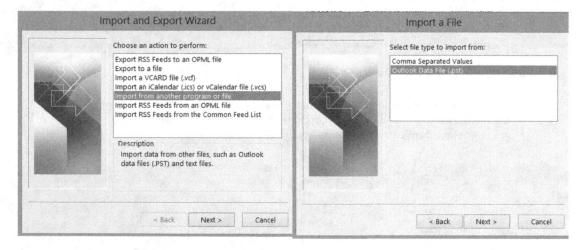

Figure 5-61. *Importing PST archives into Office 365*

7. Browse to the file to be imported (the one you exported earlier). Select **Do not import duplicates**. You want to import the PST folder into the same structure as the export. As an example, if you export the PST file as the root mailbox, you need to import it as a root mailbox (shown in Figure 5-62). You may import the e-mail account to a lower level (for example, if you are importing several e-mail accounts into one e-mail account).

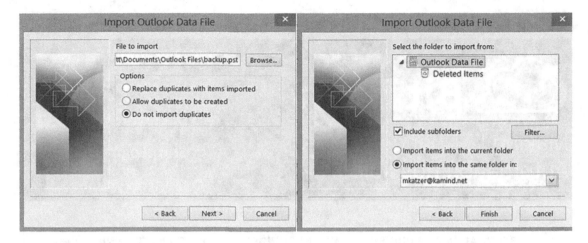

Figure 5-62. *Importing PST archives into Office 365*

The import process uploads the Outlook PST data to the Microsoft Office 365 Exchange Server. Your data will then be replicated down to your Outlook 2010. It is best that you import data using a high-speed data link, since the data will travel twice: up to Office 365 and back down to your Outlook local cache.

Migrating E-mail with BitTitan's MigrationWiz

MigrationWiz (www.migrationwiz.com) is the tool (see Figure 5-63) that is used for most of the migration from either on-premises or another hosted provider to Office 365. The tool is easy to use and allows thousands of mailboxes to move simultaneously.

Figure 5-63. *BitTitan: Mail and Data cloud Migration tools (courtesy of BitTitan)*

There are three different of migration tools that BitTitan offers. These are MigrationWiz, DeploymentPro, and User Activation. MigrationWiz is used to move mailboxes to/from Office 365. DeploymentPro is a tool configures the user's Outlook (configures desktop, moves task, Outlook cache, etc.) to a new Outlook profile linked to Office 365. User Activation is an end-user tool that integrates MigrationWiz and DeploymentPro for a hands-off migration to Office 365. The tool that you use depends on the migration approach. If you are looking for an automated migration and you have less than 25 users, then user activation is the best way to proceed. If you are using any type of SBS server (that has a local Exchange Server), you need to use either User Activation or DeploymentPro/MigrationWiz. These tools patch around the SBS service control point on the desktop. Keep in mind that any time there is an Exchange Server, you need to *uninstall* the Exchange Server at the end of the migration.

■ **Note**   There are two approaches to using BitTitan's tools: a manual migration approach using MigrationWiz and DeploymentPro, or using the User Activation automated tool. If you are migrating a small number of mailboxes, using MigrationWiz User activation saves time on the migration. The approach that we are describing here is a manual approach using MigrationWiz.

The migration approach we use is a combination of MigrationWiz and DeploymentPro. If there is an SBS server, we always use DeploymentPro. DeploymentPro configures the desktop and moves the SBS Exchange Server to the side. When we migrate larger accounts of more than 200 or 400, it depends on the migration strategy. In some cases, we use the combination tools, and in others, we use Exchange Federation; it just depends on what you are trying to achieve.

■ **Note**   If you are using MigrationWiz with DeploymentPro, and you want to upgrade the desktop Before you install clients, you need to remove the Service Control Point (e.g., CAS Autodiscover record from the Exchange Server (2007 and 2010) by running the following commands (1) to retrieve the CAS server identity <name> and (2) to set the CAS server Autodiscover record to $NULL.

(1) Get-ClientAccessServer

(2) Set-ClientAccessServer -Identity "<name>" —AutoDiscoverServiceInternalUri $NULL

After you have run the preceding commands, the Outlook clients use the DNS Autodiscover records to look up the Office 365 Exchange Server.

Using MigrationWiz

In Step 10 (earlier in this chapter), we chose a cutover migration. The easiest way to look at a migration is to use a hypothetical situation. In this example, there are ten mailboxes and a Windows server running Exchange. The migration tools that we will use are MigrationWiz and DeploymentPro. MigrationWiz moves the data and DeploymentPro configures the desktop and sets the default profile. The migration steps using these tools are as follows.

1. Log in to **www.bittian.com** and create a migration account. Confirm your account and select **MigrationWiz** (see Figure 5-64).

2. Verify that Exchange Server 2007/2010 is set to basic authentication.

3. Configure the permission for the admin user mailbox on Exchange Server.

4. Build the migration project and enter the admin credentials.

5. Load the user for migration.

6. Purchase licenses for migration.

7. (Optional). Select DeploymentPro for desktop configuration changes and send out the Configuration tool.

8. Start the mailbox migration.

9. Retry migration errors.

10. If you are using DeploymentPro, select **cutover** (either manual or scheduled) and cut over the MX records. The migration is completed.

Figure 5-64. *BitTitan: Mail and data cloud migration tools (courtesy of BitTitan)*

Step 1: Create a BitTitan Account

Log in to BitTitan (www.bittitan.com), select Products ➤ MigrationWiz (see Figure 5-65). You may purchase licenses after you log in.

Figure 5-65. *Creating an account with BitTitan for migration*

Step 2: Verify That Exchange Server 2007/2010 Is Set to Basic Authentication

If your source data is located on Exchange Server 2007/2010, you need to verify that the Exchange Server authentication is set to **Basic authentication**. To check this, select **Client Access** under Server Configuration. Highlight the server name and select **Properties**. The **Outlook Anywhere** tab should be set to Basic authentication. MigrationWiz reads and copies the user data from the mailboxes (see Figure 5-66). If you are using another hosted Exchange service, do not worry, your service is already set to this mode.

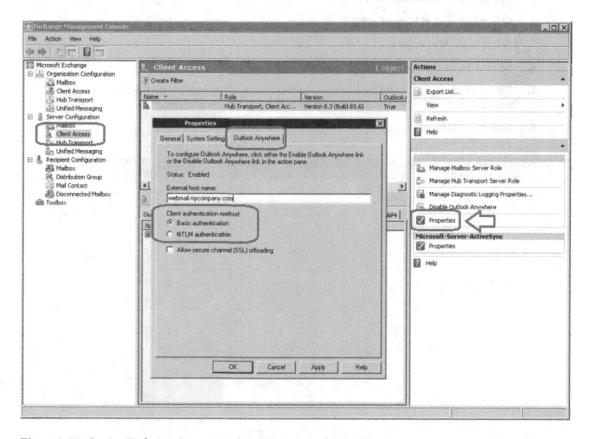

Figure 5-66. *Setting Exchange Server2007/2010 to Basic Authentication*

Step 3: Configure Permission on Exchange Server

Before you start the migration, you need to grant the administrator account on the Exchange Server permission to read all user e-mails. This is required so that you can migrate the Exchange Server e-mail account to Office 365. Follow these two steps:

1. Create a user account on the Exchange Server for migration. Search for "How do I migrate from Exchange or Office 365" on the BitTitan web site.

2. Run the Exchange Server PowerShell (as an admin) and grant permission to the user account. The PowerShell commands should look similar to the following code block.

```
Get-Mailbox -ResultSize Unlimited | Add-MailboxPermission -AccessRights
FullAccess -User UserMigWiz
```

Step 4: Build the Migration Project

Create the migration project in BitTitan. At this point, you have two admin accounts: the Office 365 Global admin account and the Exchange Server admin account (created in the previous step). We are moving data from an on-site Exchange Server to Office 365. To accomplish this, we will use the OWA mail interface to move data. Follow these steps:

1. Log in to **Migrationwiz.bittitan.com**.

2. Select **Account ➤ MigrationWiz**.

3. Select **Go to My projects**.

4. Select **Create a project** and then mailbox migration.

5. Fill out the new project information, select the source service (see Figure 5-67) and the destination service. Use the Office 365 global admin account.

6. Save the information.

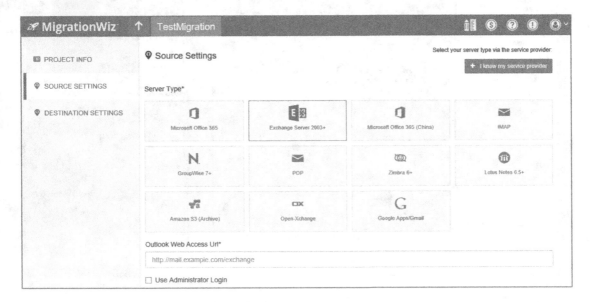

Figure 5-67. *Select Source Project (exchange) and enter OWA Url*

■ **Note**   The Office 365 global admin account must have a license assigned to the account for the services that it is accessing in Office 365.

Step 5: Load the User for Migration

Load the user e-mail addresses into MigrationWiz project to begin the migration (see Figure 5-68). You can manually add accounts or load accounts through a CSV file.

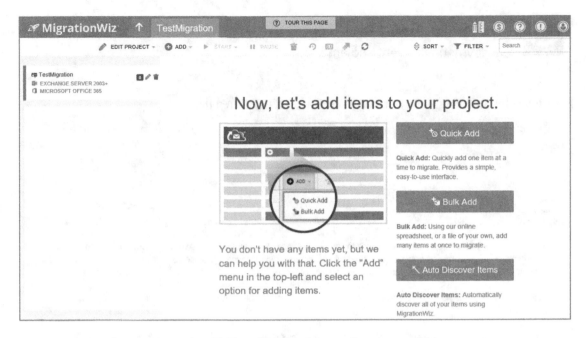

Figure 5-68. *Load user accounts into BitTitan for Migration*

Step 6: Purchase License for Migration

Once the accounts are loaded, you need to purchase the licenses. You can purchase migration licenses and deployment licenses (DeploymentPro) in any combination. Make sure that you purchase enough for your migration. Before you start the migration, verify if you are going to use DeploymentPro for the desktop configuration (see the next step). At this point, you are ready to begin the migration.

Step 7: Configure DeploymentPro (Optional)

DeploymentPro assists you in the conversion of the desktop from the local account to the Office 365 account (see Figure 5-69). Select the DeploymentPro icon from the User menu and start the process.

Figure 5-69. *BitTitan: Selecting DeploymentPro (courtesy of BitTitan)*

DeploymentPro walks you through a set of steps where you identify the account, customize your message, and send a DeploymentPro agent to the desktop (see Figure 5-70). Each user selects the DeploymentPro agent to configure the desktop. When MigrationWiz has reached the final steps, the DeploymentPro dashboard updates the status of the user configuration.

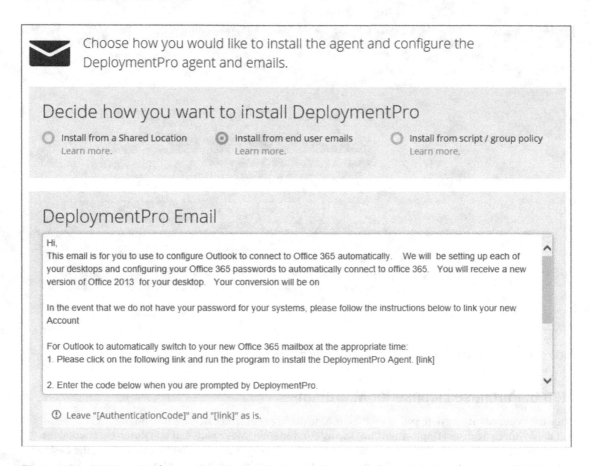

Figure 5-70. BitTitan: DeploymentPro Message Customization and Delivery Selection (courtesy of BitTitan)

At the end of the DeploymentPro setup, you have a customized e-mail with your business log that is sent out to all users that migrate to Office 365. At this time, you are ready to start the e-mail migration.

When you deploy DeploymentPro and the user installs the application, the configuration process begins. The DeploymentPro agent starts up, reports back to the administrator console, and waits until the configuration is manually started (right-click the **DeploymentPro** icon; see Figure 5-71) or you can select **Configure Outlook** from the DeploymentPro project dashboard. The advantage of using DeploymentPro is that the desktop is configured and any local Exchange Server is bypassed.

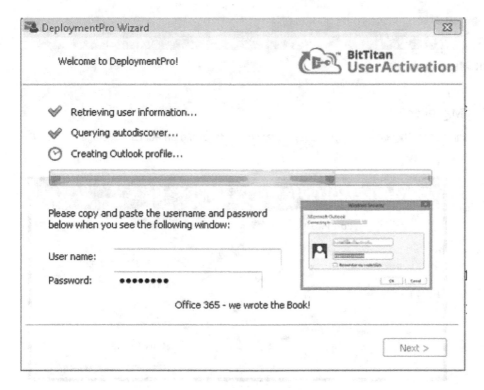

Figure 5-71. *BitTitan: DeploymentPro Configuration tool*

Step 8: Start the Mailbox Migration

Migration speed is a function of the source speed of the server where data is sourced and the destination server (where data is being copied). For example, if you are migrating from Small Business Server 2003 R2, typically you can only migrate one or two mailboxes at a time. If you are migrating from a hosted service such as Google, the limitation is on Google and Microsoft data transfers. Figure 5-72 shows a sample of the different screens that you see in a migration, after you have started.

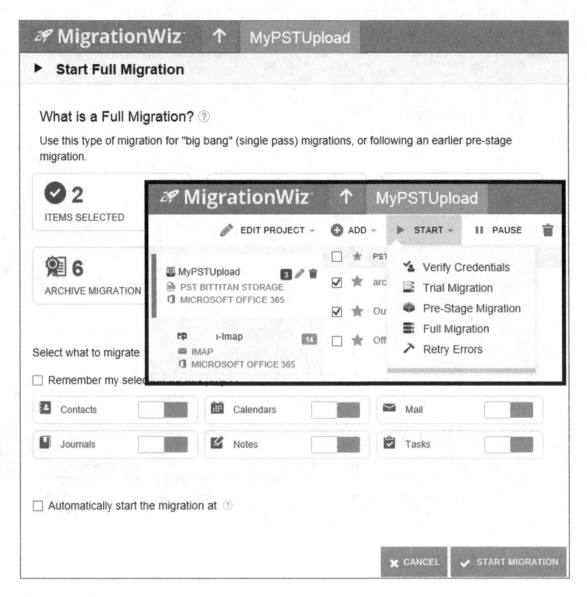

Figure 5-72. Full migration example

■ **Note** There are different ways to migrate e-mail. Typical cutover migration can be completed in stages. For example, you can start the migration and migrate only e-mail (such as all e-mails before October 31). Once the first stage is completed, you can start the final stage at cutover, and finish the migration of all e-mails, contacts, tasks, and calendar appointments. This way, the migration is completed at cutover and users do not experience any downtime or missing e-mails.

MigrationWiz provides you with statistics so that you can gauge the speed of your migration (see Figure 5-73). The most difficult part of using MigrationWiz is the configuration of the mailbox with the correct passwords.

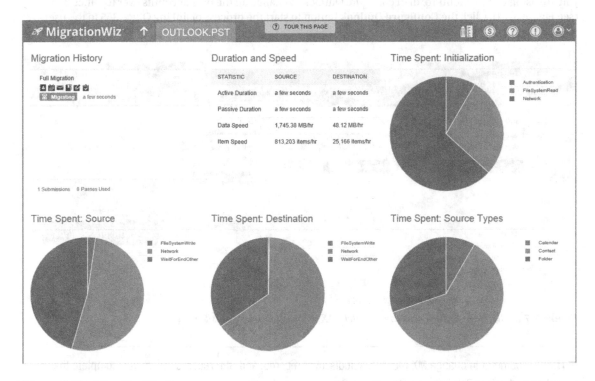

Figure 5-73. *MigrationWiz Summary screen*

When you start a migration, try one user account and verify the configuration. Once you have an account that has started to migrate, then you can start migrating the other accounts. MigrationWiz only copies data and it does not destroy the source data.

A migration includes many different types of data migration. In this example, we only used e-mail as an example. In many cases, we are emigrating data from Google Drive to Office 365, as well as older archive data in the format of a PST. If you have different data that you need to migrate, you just need to use the appropriate migration tool to move the information.

Step 9: Retry Migration Errors

After you have completed one successful pass-through on your e-mail accounts, you should rerun all of the migrations that have errors. When you select an account that has an error, select **Retry Errors**, which is an option under Start.

Step 10: Complete the MigrationWiz Migration

The migration to Office 365 is complete. The next step is to change the MX records to Office 365, and if you are using DeploymentPro, then configure Outlook to change all the user accounts over to Office 365 (see Figure 5-74). Click the **Configure Outlook** button to start the process of linking Office 365 to the user workstations.

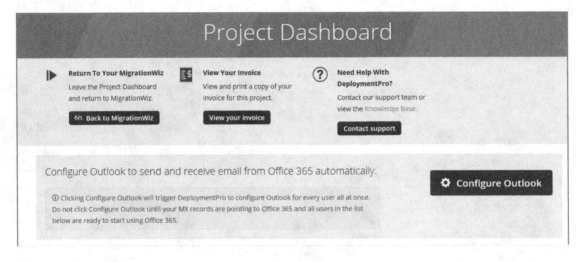

Figure 5-74. BitTitan: Mail is migrated, switch MX records (courtesy of BitTitan)

■ **Note**   You need to change MX records, Autodiscover records, and SPF records before you complete the migration and select Configure for DeploymentPro.

If you are using MigrationWiz with an on-premises Exchange Server, you need to install the registry changes to block service control point (SCP) lookup, remove the service control point from the Exchange Server, or convert the mailbox to a mail-enabled user (MEU). The registry entries required to be modified for the clients are listed next (see Microsoft KB article at https://support.microsoft.com/en-us/kb/2612922).

■ **Note**   BitTitan suggests that you upgrade 2016 after the migration or after you run DeploymentPro. We have tried this both ways, and it really depends on the organization.

Using the Microsoft Office 365 Migration Tool

MigrationWiz is a third-party tool that you can use to migrate to Office 365. However, there is also the Microsoft tool. The Microsoft Office 365 migration tool is designed to migrate up to ten mailboxes at a time. Follow these steps to access the admin screen to use the tool.

1.   Select **Office 365** in the admin center.

2.   Select **service settings**.

3. Select the **mail** option and then select **don't see what you are looking for...**, and the **Manage Additional settings in the Exchange admin center**.

4. You see the screen shown in Figure 5-75. Select **Migration** and then click the + sign. Select **Migrate to Exchange Online**. When a mailbox is migrated, the on-premises mailbox is converted to a mail-enabled unit.

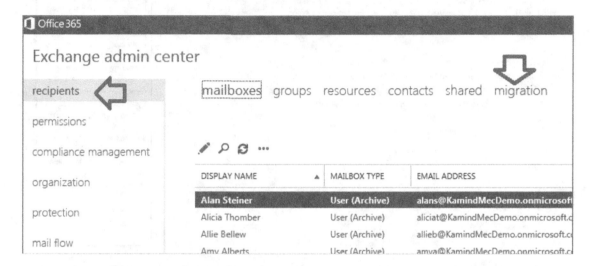

Figure 5-75. *Selecting the Office 365 Migration tool*

Your options with the Office 365 tool are limited to Exchange Servers (2003, 2007, and 2010) and IMAP. POP mail is problematic, since POP e-mail has just e-mail and no folders. Typically, if you are using POP mail, you will most likely use a PST export/import, because the POP e-mail is stored locally. We always recommend that you use MigrationWiz as the first option. It is simpler to use. In this example, we are going to use the IMAP to import mail from a non-Exchange server, and we need to build a CSV file for the usernames and passwords. To import using IMAP, select the IMAP option (see Figure 5-76).

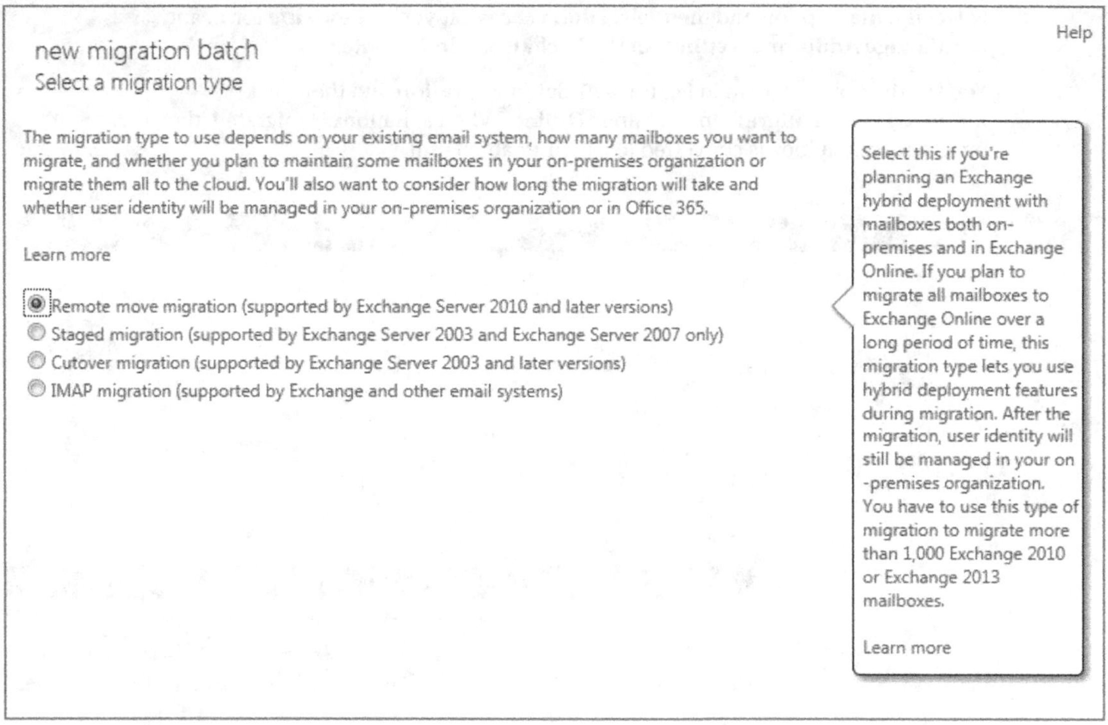

Figure 5-76. *Migrating e-mail using Office 365 e-mail migration*

■ **Note** If you do not have a third-party certificate, do not use the Microsoft mail migration tool, use BitTitan's MigrationWiz.

Provide the credentials to import the user accounts into Office 365, and create a CSV file to load the users from the source server into Office 365 (see Figure 5-77). The wizard assumes that the e-mail address of the source server is the destination e-mail address on Office 365. You need to be a global administrator to use this tool.

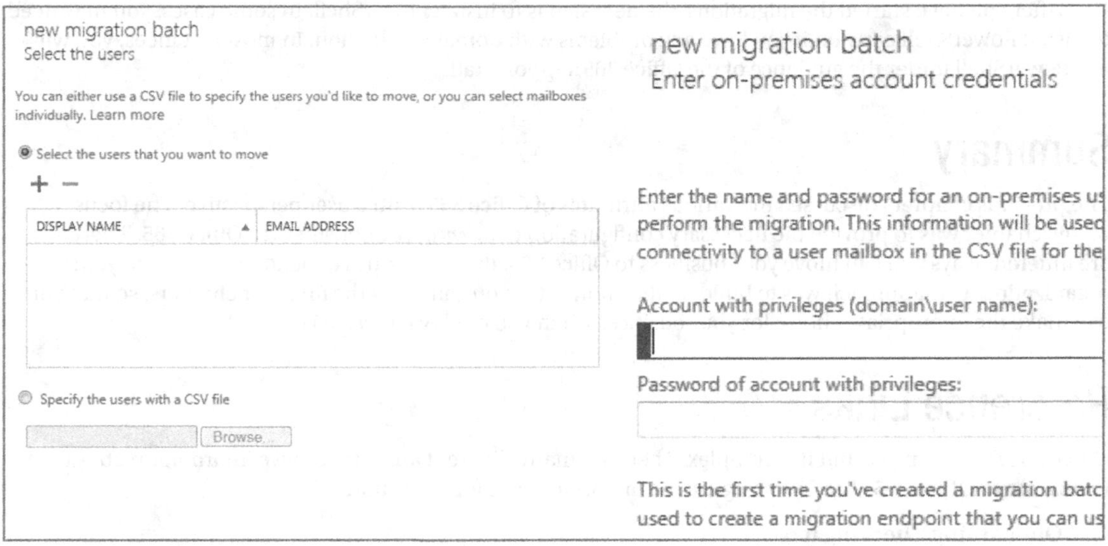

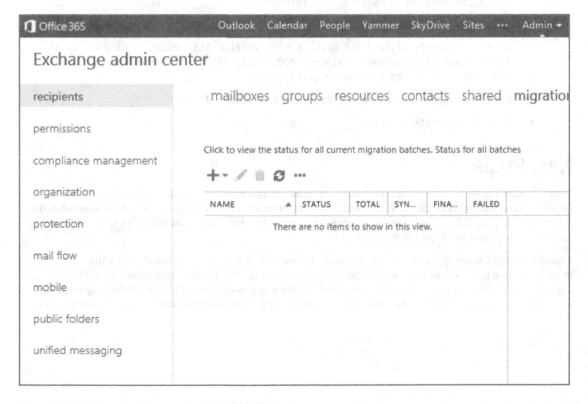

Figure 5-77. *Office 365 e-mail migration*

After you have selected **run**, Office 365 monitors the status and sends you an e-mail when the migration is completed. It lists the batch status (see Figure 5-78).

Figure 5-78. *Migration status using Office 365 migration*

After you have started the migrations, the next step is to install PowerShell. In some cases, you may need to install PowerShell early on if you have any problems with domain validation. In most instances, you will use PowerShell under the guidance of the Office 365 support staff.

Summary

The previous chapters discussed the various attributes of Office 365 from a user perspective. The focus of this chapter was to provide the necessary configuration of moving your business to Office 365. There are different ways you can move your business to Office 365; the techniques depend on the size of your organization. Our approach was to build on the knowledge you gained in the first four chapters, so that you can make the appropriate choice for your business when you deploy Office 365.

Reference Links

Office 365 seems simple, but it is complex. There are many different areas to retrieve information about how to migrate to Office 365. The following are the important links for migration.

Onboarding Checking tool

- http://fasttrack.office.com

Office 365 migration videos

- http://technet.microsoft.com/en-jm/video/office-365-jump-start-01-microsoft-office-365-overview-for-it-pros

Conversion of on-site user to mail-enabled user

- http://community.office365.com/en-us/blogs/office_365_community_blog/archive/2011/12/02/convert-exchange-2007-mailboxes-to-mail-enabled-users-after-a-staged-exchange-migration.aspx

Office 365 Migrating and Managing your business in the cloud—Update

- http://www.mattkatzer.com

Next Steps

Your Office 365 systems have been set up and configured. At this point, you understand the features of Office 365 and you are ready to move forward. However, your work is not yet complete. There is more to do, depending on your Office 365 configuration. It is recommended that you review Chapters 4, 6, and 7 after you have completed the deployment.

Chapter 4: Cloud Security Best Practices. One of the issues that all managers are faced with is the management of data and security and learning best practices. In this chapter, you explore the different capabilities of Office 365 and the monitoring that is in place to manage your Office 365 company to ensure that your data remains private. This chapter covers the most common approaches to Office 365 migration.

Chapter 6: Workstation Setup and Configuration. Office 365 supports many different systems and capabilities, depending on your business needs. The issue that IT managers constantly face is how to setup and manage the client environment. This chapter is focused on the configuration of an Office 365 desktop environment. This is the go-to reference chapter on the configuration of your desktop and mobile phones.

Chapter 7: Managing Office 365. This chapter describes the different administration centers in Office 365 and the most common tools that you use to administer Office 365. Depending on your Office 365 plan, there are five possible administration tools. This chapter focuses on the Office 365, Exchange, and Skype for Business administration centers. The chapter closes with using PowerShell to manage your Office 365 environment.

CHAPTER 6

■ ■ ■

Workstation Setup Configuration for Office 365

Office 365 is scalable for all business. An Office 365 subscription can be created for 1 user or 100,000 users. Office 365 is the only service that allows any size business to have the same capabilities as a Fortune 100 company, at a low monthly subscription. As a business owner, you are no longer restricted from using tools that were only available to large corporations. You have the same capabilities.

Once you have an active Office 365 subscription, the question always asked by users is: What do I do next? How do I configure my desktop, my smartphone, and my existing desktop? The purpose of this chapter is to describe the best-known methods in the configuration of your Office 365 subscription and desktop software. In Chapter 2, you walked through a day in the life of an Office 365 user. In this chapter, you will configure your computing device.

Office 365 Subscription Overview

The administrator (IT manager/business owner) picks one or more Office 365 plans to make up an Office 365 subscription and maps those plans to one or more users in the organization. Each Office 365 plan is designed with features to best meet the needs of businesses based upon their size or other factors. The plans are flexible and designed to allow the administrator to select plans based on the user's role in the business. As an example, your business may have a factory worker whose job function only requires occasional access to e-mail via a shared Office KIOSK computer. Why should you pay for a subscription that has features that you do not need? Office 365 configuration flexibility allows you to design your Office 365 subscription plans to match the unique characteristics of your business and the roles that your employees play in the business.

Log in to Office 365 at the portal (`http://portal.microsoftonline.com`) using the company or work credentials. Before going further into the configuration of Office 365, you need to step back and look at the two different Microsoft environments: the consumer cloud (a.k.a. Microsoft account) and the business cloud (Office 365 work account). There are different versions of Office 365—some are consumer based and some are work based. The one discussed in this chapter is the business version. If you are using a Microsoft account (or any services from Live.com), it is a consumer account, not an Office 365 account. Both accounts may use the same e-mail address. However, when you access any Office 365 service, you need to select the **Work or school account** (see Figure 6-1) when prompted to access Office 365 services.

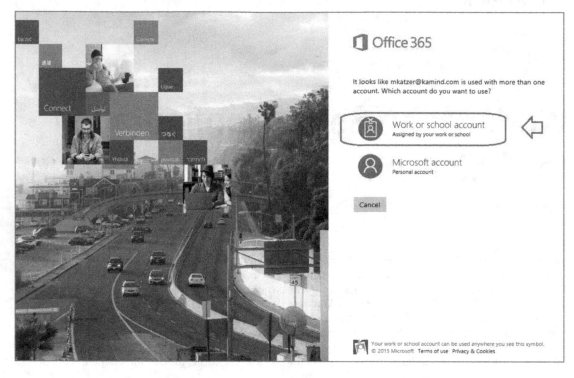

Figure 6-1. *Logging in to Office 365 with your work or school account*

■ **Note** When you log in to Office 365 and use your work e-mail address, if your e-mail address was used for any of the Microsoft consumer services, you will be promoted to pick either a Work account or a Personal (or Microsoft) account. Office 365 business is a work account.

After you log in to the Office 365 service (see Figure 6-2), Office 365 displays the features available to the user (based on the subscription plan that the administrator has assigned to the user). Each subscription plan has features that the Office 365 administrator has selected to meet the needs of business. Office 365 allows the administrator to mix and match different plans that meet the individual user's needs in the organization. The popular plans are Business Essential, Business Premium, Enterprise E1, E3, and E5 (cloud PBX using Skype for Business). There is no requirement to have everyone on the same plan; you can mix all types of subscription plans to meet the needs of the business.

Figure 6-2. *Office 365 login page*

Our approach to an Office 365 configuration is to select the subscription that best matches the roles of the employees and the needs of the organization. Office 365 supports Macs, PCs, iPads, tablets, and mobile devices. The applications shown in Figure 6-2 are a mix of CRM, Project, Visio, Power BI, and Office Professional Pro. The applications that you see may be different. The differences are based on the subscription that your administrator assigned to your Office 365 user account.

All that users need to do is log in to Office 365 (`portal.Office.com`) and verify their username and password. After you log in to Office 365, you should end up with a login screen that looks similar to Figure 6-3.

Figure 6-3. Log in to Office 365, portal.Office.com

Navigation in the portal is simple. Select the nine-block grid (upper-left corner), and select the application that you want to use. You can run Word Online and either edit the documents in the cloud or launch the local copy of Word on your desktop. If you do not have the latest version of this software, download the latest version of Office Professional Plus.

Office 365 subscriptions allow you download necessary software to your PC, Mac, laptop, tablet, or smartphone, as needed. Office 365 subscriptions allow you to download software for up to five mobile devices and five PC/MAC traditional computing devices. When you have many devices connected, the Office 365 file synchronization service, OneDrive for Business, makes it easy to manage multiple devices. OneDrive for Business syncs all of your work in process documents and shares them on all of your connected devices.

To protect information, our company deploys Windows 10 with BitLocker to encrypt the data in laptops. It no longer matters which device you use to access your latest business presentation or work product, you know that you'll have the information synchronized with all of your computing devices desktops, laptop, phones, and tablets. This is the power of productivity.

Different Versions of Office Software

Office 365 is the family name of a group of products. Under the Office 365 name, there are different versions of Office software. These include Office 365 Home and Small Business, Office 365 Standard, Office 365 Pro Plus, and the Office 365 subscription versions— Office 365 Business Premium, Office 365 E3, and Office 365 E5 subscriptions. On top of this, you have the legacy versions of Office: 2007, 2010 and 2013. The current Office version in Office 365 is Office 2016 (for Mac and PC).

The one problem that we have continuously run into is when mixing legacy desktop versions of Office with subscription versions. We always uninstall Office software on the desktop before or after we install the Office 365 subscription version. Why? Everything works better! Our help desk calls are 50% less than they were previously. Once you start using Office 365, only use the downloaded software.

■ **Note**   Office 365 has undergone many changes over the years. The most significant change has been with the software upgrades. Microsoft no longer patches Office 365 services; the service software is installed in builds. As an end user, if you want to have the latest version of Office, we no longer download the release version and apply patches, we perform an online repair and sync the desktop Office software to the latest Office 365 build. Whenever a customer calls about an Office problem, we rebuild Office. This corrects 90% of our Office support calls.

Installing Office 365 Software

Once your account has been migrated to Office 365, there isn't any installation of software to Office 365. Office 365 is a web-based service that allows you to edit, share, search, and manage information in a web console. Office 365 allows you to collaborate with fellow workers in your Office 365 company or to share information with external users who are not part of your company. Office 365 allows you to use all of these services on the Web, but you also have the ability to run Office software on your desktop, and with no online access. Office 365 allows you to have it your way: in the cloud or locally on your desktop. However, you may want to install Office 2016 desktop software.

Accessing the software application for your local use is simple. Just log into Office 365 business services, download the software, and configure your desktop environment. To download the desktop software, select the gear icon, and then select **Office 365 settings**. You can download desktop versions for your MAC or PC as needed. Remember, you can have up to five copies of desktop software in any combination, Mac or PC. After you have selected the gear icon and **Office 365 settings**, you should see the Office 365 dashboard (see Figure 6-4).

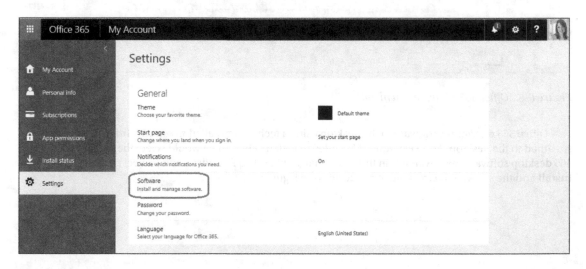

Figure 6-4. *Downloading software from Office 365*

Select **Software** to get to the different software packages that you can download. The Software option also displays the devices that you have installed Office software (you can install Office desktop software on five devices) and lets you know the number of copies that you have left to install. It is very common to have multiple devices, and now you can have those devices using the latest versions. It no longer matters if you have a Mac or PC, you can download the appropriate version for each of them. Office 365 and Windows 10 performance have given life extensions to current hardware.

Looking at the computing devices that I am using, I have two active desktops/laptops that I use daily. If I purchase a new computer, I no longer have to run down to the Office supply store and buy a version of Office for every new computing device that I use. All that I do now is log in to Office 365, download the applications that I want to use. As you can see in Figure 6-5, I have two computing devices already configured with Office desktop software and have three open licenses to use.

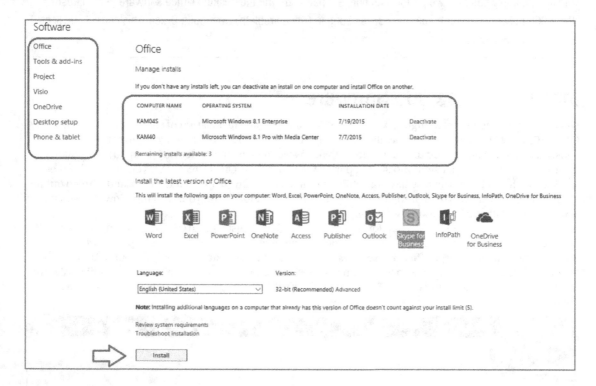

Figure 6-5. *Office 365 software downloads*

Office 365 distributes software to the desktop using a technology called *streaming*. Information is streamed to the desktop. As an example, if I wanted to install Office 365, I would select the version of Office 365 desktop software that I wanted (in this case, I have Office 2013 Pro, Visio, and Project). I then select **Install** and the software is streamed to my device (see Figure 6-6).

Figure 6-6. *Streaming Office 365 software downloads*

The streaming process installs the Office software (see Figure 6-7). Once the software is installed, I configure the applications to connect to my Office 365 services and I am off and running. If this is a duplicate computer, I also configure my OneDrive for Business. OneDrive for Business syncs all of my documents from my other computing devices to my new laptop. In the remaining sections in this chapter, you will look at the different ways of setting up your Office software, including Skype for Business (Cloud PBX) and OneDrive for Business.

Figure 6-7. *Installing Office 365 applications to your desktop*

Configuring Office 2016

At this point, you have installed Office 2016 to your desktop/laptop/Mac and you are configuring the service. The administrator has set up the Office 365 service, moved your e-mail, and verified the domain, so all that is needed to configure the Office software. Configuring Office software is a simple six-step process.

1. Start Outlook and enter your e-mail address and password.

2. Start OneDrive for Business and sync your cloud storage account.

3. Start Word and link your account to Office 365.

4. Configure OneDrive for Business.

5. Start Skype for Business and log in to the Skype for Business services.

6. Configure your smartphone.

Like any other configuration, there are always exceptions. I have outlined these exceptions in the latter portion of this chapter for your reference.

Step 1: Start Outlook and Create a New Profile

If this is a new installation of Outlook, you will see a prompt similar to what's shown in Figure 6-8. Select **New** and provide a profile name, and then click **OK** to create the profile and connect to Outlook. If Outlook does not start a new profile, follow the instructions at the end of this chapter to set Outlook to "prompt" for the profile.

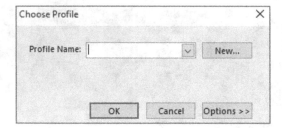

Figure 6-8. *Starting up Outlook for the first time*

■ **Note**   If this is the first time that you have connected to Outlook, open a web browser and connect to Office 365. Enter your username and password. Keep the browser window open when you configure Outlook and the process will be faster.

Step 2: Enter Your Name and E-mail Address

Select **New** (see Figure 6-8), enter a profile name, and fill in your user account information and password. Then click **Next** (see Figure 6-9).

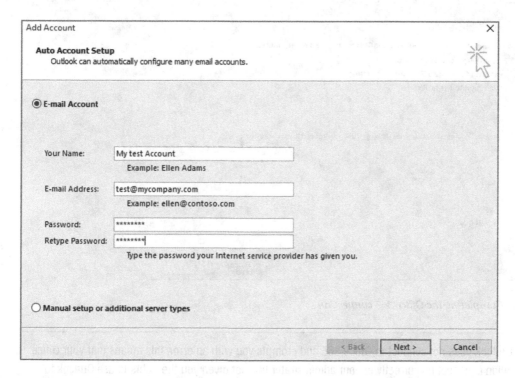

Figure 6-9. *Starting up Outlook for the first time*

Step 3: Verify the Office 365 Connection

After you have entered your credentials, you are prompted to enter your password once more, and you should see the Congratulations (see Figure 6-10) acknowledgement. If you see an error message, this means that either you entered your password incorrectly or your workstation cannot connect to Outlook. This is usually because Office 365 is not set up correctly or you are using a workstation in a business with an on-premises e-mail Exchange Server (and your e-mail account has not been migrated to Office 365).

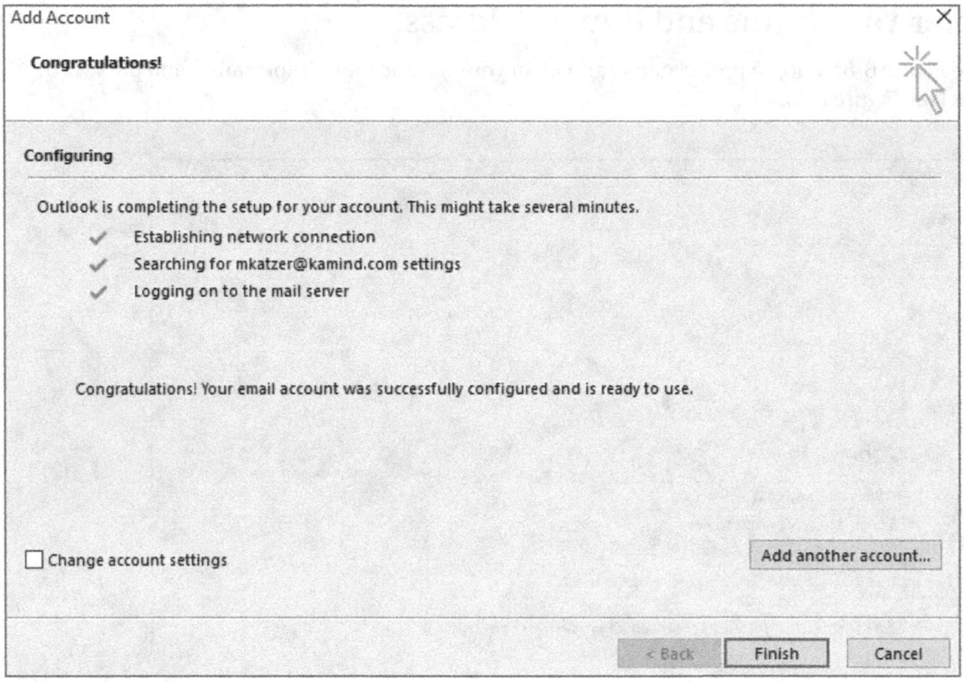

Figure 6-10. *Completing the Office 365 connection*

▪ **Note** If Outlook does not connect to Office 365 and prompts you with an error, this means that your Office 365 configuration is not set up correctly or your administrator has not given you the rights to use Outlook to connect to your Office 365 account. If you are the administrator, check the autodiscover records in your external and internal DNS. These should point to Outlook.com.

That's it! You are ready to start using Outlook with Office 365. The e-mail that you receive on your Office 365 account will be in sync with your desktop, smartphone, and tablet.

Step 4: Configuring OneDrive for Business

After you have set up Outlook to run with Office 365, or next task is to configure OneDrive for Business. Before you begin the configuration, I need to point out that there are two versions of OneDrive: a consumer version and a business version. You cannot mix these two different services. These services can coexist with each other, but they are different. To start up, go to you Start menu, and select **OneDrive for Business** (see Figure 6-11).

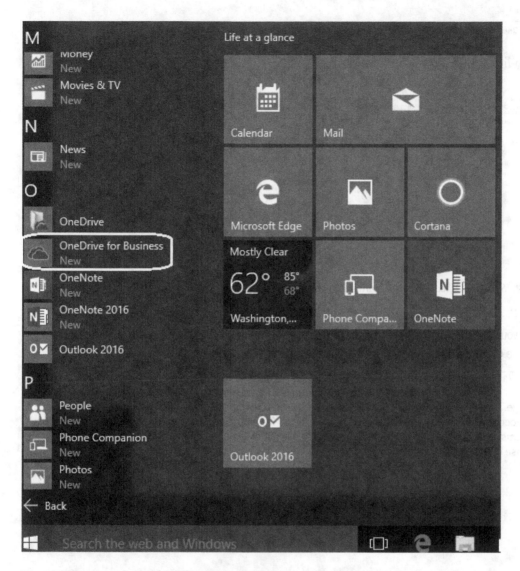

Figure 6-11. *Completing the Office 365 connection*

After selecting OneDrive for Business, it begins to connect to Office 365 and prompts you to sync your OneDrive for Business Office 365 cloud storage to your desktop. Select the **Sync Now** button (See Figure 6-12) to sync your Office 365 account

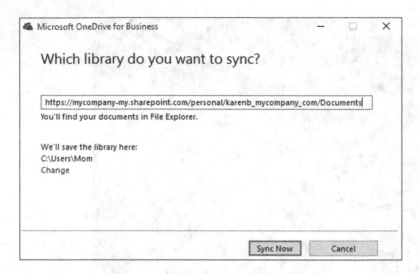

Figure 6-12. Syncing Office 365 cloud storage to your desktop

---

■ **Note**   If you have not selected the OneDrive icon in Office 365, log in to `http://portal.microsoftonline.com` and select the OneDrive icon to configure the OneDrive for Business Cloud storage.

After you have selected **Sync Now**, wait a few minutes and your desktop will be synced to Office 365 cloud storage. During the sync process, you may be requested to log in to your Office 365 service using your Office 365 account. If you also use the same e-mail address for your consumer account, Office 365 services will detect this and prompt you to select an account to use (see Figure 6-13). Always select the Work account when you use Office 365.

Figure 6-13. *Select the correct Office 365 account when prompted*

■ **Note**   The Work account is for Office 365 business accounts. The Microsoft account is for Microsoft consumer services. The information in this chapter only relates to Microsoft Office 365 business services.

After you enter your credentials, Office 365 OneDrive for Business starts syncing to your desktop system. OneDrive for Business starts the download process. After the activity bar completes (see Figure 6-14), the files begin to appear on your system. If there are any sync errors, follow the instructions and correct the problem, and then try the sync again.

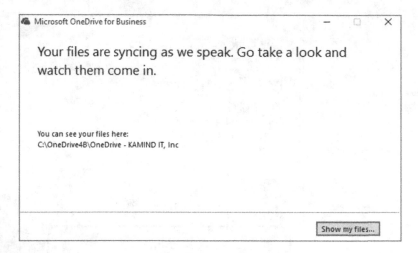

Figure 6-14. OneDrive for Business sync tool verifying data in Office 365

Once the data starts to sync to your device, you can see the status of the sync (see Figure 6-15). To check the status of OneDrive for Business, select the OneDrive for Business icons (in the desktop hidden icons). Right click on the OneDrive for Business icon and select the appropriate options.

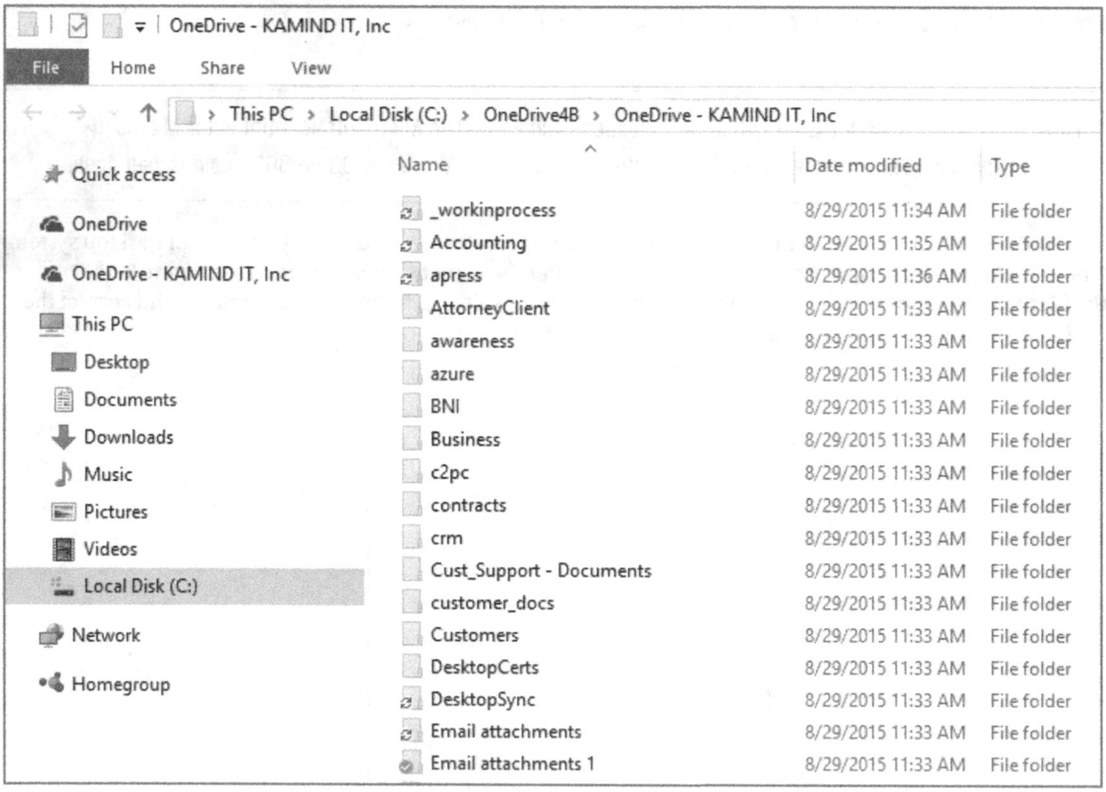

Figure 6-15. OneDrive for Business synced

There are additional options for the configuration of OneDrive for Business. I have a specific section that reviews the configuration options (in the OneDrive section). Office 365 changes every 90 days with minor updates. Some of these updates affect the Office 2016 and OneDrive for Business sync software. You can update your Office 365/OneDrive for Business software at any time by using the Online Repair feature discussed later in this chapter. Online Repair replaces the current desktop software with the latest version and at the same time syncs your desktop with the current Office 365 release.

Step 5: Configuring Skype for Business

After you configure OneDrive for Business, the next step is to configure Skype for Business or your Cloud PDX service. Configuration of Skype for Business is a start forward configuration: all you enter is your e-mail address and password.

■ **Note** The configuration setting of Skype for Business is controlled by your administrator. The public IM and external communication are enabled when you set up Office 365. If you cannot connect to an individual outside of your company, please contact your administrator to verify your Skype for Business settings.

There are two versions of Skype: Skype for Business and Skype. These products are different and have different capabilities. The main difference is that Skype is a consumer product designed for ad hoc communications. Skype for Business is integrated as part of Office 365. There two versions of Skype for Business: Standard and Enterprise. The Standard version is part of Business Essentials and Business Premium. The Enterprise version is included in all the Enterprise plans. When you start up Skype for Business for the first time, look under the apps and select **Skype for Business** (see Figure 6-16).

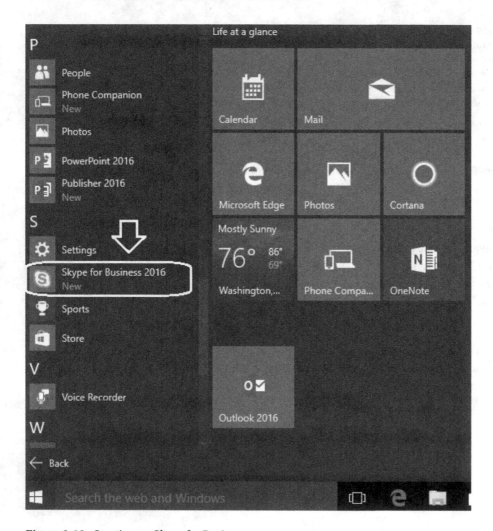

Figure 6-16. *Starting up Skype for Business*

After you have selected the Skype for Business application, enter your e-mail address and password to begin the service when the application starts (see Figure 6-17).

Figure 6-17. *Logging in to Skype service for the first time*

Once you have logged in to Skype for Business, verify that you can connect to other users outside of your company. The connectivity is dependent on the configuration of your Skype for Business service. In Figure 6-18, we are adding a Skype user to our contact list from the Skype directory.

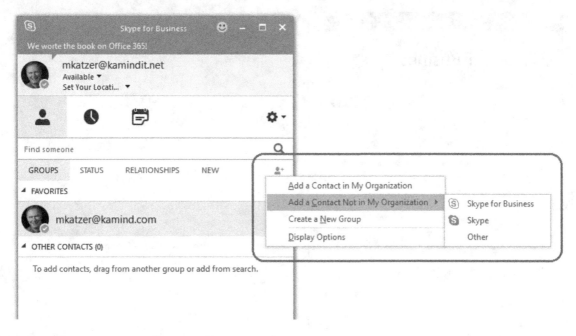

Figure 6-18. *Adding Skype (consumer) users to your contact list*

The main difference between adding contacts with Skype for Business users vs. Skype (consumer version) is permission. Skype for Business lets you add other Skype for Business users inside or outside of your organization. To add another Skype for Business user, you need an e-mail address. If they are in an Office 365 company and the company is set up for external communications, you can add their user account to your contact list. Skype consumer users need to be added via a contact request. Since Skype is free, the Skype user (or you) need to grant (or be given) permission before you can communicate to the other user.

To add a Skype user, select **Add a Contact Not in My Organization ➤ Skype** (see Figure 6-18). This action extends the Skype contacts to your Skype for Business contacts.

Once you have added a Skype (consumer user), you can add additional contacts by searching the Skype directory (see Figure 6-19). In this example, we are sending a contact request to Molly's Fund Fighting Lupus, a not-for-profit charity based in Portland, Oregon.

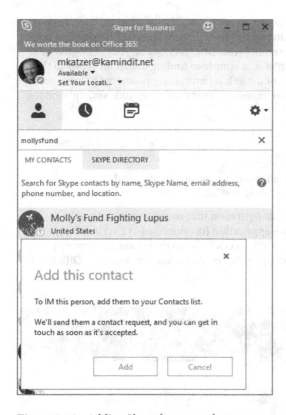

Figure 6-19. *Adding Skype (consumer) contact to your contact list*

If you have a Cloud PBX subscription, there is nothing that you need to do to configure your client. Your administration will route calls to your desktop when they are receive a call on your phone number.

Step 6: Configuring Smartphones and Tablets

Configuring your smartphone for Office 365 is simple. All you need is the same information that you used to configure Outlook: your e-mail address and password (and sometimes the Office 365 Exchange Server name: m.Outlook.com). Before you configure your smartphone, log in to Office 365 through a web browser and verify your Office 365 credentials. These are the same credentials for your smartphone and tablet (see Table 6-1).

Table 6-1. *Smartphone/Table Configuration*

Key Configuration Items
The User ID is your e-mail address
Always leave the Domain Name blank
Generic hosted Exchange Server name: **m.Outlook.com**

All smartphones and tablets require your e-mail address and password. If your administrator has not set up Office 365 correctly, you will not be able to configure your mobile device. There are two setups: one to add Office software to your smartphone and the one to configure e-mail services on your smartphone. Adding Office 365 applications to your smartphone or tablet is as simple as finding the applications in the Store and downloading the software to your smartphone (or tablet). When you are promoted to log in to Office 365 services, please use your Office 365 account and password. This configures your smartphone for the Office 365 business services. The steps are listed next.

1. Search for Office 365 in the App Store.

2. Download the application to your smartphone.

3. If you have already installed the Office applications, open the application and select **Add account**. Enter your Office 365 password and log in.

Configuration of the e-mail services depends on the configuration that you wish to use. If you downloaded and installed Office, the smartphone Outlook application (downloaded as part of Office) auto configures after login. There are two possible accounts to use to access Microsoft services: a Microsoft Account, and an Office 365 or Work Account. You use the Office 365 (or Work) account to access Office 365 services (see Figure 6-20).

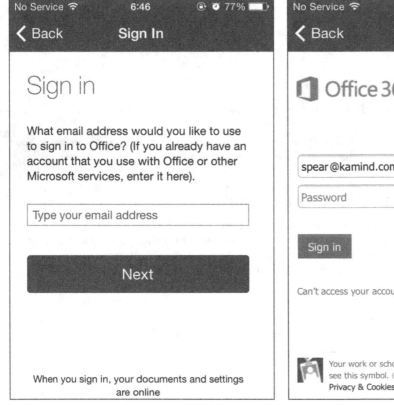

Figure 6-20. Android, iPhone, and Windows Phone prompt you for both a Microsoft account and an Office 365 account. Make sure that you use your Office 365 business account

■ **Note** iOS devices require iOS version 8.0 and above to use Office 365 and Outlook for iPhone. Android devices require Android version 4.0 or later. If your device does not support theses minimum releases, please follow the manual for your smartphone.

iPhone

The current versions of iPhones/iPads support the ability to have multiple exchange e-mail accounts. Exchange e-mail accounts are the e-mail services hosted on Office 365. Follow the steps outlined next.

1. Delete any previous account(s) that use your primary e-mail address.

2. On your iPhone or iPad, under Settings, select **Mail, Contacts, and Calendars**.

3. Press **Microsoft Exchange** to add your new account.

4. Enter your fully qualified e-mail name (e.g., info@kamind.com) in both the e-mail and username fields and your e-mail password. Click **Next**.

5. The iPhone or iPad uses the DNS records for the e-mail address (MX) feature to fill in the server box. Click **Next**.

6. Synchronize contacts and e-mail.

At this point, you have completed the necessary steps and your device will synchronize.

■ **Note** If you cannot connect (and save the connection) to your iPhone/iPad, follow these steps: (1) E-mail address and user ID are identical—the full e-mail address. (2) Enter the server name, **m.Outlook.com**. (3) Leave the domain name blank and select Next. If the iPhone configuration allows you to "save" the configuration (regardless of the error message), your phone is connected to Office 365.

Android Devices: Motorola Droid v2.2 (and Above)

Android devices vary. These instructions may be slightly different depending upon the phone's vendor (and carrier). Android uses the term "Corporate Email" or "Exchange" (in newer versions) for integrating into a Microsoft Office 365 service. If you do not see "Corporate Email," check with your phone supplier to verify that you have the latest version of the Android operating system on your phone.

1. Start by selecting **Home** and the **Settings** button (second from left). Then select **Settings ➤ Accounts & sync ➤ Add account**.

2. Select **Microsoft Exchange Active Sync**.

3. Enter your fully qualified e-mail name (e.g., info@kamind.net) and password. Click **Next**.

4. This may fail. You will see a screen to allow you to reenter your information. If this fails, then you need to do the following:

   a. Re-enter your e-mail address and duplicate this for Domain\Username (the backslash is OK). (Your password has been kept from the previous entry.)

   b. For Office 365, enter **m.Outlook.com** in **Server**. (This should be automatic, but may not be.)

   c. Keep **Use secure connection (SSL)** checked.

   d. Press **Next**.

At this point, you have completed the necessary steps and your device will synchronize.

Windows Phone 7: Office 365

Windows Phone 7 supports multiple accounts and allows you to pin. You may have multiple e-mail accounts. The following procedure connects your Windows Phone to both your Hosted Exchange and SharePoint accounts.

1. Select **Settings**.

2. Select **Office Hub**.

3. Select **Office 365 and Setup**.

4. Select **Add an Account Outlook**

5. You will receive a message that allows you access to the Team Site (Office 365 SharePoint).

6. Select **Finish**.

■ **Note**　When you access the Office 365 Team Site, you will be prompted for your username and password. Select **Always connected** to not be prompted for the password.

At this point, you have completed the necessary steps and your device will synchronize.

Windows Phone 8.1: Adding Another Exchange Account

Windows Phone allows connections to multiple Exchange Servers. The following procedure connects your Windows Phone to another Exchange Server.

1. Select **Settings**.

2. Select **Email + accounts**.

3. Select **Add an Account**.

4. Select **Outlook**.

5. Enter the e-mail address and password.

6. Select **Sign in**.

7.   If prompted that credentials are bad, check your password with **Show password**.

8.   Change the username to the e-mail address.

9.   Select **Sign in**.

10. If promoted, select **Advance**.

11. Enter the server name: **m.Outlook.com**

12. Select **Sign in**.

At this point, you have completed the necessary steps and your device will synchronize.

Windows Phone 10: Office 365 and Windows Intune (Company Portal)

The Windows Phone 10 environment is simple to add to Office 365. All that is needed is your login credentials to Office 365. Windows Phone 10 allows you to have multiple e-mail accounts and pin e-mail folders to your smartphone tiles.

The following procedure connects your Windows Phone 10 to your Office 365, OneDrive for Business, and Team Site (SharePoint) accounts.

1.   Select **Settings** (swipe from right).

2.   Select **Accounts** (see Figure 6-21).

Figure 6-21. *Windows Phone 10 settings*

3.   Select **Work Access** (see Figure 6-22).

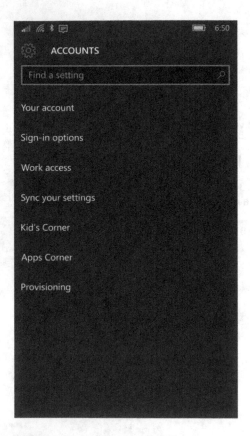

Figure 6-22. *Selecting a Work account*

4.   Enter your e-mail address and select **Connect**.

5.   If prompted, enter **Work account**.

At this point, Office 365 Mobile security settings are downloaded to your phone. Depending on the configuration, your settings may include a pin requirement and running company applications. If your phone has been configured with any Team Site settings, theses will be downloaded to your phone.

■ **Note**   When you access the Office 365 Team Site, you are prompted for username and password. Select **Always connected**.

At this point, you have completed the necessary steps and your device will synchronize.

Windows Phone 10: Adding Another Exchange Account

Windows Phone allows connections to multiple Exchange Servers. The following procedure connects your Windows Phone to another Exchange Server.

1. Select an Outlook account.

2. Select the gear icon.

3. Select **Accounts**.

4. Select the + sign to add an account.

5. Chose an account (select an account if present), or select the account type that matches.

6. Enter the e-mail address and password.

7. Select **Outlook**.

8. Enter the e-mail address and password.

9. Select **Sign in**.

10. Select the new account, and then select **Pin to Start**.

11. Change username to e-mail address.

12. Select **Sign in**.

13. If promoted, select **Advance**.

14. Enter the server name: **m.Outlook.com.**

15. Select **Sign in**.

At this point, you have completed the necessary steps and your device will synchronize.

Setup Summary

At this point, you have completed the Office 365 setup on your workstation and mobile devices. OneDrive for Business is syncing to your Office 365 cloud storage. You have linked your Skype for Business to communicate to your other team members and to the Consumer Skype users. There is nothing more that you need to do except some occasional care and maintenance of your Office 2016 software. When you see any problems with Office 2016, it's recommended that you try to rebuild the Office 2016 software (see Figure 6-23) with an "Online Repair".

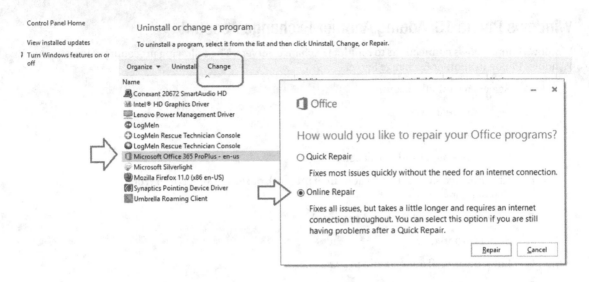

Figure 6-23. *Updating Office 2016 using the Online Repair feature*

The steps to rebuild Office 365 on a workstation or a laptop are simple:

1. Go to the Control Panel.

2. Select **Programs and Features**.

3. Find the Office 2016 software, and select.

4. Select **Change** and then **Online Repair**.

This procedure deletes the current software on your system, downloads the latest Office 2016 build from Office 365, and installs it onto your desktop system. Office 365 cloud software and Office products are built in weekly builds. When you select Online Repair, you are syncing the desktop software with the current Office 365 release.

■ **Note** Your Office 365 company is updated every 90 days with the latest release. If you find that Office Professional Plus is running slower on your desktop, then rebuild the release as described earlier.

OneDrive for Business: Planning for Personal and Team Site Document Storage

Office 365 has two great features for cloud storage: the Team Site and the OneDrive for Business cloud storage site. The questions that my KAMIND IT team are asked include: What information do you place in OneDrive for Business? and What information do you place in your Office 365 Team Site? Typically, your work product can be classified in one of two categories: current or reference/archive. Current information is what you are currently using as a work in process. Reference/archive is information that is part of an older project that you may need to access every now and then. Simply put, OneDrive for Business is a personal document storage library, whereas the Team Site is a set of company document libraries, managed by IT.

If you look at the way you work, current information is what you want to replicate to your workstation, laptop, or tablet. It is information that you need to have access at any moment to complete a task. That is the information that you place in OneDrive for Business and replicate to your device.

When you complete a project, you typically archive the project because the access is not needed on a daily basis. You are accessing the old project as needed. Completed projects should be placed in your Team Site, and not replicated to the desktop. If you are not going to access the information, why replicate the data? Documents in the Team Site still can be searched and downloaded when you need them.

As you start to use OneDrive for Business, remember these rules:

- If you exceed the limits or have a replication error, OneDrive for Business stops working.

- OneDrive for Business can replicate multiple libraries.

- OneDrive for Business is limited to 20,000 items, including folders and files. This is a Systems limit.

- Site Libraries are limited to 5,000 items, including folders and files.

- The maximum file size per library cannot be over 2GB.

- The Site Collection storage limit is 1TB.

- Site Collections per tenant is 500,000.

- The file attachment size is 250MB.

- The number of subsites (or libraries) per collection is 2,000.

■ **Note**　OneDrive for Business is undergoing constant improvement. New administrator controls are in place to restrict the OneDrive size and syncing to domain join devices (which can restrict home users from syncing corporate data). The new IT management tools include auditing of OneDrive for Business.

If you are using Office 365 and downloading one of the Office 365 subscription plans that include Office desktop software, your OneDrive software is installed and configured for your desktop as part of the installation process discussed earlier. If you are using a version of Office software that was purchased through a retail channel, and an older version of Office 2007 or 2010, or a version of Office software that was acquired under a volume license agreement, then you need to follow the steps outlined next to install OneDrive for Business on your desktop system.

Step 1: Office 365 OneDrive for Business Configuration

The Office 365 OneDrive for Business configuration is simple. You need to log in to Office 365 and select OneDrive (see the red arrow in Figure 6-24). If you have not accessed this site before, there is a five-minute configuration (first time). This action builds your OneDrive for Business site. After you have built the OneDrive for Business site, you are ready for step 2, installing the OneDrive for Business software on your desktop.

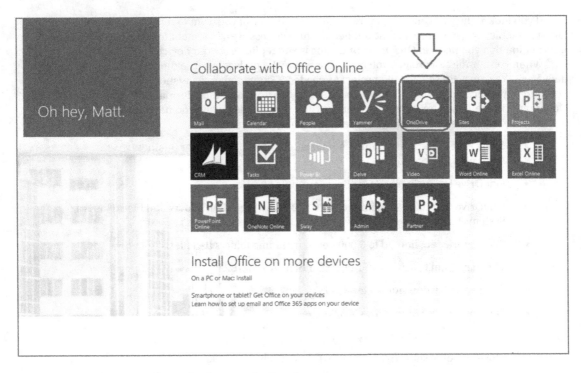

Figure 6-24. *Accessing OneDrive for Business the first time*

Once you have accessed OneDrive for Business, you should see OneDrive for Business and the sync icon displayed (see Figure 6-25). This icon is displayed on all the SharePoint sites so that you can selectively sync sites/subsites to your desktop.

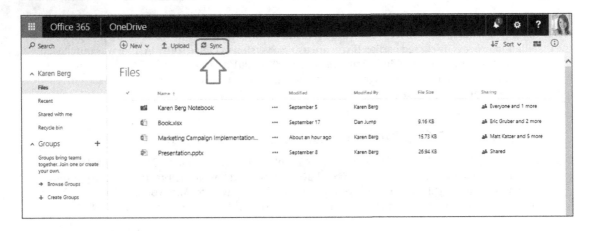

Figure 6-25. *OneDrive for Business ready to sync*

■ **Note** Do not select **Sync** until the software is installed on your desktop.

Step 2: Add OneDrive for Business to Your Desktop

There are two ways to add OneDrive for Business: as part of the Office 2016 (or Office 2013) download or as a separate download from the Office 365 site for Office 2007 or Office 2010. The simplest way to use OneDrive for Business is to install Office 2016. To download Office 2016, log in to Office 365 (at http://portal.office.com) and download the Office 365 2016 software.

1. Go to **http://portal.office.com**.

2. Sign in, selecting **Work or school account** (if prompted).

3. Click the gear icon in the upper-right corner.

4. Select **Office 365 Settings**.

5. Select **Install and manage software** (see Figure 6-26)

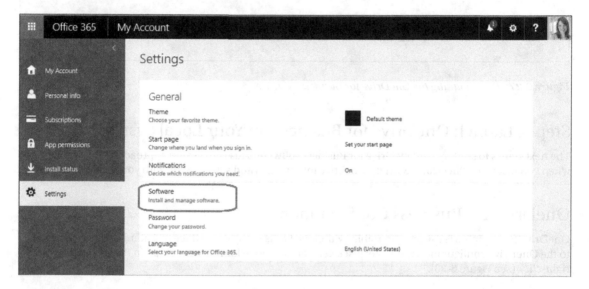

Figure 6-26. *Office 365 software download for OneDrive for Business*

Select **Install and manage software** and then select **OneDrive** (see Figure 6-27) to download the Sync tool to your desktop. Install the software onto your desktop.

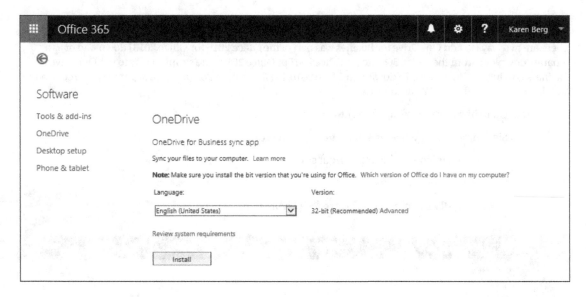

Figure 6-27. Downloading the OneDrive for Business software

Step 3: Launch OneDrive for Business on Your Local System

The next step is to start up the OneDrive for Business software. This is the same approach discussed earlier when you installed Office 2016. Start up Onedrive for Business and start to Sync with your desktop.

OneDrive for Business Configuration

OneDrive for Business is user-configurable, within the limits set by your Office 365 administrator. Access to the OneDrive configuration is simple: just select the OneDrive for Business cloud in the hidden icon and right-click (see Figure 6-28).

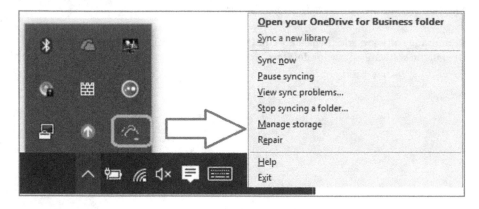

Figure 6-28. OneDrive for Business: Managing cloud syncing

You can add multiple libraries to synchronize with Office 365. However, when adding files from the Team Site, there are limits to the number of files and the size of the files that you can sync. A different Team Site location can be added from the hidden icons by right-clicking the OneDrive for Business icon, as seen in Figure 6-28. To add a different library to sync to your desktop, select **Sync a new library**. If you wish to stop the Office 365 sync or to add a different location to the sync content, right-click the OneDrive for Business icon and make the necessary changes.

■ **Note**   If you stop syncing a folder, the desktop folder will be converted to a non-synced folder. You will not lose any data in this process.

OneDrive: Checking Storage Allocation

Office 365 OneDrive for Business supports up to 1TB (or 1,000GB) of personal OneDrive storage. To determine the amount of storage that you are using, access the OneDrive status folder.

Once you have found the OneDrive for Business icon in the hidden icons (see Figure 6-29), right-click it (it's the blue cloud) and select **Manage storage**. This launches the status of the OneDrive for Business storage site. You have two options: view OneDrive for Business Storage or open the OneDrive for Business recycle bin. Select to view the **OneDrive Storage** site. The personal OneDrive storage shows the storage allocation free in MB. You have two selections: **View OneDrive for Business Storage**, and **Open OneDrive for Business Recycle Bin**.

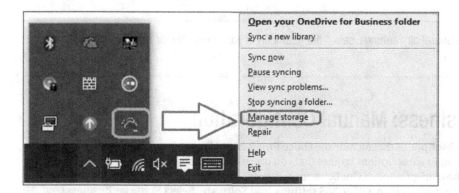

Figure 6-29. OneDrive for Business: Managing storage

Figure 6-30 shows that there is 1,024GB allocated storage and the storage used. In this case there are 1,024GB of storage left (this is a new OneDrive for Business site). OneDrive for Business has the same controls as SharePoint. The default configuration of OneDrive for Business supports versioning.

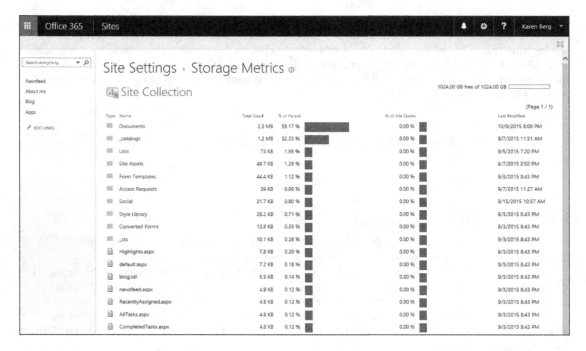

Figure 6-30. OneDrive for Business: Storage allocation

■ **Note** To access the SharePoint settings, select the gear icon in your OneDrive for Business site and select **Site settings**.

Skype for Business: Manual Configuration

Office 365 Enterprise subscriptions that include the Office Professional Plus software includes Skype for Business. However, the other subscriptions require that you download and configure Skype for Business. This is very similar to the configuration of OneDrive for Business. To access the Skype for Business software, log in to Office 365, select the gear icon, **Office 365 settings**, and **Software**. Select Skype for Business (see Figure 6-31) to install the software.

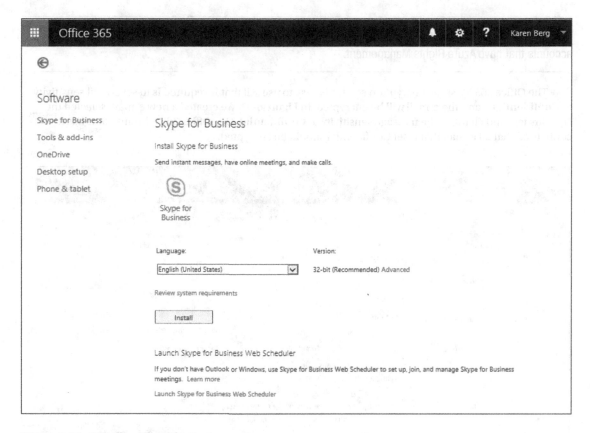

Figure 6-31. *Installing Skype for Business*

■ **Note**   Skype for Business is an optional installation for Office 365 Business Premium. The software is included with Office Pro Plus and E3/E5 subscriptions.

After downloading Skype for Business, follow the instructions to install the software. Once the software is installed, select Skype for Business and enter your Office 365 login and password to access the service.

Office 365 Encryption

Office 365 Enterprise subscriptions include Message Encryption and Rights Management. Rights Management is a service that is used to mitigate data loss, and Message Encryption is a service that is used to encrypt confidential information that is being sent via e-mail to an internal or external user via e-mail. The most common types of information that people encrypt are credit cards and other personal information. Encrypted e-mails may be read in any Office 365 e-mail address, or any e-mail address that has added Microsoft account security credentials. (Go to http://account.live.com, and select **Create an account**, and assign your e-mail address to the Microsoft account). An e-mail address without security credentials cannot be trusted.

■ **Note** Encryption is an optional service that your administrator can enable for E3 accounts and other accounts that have Azure Rights Management.

The Office 365 Message Encryption service is easy to use. All that is required is to set e-mail sensitivity to **Confidential**—and the e-mail will be encrypted. In Figure 6-32, we created a new e-mail, selected the **Options** tag, and changed the message sensitivity to **Confidential**. Our Office 365 administrator has it configured that all e-mail that is set Confidential should be encrypted.

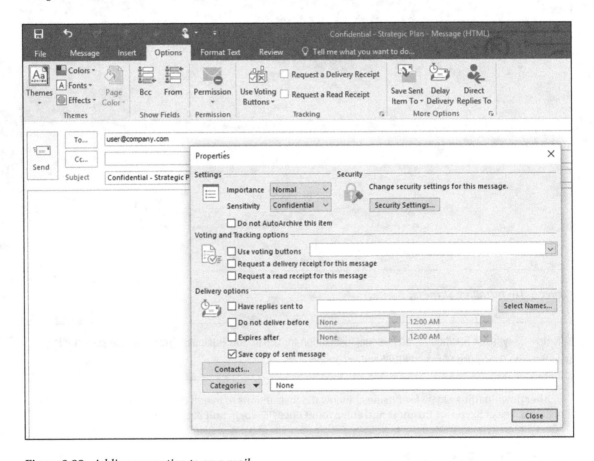

Figure 6-32. *Adding encryption to an e-mail*

When an encrypted e-mail is sent to a recipient, the user receives an e-mail with instructions to download the file and open the encryption link (see Figure 6-33).

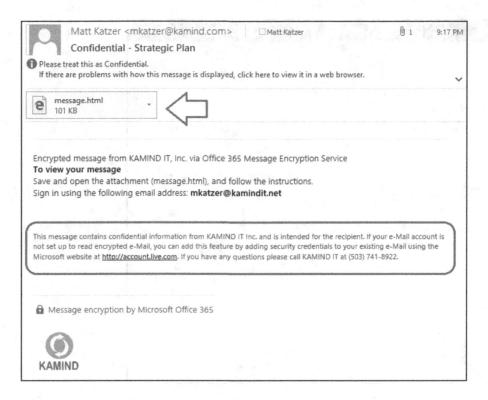

Figure 6-33. *Received an encrypted e-mail*

Once you download the file, and then save and open it, you see an e-mail notice that the message is encrypted (see Figure 6-34). To view the encrypted message, click **View your message** and open the e-mail using your e-mail account or a one-time passcode. If your e-mail account is not set up to read encrypted e-mail, you can add this feature by creating an account at http://account.live.com and assigning your e-mail address to a Microsoft account, or fall back to the one-time passcode.

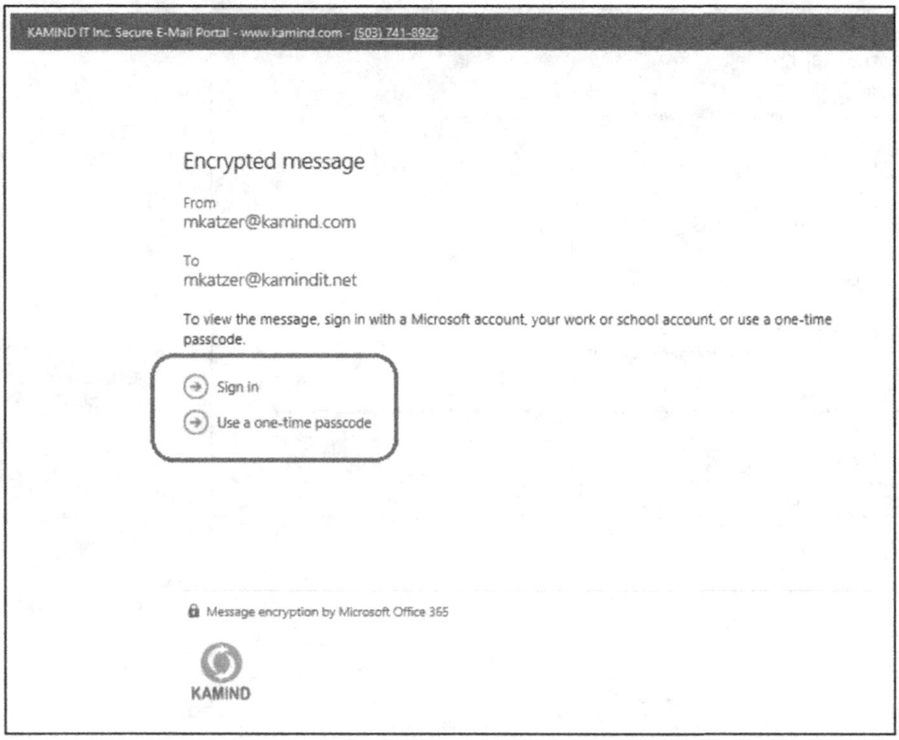

Figure 6-34. *Opening the encrypted e-mail header*

After you select the encrypted link, you can either select **Sign in** or **Use a one-time passcode**. If you want to sign in, make sure that you select the correct account to sign in to—either your Office 365 account or your Microsoft account—and open the encrypted e-mail (see Figure 6-35).

Figure 6-35. *Opening an encrypted e-mail with your Office 365 account or Microsoft account*

If you choose to select the one-time passcode, you are sent an e-mail and prompted to supply the code (see Figure 6-36).

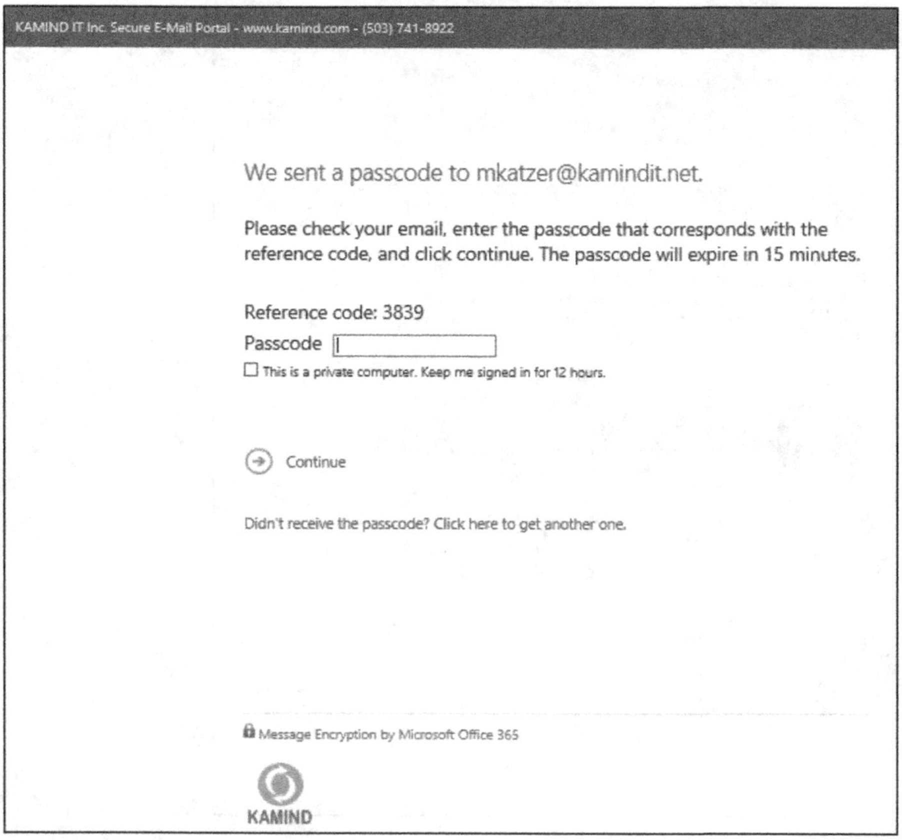

Figure 6-36. *Selecting one-time passcode instead of a Microsoft account*

The Microsoft Office 365 encryption service sends you an e-mail to the e-mail addressed that you specified in the encrypted e-mail (see Figure 6-37).

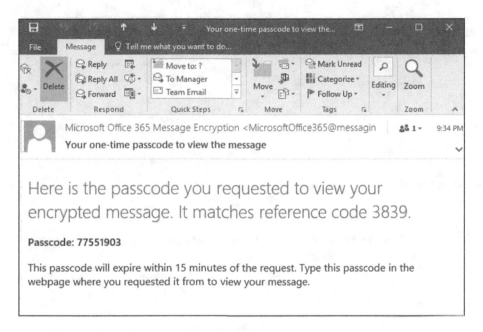

Figure 6-37. *Retrieving e-mail with encrypted passcode*

After you have entered the passcode, you can read the encrypted e-mail (see Figure 6-38). Encrypted e-mails are a persistence service. Once you receive an encrypted e-mail, it is stored in an Office 365 service so that you can access the encrypted e-mail at a later date.

Figure 6-38. *Reading the encrypted e-mail*

Office 365 Message Encryption is designed to send confidential (or private information) to external (or internal) e-mail recipients. Office 365 e-mail encryption allows the recipients to reply to the sender in the same encrypted e-mail. The message that is returned to the sender is automatically encrypted. Office 365 encryption ensures that the entire thread (or conversation) is encrypted.

Office 365 encryption also allows you to dynamically encrypt e-mail based on various rules. For example, HIPAA and PII rules are the most common rules to protect private information because they are required by federal regulations.

Office 2007/2010: Desktop Setup Configuration

Office 2007 and Office 2010 require additional software to be installed on your desktop. When you run the desktop setup (see Figure 6-39), Office 365 downloads a setup configuration tool that updates your desktop and Office software with the latest patches and security information. Office 2013 and Office 2016 were designed for Office 365 and do not require any additional desktop configuration.

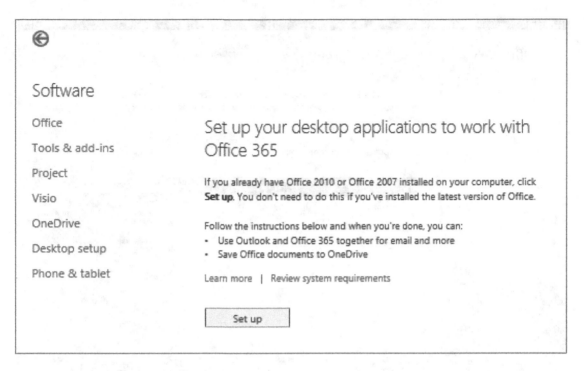

Figure 6-39. *Installing desktop setup*

To install the desktop configuration tool, select **Setup**. This action downloads the desktop configuration tool that is streamed from the Office 365 servers. Once the desktop configuration tool is installed, click **Setup** in **Set up and configure your Office desktop apps**, and then follow these next steps.

1. Click the check box beside the applications that need to be configured (see Figure 6-40). Normally, the startup process checks the correct items. Click **Continue**. Close any applications that you need to.

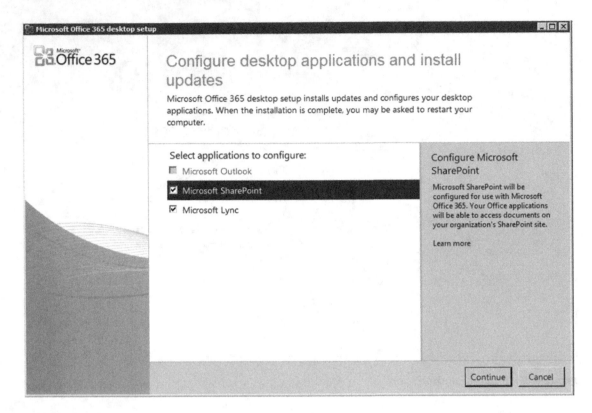

Figure 6-40. *Office 365 validation options*

2. Click **Finish** (see Figure 6-41). You might need to restart your computer.

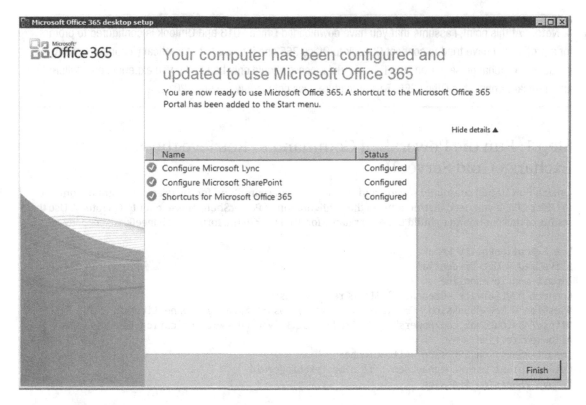

Figure 6-41. *Office 365 successful configuration update*

■ **Note** Test the desktop setup on a test system before you deploy it in a larger enterprise. I recommend that you upgrade to Office 2016. It is a much better experience for the user.

Outlook 2007/2010/2013: Manual Configuration for Office 365

There are cases where you need to manually configure the Outlook 2007/2010/2013 desktop client. Office 365 uses Microsoft Exchange 2013; it no longer uses RPC or SSL (HTTPS) to connect to the Exchange Server through the client access server. The new structure uses exchangeGUID@<compnay.com> to connect e-mail services. Since there are no longer any mail servers to configure, you need to determine the ExchangeGuid ID as the server and create the Exchange Server name to manually configure the Outlook client. To do this, read the following instructions.

■ **Note**   At this point, I assume that you have downloaded Office 2013 and Outlook is configured to prompt for a profile. You have tried to connect Outlook to Office 365 and it failed to automatically connect. Usually this is due to an exchange server on site. This manual process should only be used if you experienced a failure to automatically connect to Office 365. This procedure does not work with Office 2016.

Step 1: Run the PowerShell Command to Retrieve the ExchangeGuid Server ID

Open a PowerShell command session and run the following command for the users who cannot connect to Office 365. If you need instructions on the configuration of PowerShell, please refer to Chapter 7. Use the results of this command to build the server name for each user in the format exchangeGuid@company.com.

```
Set-ExecutionPolicy RemoteSigned
$LiveCred = Get-Credential
Import-module msonline
Connect-MSOLService –Credential $LiveCred –Verbose
$Session = New-PSSession -ConfigurationName Microsoft.Exchange-ConnectionUri
https://ps.Outlook.com/powershell/ -Credential $LiveCred -Authentication Basic –
AllowRedirection
Import-PSSession $Session -AllowClobber
Get-Recipient user@compnay.com | fl name, exchangeguid
Remove-PSSession $Session
```

Step 2: Configuration of Outlook

Change Outlook to prompt for a profile (see the following section). At this point, you have tried the automatic configuration (and verified that the autodiscover records were set up correctly). The only option left is the manual configuration of Office 2013. To begin the manual configuration, start Outlook and select **New** (see Figure 6-42) to create a new profile.

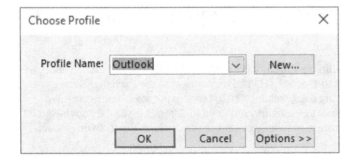

Figure 6-42.   *Outlook: Choose Profile*

If you wish to speed up the configuration of Outlook, log in to the web site at http://Office.microsoft.com before you start the manual connection process. Outlook uses a secured HTTPS connection and uses the same connection that you enter for your browser. If the automatic configuration fails, create a new profile and select the **Manual** button.

After you name your profile, save it, and then follow the wizard. Select **Microsoft Exchange Server or compatible service** and then click **Next** (see Figure 6-43).

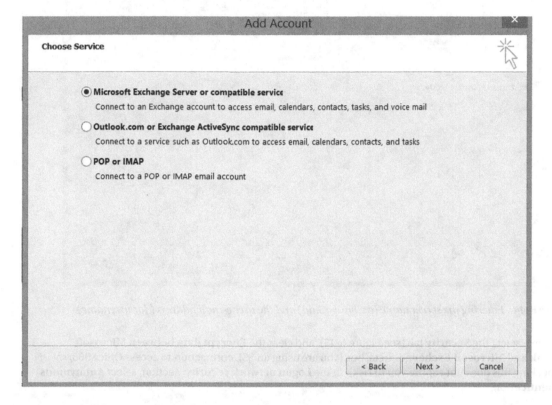

Figure 6-43. Selecting Exchange (manual configuration)

In step 1, we ran the PowerShell script to retrieve the ExchangeGuid. We appended the domain name after the ExchangeGuid to build the server name (in this format: ExchangeGuid@company.com). As an example, using the KAMIND.com domain, the server name would look like c29d8a0e-26c0-7d4a-8bd2-df1658f1f421@kamind.com. Enter **exchangeGuid@company.com** for the server (see Figure 6-44). The username for Office 365 is the user's e-mail address (the user Principal Name should be the same for Office 365). Select **More Settings** to enter the extended parameters of the connection to Office 365. *Do not select* to check the name.

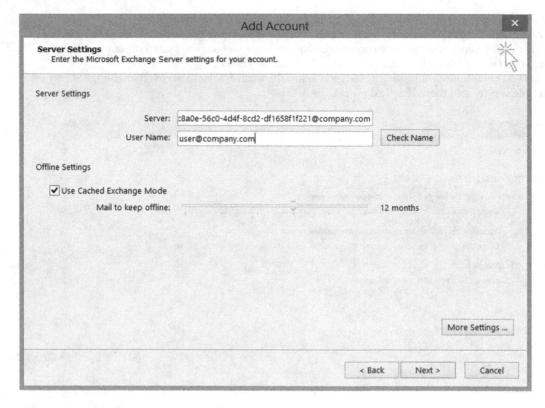

Figure 6-44. *Entering the server name (exchangeGuid) and the user e-mail address (for username)*

Next, select the **Security** tab (see Figure 6-45), and clear the **Encrypt data between Microsoft Outlook and Microsoft Exchange** check box (you are using an SSL connection to access Office 365, so unchecking this does not expose you to risk). In the **Logon network security**, section, select **Anonymous Authentication**.

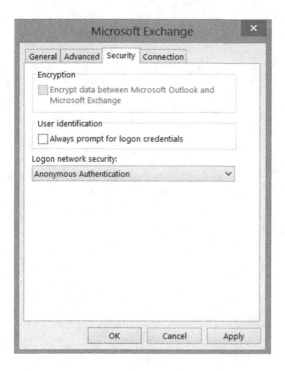

Figure 6-45. *Remove the encryption check mark, and set to anonymous settings*

Set the security to the proper values. Then select the **Connection** tab, and select the **Connect to Microsoft Exchange using HTTP** check box. Select **Exchange Proxy Settings** (see Figure 6-46) to set the connection properties.

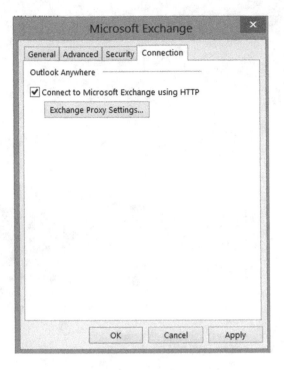

Figure 6-46. *Selecting the Exchange Server proxy*

Next, select the Exchange Server proxy settings. Enter the following settings for Office 365 Exchange Server (see Figure 6-47 and Table 6-2).

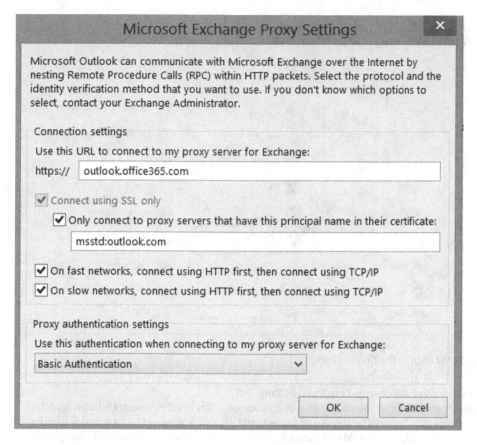

Figure 6-47. *Manual configuration of HTTPS proxy settings*

Table 6-2. *Correct Setting for HTTPS Connection to Server*

Field	Value
Proxy server	http://Outlook.Office365.com
Principal name	msstd:Outlook.com
Connected Fast/Slow	Check both check boxes (see Figure 6-47)
Authentication	Basic

Figure 6-48. *Selecting the mail in the Control Panel*

The parameters that you have changed are listed in Table 6-2.

Select **Apply**, and then **OK**. Enter the password when prompted. You need to restart Outlook, and then it should connect to Office 365. You will be requested to log in to Office 365. Restart Outlook and select the new profile that you just created. You should see Outlook connect to Office 365 and download your profile.

If Outlook does not connect, verify the parameters used in the manual connection. Usually the problem is that the server name is incorrect or that the username is wrong. Verify the parameters and try again.

Setting Outlook to Prompt for a Profile

There are cases where you need to manually configure Outlook to prompt for profile or default to a different profile. You can do this either by using the command line, with an option when you launch Outlook, or by setting Outlook to prompt for profile in the Control Panel. To set the Office 2013 or 2016 to show the prompt for a profile dialog box, use one of the following commands in the Command window.

```
Office 2013:   Prompt for profiles Options

"c:\program files\microsoft Office\Office15\Outlook.exe" /profiles

Office 2016:   Prompt for profiles Options

"c:\program files\microsoft Office\Office16\Outlook.exe" /profiles
```

If you choose to use the Control Panel to set the prompt for a profile, select the mail icon and then select the data profile properties. Follow the steps outlined next.

Step 1: Select the Control Panel

If you are using Windows 10, search for the Control Panel to bring up the screen shown in Figure 6-49.

Figure 6-49. Selecting Show Profiles in the Control Panel

Step 2: Select Mail 2016 and Configure Profile

Next, select **Show Profiles** to show the different Outlook profiles (see Figure 6-49).

Step 3: Set the Profile Option to Prompt

Select **Prompt for a profile to be used** (see Figure 6-50).

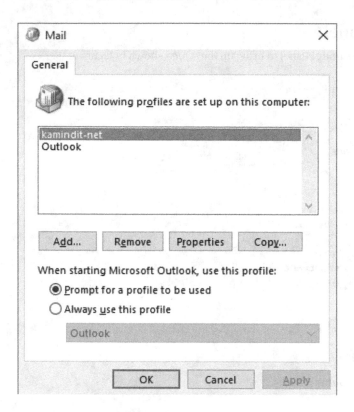

Figure 6-50. *Setting the prompt for a profile options*

You can either create a new profile at this stage and set it the as the default, or select **Prompt for profile** and allow the user to create a new profile when Outlook is started.

Summary

I have been asked about the simplest way to describe Office 365. From my perspective, it is a business process change. In previous chapters, we reviewed cloud security and looked at the applications in Office 365. I wanted to wrap up this chapter with a view of how simple it is to use Office 365, and share with you some hard-earned configuration lessons. As you look back on what you have accomplished in your own Office 365 company, it is amazing what you can do with the cloud. The one phrase that I can use to sum up Office 365 and this chapter? It simply "just works"—as it always should have done.

Reference Links

There is a lot of information about Office 365 on the Web, but the issue is finding the right site. The information contained in this chapter is a combination of our team's experience in doing deployments and the knowledge of support information that has been published by third parties.

Office 365 Learning Center

- http://Office.microsoft.com/en-us/Office-home-for-Office-365-FX102821134.aspx

Office 365 Documents and Training Videos

- http://fasttrack.microsoft.com

Using Office 365 OneDrive for Business

- http://www.youtube.com/watch?v=c74OqwWR-cs

Adding OneDrive for Business for Office 2010 and 2007

- http://www.microsoft.com/en-US/download/details.aspx?id=39050

Get help with Office 365

- http://www.kamind.com

Update information from Office 365: Migrating and managing your business in the cloud

- http://www.mattkatzer.com

Next Steps

Your Office 365 systems have been set up and configured. At this point, you understand the features of Office 365 and you are ready to move forward. However, your work is not yet complete. There is more to do depending on your Office 365 configuration. It is recommended that you return to Chapters 2, 3, and 4 and review the user configuration.

Chapter 3: The Apps. Office 365 is owned by the business, and the data is only available to the business for Business use. Office 365 takes advantage of social enterprise through the different data mining capabilities that are present in services like Gmail, Dropbox, Facebook, LinkedIn, and other social media sites. Those capabilities are applied to your Office 365 site to improve your business productivity. This chapter describes Office 365 apps and discusses how you use them in your business to improve communications and productivity.

Chapter 4: Cloud Security Best Practices. One of the issues that all managers are faced with is the management of data and security and learning best practices. In this chapter, you explore the different capabilities of Office 365 and the monitoring that is in place to manage your Office 365 company to ensure that your data remains private. This chapter covers the most common approaches to Office 365 migration.

Chapter 5: Office 365 Deployment Step by Step. The secret to a successful deployment to Office 365 is picking the correct plan that supports your business. The key to a successful migration to Office 365 is the planning and purchase process. Once you select a plan, your primary consideration must be to ensure that the migration process is seamless for your organization. This chapter describes the basic purchase information and it details the choices. It concludes with information about pre-deployment, deployment, and post-deployment.

CHAPTER 7

■ ■ ■

Managing Your Office 365 Deployment

Previous chapters discussed how to move your business to Office 365. This chapter is focused on the administration of Office 365. Time is money, and as an administrator, you are looking for the simplest way to accomplish a task. This chapter outlines the common tasks that administrators are asked to perform in the administration of Office 365. These tasks range from renaming users to adding e-mail aliases, to creating shared mailboxes, to changing the subscription type. There are four different ways to administer Office 365: the Office 365 administrator center, PowerShell, the cloud-based tool Nuvolex (www.Nuvolex.com), and the local Active Directory managed from your Windows Server. Let's review these management tools—with the exception of the local Active Directory management, which is beyond the scope of this chapter.

Office 365 Administration Overview

As an administrator, you'll find that your company needs different components and applications for the different business roles of the employees in your business. Office 365 allows you to add different components to your subscription. In some cases, your business needs change and you'll be in a situation where you have too many licenses (or too few). You can easily change your subscription mix. To see the additional options available for your subscription, select **Billing ➤ Subscriptions** (see Figure 7-1). If you are interested in reducing the subscriptions, then select **More actions** and the appropriate option. If you are looking at the different subscription options, select **Add subscriptions**. The process of adding components (or applications) is simple: you purchase the subscriptions (select **Buy now** or **Start free trial**; see Figure 7-2) that meet your needs and add the purchased licenses to the user account.

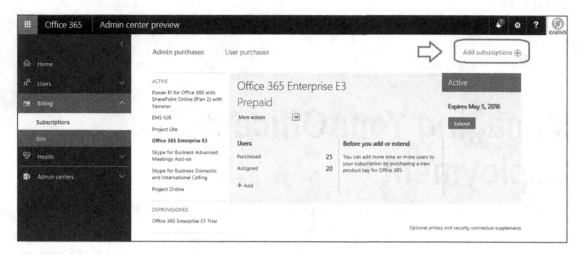

Figure 7-1. *Admin center: purchase options Office 365*

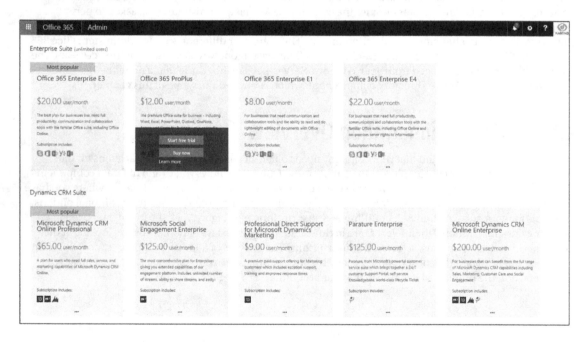

Figure 7-2. *Admin center: purchase options Office 365*

Global administrator is the first account created when you sign up for Office 365. The global administrator account has full access to all Office 365 resources. You can use the PowerShell environment to configure capabilities, or you can use the graphical interfaces in the various admin centers (Exchange, Skype for Business, or SharePoint) to manage Office 365 capabilities. The only rule to remember is this: to change features using PowerShell or in the administration graphical interfaces, you must have a license (such as Exchange, Skype for Business, SharePoint, or other centers) provision to the account that is being used to change that feature. If a global administrator's account tries to change features on a subscription area that the account is not licensed to use, that action will not be permitted. In some cases, the global administrator is denied access to the GUI command options (access to the eDiscovery Center, for instance). Partners with delegated administrator rights do not have a license and cannot access a user's data. In some cases, the PowerShell commands will fail (with no failure notice).

■ **Note** Only selected Microsoft Partners have the ability to offer delegated administrator services to their customers. The global administrator must approve the rights to a Microsoft Partner to act as a delegated administrator. Microsoft Partners that have delegated administration capabilities have earned rights to use this service offering.

A good example is using PowerShell to set up a shared mailbox for smartphones. If you *do not* have an Exchange license assigned to the global admin account, the Exchange PowerShell scripts will fail when they make a set-mailbox call. There are many different commands that you can use to manage Office 365 with PowerShell (see Figure 7-3).

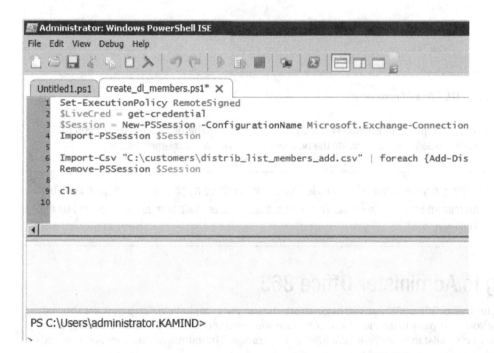

Figure 7-3. PowerShell command to add members to distribution list

For example, you can use PowerShell to administer Office 365 (see Figure 7-3) or you can use the GUI interface (see Figure 7-4). Both interfaces provide the same results, but one is much more scalable than the other is. As an administrator, you use both interfaces. The only rule to remember is that you must have a license assigned to the account that you are using to grant permissions to the user accounts.

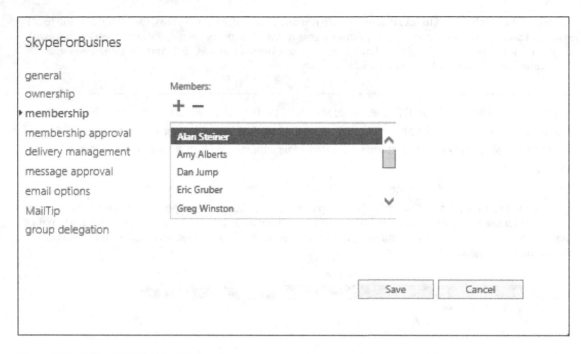

Figure 7-4. *Office 365 DL list: add members*

The objective of this chapter is to provide you with the tools and capabilities necessary for you to administer your own Office 365 site and provide the best level of service to your organization.

■ **Note**   If you have Directory Synchronization enabled, you cannot edit some properties of a user's mailbox, because it's out of the current user's write scope. This means that the user mailbox must be managed by the on-premises Active Directory.

Preparing to Administer Office 365

Once you have purchased Office 365, you can begin to administer the company. In Chapter 5, we showed you how to move your company to the cloud and configure your mail services. At the end of the migration steps, we included a checklist to verify your Office 365 configuration. This administration section is based on the assumption that you have completed this step.

Final Checklist

This information is reprinted from the previous chapter. If you have not verified your configuration, please do this now. These configuration options are discussed in each of the setup and migration steps.

1. If you have desktop Office 2007/2010 and are using Outlook 2007/2010 (and you are not using Office 2013/2016), run the desktop upgrade for Outlook 2007/2010 from the Office 365 software download. If you do not do this, Outlook 2007/2010 will stop working.

2. Check the domain configuration. If you have any actions to complete (under the action header), please complete them before you move forward.

3. Verify that your Office 365 domain is set to Authoritative and is not shared for e-mail. (This will only be set if you have run a test group).

4. Verify that you have placed a local DNS record in your on-premises DNS server. You need to add an Autodiscover CNAME to your **internal DNS** that points to **autodiscover.outlook.com**.

5. If you have an on-premises Exchange Server, and you have migrated to Office 365, set the Autodiscover record to **$NULL** with the following command (note that, once set, local clients cannot autodiscover the local Exchange Server):

   ```
   Set-ClientAccessServer -Identity "<name>" -AutoDiscoverServiceInternalUri $NULL
   ```

6. Extend the 14-day delete holding time to a 30-day delete holding time. Run the PowerShell command.

   a. Extend the 30-day delete for a mailbox.

   ```
   Set-mailbox user@contoso.com -retaindeleteditemsfor 30
   ```

   b. Extend the 30-day delete for the organization.

   ```
   Get-mailbox | Set-mailbox -retaindeleteditemsfor 30
   ```

7. Enable the audit logs on all users' mailboxes. The default logs are kept for 30 days and can be extended to multiple years.

   ```
   $UserMailboxes = Get-mailbox -Filter
   {(RecipientTypeDetails -eq 'UserMailbox')}

   $UserMailboxes | ForEach
   {Set-Mailbox $_.Identity -AuditEnabled $true}
   ```

8. The default retention policies *are not enabled* until the archive is enabled. If you *enable the archive* on a user mailbox, the retention polices begin to execute. For example, the default retention policy is two years. When the retention policy executes, e-mail is deleted.

9. Verify the retention tags in the retention policy and remove or create a new policy.

10. Verify that you have enabled Yammer on your subscription. To enable Yammer, select **Dashboard**, followed by included services, and then the primary domain for the Yammer Enterprise configuration.

11. Verify that you have transferred all of the distribution groups and contacts over to Office 365.

12. Enable Azure AD and create an Azure account. Different partners provide different capabilities for migration. KAMIND IT enables Azure AD and Microsoft Enterprise Mobility Services (EMS) as part of all migrations to Office 365.

13. (Optional.) Create a global admin account to be used by the Nuvolex software. Nuvolex is a third-party software package (discussed later in this chapter) that simplifies the administration of Office 365 and Azure.

■ **Note**   Nuvolex has been mentioned many times in this section. Nuvolex is a cloud admin tool that KAMIND IT uses to manage accounts with least privileges. Nuvolex does not allow you to manage Office 365 users that the administrator is not granted permission to administer.

Common Office 365 Administration Tasks

Office 365, in our example, has nine administration centers: Office 365, Exchange, Skype for Business (Skype for Business), SharePoint, CRM, Power BI, Compliance, Azure AD, and Bing Places for Business. You can reach the admin center by selecting the **A** (see Figure 7-5). In our example, we have an E3 subscription, Power BI, and Intune extensions. Your subscription may have a different number of applications, depending on your licenses and the additional administration centers that are added, based on the optional subscriptions. This chapter focuses on the areas of administration in Office 365 using Exchange and Skype for Business. The other administration centers (CRM, Power BI SharePoint, Compliance and Data Loss Prevention, and Exchange Online Protection) are beyond the scope of this chapter. What we have included here are the most common questions that we have been asked about Office 365.

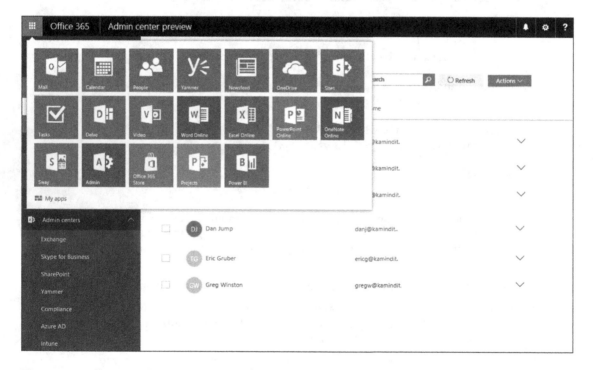

Figure 7-5. *Office 365 admin center preview (with CRM and Power BI option)*

The Office 365 administration areas that we address are Office 365 dashboard and licenses, Exchange administration (see Table 7-1), and Skype for Business/Skype administration (see Table 7-2). We have included information on the configuration of PowerShell and wrap up this chapter with an overview of Nuvolex, our cloud administration tool. We use PowerShell to configure some functions that are not in the Office 365 GUI, such as OneDrive for Business. At any time that you need to get back to the home page in the administration center, select the nine-block grid in the upper left-hand corner, or select Office 365 in the admin panel. The grid allows easy movement to the different Office 365 functions.

Table 7-1. *Office 365 Administration Functions*

Task	Description
Administration roles	Office 365 supports five different administrator roles: global administrator, billing administrator, user administrator, service administrator, and password administrator.
Domain verification (and DNS review)	Domain verification, DNS review, and service record management.
Adding , deleting, and restoring users	Account creation and user management.
Renaming users (no Exchange mailbox)	Simple steps to rename a user account and change the e-mail address with little impact on the user.
Adding/changing licenses	Subscription/license management.
Security groups	Domain security groups management for federated services.
Partner delegated administration	Partner administration management.

Table 7-2. *Exchange Administration Functions*

Task	Description
Exchange administration roles	Review of the different Exchange roles for managing Office 365.
Default user role	Explains the default user roles and permissions.
Conference Room/Resource Room	Explains how to set up and manage a conference room.
Changing a user name and e-mail address	Changing an e-mail is a two-step process. This is how you change the e-mail address of the user accounts.
Adding a user alias	Adding an alias e-mail or changing the default e-mail address.
Shared mailbox	Explains how to create a shared mailbox for the smartphone or Outlook.
Creating a distribution group	Explains the different Office 365 distribution groups.
Sending e-mail from an alias e-mail address	Allows the user to send an e-mail from a different e-mail address than the user's own e-mail address.
Smartphone management	User configuration options for Exchange.
Troubleshooting: Autodiscover	Desktop configuration to ignore Exchange Server.

User accounts can be synchronized in two ways in Office 365: through a manual process (single user load/bulk load) or via Active Directory Synchronization accounts created through an Active Directory process that can only be managed by on-premises Active Directory tools.

There are different types of administrative accounts on Office 365. The root account (the first account that was created when you purchased Office 365) is a global administrator account. You can create additional global administrator accounts to manage Office 365. Global administrator accounts do not need a license to perform global administration functions. However, the global administration account does require a license to perform administration functions at the functional level. For example, if you wish to configure Exchange services or Skype for Business services, you need Skype for Business and Exchange licenses assigned to the account. The same is the case with SharePoint. If you do not have a license, or if you are running Active Directory Synchronization, you cannot configure the functions of the service, only the global access controls for the service. Table 7-2 shows a listing of the common Exchange functions that you use to manage Office 365.

■ **Note**   If you are using Directory Synchronization, Exchange functions are controlled by the on-premises Active Directory or by using the Nuvolex cloud administration tool.

Skype for Business allows you to communicate internally without any configuration. The normal configuration is the enabling of communications with external users (Skype and smartphones). The problem is external communication. The administration topics in Table 7-3 are the configuration changes that are required to address these communications across different external domains. Figure 7-6 is a snapshot of the common Skype for Business configurations that can be changed by a global administrator.

Table 7-3. *Skype for Business Administration Functions*

Task	Description
Setting up Skype for Business	Enabling Skype for Business to communicate with non-company users
Adding Skype voice and porting phone numbers	Adding Skype voice local and international calling
Configuration dial-in conferencing	Adding dial-in conferencing for Skype for Business users
Communicating with Skype users	Step-by-step instructions to enable Skype for Business to Skype integration
Restricting Skype for Business users capability	Restricting Skype for Business capabilities in the admin center

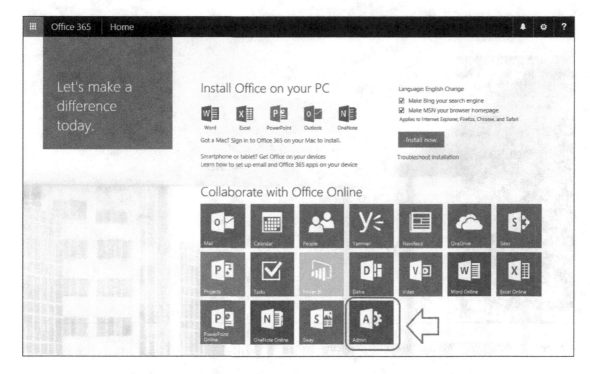

Figure 7-6. *Dashboard after logging in as an administrator*

In addition to the administration section, we have also included an overview and usage section on PowerShell and Nuvolex. PowerShell is extremely useful if you have to implement unique functions, or have to repeat a set of tasks multiple times. Nuvolex is used to simplify administration of Office 365 for Tier 3 help-desk support. Office 365 may be completely administered from PowerShell, and our discussion is not a complete list. The objective of this chapter is to show you the various options you can use in managing Office 365.

Office 365 Administration Center

The Office 365 administration consoles are easy to access once the user logs into Office 365 (see Figure 7-6). Once you have selected the admin console, select the admin center (see Figure 7-7). The admin center only shows the admin console for the licenses that have been activated for Office 365. For example, if the Skype for Business licenses are not purchased, there is no access to the Skype for Business admin center. The Office 365 admin center is used to administer global functions. These oversee permissions, security groups, domain management, and support and system health. However, the Office 365 admin center is also limited if Directory Synchronization is enabled. When Directory Synchronization is enabled, Office 365 acts as a backup to the on-premises Active Directory. In this case, only those functions that are not on the on-premises servers can be modified by Office 365.

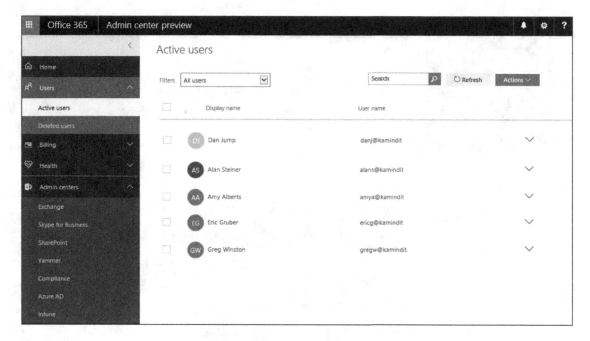

Figure 7-7. *New Office 365 admin center preview*

■ **Note** Office 365 will soon look similar to Windows 10 and Office 2016. To help with the transition to the new admin center, we are using the preview center. Most of this chapter is focused on the individual administration centers.

Accessing the Office 365 admin center is simple: just log in to Office 365. If you have the permissions, you will land at the main page. Select the **Administration** dashboard (see Figure 7-6). If your permissions are limited, your menu options will be limited to reflect your privileges. Admin center access is based on the permission settings. Office 365 plans have different administration centers and configuration options. To access the administration area for Office 365, select **Admin** and then select the appropriate **admin center** you wish to use (see Figure 7-7 and Figure 7-8).

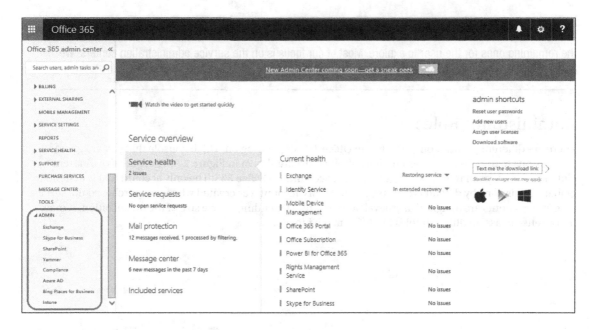

Figure 7-8. *Overview of the old Office 365 administration center*

The functionality of both administrator centers is the same, however; the look is cleaner in the new center, and it is easier to find things. For example, look at changing the subscription mix (described earlier). The new center allows you to change the subscription mix in one place; the old center requires you to change the subscription information in four different places. The new admin center has all of the subscriptions in the same place. This makes it simpler to administer Office 365.

■ **Note**   Are you missing the new admin center look? It is easy to add. In the old Office 365 admin center, select services, then Update. Enable Update for the entire organization.

The Office 365 administration center is organized into separate administration centers. The main center is the Office 365 dashboard. This supports the most common administration function. Earlier we discussed the different types of administrators. Different versions of the administration dashboard appear in Figures 7-7 and 7-8. The key areas that we will focus on are the Users (new admin center preview), External Sharing, Domain, and Service Centers.

The global administrator sees all administrator options and has the ability to configure the administration centers, such as Exchange, Skype for Business, SharePoint, Yammer, Compliance, Azure AD, and Intune. Other service centers are added based on the optional subscriptions that were purchased. For example, if you purchased Dynamics CRM, this would be added to your subscription. In this case, we added Windows Intune licenses to our Office 365 tenant. Once you have selected the administration dashboard, you can select the different administration centers that you need to configure your Office 365 company. These areas are organized as sections later in this chapter.

> ■ **Note**   We review the key administration configuration areas that are important for Office 365, and leave the remaining ones for the user to explore. Most of our focus is on the service administration centers. We recommend that the user explore the admin center preview.

Administrator Roles

There are different permission structures in Office 365, depending on which console that you are given permissions to use. The basic permissions of Office 365 are shown in Figure 7-9. There are five different global permissions that may be assigned to user accounts on Office 365. The only account that is assigned global permissions by default is the first account. This account was created when you purchased the service. All other accounts are assigned user-level permissions. Depending on the size of the organization, it may make sense to assign different roles for different job functions.

Office 365 admin roles

Permission	Billing admin	Global admin	Password admin	Service admin	User management admin
View organization and user information	Yes	Yes	Yes	Yes	Yes
Manage support tickets	Yes	Yes	Yes	Yes	Yes
Reset user passwords	No	Yes	Yes; with limitations. This admin can only reset passwords for non-admins.	No	Yes; with limitations. This admin can't reset passwords for billing, global, and service admins.
Perform billing and purchasing operations	Yes	Yes	No	No	No
Create and manage user views	No	Yes	No	No	Yes
Create, edit, and delete users and groups, and manage user licenses	No	Yes	No	No	Yes; with limitations. This admin can't delete a global admin or create other admins.
Manage domains	No	Yes	No	No	No
Manage organization information	No	Yes	No	No	No
Delegate admin roles to others	No	Yes	No	No	No
Use directory synchronization	No	Yes	No	No	No

Figure 7-9. *Office 365 administrative roles (courtesy of Microsoft)*

Microsoft's approach is to follow administration management similar to on-premises Active Directory. Active Directory Synchronization and Active Directory Federation Services are used to "sync" the AD environment to Office 365. The Office 365 (and Azure) permissions are global in design, and the individual admin centers are used to restrict permissions. For example, global administrators have all rights, but in order to access eDiscovery data, they need to be placed in the appropriate Exchange administration permission groups. Smaller companies do not need to have such distributed administration rights and tend to be less granular. Small organizations typically assign three roles: global administrator, billing administrator, and password administrator.

Step back and look at your company and the different roles you can assign to personnel in your company. Microsoft's security model is to assign the least role possible and to grant basic permissions that are required to complete the job. When you assign roles, look at Figures 7-9 and 7-10, and verify that you are providing access at the appropriate level needed to execute the administrative task. Table 7-4 has detailed descriptions of the different administrator rights. At KAMIND IT, we use Nuvolex to restrict administration rights. This provides a better-managed help desk, where we can assign limited rights to our support personnel.

Office 365 admin role extensions

Office 365 admin role	Role in Microsoft Exchange Online	Role in SharePoint Online	Role in Lync Online
global admin	Exchange Online administrator Company administrator	SharePoint Online administrator	Lync Online administrator
billing admin	N/A	N/A	N/A
password admin	Help Desk administrator	N/A	Lync Online administrator
service admin	N/A	N/A	N/A
user management admin	N/A	N/A	Lync Online administrator

Figure 7-10. *Permission mapping between Office 365 and different services (courtesy of Microsoft)*

Table 7-4. *Office 365 Role Descriptions*

Role	Description
Global administrator	This is the company administrator. Users in this role have access to everything or the permission to add them to a dedicated role where they do not have permission (such as discovery management).
Billing administrator	Access to all financial transactions. Delegated partners do not have access to this information.
Password administrator	They can reset only passwords of users and other administrators at the same level of permissions.
Service support administrator	This is a limited administration role. Users in this rule can only view the portal and assign support tickets. Typically, users that are assigned this role have a different role assigned to the different subsystems, such as Exchange (see Figure 7-7).
User management administrator	These users can assign licenses and passwords but cannot make changes to other admin accounts that have more privileges than they do.

■ **Note** Global administrators are assigned all rights by default. A global administrator can grant themselves the rights to read any users mailbox by simply opening a mailbox other than their own. Business owners are cautioned to grant these rights only to those that need them.

The typical Office 365 configuration leaves one account (usually the root account—the initial Office 365 account) as a global admin user without any user licenses. Some organizations leave this as a global admin account, and others use it as a user account. Regardless of what you do, the first account is the root account. The root account should never be used as a user account. The root account in Office 365 is the base account that is used to create all the different services that are linked to the Office 365 tenant. As Microsoft has deployed new versions of Office 365, the dependence of the root account has been minimized. We recommend that you do not delete or assign a user to this account.

In the past, the first account was a sacred account, and many Office 365 services depended on this account. Microsoft addressed the dependency of the first account by creating a new internal Office 365 group known as the *company administrators*. All global admins are members of the company administrator group. This group is where the base permissions are assigned in Office 365. This internal account reduces the criticality of using the root account as a user account.

Our approach in setting up Office 365 customers has changed over the years. Along with the change, we always recommend the following configuration for our new Office 365 clients. There are additional measures you can take in the configuration of your Office 365 company. Some of these were discussed in our security chapter. Our typical configuration for Office 365 includes the following.

- Enable 360-day auditing for all delegated administration and administration access (see the PowerShell sections).

- Enable EMS productivity suite with extended security analytics.

- Deploy two-factor authentication on global admin accounts.

- Do not use a global admin account for any user e-mails.

- Set passwords to change every 90 days.

- Review the EMS logs weekly and look for problem.

The Office 365 administration functions that are covered in the configuration sections are dashboard, setup (discussed in a previous chapter), users' admin center (preview), external sharing, and domain setup/configuration. The services section covers the different administration centers.

Config: Adding, Deleting, and Restoring Users

Office 365 supports many features that you can configure through the Office 365 user interface. Some actions (such as setting conference room permissions) are only available using PowerShell. If you are running Federation Services (large organizations), you can use your on-premises tools for Exchange 2010/2013/2016 or Active Directory tools to configure services (and sync those changes into the cloud. Our focus in this chapter is on the user configuration of Office 365 using the Office 365 interface.

There are four primary user operations for administration:

- Adding single users via the user interface

- Bulk-adding using a CSV file and the GUI interface

- Deleting users

- Restoring users

If you need to assign user passwords, you need to use the PowerShell commands. Typically, we load the users using the bulk load options, and then we assign the passwords using PowerShell. If you have a federated server (using DirSync or ADFS), you need to assign those passwords using the on-premises Active Directory server.

Users: Adding Users via the User Interface

Log in as an administrator (at www.office365.com or http://portal.microsoftonline.com) as shown in Figure 7-9. Click the nine-block grid (at the top left). Next, click **Admin ➤ Admin center preview ➤ Users ➤ Active users**. Select the **Actions** (see Figure 7-11), then select the **+ Add users** to add a new user.

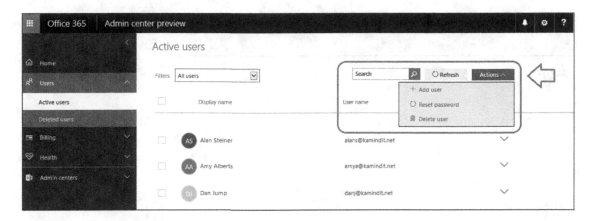

Figure 7-11. Adding users to Office 365

Fill in the information for the user and create the account. The minimum information you need to create a user is the username (first, last), e-mail address, and subscription product. There are additional configuration options on user accounts (contacts, password, products, and administration roles). There are four steps to setting up a user account.

1. Set up the user name and primary e-mail address.

2. Set the user password.

3. Set the user administration permission (no administrator rights is the default).

4. Assign a license.

These steps are reviewed next.

Step 1: Add User Information and E-mail Address

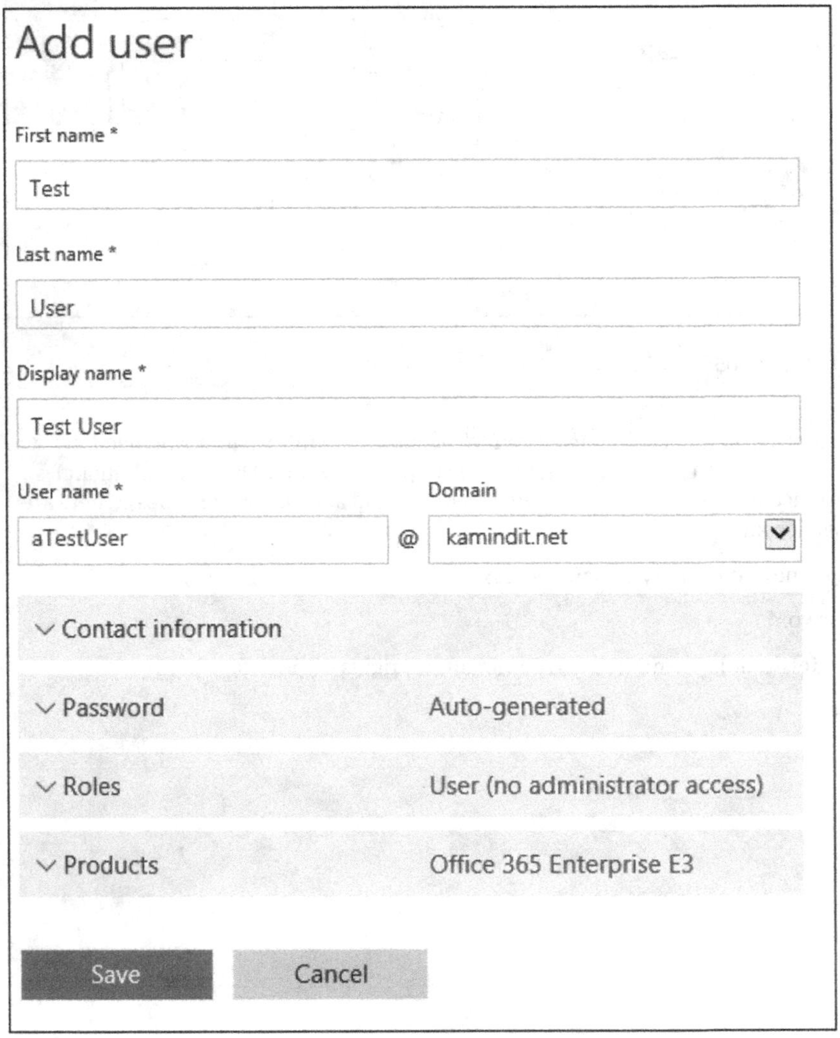

Figure 7-12. *Add the user information*

Step 2: Add Password Information

It is important that you change the default password policy when you create a new user. There are cases where you need to set the password when the account is created, and cases where you need to have the user rest the password. Our recommendation is that you always have the user set their own password (see Figure 7-13).

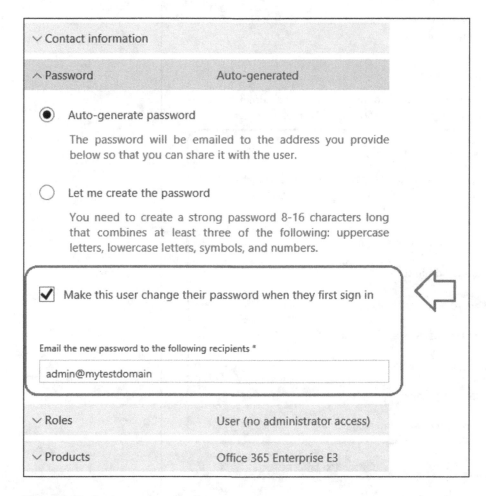

Figure 7-13. *Setting password policy*

Step 3: Assign Administration Roles

When you add the user, you can assign the role for the user (see Figure 7-14). Only global administrators can assign administrator roles. If you assign a user admin rights, you need to supply a mobile phone number in the contacts, otherwise you cannot create a new account. All administrator users must have a cell phone that receives calls.

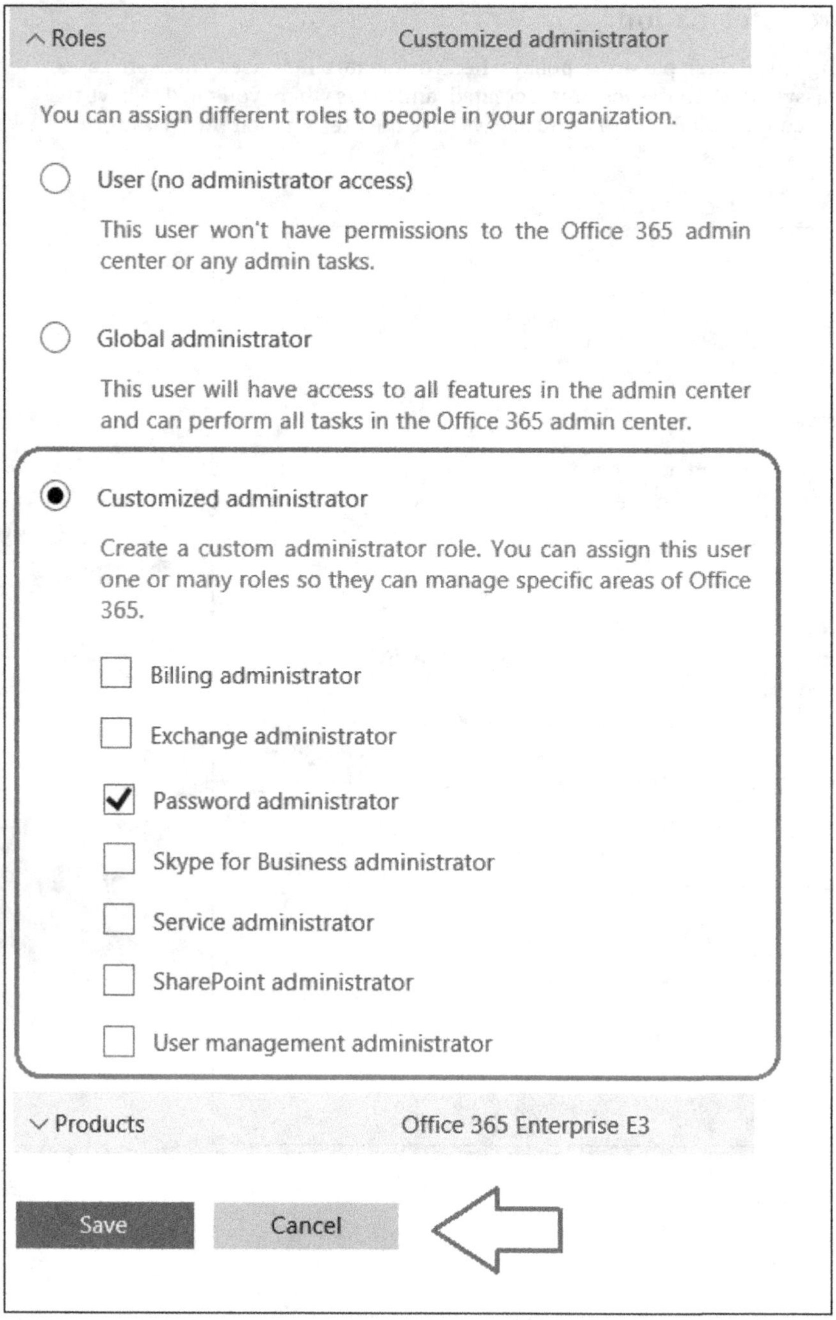

Figure 7-14. *Assigning the admin user*

Step 4: Assign the Licenses to the User

You can assign any valid license to the user. You can also selectivity assign access to the various Office 365 services (see Figure 7-15). Select **Save**. You have created the user account.

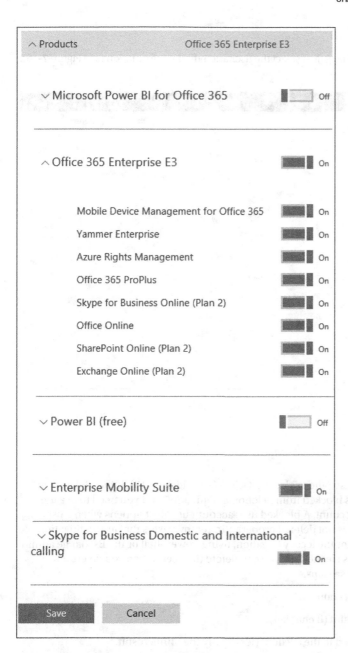

Figure 7-15. *Assigning the license to the user*

In Figure 7-15, we assigned E3 licenses with the Enterprise Mobility Suite (EMS) and Skype for Business. As an administrator, you can selectively remove access to different licenses. To remove capabilities, just move the option switch to Off.

Users: Changing User information

You can also change any information about a user. Just select the user and edit the information (see Figure 7-16).

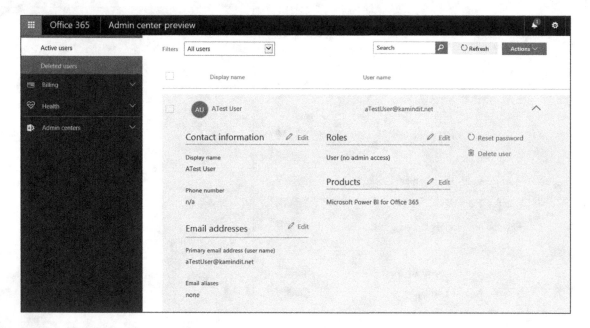

Figure 7-16. *Changing user information*

Users: Deleting

Deleting users is as simple as selecting the user, then selecting Delete (see Figure 7-17). If the "delete user" trashcan icon is not present, then the user is blocked from deletion in Office 365 and you need to use the PowerShell command to remove the user account. A blocked user account usually happens when a user is placed on legal hold, or when an account was not deleted properly. To remove users that are on litigation hold, you need to remove the in-place hold or the legacy litigation, using PowerShell or the Exchange admin center. Once the in-place or litigation hold is cleaned up, you can delete the user. When you delete an account, we recommend that you follow these steps.

1. Remove any legal hold on the account.

2. Disable the archive on the account (if enabled).

3. Remove any e-mail alias assigned to the account (leave only the onmicrosoft. com name and SIP).

4. Set the user account to the onmicrosoft.com name as the **Primary Address**.

5. If you do not want to keep e-mail (or move e-mail to another account), then remove all licenses from the account.

6. Delete the account. (If you deleted the account, mail will be deleted!)

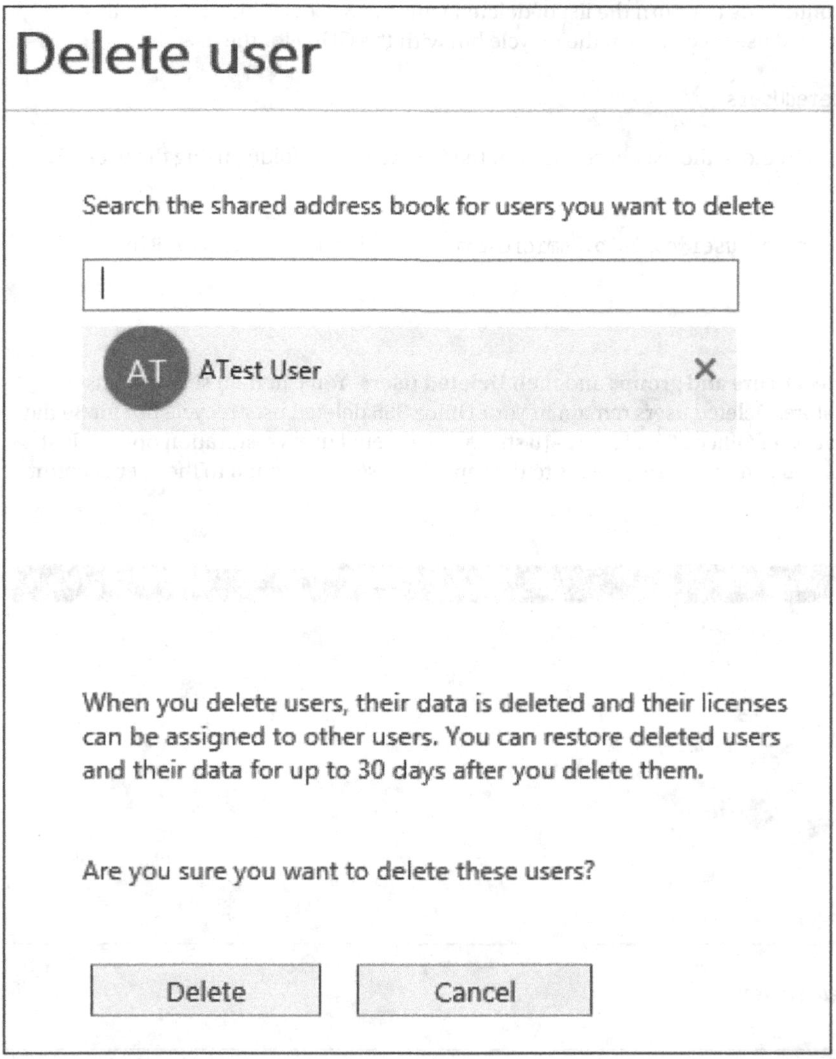

Delete user

Search the shared address book for users you want to delete

| |
| |

AT   ATest User   ✕

When you delete users, their data is deleted and their licenses can be assigned to other users. You can restore deleted users and their data for up to 30 days after you delete them.

Are you sure you want to delete these users?

| Delete | | Cancel |

Figure 7-17. Deleting a user account

■ **Note**   Before you remove the user account (as suggested earlier), verify that you have the OneDrive for Business data backed up. Removing the e-mail address may delete the user's OneDrive for Business data.

Deleted users can be recovered up to 30 days and are located in the Deleted Users folder. If you wish to remove the user from the Office 365 Deleted Users folder, run the following PowerShell command to purge the user account. If you have not set up PowerShell, see the PowerShell section at the end of this chapter. These PowerShell examples are code snippets and require the necessary credentials to execute (see the PowerShell section for detailed information on setup).

PowerShell provides commands to return the list of deleted Office 365 users. This PowerShell command returns all the deleted user accounts in the recycle bin with the GUID for the user.

```
Get-MsolUser -ReturnDeletedUsers
```

PowerShell commands to remove the user account from the Deleted Users folder, using the user e-mail address.

```
Remove-MsolUser -User <such as user@contsto.onmicrosoft.com> -RemoveFromRecycleBin
```

Users: Restoring

To restore deleted users, select **Users and groups** and then **Deleted users**. You can then select the user account that you wish to restore. Deleted users remain in your Office 365 deleted user recycle bin for 30 days, depending on the configuration of Office 365. Figure 7-18 shows the deleted users restoration option. Just select the user, then restore. You can only restore users to the same license provisioned to the user account when the account was deleted.

Figure 7-18. *Restoring a deleted user*

■ **Note**   If you attempt to restore a user and it fails due to account being managed by a different service, use the `RestoreMsolUser` PowerShell command to restore the user account.

Users: Renaming

Renaming a user display name is a simple process: select the user account from the Office 365 admin center, followed by **Actions**, and then the property that you want to change (see Figure 7-19).

Figure 7-19. *Changing a user's properties*

Once you select the edit function, select the area that you wish to change. For example, you can select the details and change the user name or domain as the primary login address (see Figure 7-20) of the user.

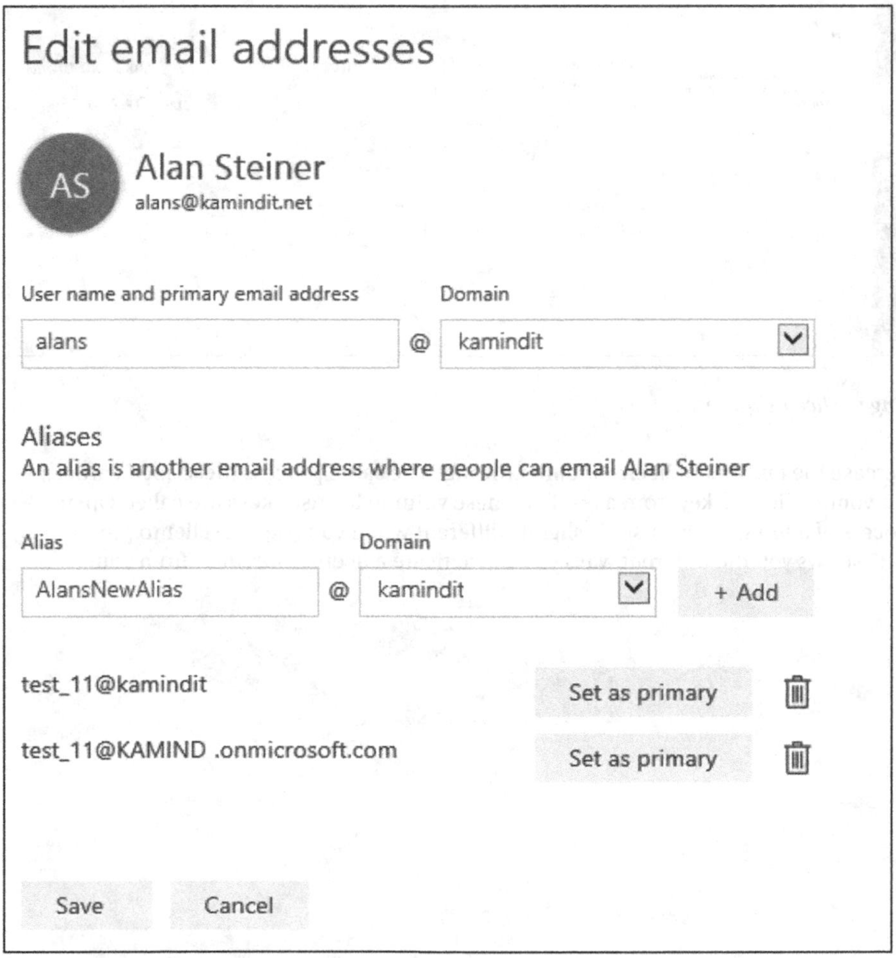

Edit email addresses

AS   Alan Steiner
alans@kamindit.net

User name and primary email address   Domain

| alans | @ | kamindit ▾ |

Aliases
An alias is another email address where people can email Alan Steiner

Alias   Domain

| AlansNewAlias | @ | kamindit ▾ | + Add |

test_11@kamindit   Set as primary   🗑

test_11@KAMIND .onmicrosoft.com   Set as primary   🗑

Save   Cancel

Figure 7-20. *Editing the user e-mail address and login domain*

■ **Note**   If you wish to change the user e-mail address to a different alias, you can do that in the Office 365 admin center (if the alias e-mail address exists in the user account). If the e-mail alias does not exist, any change you make will fail.

Billing: Adding/Changing and Decreasing Licenses

There are multiple ways that you can change license numbers in Office 365. Microsoft allows you to change the existing license quantity, add new licenses via purchase URL, add new licenses via the purchase option, or purchase a volume licenses key from your Microsoft Partner. Reducing licenses is simple in the administration portal (see Figure 7-21); just select the **Subscription** sidebar menu option and the subscription that needs the license quantity adjusted.

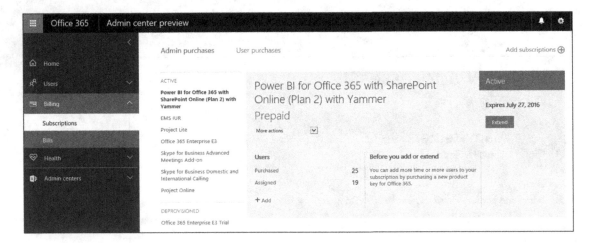

Figure 7-21. *Changing the license quantity*

You may also increase the number of licenses, either through the same process (described earlier), or you can purchase a volume license key from a reseller. These volume licenses keys are called Open License keys. The process of adding the licenses is slightly different when you use a reseller to purchase the license. Figure 7-22 shows you the different ways you can activate a license purchase from your Microsoft Partner.

> **Type of new Licensing ID:** OPEN
>
> **How to activate your Online Services:**
>
> 1. Please obtain your Product Key from VLSC. The Online Service Activation (OSA) Keys can be found at either of the following locations from the VLSC Homepage:
>   - **Download & Keys** > find the Product/Service name > click **Key**
>   - **Licenses** > **Relationship Summary** > Click on the License Number > **Product Key**
> 2. Copy the Keys and activate at the below Online Product Portal :
>   - For Office 365 activation http://www.office.com/setup365
>   - For Windows Intune activation www.microsoft.com/windowsintune/open
>   - For Windows Azure activation http://azure.microsoft.com/offers/azure-open/

Figure 7-22. *Different types of open subscription activation and links*

■ **Note**   Always check with your Microsoft Partner before you add licenses. Microsoft offers different incentives on licenses depending on when the purchase is made.

When you purchase an Open Licenses from a partner, you retrieve the subscription license number from the volume licenses center (www.microsoft.com/licensing) and select the appropriate link to start the activation process (see Figure 7-23). You must be a global administrator to add the Open License key to your Office 365 environment.

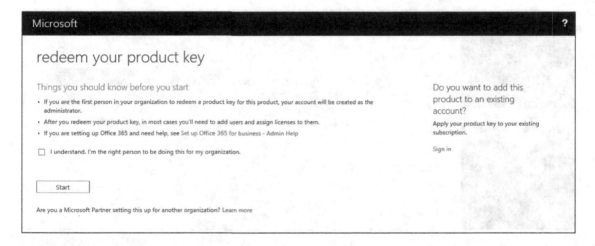

Figure 7-23. *Activating the Open License key*

Follow the wizard and the new subscription will be added to your environment. If you purchase multiple licenses of the same license type (E3 Open subscription), all the licenses are polled together as one license group. In Figure 7-24, we are adding 25 licenses. If there are multiple licenses added on the same date, Microsoft gives you the option to group the licenses together for a common renewal date.

Figure 7-24. Grouping licenses together

Once you have added the licenses to your Office 365 subscription, the new licenses are updated in your subscription portal (see Figure 7-25). We recommend that you always add the licenses before you add users.

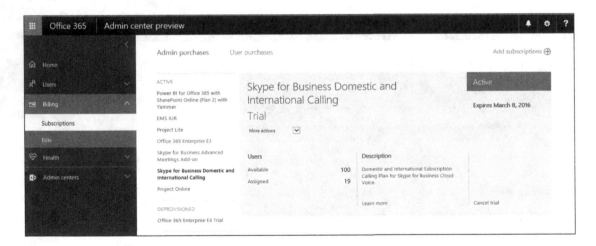

Figure 7-25. Adding new Skype for Business domestic and international calling licenses to Office 365

Config: Password Expiration

Office 365 allows you to configure password policy to allow password changes between 14 and 730 days. Typically, password policy is set to 90-day expiration and with a 14-day warning. To change the password policy (or to enable multi-factor authentication), select **Active users** on your dashboard, and then select **Change now** (see Figure 7-26).

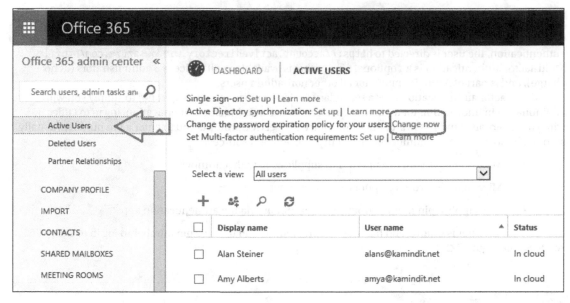

Figure 7-26. *Changing password policy*

Once you have selected the change password option, set the password policy for your organization. We recommend that you leave the default (change passwords every 90 days), unless you are planning to enable the multi-factor authentication password option. Changing the password is simple: select the new password option and select **Save** (see Figure 7-27).

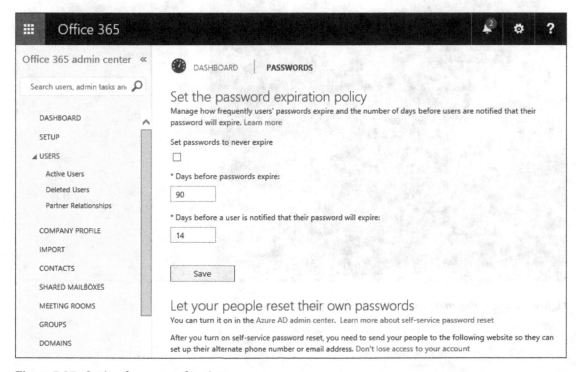

Figure 7-27. *Setting the password option*

Config: Password Multi-Factor Authentication

Office 365 has integrated multi-factor authentication with Azure. When you enable a user for multi-factor authentication, the user is directed to `https://account.activedirectory.windowsazure.com/profile/`. Multi-factor authentication is an optional service that is available to all Office 365 administrators (at no charge), and is part of Azure Premium for all other non-admin users.

Multi-factor authentication uses a secondary device (such as your smartphone) to supply you with additional login information for a Microsoft service. To use multi-factor authentication, log in to Office 365 with your username and password. Microsoft Office 365 service prompts you to enter a pin number (usually six or eight digits). The pin number comes from three different sources.

- Microsoft calls your cell phone and supplies you with a number

- Microsoft texts your cell phone with a number

- You supply a pin number from your smartphone via the authentication app

The pin number is unique and has a very short lifetime. You use this pin number to log in to Office 365 services (see Figure 7-28).

Figure 7-28. *Logging in to Office 365 with multi-factor authentication enabled*

There are two ways that you can set up multi-factor authentication: log in to Azure and enable multi-factor authentication, or log in to Office 365 and select **Users ➤ Active Users ➤ Multi-factor authentication ➤ Set up**. Either way works and uses the same Azure service. Microsoft Azure prompts you to log in again before you can enable multi-factor authentication.

■ **Note**   In the previous Office 365 setup/configuration chapter, we instructed you to enable Azure AD. Azure AD maintains the user identify for Office 365 and is used to handle multi-factor authentication for Office 365 services.

Setting up the multi-factor authentication is straightforward. Log in and select **Admin center ➤ Active Users ➤ Set up** (see Figure 7-29). Office 365 will direct you to Azure to authenticate your credentials. All user identities are managed in Azure. To set up multi-factor authentication on a user account, follow the steps outlined next.

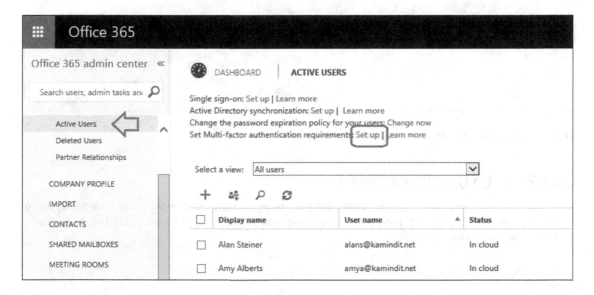

Figure 7-29. *Selecting multi-factor authentication*

Step 1: Enable the Users

Select the user to enable multi-factor authentication, and set the policy (see Figure 7-30). Then select **Enable** to set up the multi-factor authentication properties.

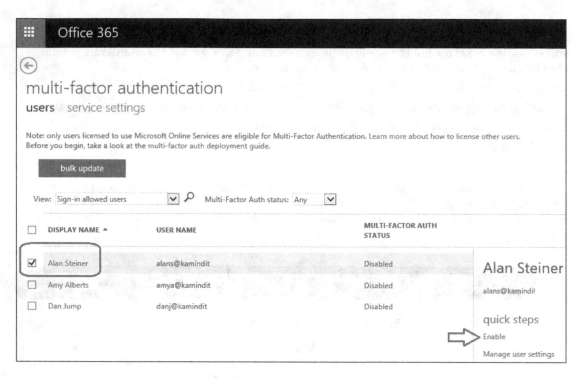

Figure 7-30. *Selecting users for multi-factor authentication*

Step 2: Set Up User Credentials

After you have enabled the user (select **enable multi-factor auth**), have the user log in to Office 365 to set up the credentials (see Figure 7-31). If you wish to set up the credentials for the user, you need their smartphone and login credentials for Office 365.

Figure 7-31. *Enabling multi-factor authentication*

The next time the user logs in to Office 365, they are informed of the setup to the new services (see Figure 7-32).

Figure 7-32. User setting up multi-factor authentication

Step 3: Authenticating Smartphones

Azure is used to authenticate the service for Office 365. The authentication service is an international service and requires that you own a phone that can receive a text message for login or can install an office authentication app on your smartphone. You need to pick the service that makes business sense (see Figure 7-33). If your phone does not receive text messages, you can elect to have Microsoft call your native language.

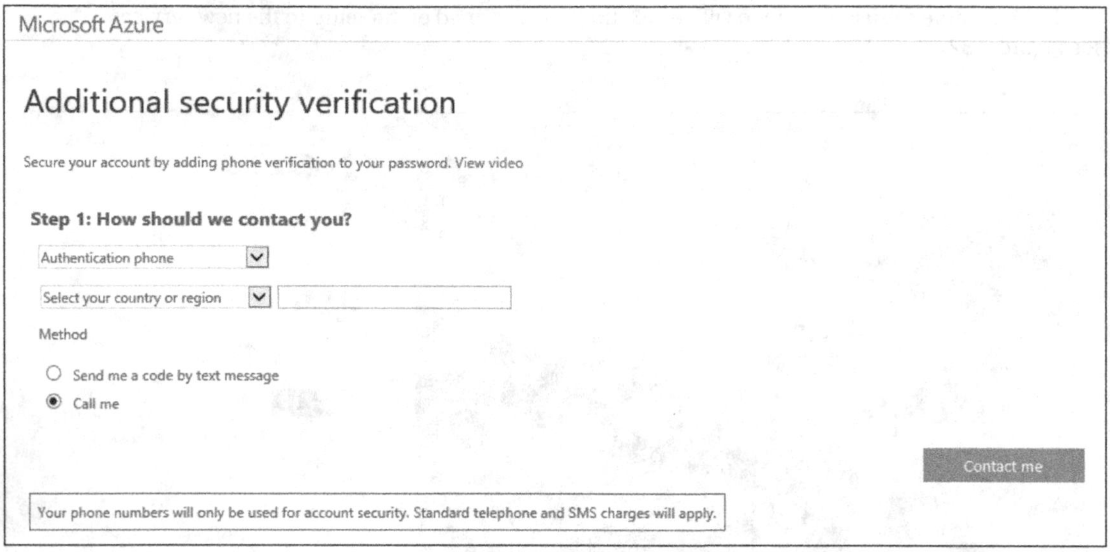

Figure 7-33. *Setting up the service for login*

Once you have verified your smartphone with Microsoft, you are supplied with a security token to allow your mobile device to access the Office 365 account. This passcode is unique and is used to configure the mobile applications that do not use two-factor authentication (see Figure 7-34). Use this passcode as the new password for your mobile applications that access Office 365 services. Select **Done** when completed.

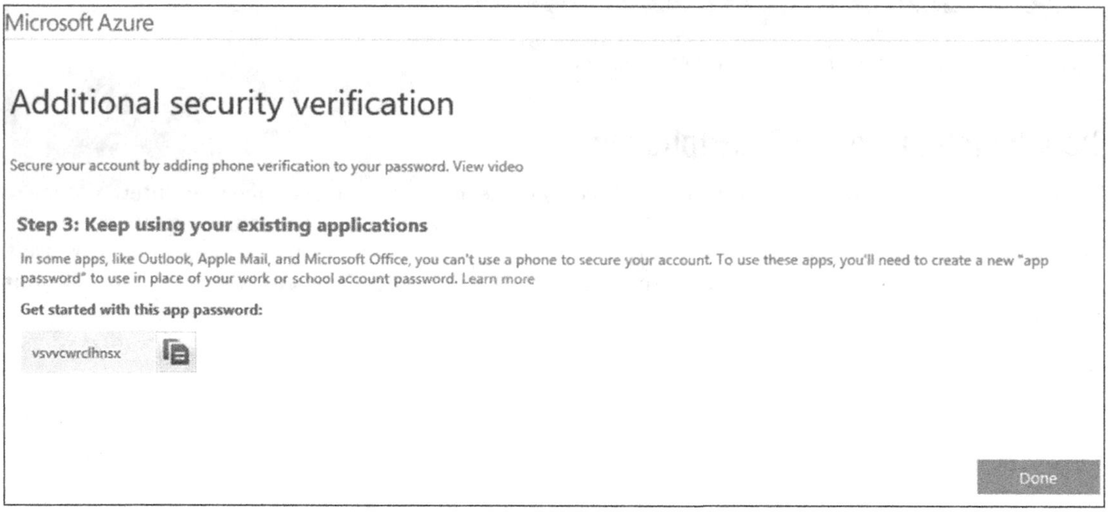

Figure 7-34. *Setting a new password for your mobile application*

Step 4: Testing the Service

Log in to the Office 365 service at **https://portal.microsoftonline.com**. Office 365 will text or call your cell phone with the authentication password (see Figure 7-35).

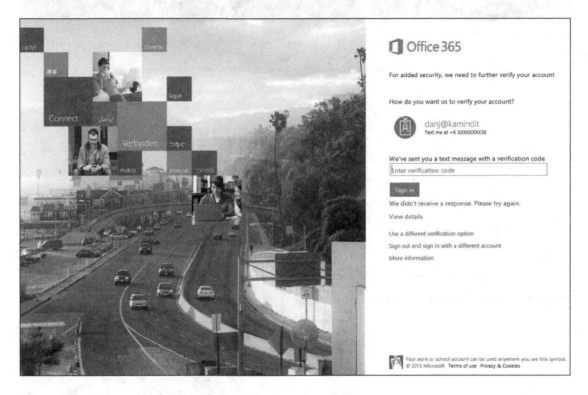

Figure 7-35. *Testing multi-factor authentication*

Config: Groups (Office 365 and Security Groups)

Groups are used to manage permissions globally in Office 365. There are different ways to use security groups. You can use security groups to filter users and administrator permissions (useful in large organizations). You can also use security groups to manage permissions for different services. SharePoint (as an example), can either use security groups to grant permissions to various site libraries for users. You can use SharePoint security permissions to restrict access to different libraries in SharePoint. For example, in large organizations, you can create a security group to isolate users from each other, and use security groups to manage access to different federated services (such as Intune and Azure services). There are different ways to use security groups, depending on your business needs. Some organizations use security groups to manage SharePoint services. For example, a SharePoint site is designed and security groups are created to assign permissions to different areas. The global administrator adds accounts to the different security groups, depending on the business requirements. The users added to the security groups inherit the permissions necessary to access the functional areas in SharePoint.

Creating security groups is easy. Sign in as an administrator. Click **Admin/Office 365** and then click **GROUPS** (see Figure 7-36). Click the + to add a new Office 365 group or a security group (see Figure 7-37).

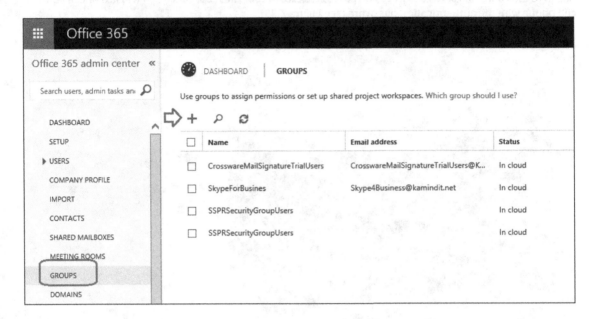

Figure 7-36. *Selecting or creating a new security group*

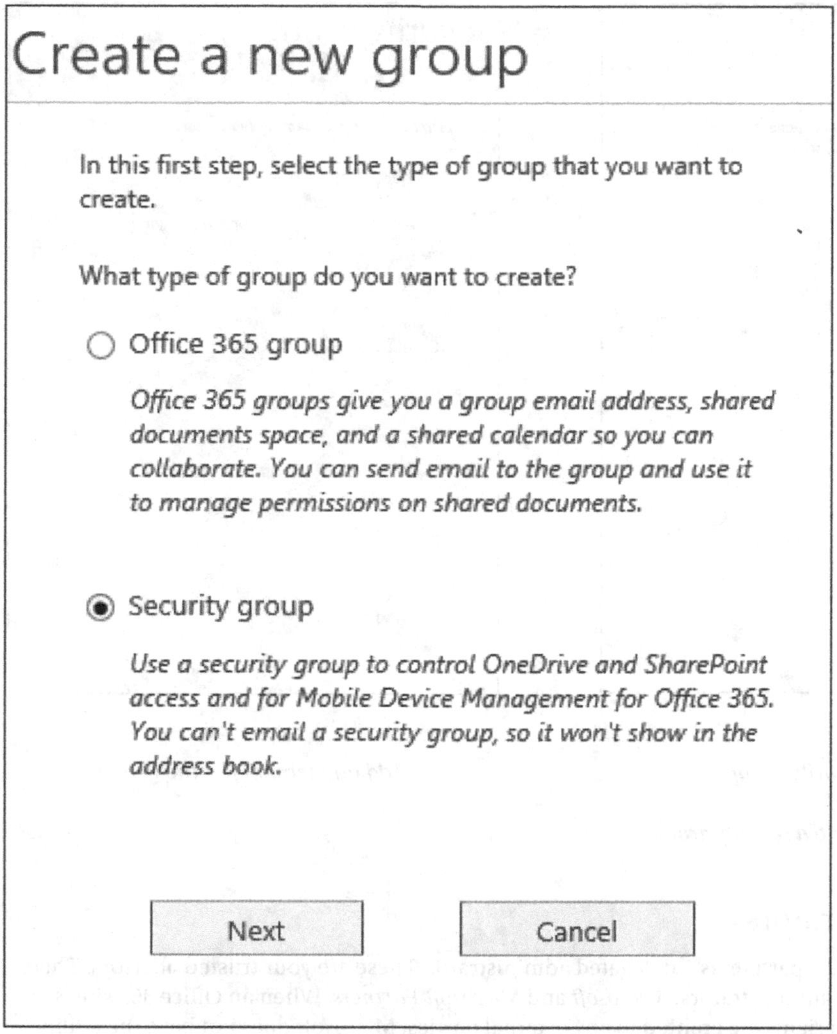

Create a new group

In this first step, select the type of group that you want to create.

What type of group do you want to create?

○ Office 365 group

Office 365 groups give you a group email address, shared documents space, and a shared calendar so you can collaborate. You can send email to the group and use it to manage permissions on shared documents.

◉ Security group

Use a security group to control OneDrive and SharePoint access and for Mobile Device Management for Office 365. You can't email a security group, so it won't show in the address book.

Next	Cancel

Figure 7-37. Adding to a security group

The security group wizard walks you through the steps for setting up a new security group (see Figure 7-38). It shows the account members that are in the security group and those members that can be added to the security group. Click **Members** to see the list. Once you have added all the members, be sure to click **Add Members** (at the bottom of the screen) to save the group.

Creating a security group

Adding members to the group

Figure 7-38. *Adding users to a security group*

Partner Administrators

Partner Relationships adds a partner as a delegated administrator. These are your trusted advisors. There are two types of delegated administrators: *Microsoft* and *Microsoft Partners*. When an Office 365 site is created, no administration rights are granted to any external parties. Microsoft does not have the ability to access user data, unless that right is granted by the account owner. There are two types of partner administrators: delegated administration from a Microsoft Cloud Advisor and a Microsoft Cloud Solution Provider (see Figure 7-39).

Figure 7-39. *Types of Microsoft Cloud Partners*

The account owner (global admin) can add (or delete) Cloud Solution Advisors and add (or delete) the Cloud Solution Providers as needed, with some caveats.

- Cloud Solution Advisors are partner global administrators and need to purchase licenses through Microsoft or a third party. You can add/remove these advisors as needed.

- Cloud Solution Providers are partner global administrators and provide licenses to Office 365 customers through a partner administrator. You cannot remove these providers unless you have removed the licenses provided by these providers.

Cloud Solution Providers (CSP) are different from Cloud Solution Advisors (CSA). For example, KAMIDN IT CSP offerings are listed at http://www.kamind.com/csp. Keep in mind, that if you purchase licenses through a CSP, your Microsoft account is managed by the CSP, not Microsoft.

Config: External Sharing

The administrator uses external sharing to manage external access to manage Office 365. Office 365 is designed for collaboration. As an administrator, you control how SharePoint (a.k.a. sites), calendars, and Skype for Business are shared. There are two steps to manage collaboration: enabling the service for external users (set these options on/off) and configuring the local options (Sites, Calendar, and Skype for Business). Global options are managed in the External Sharing administration center. If you disable the global options, then the local service options will not have those external feature options. You should configure the services, as shown in Figure 7-40, for external sharing.

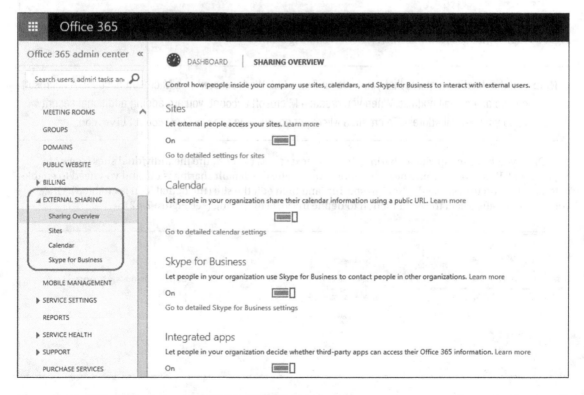

Figure 7-40. Office 365 admin center: External Sharing settings

Config: External Sharing, Sites

Office 365 SharePoint services support Team Sites and OneDrive for Business. The "sites" sharing controls are used to enable these services for external access. As an administrator, you have two choices (see #1 in Figure 7-41) for sharing: enabling to require authentication (no anonymous guest links) and requiring users to log in to the service.

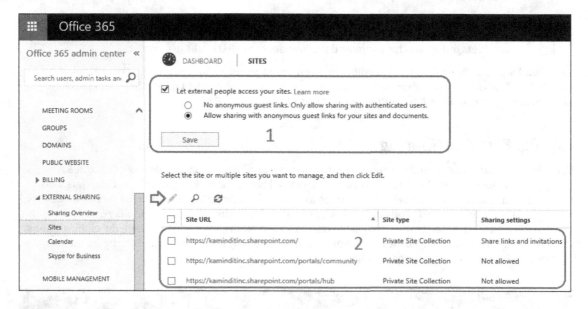

***Figure 7-41.** Office 365 Admin Center: External Sharing settings*

■ **Note**   Authentication requires that you have an Office 365 Work account or a Microsoft account. A Microsoft account can be any e-mail address. When you create a Microsoft account, you are adding additional security credentials to your e-mail address. To create a Microsoft account, go to `http://account.live.com`.

Once you have set up global sharing, then the next step is to configure the individual sites (see #2 in Figure 7-41). When you create a new SharePoint Team Site, the default sharing is off, and you need to enable it as a user. To do this, select the "site" in sharing, and then edit the site (the pencil icon is enabled). Once you select the site, select the edit function to define the level of sharing (see Figure 7-42).

Site URL	Site type	Sharing settings	
☑ https://kaminditinc.sharepoint.com/	Private Site Collection	Share links and invitations	https://kaminditinc.sharepoint.com/
☐ https://kaminditinc.sharepoint.com/portals/community	Private Site Collection	Not allowed	
☐ https://kaminditinc.sharepoint.com/portals/hub	Private Site Collection	Not allowed	5 external users. Manage external users for this site
☐ https://kaminditinc.sharepoint.com/search	Private Site Collection	Not allowed	
☐ https://kaminditinc.sharepoint.com/sites/AppCatalog	Private Site Collection	Not allowed	quick steps
☐ https://kaminditinc.sharepoint.com/sites/apps	Private Site Collection	Not allowed	Details

***Figure 7-42.** Managing external sharing on Team Site and OneDrive for Business*

This is how an administrator manages the external access to different sites. Administrators have the permission to set the allowed sharing (with logins, without logins, or disabled altogether). Administrators also have the ability to manage the external users that have shared documents.

Config: External Sharing, Calendar

Administrators can also control the way calendars are shared. For example, you may want to openly share information with external users to see the details in your calendar when you get a meeting invite. Likewise, you may want to restrict the information to free/busy. The settings in Figure 7-43 apply to all users globally, regardless of their individual settings.

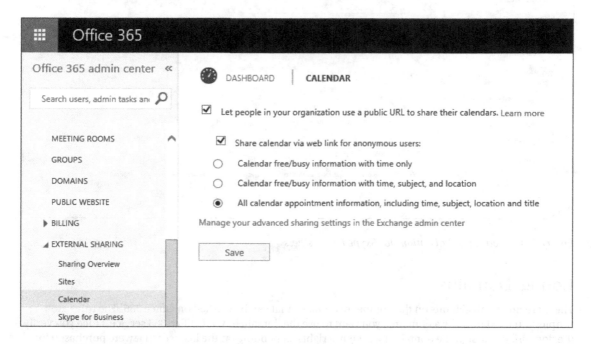

Figure 7-43. *Managing external sharing of calendar for Office 365 users*

Config: External Sharing, Skype for Business

Skype for Business is the business version of Skype. Business users can communicate to other business users by using an e-mail address, if the sharing is enabled in the Office 365 account. Skype users can only communicate to Skype for Business users if the administrator has allowed this option. In both cases, you need to have the e-mail address of the user to speak with them. If you purchased the Skype for Business calling plans, we'll walk you through the configuration steps later in the chapter. The basic sharing configuration (allowing you to speak with other Skype for Business users and Skype users) are controlled as shown in Figure 7-44.

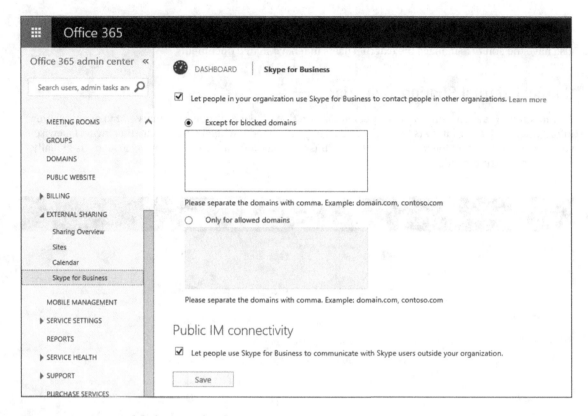

Figure 7-44. *Setting global options for Skype For Business*

Config: Domains

There are no practical limits on the number of domains that can be verified on Office 365. The rules are simple: you need to verify a domain if you want to use the domain in your Office 365 service. Once you verify the domain, you assign the domain different use rights, depending on the licenses that were purchased for your Office 365 services.

In an earlier chapter, we added a new domain, configured the DNS, and assigned the domain to be used with specific services (see Figure 7-45). This allows administrators to restrict services on domains. Adding a domain is very straightforward: just add the domain (see Figure 7-46) and enter the necessary record changes in the DNS (please refer to the steps in Chapter 5). When you add the domain, it is very easy to follow the wizards; just be careful with the options that you select. We typically use a manual approach to adding DNS records once an Office 365 account is active.

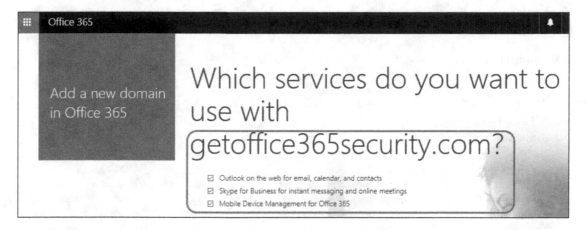

Figure 7-45. *Setting the service option for the new domain*

Figure 7-46. *Adding a new domain to Office 365*

Config: Domains: Troubleshooting

Once you have added the domain, Office 365 constantly verifies your DNS and highlights the invalid DNS records. Fixing the records is easy: just select the domain (see Figure 7-46) and then select **Fix Issues**. If there are any issues present or a configuration that you can use, Fix Issues is available as an option. In Figure 7-47, the incorrect records are highlighted with a red X. Correct these records in your DNS records and verify them until all the records have a green check mark.

Add these DNS records for getoffice365security.com at NetworkSolutions. Why do I need these records?

MX records

Priority	Host name	Points to address or value	TTL	
0	@	getoffice365security-com.mail.protection.outlook.com	3600	✗ What do I fix?

CNAME records

Host name	Points to address or value	TTL	
autodiscover	autodiscover.outlook.com	3600	✗ What do I fix?
msoid	clientconfig.microsoftonline-p.net	3600	✓
enterpriseenrollment	enterpriseenrollment.manage.microsoft.com	3600	✓
enterpriseregistration	enterpriseregistration.windows.net	3600	✓
sip	sipdir.online.lync.com	3600	✓
lyncdiscover	webdir.online.lync.com	3600	✓

Figure 7-47. Fixing the DNS records

Exchange Admin Center

Office 365 administration sites (shown in the admin center) are added based on licensed purchased. Exchange (e-mail services in Office 365) is a licensed subscription option. The global administrator has access by default, but different administrator access may be disabled if their roles do not permit them access. Role-based permissions are controlled in the Office 365 Exchange admin center (EAC), which is located under Admin ➤ Exchange (see Figure 7-48). All the commands in the following section assume that you are operating in the Exchange administration section.

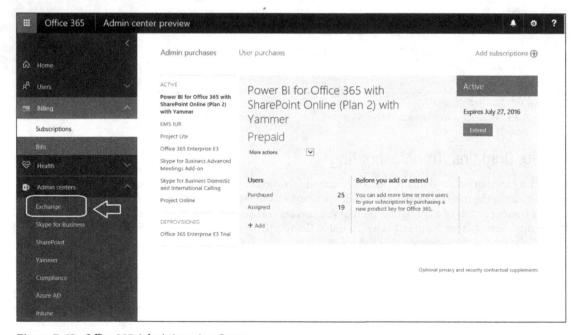

Figure 7-48. Office 365 Administration Center

Select **Exchange** (under admin centers). This is the location to manage the user account with advanced mail flow and mailbox features (see Figure 7-49). If the account is synced via Active Directory, some of these features need to be managed through the on-premises Active Directory center.

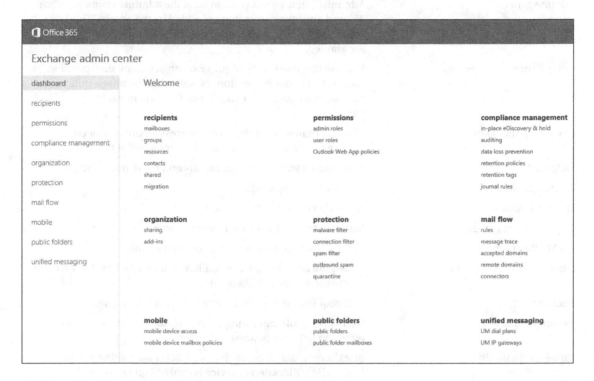

Figure 7-49. *Office 365 Enterprise Exchange admin center (EAC)*

Exchange Administration Roles

The Exchange admin center includes a number of administration roles. These roles are used to assign various subtasks to users. The Office 365 global administrator is an organization administrator. The global administrator may not have permission in some Exchange roles; however, the global administrator can add be added to that role, but that action is audited. In large organizations, the global administrator accounts are controlled and user accounts are modified with administrator permissions based on the job roles. For example, a large company may create a security group of users from one location, and the Exchange administrator is a user in that security group. The Exchange administrator functions are limited to that location, as defined in the security group. This is in contrast to a global administrator who has access to all accounts.

Table 7-5. *Exchange Administrator Roles*

Exchange Server Role	Description
AdminAgents	Administration agents contain all of the administrators in Office 365 and any other users that are added by the admin. This is where the base Exchange administration permissions are granted.
Compliance Management	Users in this role can configure Exchange compliance policies, such as Data Loss Prevention, as well other Exchange policies or compliance issues (see compliance function in Exchange admin center).
Discovery Management	This role manages the discovery process. In order to access discovery information, you must be a member of this role.
Help desk	This manages view-only operations and password resets.
HelpdeskAdmins	Manages the help desk.
Helpdesk Agents	Agent that operates the help desk.
Hygiene Management	Manages the Exchange transport services.
ISVMailboxUsers	Third-party application developer mailbox role.
Organization Management	Allows full access to all user mailboxes for any administrative role except for discovery management.
Recipient Management	Role required to move mailboxes in hybrid deployment.
Records Management	Users in this role can configure compliance features such as retention tags and policies.
Rim-MailBxAdmins	Blackberry Mailbox access for BlackBerry messaging servers (only valid if BlackBerry service is enabled on Office 365).
TenantAdmins	Legacy admin role for management of Exchange tenants.
UM Management	Universal messaging management role to integrate necessary functions for Enterprise Voice with Skype for Business.
View-Only Organization Management	View-only privileges for Exchange organization. Users in this role cannot modify any Exchange properties.

In larger organizations, different roles are assigned in Exchange. But in small organizations, there are only two roles that are commonly used: the company administrator role (global admin via the AdminAgent role) and the discovery management role. The global admin does not have access to discovery management unless that role is granted and permission is granted in the discovery SharePoint center.

You can assign any of the administrator roles in Table 7-7 to the user mailbox. Our recommendation for assignment of user permissions follows this model:

1. Build a security group for the accounts that will be managed. The user who will manage these accounts should be in the security group.

2. Assign the user Exchange administration permission to the selected account in the newly created security group (see Figure 7-50).

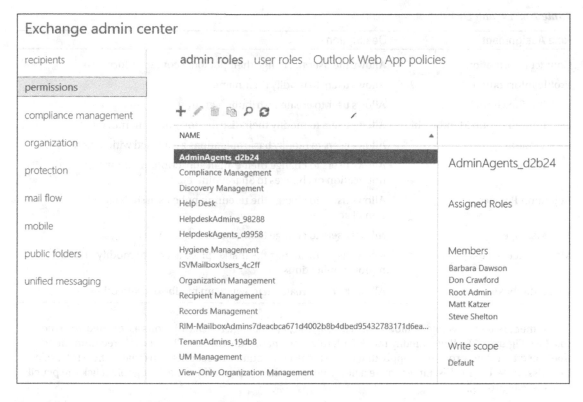

Figure 7-50. *Assigning administrative permissions*

Once you have assigned permission to the user to manage Exchange users, you can create necessary user roles (if needed) to manage the group.

Default User Role Defined

All users have a default role assigned to them when they are added to Office 365. The default user role defines the characteristics that the user has in accessing the Exchange mail system. For example, Outlook web access is defined as a user role. If you don't want to have users access the web mail, you can remove these privileges. The user roles that you can change are listed in Table 7-6.

Table 7-6. *Default User Role Assignments*

Role Assignment	Description
Contact Information	Allows the user to change their personal contact information
Profile Information	Allows users to modify their name
Distribution Groups	Allows user to create distribution groups
Distribution Group Membership	Allows users to modify their distribution group memberships
Base Options	Allows users to modify basic operations associated with their mailboxes
Subscriptions	Allows users to change their e-mail subscription options (such as notification of changes to SharePoint, etc.)
Retention Policies	Allows users to change the retention policies associated with their e-mail account
Text Message	Allows users to change their text message (IM) settings
Marketplace Access	Allows users to change the marketplace access to modify or add remote applications
Team Mailboxes	Allow users to create their own team mailboxes with other users

Either create a new role or modify the existing role, and change the permissions associated with the role (see Figure 7-51). If you modify the default role, you change the role for all users. It is recommended that you create a new role, then apply that roll to the user account (or accounts). To create a new role, select **Permission ➤ User roles**. Either create a new role (click the +), or modify the existing role (click the pencil icon) (see Figure 7-52).

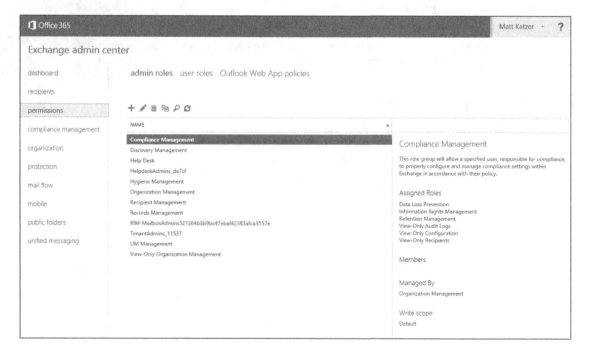

Figure 7-51. *Editing user roles in Office 365*

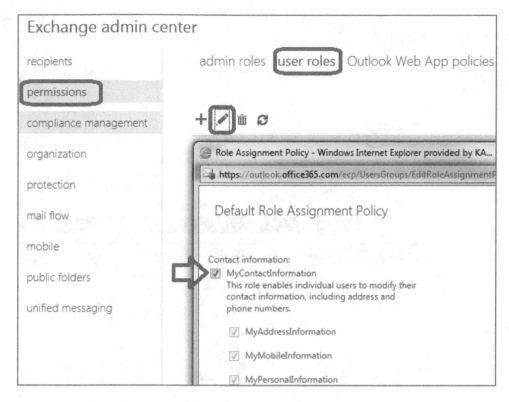

***Figure 7-52.** Changing the default user role*

If you create a new role for a user account that is different from the other default role, you need to apply the new role to the user account. Select the **Recipients ➤ Mailboxes** and then the user account. Edit the account and assign the role (see Figure 7-53).

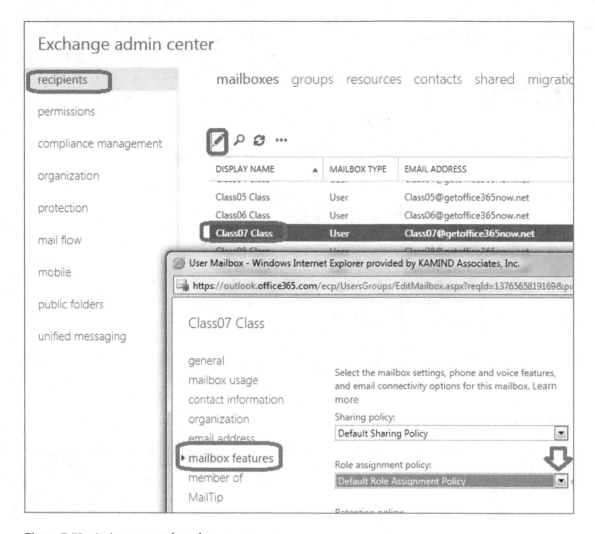

Figure 7-53. *Assign a new role to the user account*

Exchange: Conference Room, Configuration

Office 365 provides a resource called *meeting room*. Meeting rooms are used to control resources that are limited and need to be managed through scheduling. To set up a meeting resource, log in to Office 365 as an administrator and select **Admin center ➤ Exchange ➤ Exchange admin center (EAC)**.

Creating a conference room is simple. After you have selected the EAC, select **recipients ➤ mailboxes** (in the drop-down dialog box in Figure 7-54), and select **Room mailbox**. This sets up the meeting room with a default configuration (if the meeting room is being used, it shows a busy status). There are additional configuration changes that can be made on conference rooms, but there is no GUI interface. These changes would need to be made using PowerShell.

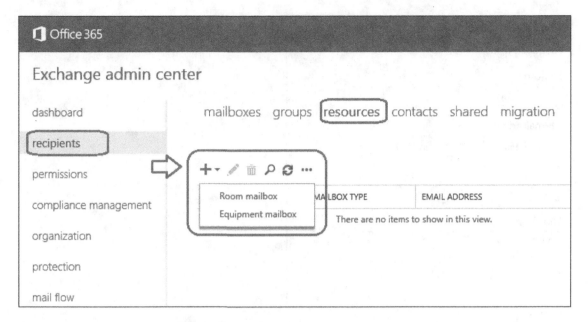

Figure 7-54. *Creating a new conference room*

When you create the meeting room, the first order of business is to assign users that have permission to book the meeting room. These users are called *delegate users*. You have two options on meeting rooms: allow all users to book meeting rooms (default) or allow restricted users to book meeting rooms. Provide the name of the meeting room and select the appropriate option, and then click **OK** (see Figure 7-55).

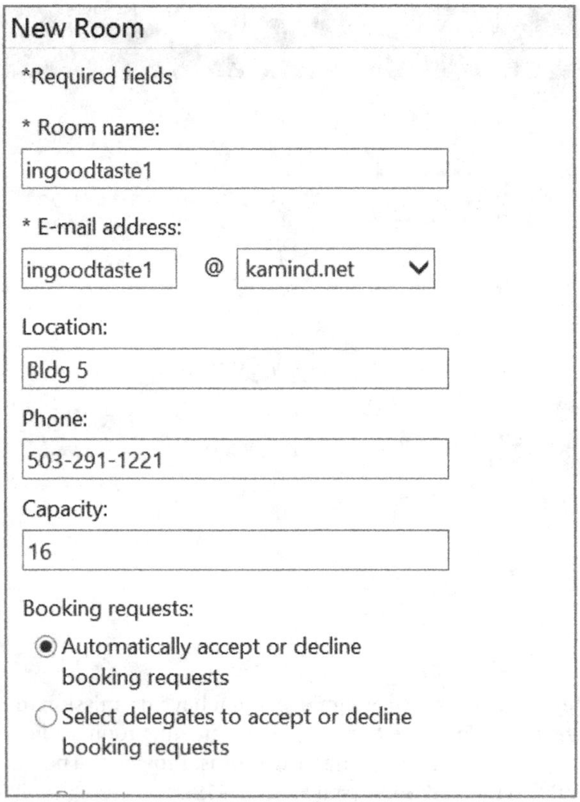

New Room

*Required fields

* Room name:

```
ingoodtaste1
```

* E-mail address:

```
ingoodtaste1      @    kamind.net        ∨
```

Location:

```
Bldg 5
```

Phone:

```
503-291-1221
```

Capacity:

```
16
```

Booking requests:

◉ Automatically accept or decline
   booking requests

○ Select delegates to accept or decline
   booking requests

Figure 7-55. *Configuring a conference room*

The room is configured with the default setting showing only a busy status. Meeting rooms are very versatile. You can use this function to reserve any type of resource, such as equipment. Remember, meeting rooms are a single device, and a meeting room resource manages multiple objects. To use meeting rooms to manage multiple objects, you need to create a meeting room for each device. After you have created the room, you can modify the capabilities of the room based on your needs (see Figure 7-56).

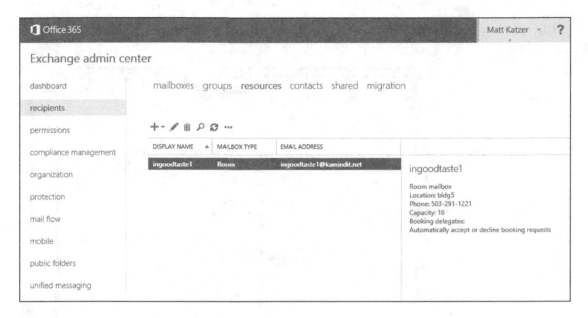

Figure 7-56. *Reviewing conference room characteristics*

Exchange: Conference Room, PowerShell Modification

Conference and resource rooms provide the basic configuration for use, but there are additional configuration options that can only be done using PowerShell. For example, the default configuration hides the meeting status and ownership. If you want to make those available, you need to run the following PowerShell commands (see the sections on PowerShell setup toward the end of this chapter).

Set full details of a conference room using PowerShell:

```
Set-CalendarProcessing -Identity ingoodtaste1 -AddOrganizerToSubject $true -DeleteComments
$false -DeleteSubject $false
```

Set limited details of a conference room using PowerShell:

```
Set-MailboxFolderPermission -AccessRights LimitDetails -Identity ingoodtaste1:\calendar
-User default
```

■ **Note** If you wish to approve conference room use, the email address of the "approver" must have fully delegated rights over the conference room resource mailbox.

Exchange: Adding an Alias E-mail Address to a User

It is simple to add an alias e-mail address. Just select the Exchange admin center, highlight the user account, click **Edit**, and select the e-mail address (see Figure 7-57). Enter the new e-mail "alias" address for the user. The domain must be verified in Office 365; otherwise, the alias will not be added.

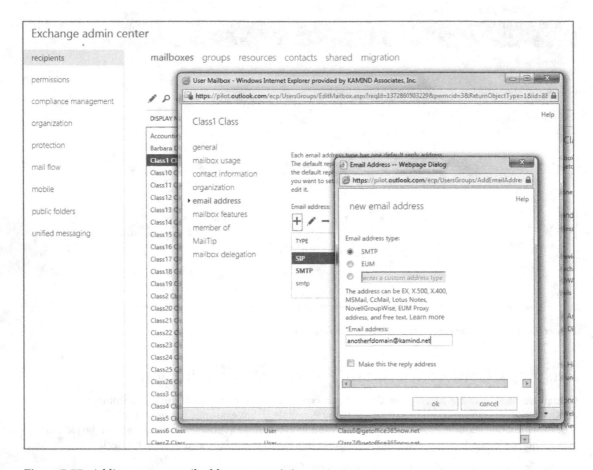

Figure 7-57. *Adding a new e-mail address to an existing account*

Exchange: Changing a User E-mail Account Primary Domain

Office 365 supports multiple domains and multiple user e-mail aliases per an account. In some cases, an Office 365 organization may need to change to a new domain (e.g., after a company merger or branding change). Making the change for all users is not difficult: all that is required is to verify the domain (set the MX records and Skype for Business records), add the domain to the existing users, and set the reply address to the new e-mail alias. What you cannot do is change the xxx.onmicrosoft.com domain. If you need to change it, you must migrate to a new Office 365 organization. To make this change, follow the steps outlined next.

Step 1: Validate the New Domain

Complete a validation for the new domain with the domain intent set to Exchange and Skype for Business. Follow the instructions discussed in Chapter 5 and in this chapter's "Config: Domains" section.

Step 2: Add the User Alias and Set the Reply Address

Add the new e-mail alias to all the users needing a domain change. If a user's primary e-mail address is changing, then select the **Make this the reply address** option. This changes the user's primary login address to the new domain. This step is no different than changing the user's e-mail address to a new address (as discussed earlier).

■ **Note**   When the reply e-mail address is changed, the Outlook user is requested to log in with new credentials. Outlook recognizes that the user profile is the same and links the existing Outlook mailbox to the corrected e-mail address.

Exchange: Adding Shared Mailbox

There are two methods for adding a shared Exchange mailbox. The approach you use depends on the capabilities that you want the mailbox to have. If you need to receive information on a mobile device, or if you require the mailbox as an archive for long-term storage, then you need to use a licensed mailbox. If you do not need these features and you only want to have access via Outlook, then the mailbox does not need to have a license. We have outlined the choices in Table 7-7.

Table 7-7. *Shared Mailbox Options*

Approach	Cost (monthly)	Data Size	Capabilities
Shared licensed mailbox	$4–$8	25GB with 25GB or 100GB archive	Can be received on smartphones (active sync support)
Exchange shared mailbox	$0	5GB limit	No active sync

The key decision factor for most users is to receive the information on smartphones. This requirement dictates that you use an Office license rather than a free, shared mailbox.

Exchange: Shared Mailbox, Using with a Smartphone and Outlook

Smartphone devices require an active sync connection. You add a shared mailbox the same way you add a mailbox to Office 365. The only issue is that you must assign delegated rights to the users who wish to use the mailbox. This is the same for all user mailboxes. Once a mailbox has been created, you need to assign share rights to the mailbox.

To add a shared mailbox, follow these steps:

1. Purchase an Exchange Plan 1 (or Plan 2) mailbox.

2. Assign a user account to the Exchange e-mail account.

3. Assign user-delegated rights to the mailbox.

In the Exchange admin center, highlight the user account, click edit (the pencil icon), and then **Select e-mail address** (see Figure 7-58). Select **Mailbox delegation** and then add the user for both **Full Access** and **Send on Behalf**. Click **OK** when done. The mailbox is modified.

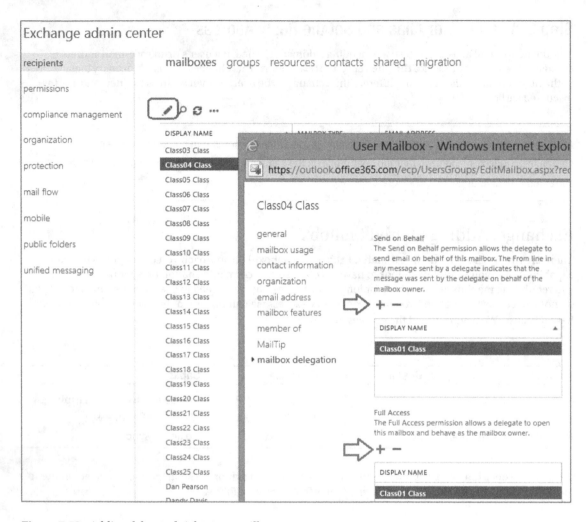

Figure 7-58. *Adding delegated rights to a mailbox*

Exchange: Shared Mailbox, Using Only with Outlook

If you need to add a shared mailbox for use only with Outlook (and you do not want to use a license), you can create a shared mailbox in the Exchange admin center, and then add the user as a delegated user to the mailbox (as shown in Figure 7-59).

Figure 7-59. *Adding a free shared mailbox*

In the Exchange admin center, select **Shared**. Create a shared mailbox. In this case, we created a mailbox called CompanyCal (see Figure 7-44). Select the mailbox and then **Mailbox delegation**. Add the users who will access the shared mailbox (see Figure 7-58). Click **OK** when completed. The shared mailbox will appear in Outlook for each user added as a delegated user.

Exchange: Shared Mailbox, Using PowerShell

In some cases, you need to use PowerShell to set up and configure a shared mailbox. You need to run two PowerShell commands: one to set the permission and the other to set the behavior of the shared mailbox. Once you have modified the shared mailbox, the configuration is updated in the Outlook client at the next login. In this example, **Identity** is the shared mailbox, and **User** and **Trustee** mean the person who has access to the shared mailbox.

Step 1: Add the Recipient Permissions

```
Add-RecipientPermission -Identity user@kamind.com -Trustee trusted@kamind.com -AccessRights SendAs
```

Step 2: Add Mailbox Access Permissions

```
Add-MailboxPermission -Identity user@kamind.com -User trusted@kamind.com -AccessRights
FullAccess -InheritanceType All
```

Exchange: Adding a Distribution Group

There are three different types of distribution groups: distribution groups, mail-enabled security groups, and dynamic distribution groups. When you add a group (see Figure 7-60), you select a group based on the business role that you wish the group to perform.

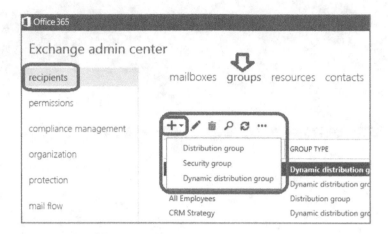

Figure 7-60. *Adding a distribution group*

There are different view types for groups, and the group that you use comes down to management view. In general, security groups are not mail-enabled and are managed externally to the Exchange admin center. Security groups are created in the Office 365 administration center and are managed from Office 365, not the Exchange admin center. Typically, you create a distribution group, or if you are a large organization, you create a dynamic distribution group.

Table 7-8. *Distribution Group Types*

Group Type	Description
Distribution group	Distribution groups are mail-enabled groups. An e-mail that is sent to the distribution group is sent to all members.
Security group	Security groups are groups that are used to grant permissions. In some cases, these may be mail enabled. It is recommended that you do not use mail-enabled security groups.
Dynamic distribution group	A distribution group that has a variable number of members based on filters and conditions in Active Directory.

Step 1: Create the Distribution Group

In the Exchange admin center, select **recipients** and **groups** (see Figure 7-61). Add the group by clicking the + and then select the distribution group to be added.

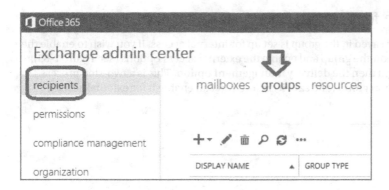

Figure 7-61. *Adding a new distribution group*

Step 2: Define the Distribution Group

Fill in the information about the distribution group. When you first create the group, leave the defaults in place. You must specify an owner of the group and any initial members that you wish to add (see Figure 7-62).

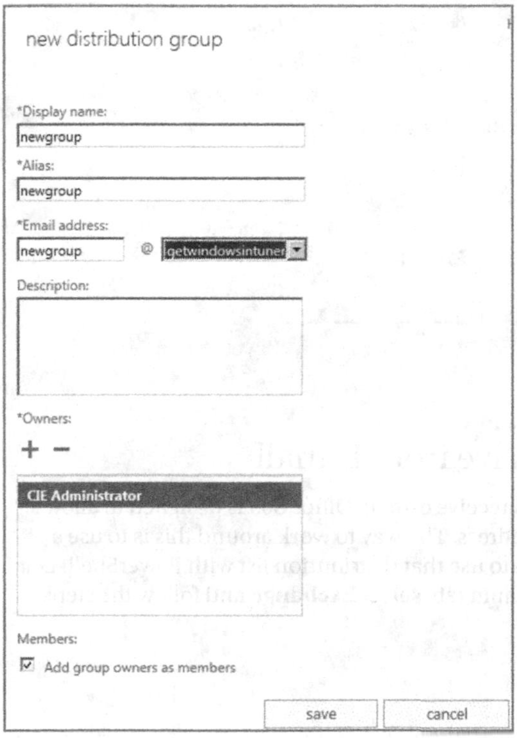

Figure 7-62. *Defining the distribution group*

Step 3: Enabling the Group for External Access

After you have created the group and saved it, the group is set up for internal access. If you wish to enable the group for external access, you must edit the group and enable the external access options (see Figure 7-63). Select the group, followed by **Edit**, and then the **delivery management** option. This is a two-step process. You must create an internal distribution group (and save it) before you can enable it for external access.

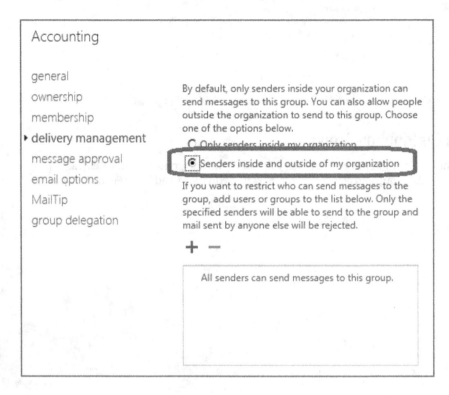

Figure 7-63. *Settings for external delivery*

Exchange: Using Alias to Send to/Receive from E-mail

You may want to use a different e-mail address to send and receive e-mail. Office 365 is designed to allow only one e-mail address to be used: your primary e-mail address. The way to work around this is to use a distribution list and to grant a user account full permission to use that distribution list with PowerShell. Log in to the Office 365 administration center and under the Admin tab, select **Exchange** and follow the steps outlined next.

Step 1: Create the Distribution Group

In the Exchange admin center, select **Recipients ➤ Groups** and click the + to add the distribution group. Use the e-mail alias as the distribution group name.

Step 2: Configure the Group Being Added

Since this is a personal alias, add a description and complete the additional steps for the configuration of the group (see Figure 7-64).

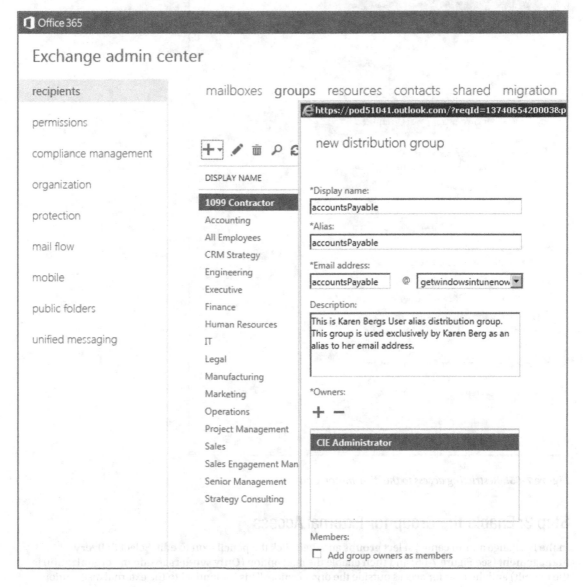

Figure 7-64. *Adding a distribution group*

Add the user and select the membership options. Since this is an e-mail alias (i.e., an internal group), it is recommended that you restrict it to the individual that is using the group (see Figure 7-65).

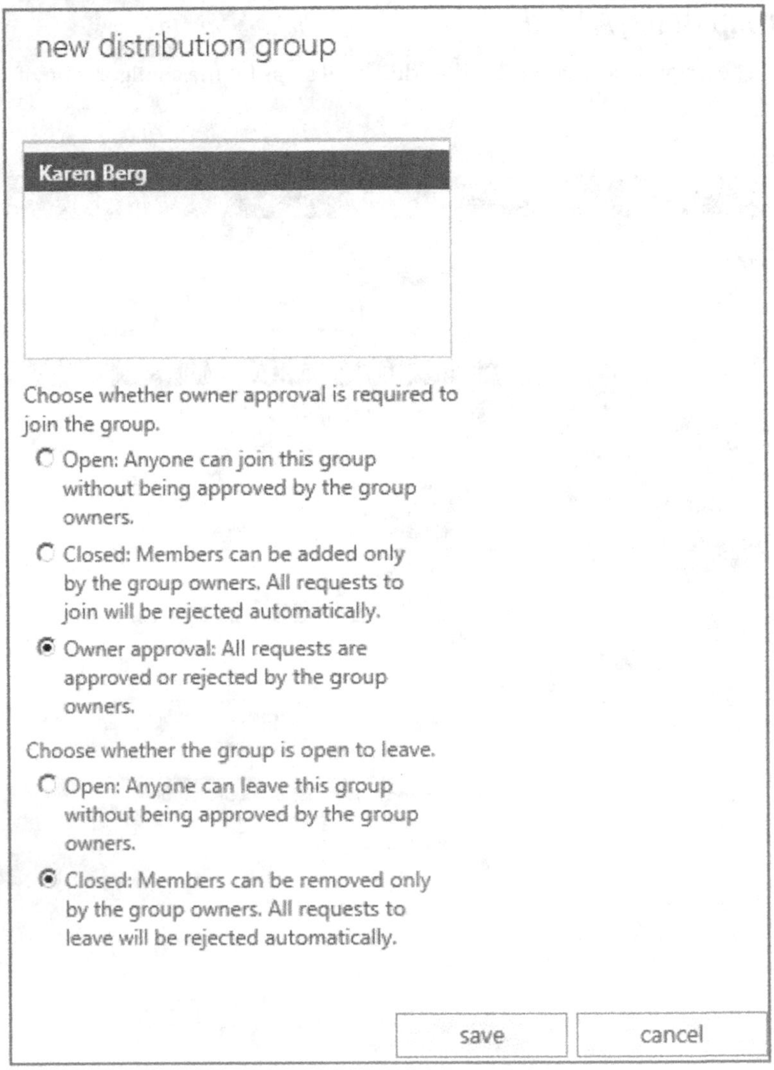

Figure 7-65. *Restricting access to the distribution group*

Step 3: Enable the Group for External Access

In the Exchange admin center, select **groups** and then click the pencil icon to edit. Select **delivery management** (see Figure 7-66) and then enable the mail option (**Only senders inside my organization** is the default) and the user for access outside the organization. This is identical to the external distribution groups discussed earlier.

Figure 7-66. *Enabling the group for external access*

Step 4: Grant Permission to the User

The final step is to grant permission to the user. There are two ways to do this: either through PowerShell or by using the Exchange admin center. Select the **In the Exchange admin center** option, select **groups**, and then click the pencil icon to edit. Select **group delegation**. You need to enter the user account for both **Send As** and **Send on Behalf** (see Figure 7-67). Click **OK**. The user is now able to use the From address in Outlook, or in the Outlook Web App, to send e-mails using the alias e-mail address.

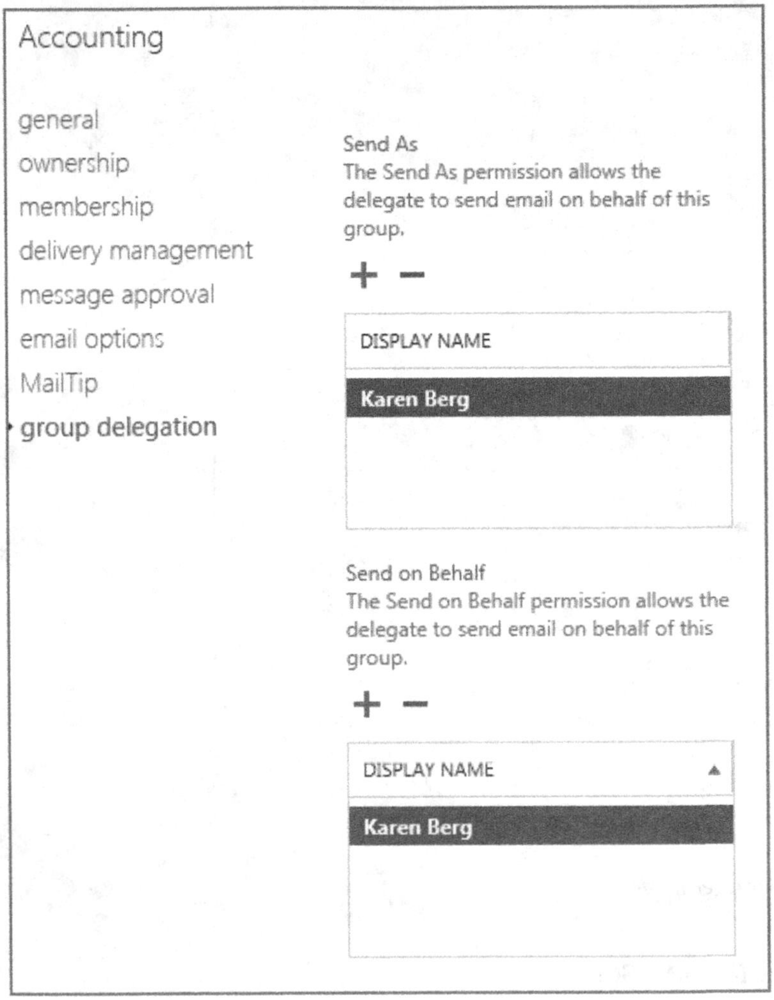

Figure 7-67. *Setting Send on Behalf options*

You can also grant permissions using the PowerShell commands for a shared mailbox. In this case, you are using a distribution list and granting full access for its use. Execute the PowerShell command and give access rights to the user mailbox. The shared mailbox PowerShell command is as follows:

```
Add-RecipientPermission -Identity myfakee-mail@domain.com -Trustee myrealeamil@domain.com
-AccessRights SendAs
```

Step 5: Verifying Outlook Configuration

The final step is to send an e-mail from Outlook to verify that you can send a message from an alias. In order for this to work, you must select the e-mail distribution group you created earlier. In our example, we used Get365. Select **Get365** from the group e-mail address book. (If you manually type the e-mail address in, this will fail.) To send an e-mail alias from Outlook, follow the steps outlined next:

1. Open Outlook and select the **From ➤ Other e-mail address** (see Figure 7-68).

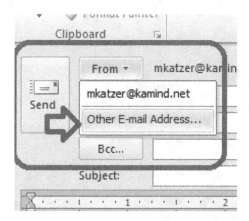

Figure 7-68. *Selecting From / Other e-mail address*

2. In the From box, select **From** and find the distribution alias (see Figure 7-69).

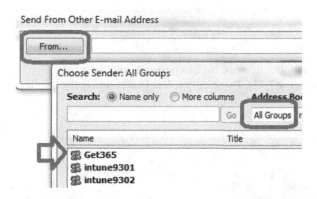

Figure 7-69. *Selecting the alias address Get365*

3. Click **OK** to send the e-mail.

After selecting **Other E-mail addresses**, select the distribution group (see Figure 7-69). You cannot enter the distribution group name in the address bar. The e-mail will not be sent.

317

Smartphone Management from Exchange

Smartphone devices are controlled with Exchange active sync. The default configuration is to allow users to control their smartphone using **Outlook Web App ➤ Options**. If you desire to control these options at an administration level, you access this information via the Exchange admin center (EAC), under the mobile option (see Figure 7-70).

Figure 7-70. *Mobile device access control*

You can also enable detailed control options on mobile devices, such as password requirements, password complexity, and encryption options (see Figure 7-71). These options are in addition to the Intune mobile device management policies.

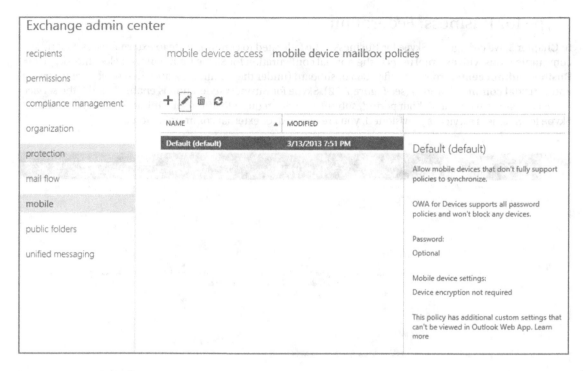

Figure 7-71. *Mobile device policies*

Many organizations wish to limit what users can do with smart devices. In some cases, you may restrict all users from using mobile devices; this is a business planning issue. It is best to define the business polices and implement them during deployment. The important point here is that you can control mobile device access to information, if needed.

Skype for Business: Administration

Skype for Business is a fully featured communications tool that supports file sharing, web conferencing, voice communications, and many other features (very similar to Skype, but with many more features). Skype for Business integrates into Microsoft Exchange and acts as a phone switch for incoming voice calls. Large organizations use Skype for Business as desktop phone replacements, and allow their users to deploy Skype for Business clients on any mobile or desktop device. Smaller organizations use third-party services such as Connect Solution (www.coso.com) to handle incoming phone calls. Skype for Business supports Enterprise voice (both people can talk at the same time). There are many different characteristics of Skype for Business; it is a powerful and popular business communication tool, and the data it accesses is encrypted between parties.

■ **Note**　If you are having trouble with file transfer on Skype for Business clients, download a new version of Skype for Business client from Office 365 or run the Online Repair on the Office 2016 installation. Please refer to the "Workstation Configuration" section in Chapter 6.

Skype for Business: Federation

In Chapter 5, we configured Skype for Business to be federated to communicate to external users. Open communications with external users is the normal configuration for Skype for Business. Select the **Skype for Business admin center** from the Office 365 dashboard (under the Admin tab), and then select **organization** and **external communications** (see Figure 7-72). Skype for Business federation is enabled, and if the service is not configured within a 12-hour period, submit a service request to Microsoft Online Services. Once the Skype for Business service is provisioned, you are enabled for external communications.

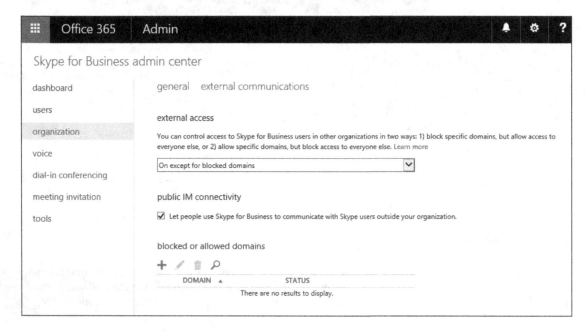

Figure 7-72. *Enabling external communications*

■ **Note** It is recommended that you have verified the domain prior to enabling Skype for Business federation. If you enable the onmicrosoft.com domain, there may be some service downtime when you switch over to the verified domain.

Skype for Business: Voice

Skype for Business supports domestic and international voice. The configuration requires that that you have properly set up and verified the DNS. Skype for Business allows you to port numbers to the service or to generate the necessary numbers for your users (see Figure 7-73).

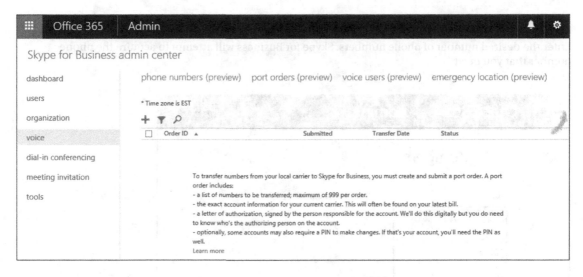

Figure 7-73. *Skype for Business admin center*

The configuration requires that that you have properly set up and verified the DNS. There are two phases to configure Office 365 Skype for Business voice. First, add the phone numbers and assign them to users.

Step 1: Adding Phone Numbers

Adding phone numbers is a straightforward process. Select the phone number option, followed by the +, and then add the new numbers (see Figure 7-74).

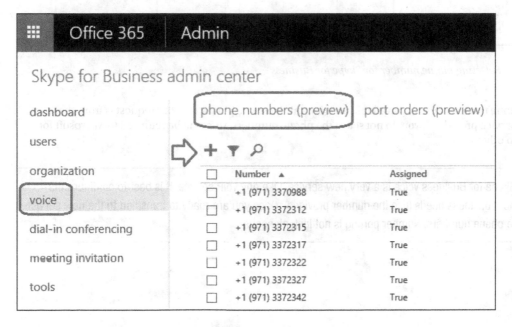

Figure 7-74. *Adding numbers in the Skype for Business admin center*

The Skype for Business rollout in the United States is phase released. Not all states and cities are being supported. You can check your location to see if a phone number is available (see Figure 7-75). Enter the desired number of phone numbers. Skype for Business will attempt to acquire the phone number that you need.

Figure 7-75. *Selecting phone number for Skype for Business*

The phone numbers are only available for a few minutes. The phone number request is from the telephony service provider. If you do not select the phone numbers, they will be returned to Microsoft for allocation to other users.

■ **Note**   Skype for Business voice is a very new service. Like any VoIP service, it is best to configure the service to meet business needs (use the number provided). Once you are ready to transition to the new service, then port the phone numbers. Number porting is not instantaneous.

Step 2: Adding an Emergency Response Location

Once you have your phone number, you can set an emergency response location (see Figure 7-76).

Figure 7-76. *Assigning emergency location*

Step 3: Adding Phone Numbers

Once you have your phone number, the next step is to assign the phone number to the different user accounts. Select the user account (see Figure 7-77) and assign one of the phone numbers you allocated from the previous step.

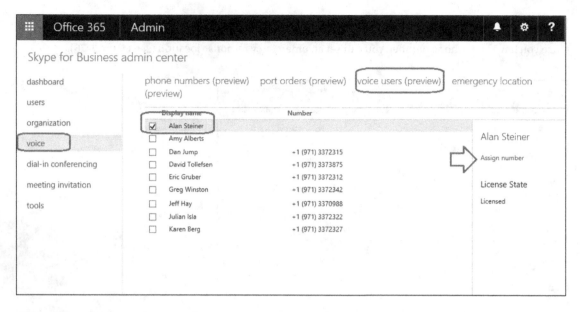

Figure 7-77. *Assigning phone numbers to users*

Once you assign the phone number to the user, you have completed the configuration of Skype for Business voice system. The **save** button is enabled if the emergency location has been identified (see Figure 7-78).

Figure 7-78. *Assigning phone numbers in Skype for Business*

Step 4: Verifying that Voice Has Been Provisioned

Have your user log out of Skype for Business and then log back in. The "dial paid" will show up once the user logs back in to the service (see Figure 7-79).

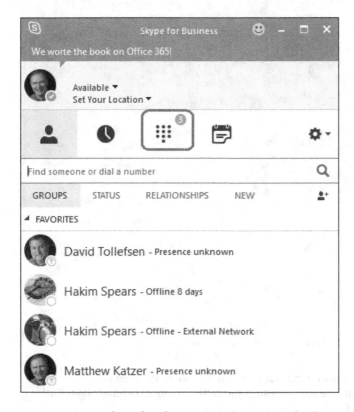

Figure 7-79. *Verifying that the voice number is set up for the user Skype for Business client*

At this point, you are ready to use the service. There are additional configurations of voice systems that you may want to have the user complete. For example, we let our desk (Skype for Business) and our smartphones ring at the same time. To access the ring options, select **Tools ➤ Options** (under the gear; see Figure 7-80), and then adjust the time length for the phone to ring.

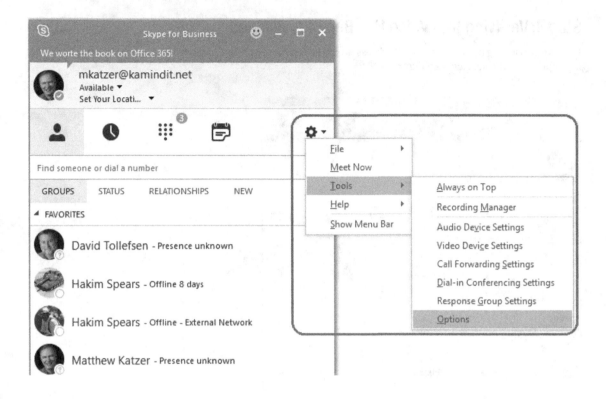

Figure 7-80. *Accessing the Skype for Business options*

We have found that setting the phone number to ring for 35 seconds is about the right amount of time to have the phone ring on your cell phone (and be able to answer the call). You set this option under **Call forwarding** in your Skype for Business client.

■ **Note**   Make sure that you test the ring delay for voice mail. The default setting, 20 seconds, is too short to ring to a third number; 35 seconds is a better ring delay to launch Skype for Business on your cell phone and to answer the call (see Figure 7-81).

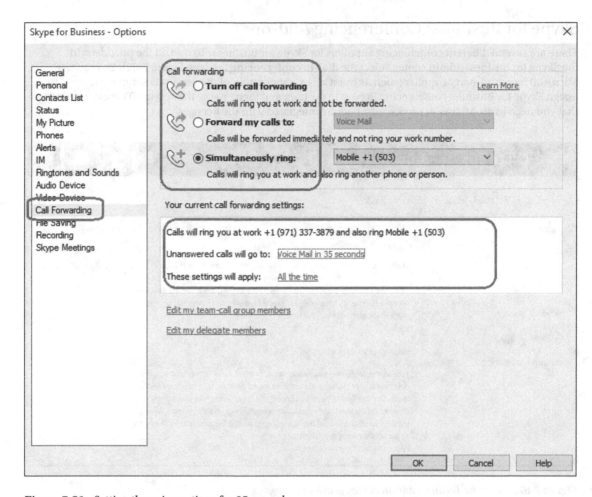

Figure 7-81. Setting the voice options for 35 seconds

Step 5: Porting the Phone Numbers

After you have tested the service, you are ready to port your phone number to the service. In the Skype for Business admin center, select voice and port numbers. This is not an instantaneous process.

■ **Note** Porting phones number is interesting. In the Portland (Oregon) area, we have phones that are caught in an artificial rate district. What happens is that you are charged a forwarding fee and your number is locked for transfer. What has worked for us in these cases is to port the number to a cell carrier, wait a month, and then port the number to Skype for Business. Please refer to your state laws on what you can legally do in your state regarding number porting.

Skype for Business: Conferencing Add-on

There are several different conferencing suppliers for Skype for Business. To find all the providers, in the Skype for Business admin center, select the **dial-in conferencing** tab (see Figure 7-82). You can use Microsoft or a third-party supplier (such as InterCall). Configuration of the service is simple: you need to assign Skype for Business conferencing license to the user, and then enable the service. There is nothing else that you need to do. Microsoft service numbers are integrated with the licenses.

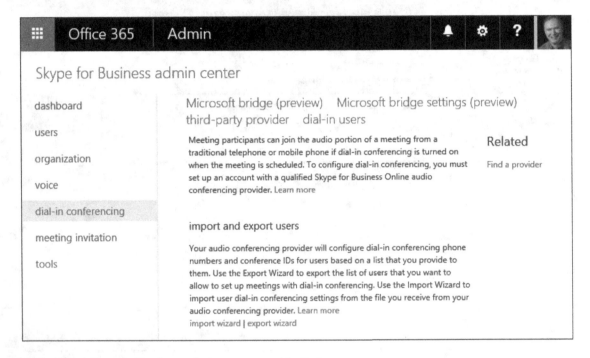

Figure 7-82. Skype for Business admin center, provider listings

If you are using a third-party provider, enter the dial-in information for the user account under "dial-in users" (see menu item in Figure 7-82). Your teleconferencing bridge number is enabled and automatically generated with an Outlook calendar invite, as long as Skype for Business is installed and running on your desktop.

■ **Note** Skype for Business requires that your DNS supplier support service records (SRV). If your DNS supplier does not support SRV, you need to move your DNS hosting services to a different service.

Yammer

Yammer is a service that is included with Office 365 Enterprise subscriptions. Yammer acts as an internal social media site or discussion board. Yammer content is owned by the company deploying Office 365. This allows an organization to own the social content (and not use a public site, like Facebook) for internal company issues. Yammer is a replacement for SharePoint newsfeed.

Access to Yammer is simple: if the user access is "licensed," the user selects the Yammer link from the Office 365 web interface. Yammer user accounts are then synced from Office 365 to Yammer. Once you select the link, you can either invite users to join the Yammer network or let each user join on their own initiative. Once your users have joined Yammer, the operation is similar to Facebook, except the data is internal to your company and is owned by the company; it is not in the public domain (see Figure 7-83).

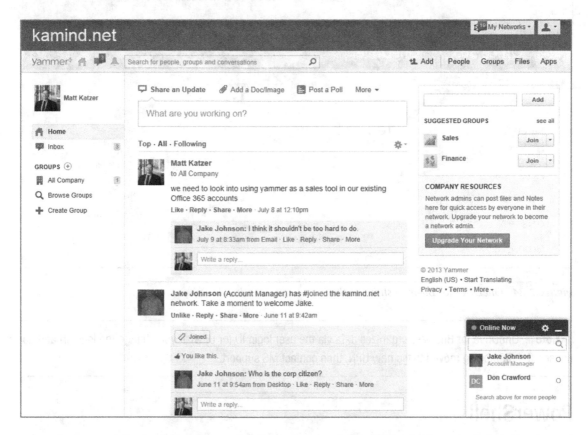

Figure 7-83. *Yammer social media home page (sample shown is from the author's company, KAMIND)*

We have only touched on a few areas that are most common in the configuration of an Office 365 company. There are many more issues that you may run into.

OneDrive for Business

OneDrive for Business is organized based on the user's UPN. What this means is that data is stored under the user's primary e-mail address. The way that OneDrive for Business is stored is how the data is stored on Office 365. For example, a OneDrive site is in an `https://<domainname>-my.sharepoint/personal/user_domainname_com` format. If you change the user's UPN (a.k.a. e-mail address), it takes up to 48 hours for the data to be remapped to the new UPN.

Looking at Figure 7-84, the OneDrive for Business UPN is the user id karenb@kamindmec50. onmicrosoft.com. If you change the UPN to karenb@kamindmec50.com, it will take up to 48 hours for the data to appear under the new UPN, karenb@kamindmec50.onmicrosoft.com.

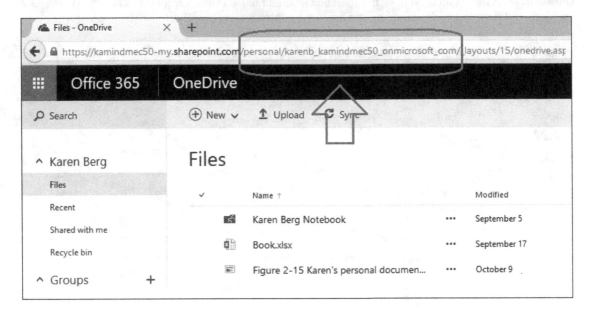

Figure 7-84. *OneDrive for Business showing the users login ID (a.k.a. UPN)*

■ **Note**   OneDrive for Business organizes data via the user login ID (or UPN). If you change the login ID and do not see the data being moved to the new UPN, then contact MS support.

PowerShell

Earlier, we briefly discussed PowerShell and the capabilities that it provides. PowerShell is required for any bulk changes that you need to perform, or for special commands that are not part of the Office 365 admin console. Typically, we recommend that if your organization has more than ten accounts, then you may find it more convenient to use PowerShell. The account that you will use for PowerShell management is the global admin user account. The account must have a license in the area that the PowerShell command is executing. For example, if you are using Exchange PowerShell commands, the global admin account must have an Exchange license assigned. If the license is not assigned, then the PowerShell command will fail. The simplest way to install the latest version of PowerShell is to select the **Single sign-on** option (see Figure 7-85). This is the same process used in Chapter 5.

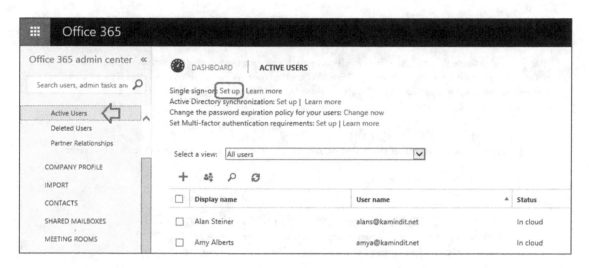

Figure 7-85. *Selecting single sign-on to install PowerShell*

■ **Note**   PowerShell installation requires that you install both (1) Microsoft Online Services Sign-In Assistant for IT professionals RTW (from the Microsoft download site) and (2) the Azure PowerShell module (from the Office 365 tenant).

If you have not installed the Microsoft Online Services Sign-In Assistant for IT professionals RTW, do that now. Go to www.microsoft.com, download, and search for the sign-in services assistant. PowerShell commands will not work unless the sign-in assistant is installed.

The latest version of Azure PowerShell can be downloaded from the Office 365 tenant. After you have selected **Set up** (see Figure 7-85) and step 3, **Install PowerShell** (see Figure 7-86), the PowerShell installation verifies the updates required to support Azure PowerShell. The only option we are interested in is the installation of PowerShell on your desktop systems. Select the correct version (32-bit or 64-bit) for your system.

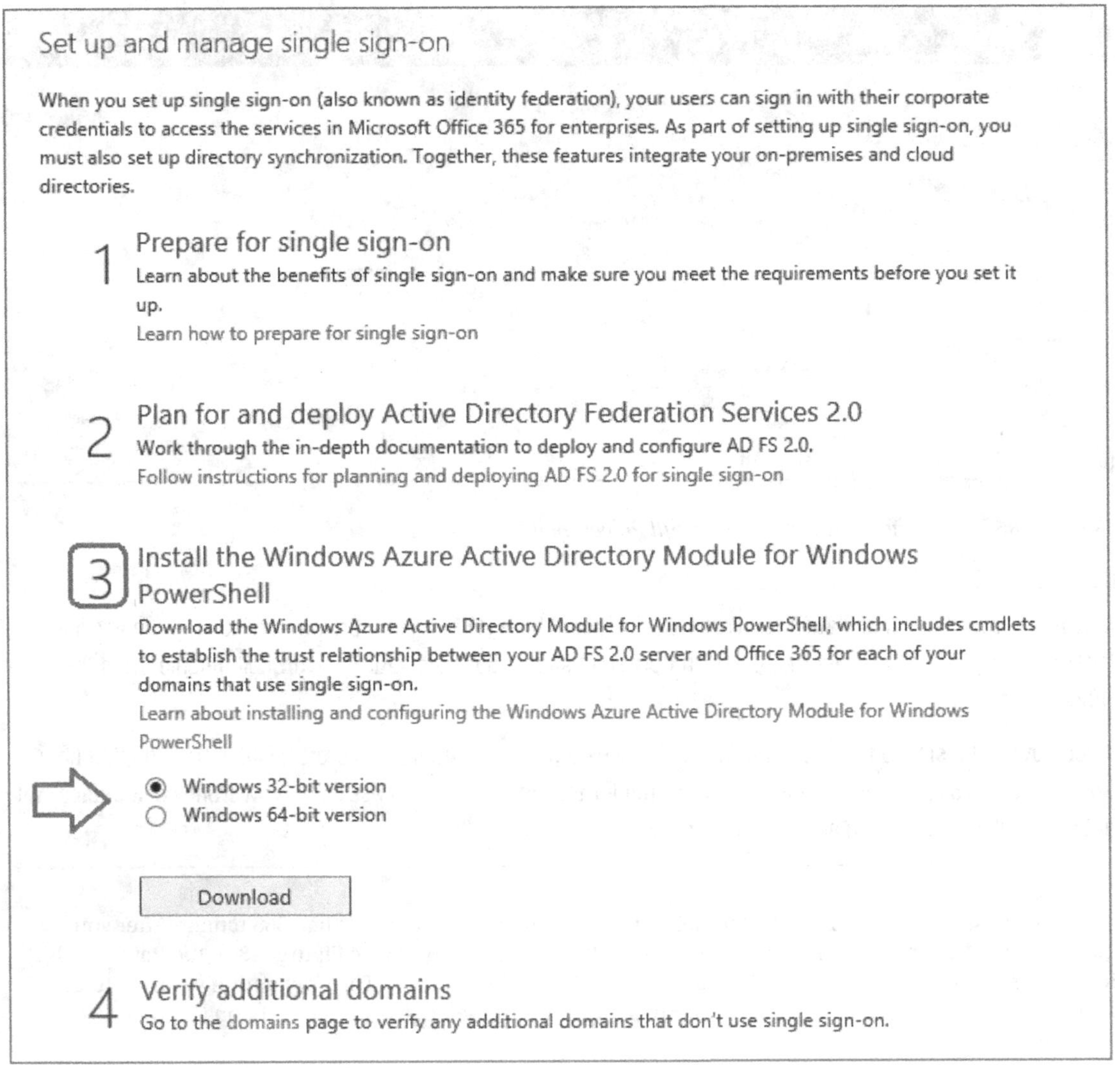

Set up and manage single sign-on

When you set up single sign-on (also known as identity federation), your users can sign in with their corporate credentials to access the services in Microsoft Office 365 for enterprises. As part of setting up single sign-on, you must also set up directory synchronization. Together, these features integrate your on-premises and cloud directories.

1 **Prepare for single sign-on**
Learn about the benefits of single sign-on and make sure you meet the requirements before you set it up.
Learn how to prepare for single sign-on

2 **Plan for and deploy Active Directory Federation Services 2.0**
Work through the in-depth documentation to deploy and configure AD FS 2.0.
Follow instructions for planning and deploying AD FS 2.0 for single sign-on

3 **Install the Windows Azure Active Directory Module for Windows PowerShell**
Download the Windows Azure Active Directory Module for Windows PowerShell, which includes cmdlets to establish the trust relationship between your AD FS 2.0 server and Office 365 for each of your domains that use single sign-on.
Learn about installing and configuring the Windows Azure Active Directory Module for Windows PowerShell

◉ Windows 32-bit version
○ Windows 64-bit version

[Download]

4 **Verify additional domains**
Go to the domains page to verify any additional domains that don't use single sign-on.

Figure 7-86. *Installing Office 365 PowerShell*

Once you have installed Office 365 PowerShell, launch the PowerShell module and enter the following commands:

```
Set-ExecutionPolicy RemoteSigned
$LiveCred = Get-Credential
Import-module msonline
Connect-MSOLService -Credential $LiveCred -Verbose
Get-MsolGroup
```

The results of running these commands should be similar to Figure 7-87.

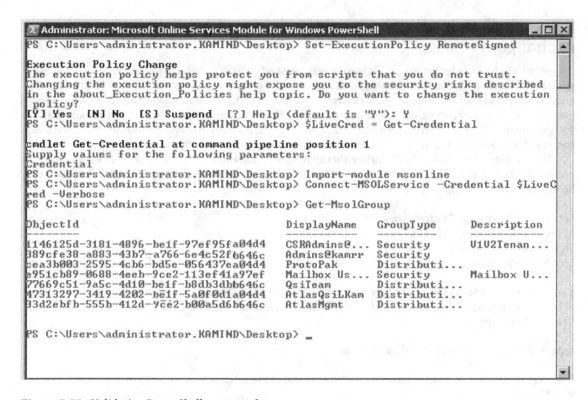

Figure 7-87. Validating PowerShell commands

You have completed the base PowerShell setup; now use the preceding command to validate the installation. If the command does not work, you have installed the PowerShell GUI incorrectly, or there is a lack of permissions, or you have not installed the desktop connector for Office 365. Using PowerShell requires administrative privileges and a license to be assigned to the account that is using PowerShell commands.

PowerShell: Setting Up for Skype for Business and SharePoint

There are different versions of PowerShell installations for Skype for Business Online, SharePoint Online, and other Microsoft Online Services (such as BI and CRM). For those services, you need to install the appropriate Active Directory services. These additional PowerShell modules are available from the Microsoft download center (www.mmicrosoft.com/download).

- Skype for Business PowerShell: Windows PowerShell module for Skype for Business Online

- SharePoint PowerShell: SharePoint Online Management Shell

These additional commands are described in the following sections. Before you can use the commands, you must download and install the PowerShell extensions.

PowerShell: Using the Standard Header for MS Online Services and Exchange

PowerShell can be complex for any user. When using PowerShell with Office 365 and Exchange, you need to use a standard PowerShell header. This standard header allows you to connect directly to the Office 365 administration interface and make the necessary changes. However, if you do not set up the commands correctly with the remote interface execution parameters, the PowerShell command will fail. The only issue is that the user account that you log in to (for Office 365) must have a license assigned to it. The licensed user can only execute the PowerShell commands for Office 365 that the user admin account is licensed to use; otherwise, it will fail.

We use a standard PowerShell interface that allows the command to run in a PowerShell command prompt, or the integrated systems editor (ISE). The standard command interface (or PowerShell header) can be invoked with this script:

```
Set-ExecutionPolicy RemoteSigned
$LiveCred = Get-Credential
Import-module msonline
Connect-MSOLService -Credential $LiveCred -Verbose

$Session = New-PSSession -ConfigurationName Microsoft.Exchange-ConnectionUri
https://ps.outlook.com/powershell/ -Credential $LiveCred -Authentication Basic -
AllowRedirection

Import-PSSession $Session -Allow Clobber

# Insert Other Power shell commands before remove PSSession
#*********
# PowerShell Commands go here
#*********

#Clean up and close the session
Remove-PSSession $Session
```

Once you have verified the functionality of the header script, you are ready to make the necessary changes in Office 365. This section of the administration maintenance manual lists the type of problems encountered and the PowerShell solution. All that is needed for the user to execute these commands is to use an account—with global administrator rights—that is licensed with an appropriate subscription (such as Exchange, SharePoint, etc.).

PowerShell: Not Remotely Sign Error

The first time you run PowerShell, you may get the error "not remotely signed." To correct this error, you need to enable PowerShell on your system.

1. Start Windows PowerShell as an administrator by right-clicking the Windows PowerShell shortcut and selecting **Run as administrator**.

2. The WinRM service is configured for manual startup by default. You must change the startup type to **Automatic** and start the service on each computer that you want to work with. At the PowerShell prompt, you can verify that the WinRM service is running using the following command:

   ```
   get-service winrm
   ```

The value of the Status property in the output should be Running.

a. If the value is not running, you can start the service from the command prompt:

```
sc config winrm start= auto
start winrm
```

b. To configure Windows PowerShell for remoting, type the following command:

```
Enable-PSRemoting –force
```

Mail flow should resume in the next two to four hours.

PowerShell: Winmail.dat Problem

Let's say the e-mail is being sent externally to users in an RTF mime format, and the users cannot read the e-mail and see a winmail.dat file. The winmail.dat file appears on the client e-mail because Outlook (on the sender) is not installed correctly, or there is another Outlook add-in (on the sender) that is preventing the e-mail from being converted to text. To resolve this issue, either disable the Outlook add-ins (on the sending device) or uninstall and reinstall Office 2007/2010.

If this fails, then as a last resort you can force the Office 365 Exchange Server to send only pure text e-mail. This command forces the e-mails to be sent out as pure text format:

```
Set-MailContact <ExternalE-mailAddress or GUID> -UseMapiRichTextFormat Never
```

Verify that the mail format was applied:

```
Get-MailContact | Select <ExternalE-mailAddress or GUID> | Select UseMapiRichTextFormat
```

These commands will only display the user e-mail address if it supports RTF format; otherwise, it will display other options.

PowerShell: Enable Audit

The Audit command turns on full tracking for any access to a mailbox. To change the audit state on a mailbox, run this command:

```
Set-Mailbox <Identity> -AuditEnabled $true
```

Set multiple mailboxes for audit:

```
$UserMailboxes = Get-mailbox -Filter {(RecipientTypeDetails -eq 'UserMailbox')}
$UserMailboxes | ForEach {Set-Mailbox $_.Identity -AuditEnabled $true}
```

PowerShell: Verification of Audit Logs

Run the following command to verify the audit log configuration and the time limit configuration. Administrator audit logs are on by default; mailbox logs are off by default. Audit logs are enabled for 15 days.

```
Get-AdminAuditLogConfig
```

335

PowerShell: Mailbox Audit Log search

To perform an audit log search in PowerShell, use the following command (it requires that auditing be enabled on the mailbox in question):

```
New-mailboxAuditLogSearch -Mailboxes user@domain.com –Startdate 1/1/2010 –EndDate 12/31/2013
-StatusMailRecipients manager@domain.com
```

PowerShell: Passwords Forever

Passwords can be set from the user interface. However, when you reset a password, all passwords revert to the 90-day password reset.

```
Get-MSOLUser | Set-MsolUser -PasswordNeverExpires $true
```

■ **Note**   If the user's password is reset, the policy changes back to 90 days. If you want the forever policy applied, you need to set it again with PowerShell, and every time you reset a password. The Office 365 interface allows passwords to be fixed for up to 720 days.

PowerShell: Get Mailbox Statistics

This command retrieves all of the usage data about the user:

```
Get-Mailbox | Get-MailboxStatistics | Select-Object DisplayName,StorageLimitStatus,TotalItemSize
```

PowerShell: Enable Litigation Hold–No Notice

There are different legal holds—with notice and without notice. This command places a mailbox on legal hold with no notice given to the end user:

```
Get-Mailbox -ResultSize unlimited | Set-mailbox -LitigationHoldEnabled $true
```

PowerShell: Review Permission Assigned to a Mailbox

This command retrieves all of the permission information about the user:

```
Get-MailboxPermission -Identity user@domain.com
```

PowerShell: Review the Management Role Assignment to a User Account

This command retrieves all of the permissions assigned to different roles in Office 365:

```
Get-ManagementRoleAssignment- -Enabled $True -Delegating $True
```

PowerShell: Display All Mailbox Forwarders

The following commands retrieve information about the mailbox forwarders and allow you to turn them on or off.

Display all mailbox forwarders:

```
Get-Mailbox | Where {$_.ForwardingSMTPAddress -ne $null} | Select Name,
ForwardingSMTPAddress, DeliverToMailboxAndForward
```

Turn off all mailbox forwarders:

```
Get-Mailbox | Where {$_.ForwardingAddress -ne $null} | Set-Mailbox -ForwardingAddress $null
```

Turn off a single mailbox forwarder:

```
Set-Mailbox <e-mailaddress> -ForwardingSmtpAddress $null
```

PowerShell: Change Mailbox Permissions

The mailbox permission command is very useful; you can use this on any e-mail-enabled item (such as distribution groups):

```
Add-MailboxPermission -Identity public@kamind.com -User john@kamind.com -AccessRights
FullAccess -InheritanceTypeAll -Confirm:$false
```

```
Add-RecipientPermission -Identity public@kamind.com -Trustee rajk@kamind.com -AccessRights SendAs
```

PowerShell: Change the User Principal Name on a User Account

After you configure AADConnect, you may run into a situation where the user account name has not synced correctly to Office 365. This is usually because the e-mail address is not set up in the on-premises Active Directory or the UPN is missing in the root of the Active Directory. If you have corrected the on-premises AD and the user's principal name has not changed, then run the following PowerShell command:

```
Set-MSOLUser -UserPrincipalName user@domain.onmicrosoft.com -NewUserPrincipalName user@domain.com
```

■ **Note** The Office 365 account has the Active Directory from the on-premises server. Make sure that you check the configuration of the Active Directory to make sure that the user's e-mail address is in the correct field and the UPN is set for the AD login. If you need to execute this command, there is a configuration problem in the local Active Directory.

PowerShell: Assign License to a User Account

After you have directory-synced an account, there may be a need to bulk-assign licenses via PowerShell. To complete this, you need to execute the following two PowerShell commands. There are additional PowerShell commands that you also need to run to retrieve the subscription SKUs to use this command. The licenses types must be active.

```
Set-MSOLUser -UserPrincipalName user@domain.com -UsageLocation US
Set-MSOLUserLicense -UserPrincipalName user@domain.com -AddLicenses
{tenantid}:ENTERPRISEPACK
```

PowerShell: Purging Users in the Delete Bin

There are cases where you need to remove users that have been deleted in Office 365. A deleted user is retained in Office 365 for 30 days, which allows you to easily restore the user account to the same subscription that the account had prior to deletion. If you need to delete all user data, use these PowerShell commands to perform this action:

```
#Get a list fousers in the RecyleBin
Get-MsolUser –ReturnDeletedUsers

#Purge all users from RecyleBin
Get-MsolUser –ReturnDeletedUsers | Remove-MsolUser –RemoveFromRecycleBin –force
#Purge a user from the RecyleBin
Remove-MsolUser -UserPrincipalName testmatt@testmatt.com –RemoveFromRecycleBin –force
#Restore a user from the recycle bin
Restore-MsolUser -UserPrincipalName testmatt@testmatt.com
```

PowerShell: Bypass Spam Filtering for E-mail

Allow all mail to be sent to a mailbox without filtering e-mail by using Exchange Spam Confidence Level (SCL) for e-mail processing. This command accepts all incoming e-mail that is processed by Office 365 Exchange Transport server role:

```
Set-ContentFilteringConfig –Bypassedrecipients public@kamind.com
```

PowerShell: Extend the Purges Folder to Greater Than 14 Days

E-mail in Office 365 is deleted from the Purges folder after 14 days, once the user has selected the item in the Delete folder. You can extend this to 30 days with the following commands.

- Extend 30-day delete for a mailbox:

  ```
  Set-mailbox user@contoso.com –retaindeleteditemsfor 30
  ```

- Extend 30-day delete for the organization:

  ```
  Get-mailbox | Set-mailbox –retaindeleteditemsfor 30
  ```

PowerShell: Meeting Room Configuration

To make meeting rooms more useful, you need to add additional user information about the meeting room. The only way to add these capabilities is to use PowerShell to extend the meeting room options. This example uses the "ingoodtaste1"meeting room.

Set the conference room to show "limited details–free & busy":

```
Set-MailboxFolderPermission -AccessRights LimitDetails -Identity ingoodtaste1:\calendar
-User default
```

Cloud Solution Provider: Office 365

The Microsoft Cloud Solution Provider (CSP) is where the Microsoft Partner manages the Office 365 subscription billing and support rather than using Microsoft services. CSP providers support a variety of different options for Office 365. Figure 7-88 shows the KAMIND IT CSP program designed around Office 365 Business Premium, E3, and the Skype for Business Cloud PBX (E5) solution.

KAMIND IT Cloud Packages

	O365 Core	O365 Secure	O365 Ultimate
Office 365 license (incl)	Business Premium	E3	E5
Malware Protection	✔	✔	✔
Admin support	✔	✔	✔
KAM Signature	✔	✔	✔
Training Vouchers	✔	✔	✔
Webinars	✔	✔	✔
Library of tech notes	✔	✔	✔
Office Suite	✔ Std	✔ Pro	✔ Pro
EMS		✔	✔
Email encryption		✔	✔
Compliance		✔	✔
Audit log		✔	✔
Cloud PBX			✔
KAM Cloud Backup			✔
KAM Cloud Sync			✔
KAM Cloud Admin			✔
Client Monitoring			✔
Fast Track			✔

Figure 7-88. *KAMIND IT CSP program offering (www.kamind.com/csp)*

■ **Note**   Office 365 Cloud PBX (E5 subscriptions) works very well for businesses with less than 51 seats. For better performance, if your organization has more than 51 employees, you need to use Azure Express Route to link the on-premises network to Office 365/Azure.

Nuvolex: Managing Office 365

One of the newest third-party administration tools is Nuvolex (see Figure 7-89). It is designed to reduce Office 365 administration costs. It is a graphically based, best-of-class administration tool that makes managing a large number of Office 365 sites and users simple.

Figure 7-89. *Nuvolex home page (www.nuvolex.com)*

Nuvolex provides the same capabilities as Office 365, but extends them by targeting the most common set of features that administrators and MSP use to manage Office 365. Nuvolex is designed to allow you to manage administrator actions. For example, support staff is organized by skills: Tier 1, Tier 2, and Tier 3. The entry-level skills are classified as Tier 3. If you are not using a tool like Nuvolex, you need to assign your Tier 3 support staff with global administration rights. This may cause a compliance issue since global administrators have full access to all company information. This is where Nuvolex helps the Office 365 administrator.

Most Tier 3 help desk administrators are assigned limited rights. Nuvolex allows you to assign limited rights to Tier 3 administrators (see Figure 7-90). In this situation, the Tier 3 individuals have the ability to perform calendar sharing, password reset, and e-mail alias creation. However, they do not have other rights on the management of accounts or access to different types of accounts.

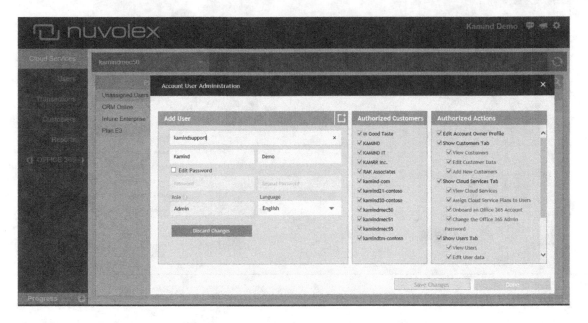

Figure 7-90. Nuvolex custom permissions

Likewise, Tier 1 and Tier 2 support staff have different rights based on their skill sets. One of the main issues that Nuvolex solves is the ability to reduce administration rights in the management of Office 365. Office 365 allows you to limit administrators to six different types of administrator roles (see Figure 7-91). These administration rights are global across all users. Nuvolex provides a finer level of granularity across accounts, users, and administration rights.

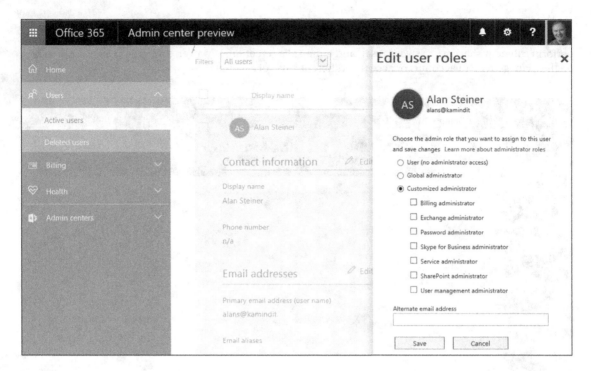

Figure 7-91. *Office 365 limited permission*

As a Tier 1 administrator, you want to reduce the rights that your support staff has in managing user accounts. This allows you to scale help desk support personnel by salary or skill levels, while reducing the risk of the Tier 3 support staff accessing information that they are not entitled to see (such as HR payroll). Tier 3 supports personnel, typically by managing calendar access permission, e-mail aliases, and so forth, and their rights need to be restricted to job function. For example, you may want to restrict password reset to Tier 2 or other support staff (those that are more trusted). Nuvolex allows you to do that in a very granular way, as compared to Office 365, which is grant-all or deny-all access (see Figure 7-92).

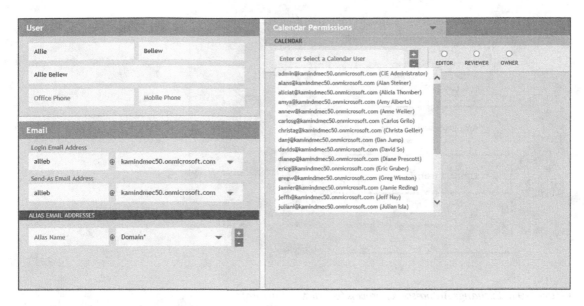

Figure 7-92. *Nuvolex limited access permission example*

Troubleshooting: Autodiscover

Autodiscover allows an Outlook client (including your laptop and your smartphone) to discover the location of the Office 365 Exchange e-mail server, and to automatically connect to that server (see Figure 7-93). You need to insert the Autodiscover record in the external DNS and the internal DNS. Both records should point to outlook.com.

Type	Priority	Host name	Points to address	TTL
CNAME	-	autodiscover	autodiscover.outlook.com	1 Hour

Figure 7-93. *Autodiscover record value*

■ **Note** Outlook clients (Mac and PC) use Autodiscover to find the mail server. Smartphones use the MX records.

The Autodiscover process is outlined in Figure 7-94. When an internal client looks up an Autodiscover record, it first determines the Autodiscover record through Active Directory. If the client is external, it looks up the Autodiscover record from the DNS.

Figure 1   The Autodiscover service process for internal access

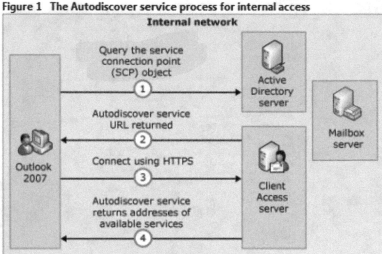

Figure 7-94. *Exchange Autodiscover process (courtesy of Microsoft)*

If you are on site and you are trying to connect to the Office 365 Exchange Server, the Outlook client uses the Exchange Service Control Point connection object to attach to the local Exchange Server and bypass the external Autodiscover look up. If you have chosen not to use Microsoft migration tools, you need to block the local clients from finding the on-site Exchange Server in the autodiscovery process, or convert the mailboxes to a mail-enabled user (MEU). The registry entries that must be modified for clients are listed next (see https://support.microsoft.com/en-us/kb/2612922).

1. Navigate to the following registry key:

    `HKEY_CURRENT_USER\Software\Microsoft\Office\12.0\Outlook\AutoDiscover`

2. Set the following values for the Value Names listed:

    ```
    "PreferLocalXML"=dword:1
    "ExcludeHttpRedirect"=dword:0
    "ExcludeHttpsAutodiscoverDomain"=dword:1
    "ExcludeHttpsRootDomain"=dword:1
    "ExcludeScpLookup"=dword:1
    "ExcludeSrvLookup"=dword:1
    "ExcludeSrvRecord"=dword:1
    ```

Troubleshooting: Creating a Bootable USB Stick

To create a bootable USB memory stick, you need to expand the ISO image from the Windows 10 download. The following are the tools that you need to create a bootable device:

- A Windows 7 PC with a USB port

- A USB memory stick with a size greater than the ISO image (4GB or 8GB)

- An ISO unpack utility such as Roxio or MagicDisc (download from the Web)

344

Any memory stick can be used, just make sure the size is larger than the ISO media. The memory sticks that we use are typically 8GB. This allows us to build a USB stick with the Windows 10 software and have enough room to add additional support files.

Preparing the USB Memory Stick

Preparing the memory stick is very straightforward. Open a CMD window in Windows 7 (64-bit), Windows 8, or Windows 10. Enter the following commands:

```
DISKPART (enter)
LIST DISK (enter) – this will list the disk devices, such as the USB stick
SELECT DISK 5 (in our case, the USB was listed as device 5)
CLEAN
CREATE PARTITION PRIMARY
SELECT PARTITION 1
ACTIVE
FORMAT FS=NTFS QUICK
ASSIGN
EXIT
```

At this point, the USB memory stick is prepared to install the Windows software.

Unpacking the ISO Software

Once you have built the memory stick, you need to copy the files over to the USB device. Copy all files, including hidden and system files. We use Magic ISO to copy the files (see Figure 7-95) from the ISO image to the USB device.

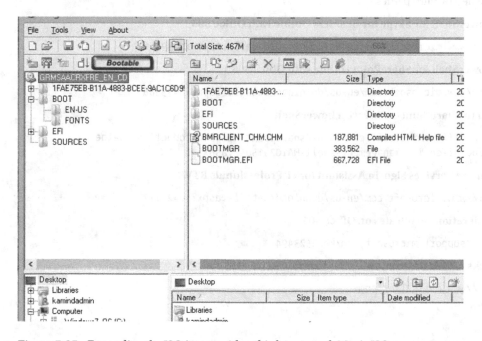

Figure 7-95. *Expanding the ISO image with a third-party tool, Magic ISO*

Setting a Bootable UBS Memory Stick

Earlier, you copied files to the USB device. At this point, you need to set the USB device to be bootable. You can do this from the USB device or the PC. The setting of the boot sector must be made from the boot directory. To set the boot drive, do the following:

1. Open a CMD window (as an administrator).

2. Change to the drive letter of the USB memory stick.

3. Change directory to the boot directory on the memory stick

4. Run the command BOOTSECT.EXE /NT60 ?: (where ? is the USB drive letter).

Now boot the USB and test the boot image. Reboot your PC with the memory stick installed.

Summary

Office 365 administration is a very large topic and many books could be written to cover this topic. The objective here was to provide you with an overview on how to administer Office 365. I wanted to provide you with exposure to the new tools and techniques so that you can see how easy it is to manage and secure Office 365 with tools like Nuvolex. As you begin to work with Office 365, remember the PowerShell section and the common header. Office 365 is about productivity and management of company resources.

Reference Links

There is a lot of information about Office 365 on the Web; the issue is finding the right site. The information contained in this chapter is a combination of our experiences in doing deployments and support information published by third parties.

Installing PowerShell for Skype for Business Online with Office 365

- http://www.microsoft.com/en-us/download/details.aspx?id=39366

Installing PowerShell for SharePoint Online with Office 365

- http://www.microsoft.com/en-us/download/details.aspx?id=35588

Introduction to SharePoint Online with PowerShell

- http://office.microsoft.com/en-us/sharepoint-help/introduction-to-the-sharepoint-online-management-shell-HA102915057.aspx

Microsoft Online Services Sign-In Assistant for IT Professionals RTW

- http://www.microsoft.com/en-us/download/details.aspx?id=28177

Updating Federation certificates on Office 365

- http://support.microsoft.com/kb/2523494

Tips and tricks for administration

- http://www.mattkatzer.com

How to set up a certificate on IIS 7.0

- http://www.iis.net/learn/manage/configuring-security/how-to-set-up-ssl-on-iis

Office 365 service level permissions

- http://community.office365.com/en-us/wikis/manage/535.aspx

Exchange 2013 Role Overview

- http://help.outlook.com/en-us/exchangelabshelp/ee441216

Exchange 2013 Built-in Roles

- http://technet.microsoft.com/en-us/library/dd351266(v=exchg.150).aspx

Next Steps

Your Office 365 systems have been set up and configured. At this point, you understand the features of Office 365 and are ready to move forward. However, your work is not yet complete. There is more to do depending on your Office 365 configuration. It is recommended that you review Chapters 3, 4, 5, and 6 in preparation for deployment.

Chapter 3: The Apps. Office 365 is owned by the business and the data is only available to the business for the business use. Social enterprise in Office 365 takes advantage of the different data mining capabilities that are present in public services like Gmail, Dropbox, Facebook, LinkedIn, and other social media sites, and applies those capabilities to your Office 365 site to improve your business productivity. This chapter describes the use of Office 365 applications and Power BI.

Chapter 4: Cloud Security Best Practices. One of the issues that all managers are faced with is the management of data and security and learning best practices. In this chapter, you explore the different capabilities of Office 365 and the monitoring that is in place to manage your Office 365 company to ensure that your data remains private. This chapter covers the most common approaches to Office 365 migration.

Chapter 5: Office 365 Deployment Step by Step. The secret to a successful deployment to Office 365 is picking the correct plan that supports your business. The key to a successful migration to Office 365 is the planning and purchase process. Once you select a plan, your primary consideration must be to ensure that the migration process is seamless for your organization. This chapter describes the basic purchase information and it details the choices. It concludes with information about pre-deployment, deployment, and post-deployment.

Chapter 6: Workstation Setup and Configuration. Office 365 supports many different systems and capabilities, depending on your business needs. The issue that IT managers constantly face is how to set up and manage the client environment. This chapter is focused on the configuration of an Office 365 desktop environment. This is the go-to reference chapter on the configuration of your desktop and mobile phones.

CHAPTER 8

■ ■ ■

Glossary

The following terms are covered in this book.

AAAA record: Part of the Domain Name System (DNS). Normally, it returns a 128-bit IPv6 address.

Active Directory (AD): Active Directory is a database designed to store information about your Microsoft network environment, including users, groups, passwords, user contact information, and network configuration. It is normally replicated across your network.

AAD Connect: The Azure Active Directory Connect tool allows you to link on-premises (or Azure) Active Directory to Office 365. This allows seamless integration to Office 365 resources, such as password reset and password synchronization.

AD FS: Active Directory Federation Services extends Active Directory to off-premises applications and systems (outside the firewall). AD FS allows single sign-on.

alias: An e-mail address that points to another e-mail address. People outside the system can e-mail to an alias address. You can have as many alias addresses as you wish in Office 365.

app: A component of Office 365 business subscriptions. Apps have a single-purpose focus.

App Store: An application-marketing place where applications may be purchased to extended Office 365. Apps may be added on a per-user or a company basis in Office 365.

A record: Part of the Domain Name System (DNS). Normally, it returns a 32-bit IPv4 address.

Autodiscover: Part of the Domain Name System (DNS). Autodiscover describes the name (IP address) of the location that a program such as Outlook can find the Exchange Server for a given e-mail account. Implemented as a CNAME record, it may have to be implemented on a DNS local server, as well as at the domain registrar. For Office 365, the initial Exchange Server address is autodiscover. outlook.com.

Azure: The Microsoft cloud platform that manages all computing activities for Microsoft. Office 365 and other third-party public clouds are cloud applications that are hosted in Azure.

BPOS: Business Productivity Online Standard Suite (the previous name and version of Office 365).

browser: Web browser, such as Internet Explorer, Firefox, Chrome, or Safari.

cloud: Any off-premises service that is maintained by a third party. Examples include Hotmail and the Microsoft Online Services: Office 365.

Cloud App Discovery: An Azure service (part of Enterprise Mobility Suite) that deploys an agent on the user's desktop to determine the applications that are being used. This tool is useful in determining which applications need to be included as a shared resource across Office 365 users.

Cloud backup: A third-party service that backs up e-mail, OneDrive for Business, and SharePoint documents to a cloud service for recovery to Office 365.

Cloud PBX: The Skype for Business phone service that may or may not be integrated into a company's office communications systems (or PBX). Cloud PBX may be deployed in hybrid or stand-alone mode in Office 365.

Cloud Solution Provider: A Microsoft cloud partner that offers cloud solutions that include Office 365 for its customers. A CSP bills Office 365 services on behalf of its customers.

CNAME record: Part of the Domain Name System (DNS). The alias of one name to another.

coexistence: In a coexistence migration, the mail flow (via the MX record) remains through the original e-mail server as test groups are migrated to Office 365. Mail flow is redirected to Office 365 at the end of the migration.

content type: A content type defines the attributes of a SharePoint list item, a document, or a folder. There is a content type per site collection. It could be considered as a "collection of columns for reuse" in other lists or document libraries. Content types are inherited.

core business software: The software that is the heart of the business. This could be the point-of-sale software for a retail store or the order-tracking system for a warehouse. The software that runs the business.

CSP: See Cloud Solution Provider.

cutover: In a cutover migration, the mail flow (via the MX record) is redirected to Office 365 for the entire organization at one time.

Data loss prevention: A machine learning process that reviews all business communications based on a set of rules that can permit or block information to third parties. DLP is used to prevent the distribution of information to users outside of an organization.

Delve: A machine-learning tool that looks at all of the users' business documents and organizes them in a way that is relevant to what is trending with users.

DirSync: Directory Sync allows an Active Directory to be synchronized to another Active Directory. In the Office 365 world, an on-premises Active Directory is synchronized (now including passwords) to the Office 365 Active Directory for your tenant. This has been replaced with by AAD Connect.

distribution groups: Distribution groups (formerly known as distribution lists) are lists of e-mail addresses. E-mailing to a distribution group sends the e-mail to each user in the group. A distribution group can be for internal e-mail only or available to the outside world.

DLP: See Data loss prevention.

DNS: Domain Name System; also the protocol used by the Domain Name System. Used to look up additional information (or translate) a name to an IP address. See also A record, AAAA record, CNAME record, MX record, SPF record, SRV record, TXT record, and www record.

document: A Word, Excel, PowerPoint, or other type of file within a SharePoint document library. A document may have independent permissions.

document library: A set of documents within a SharePoint site. In many ways, a document library is a specialized list that contains the document and associated metadata. A document library is separate from a page but usually is displayed on a page. When you select and display a specific document library, the page ribbon shows actions that can be performed in the document library or the folders and documents within it, such as setting permissions or deleting an item. A document library may contain folders and documents.

Document Set: A feature in SharePoint Server 2013 that enables an organization to manage a single deliverable, or work product, that can include multiple documents or files. A Document Set is a special kind of folder that combines unique Document Set attributes—the attributes and behavior of folders and documents—and provides a user interface (UI), metadata, and object model elements to help manage all aspects of the work product.

domain name: Often referred to as "custom" or "vanity" domains, this is the name of an organization on the Internet, used for its e-mail and web site. A domain name is maintained (and reported to the rest of the world) by a domain registrar. Examples of domain names are kamind.net, microsoft.com, and getoffice365now.com.

domain registrar: An organization that maintains your domain information; for example, eNom, Network Solutions, or GoDaddy. See also DNS.

EBS: Essential Business Server.

e-mail migration: The process of moving existing (historical) e-mail to a new e-mail service.

EMS: See Enterprise Mobility Suite.

Enterprise Mobility Suite: A suite of software from Microsoft that helps to manage and monitor user identity (access to cloud resources) and information rights (how those resources are used).

Essential Business Server: A configured three-server solution (Exchange, SharePoint, Systems Center) for companies with 75 to 400 employees. Microsoft canceled this offering on March 4, 2010. One of the factors was the cost per employee, as compared with the Microsoft cloud offering.

Exchange Federation: A mechanism for trust between Exchange servers.

Exchange Federation remote mailbox move: A form of e-mail migration between federated Exchange servers. In Office 365, this is normally between an on-premises Exchange server and the Office 365 Exchange server(s) of your tenant.

Exchange Online Protection (EOP): A Microsoft service that filters incoming e-mail for spam and viruses. Formerly known as Forefront Online Protection for Exchange (FOPE), this service is included in the hosted Exchange area of Office 365. Several controls can be used to customize the service.

Exchange public folders: A method of sharing information within an organization, using Exchange Server as the database. Contrast with SharePoint.

Exchange Server: A Microsoft Services software product that receives, stores, and forwards e-mail (and other information, such as calendars, contacts, and folders) for an organization. A user typically sees the e-mail, calendar, and contacts through a client, such as Outlook, or through a web browser. Hosted Exchange servers are maintained by an external service, such as Office 365.

.exe file: Executable file. These cannot be stored (directly) in SharePoint; use a .zip file.

external contacts: External contacts are contact information about people outside an organization.

FastTrack: A service that speeds the onboarding and education of Office 365 customers on Office 365.

Firewall: An appliance that monitors and inspects Internet traffic according to a set of rules that filer or block Internet communication and protects local computer resources form public (Internet) access.

folder: Similar to a folder on your PC. Part of a SharePoint document library. Folders may have independent permissions. A folder contains documents.

FTP: File Transfer Protocol. When implemented by an FTP server, it is a method used to share files. There are security and usability issues. See SharePoint as an alternative.

Hybrid coexistence: Hybrid coexistence could be considered as a type of migration. In the Office 365 context, an organization's e-mail can be stored in the organization's on-premises Exchange Server or the Office 365–hosted Exchange Server for the tenant. After establishing Exchange Federation, an administrator can move users' e-mail boxes to and from the cloud.

immutability: The preservation of data in its original form is "immutable" (cannot be changed) and is kept in a form that is discoverable.

Intune: A device management tool that manages the company computing assets (phones, tables, laptops, Macs, or PCs). Intune is used to manage mobility devices' access to company business information.

IP address: Internet Protocol Address. The numeric address of a device or service.

KAMIND IT: IT cloud advisors (see www.kamind.com).

legal hold: Legal hold is an action that is placed on a mailbox to meet compliance requirements for future discovery and searching.

list: A set of items within a SharePoint site. You can think of a list as a bunch of rows and columns with a data value potentially at the intersection, like a spreadsheet. There are specialized lists that have special properties. A list is distinct from a page but usually is displayed on a page. When you select and display a specific list, the page ribbon shows actions that can be performed on the list or items in it, such as setting permissions or deleting an item. Special list types include Task List and Calendar List.

Lync: See Skype for Business.

mail flow: Mail flow describes how a particular piece of e-mail flows from the sender to the receiver. See also MX record.

metadata: Additional data stored about/with a SharePoint item; for example, the date and author of a document. This data is searchable.

Microsoft Domain Name: The prefix for .onmicrosoft.com. This is also the basis of your SharePoint site; for xxx.onmicrosoft.com, the SharePoint site is xxx.sharepoint.com. This cannot be changed, nor can it be moved between different Office 365 plans.

Microsoft Online Services: Services provided by Microsoft, including Office 365 and Windows Intune.

migration: Copying data (typically e-mail, calendar entries, and contacts) from your existing environment to Office 365.

MX record: Part of the Domain Name System (DNS). An MX record tells the outside world the location of your mail service (name or IP address).

Office 365: The brand for the collection of Microsoft Cloud Services. Office 365 includes hosted Exchange e-mail, Lync Enterprise voice, SharePoint, and several software options. It is generally considered Software as a Service.

Office 365 ProPlus: The current version of Office Professional, presently Office 2013. This is the full Office product and can be installed on up to five devices (under the same login), such as your work desktop, laptop, a Mac, and a home computer.

Office 365 Wave 14: A version first released in July 2012.

Office 365 Wave 15: A version first released in March 2013.

off-premises: Often used as a synonym for *cloud*, this actually denotes hardware devices and software that are located outside of your company location (off-site).

on-premises: This generally refers to equipment, computing resources, or people that are located at a company location (as opposed to at home or on the road).

on-site: People or equipment that is located at a company location (as opposed to at home or on the road). Usually a synonym for on-premises.

OneDrive: The consumer version of OneDrive for Business. OneDrive is a file sync tool and does not incorporate version control or business data mining.

OneDrive for Business: Stores business documents in a structure manner that allows full searching and access using the Office 365 machine learning tools. The OneDrive for Business configuration maintains a version history of up to 500 copies of a document.

OneNote: A note-taking tool that allows any form of communications to be recorded in a business document called a notebook. Business communications include voice, typed and scribed notes, pictures, and links to other business communications.

Outlook profile: The Outlook client reads Outlook profiles that contain the e-mail accounts that are to be included in this execution of Outlook.

OWA: Outlook Web App

page: A SharePoint page is what you see with your web browser. You can have multiple pages within a site. Generally, a site presents a default page that users will think of as "the site."

permissions: The "who can do it" aspect of SharePoint. Permissions are set on a site, list, document library, and so forth. Permission levels include None, Read, View, Contribute (Read and Write), and more. A particular user must have "permission" to do that activity on that item; for example, the ability to update the item.

pilot/test group: A group of users who are to be migrated. The first pilot/test group should include both raving fans and naysayers, and it should be designed to test a combination of user needs to ferret out issues early in a migration.

POP mail: POP stands for *Post Office Protocol*. It is a protocol (method) of transferring e-mail from an e-mail server to an e-mail client. In a practical sense, each e-mail client receives its own copy of the e-mail. The effect is that you must frequently delete an e-mail from each client after it has been received. Contrast this with Exchange Server, where e-mail is stored on the server, and the protocol allows an action (such as deletion or movement to a folder) on an e-mail to be reflected immediately on Exchange Server.

Power BI: Organizes information contained in one or more spreadsheets in a visual manner to speed business decisions.

PST Export/Import: A PST file (the file extension for an Outlook personal information store file) stores e-mail on your computer. It can contain archived e-mails or current POP mail. Export is a process in Outlook that copies e-mail from a mailbox to a PST format file. In the context of Office 365, PST Import is the Outlook process that copies a PST file to the Office 365–hosted Exchange Server. It is a method of e-mail migration.

PSTN: Public Switch Termination Network. This is your traditional wired phone systems for homes or business.

push install: An automated installation that is set up by IT to push updates to the desktop, with no user interaction. Software updates are pushed and automatically installed.

S4B: See Skype for Business.

security group: A security group is a type of Active Directory object that can be used to grant permissions in SharePoint.

Selective wipe: A security process where Intune (part of EMS) selectively wipes business information from a mobile device.

Single user identity: A service provided by EMS that allows Office 365 to manage third-party credentials such as Google Docs, Salesforce.com, and other cloud offerings using the users Office 365 credentials. This allows a single user login for all resources.

SharePoint: SharePoint is Microsoft's document-storage and content-management tool. SharePoint was first released in 2001. Originally, SharePoint was used as an enterprise's on-premises intranet. SharePoint is fundamentally a web server that presents web pages to your browser (Internet Explorer, Firefox, Chrome, Safari, etc.). The SharePoint data (structure, permissions, sites, your documents, etc.) is hosted on SQL Server, which is maintained by Microsoft within its secure environment.

single sign-on: SSO lets users log in to an organization's computing resources with a single ID, using Active Directory Federation Services (AD FS).

site: A SharePoint site is a collection of SharePoint "apps" and Web Parts (components), such as document libraries, lists, tasks, blogs, pictures, templates, and text that are presented to a user at a particular URL as a page. A site is within a particular site collection. An example is a project site.

site collection: This is a collection of SharePoint sites. With the Enterprise plan, you may have multiple site collections within your tenant. Site collections have sets of properties that are the same for all sites within a site collection; they may be different between site collections.

site contents: The contents of a SharePoint site. The site contents page shows lists, libraries, and other apps and subsites that are associated with this site. This page is a helpful reference to your site structure. Access to this screen appears as a link on a site page or as a drop-down choice under the "gear" icon at the top right of the screen. Only items that you have permission to see will show.

Skype for Business: A communications client tool included in Office 365 that supports text, voice, and video communication with a whiteboard, shared programs, PowerPoint, shared monitors, and polls to one or more people. It can be used for planned or ad hoc meetings, person-to-person communication, and remote support.

SPF record: Part of the Domain Name System (DNS). *Sender Policy Framework* is an e-mail system to help prevent e-mail spam. The SPF record (normally implemented as a TXT record) describes which hosts are allowed to send from the domain. In Office 365, the sender is `spf.protection.outlook.com` for your domain.

SRV record: Part of the Domain Name System (DNS). An SRV record describes the location (protocol and port) for a given service at a host. Office 365 Lync requires two SRV records for correct implementation.

SSO: Single sign-on provides a single sign-on to an organization's computing resources, using Active Directory Federation Services (AD FS).

subsite: A SharePoint subsite is simply a site under (within) a site. You can nest sites until you confuse yourself.

SWAY: An Office 365 application that allows you to express your ideas across any device. SWAY is future replacement to PowerPoint for presentations and is included Office 365 business subscription with the Office component.

tenant: This is your Office 365 account, including hosted Exchange, Lync, SharePoint, and Office 365 Active Directory. The first account that you create when you first purchase Office 365 is the "owner" of your tenant. This account should be an admin account, not a person. This account does not normally require an Office 365 license. Relating to SharePoint, all of your site collections are within your tenant. You can have any number of domains within your tenant (with e-mail accounts), but you will have only one root SharePoint URL: `https://xxxx.sharepoint.com`.

TXT record: Part of the Domain Name System (DNS). A TXT record can contain any type of text. See SPF record. For Office 365, a TXT record is also used to prove domain ownership. (A specific TXT record is added by the domain registrar for your domain.)

2FA: See Two-factor authentication.

Two-factor authentication: Part of EMS that manages access to Office 365 and Azure information resources. 2FA uses two parts of the security rule "something you know (knowledge), something you have (device), and something you are (bio)." Typical 2FA uses a smartphone with a pin number that changes and a password to grant access to computing resources.

URL: Universal resource locator. The specific universal address for a web page, it is essentially a specific location within a domain within the World Wide Web. (This doesn't necessarily mean that you can see it from anywhere; there can be security restrictions.) Examples are `https://kamindit.sharepoint.com`.

virtualization: A server or desktop operating system running on a virtual host. The server or desktop operating systems are running in a hardware-agnostic mode, because the hardware services are supplied by the virtual host.

Web Part: SharePoint components that can be inserted into a page (part of a site). Web Parts are very powerful and can interact with other sites and data outside of SharePoint.

web site: A SharePoint web site is a specialized site collection that can be seen by the outside world (public facing) through a standard URL (such as `http://getoffice365now.com`). You may only have one web site within a tenant.

www record: Part of the Domain Name System (DNS). It provides the name or IP address of a web server for a given domain name.

Yammer: A business communication tool where the business information is owned by the company that allows users to express and share information in an unstructured manner. Yammer is sometimes referred to as the internal Facebook of the business. Yammer information is data mined by Delve for the internal use of the company.

Index

■ R

■ S, T

■ U, V

■ W, X

■ Y, Z

Get the eBook for only $5!

Why limit yourself?

Now you can take the weightless companion with you wherever you go and access your content on your PC, phone, tablet, or reader.

Since you've purchased this print book, we're happy to offer you the eBook in all 3 formats for just $5.

Convenient and fully searchable, the PDF version enables you to easily find and copy code—or perform examples by quickly toggling between instructions and applications. The MOBI format is ideal for your Kindle, while the ePUB can be utilized on a variety of mobile devices.

To learn more, go to www.apress.com/companion or contact support@apress.com.